MAYDAY
1971

MAYDAY
1971

A WHITE HOUSE AT WAR, A REVOLT IN
THE STREETS, AND THE UNTOLD HISTORY
OF AMERICA'S BIGGEST MASS ARREST

LAWRENCE ROBERTS

Houghton Mifflin Harcourt
Boston   New York
2020

For information about permission to reproduce selections from this book, write to trade.permissions@hmhco.com or to Permissions, Houghton Mifflin Harcourt Publishing Company, 3 Park Avenue, 19th Floor, New York, New York 10016.

hmhbooks.com

Library of Congress Cataloging-in-Publication Data
Names: Roberts, Lawrence, (Journalist) author.
Title: Mayday 1971 : a White House at war, a revolt in the streets, and the untold history of America's biggest mass arrest / Lawrence Roberts.
Other titles: White House at war, a revolt in the streets, and the untold history of America's biggest mass arrest
Description: Boston : Houghton Mifflin Harcourt, 2020. |
Includes bibliographical references and index.
Identifiers: LCCN 2019033950 (print) | LCCN 2019033951 (ebook) |
ISBN 9781328766724 (hardcover) | ISBN 9781328766748 (ebook)
Subjects: LCSH: Vietnam War, 1961–1975 — Protest movements — United States. |
Demonstrations — Washington (D.C.) — History — 20th century. |
Mall, The (Washington, D.C.) — History — 20th century. | Government,
Resistance To — United States — History — 20th century. | Washington (D.C.) —
History — 20th century. | Civil disobedience — United States — History —
20th century. | Militarism — United States — History — 20th century. |
United States — Politics and Government — 1969–1974.
Classification: LCC DS559.62.U6 R63 2020 (print) | LCC DS559.62.U6 (ebook) |
DDC 959.704/31 — dc23
LC record available at https://lccn.loc.gov/2019033950
LC ebook record available at https://lccn.loc.gov/2019033951

Book design by Emily Snyder

Frontispiece: Map by Mapping Specialists, Ltd.
Part 1 March 1971: Washington Star photo by Bernie Boston / Reprinted with permission of the DC Public Library, Star Collection © Washington Post
Part 2 April 1971: Washington Star photo by Bill Perry / Reprinted with permission of the DC Public Library, Star Collection © Washington Post
Part 3 May 1971: Reprinted with permission of the DC Public Library, Star Collection © Washington Post

Printed in the United States of America
DOC 10 9 8 7 6 5 4 3 2 1

For Nancy and Jacob

Whenever American institutions have
provided a hysterical response to an emergency
situation, we have come later to regret it.

— JUDGE HAROLD H. GREENE

Contents

MAY 1971

Washington
in the Spring of 1971

Georgetown University

Key Bridge

LANIER PLACE NW

Dupont Circle

Mayday Tribe house

.1029 Vermont Avenue

Washington Coliseum

Superior Court

U.S. Courthouse

Justice Department

White House

THE ELLIPSE

George Washington University

Selective Service headquarters

Watergate

Roosevelt Bridge

Memorial Bridge

Lincoln Memorial

WEST POTOMAC PARK

Washington Monument

NATIONAL MALL

Vietnam Vets campground

Supreme Court

United States Capitol

RFK Stadium

Mayday Detention Camp

Anacostia River

Potomac River

Jefferson Memorial

14th Street Bridge

ARLINGTON NATIONAL CEMETERY

Key People and Events

A NOTE TO READERS: The events described herein involved thousands of participants and touched many more lives. By necessity I have chosen key people to represent the whole. Within that group are eight who played particularly interesting roles. The story you will read is told largely through their eyes. The eight are highlighted below in boldface. To help you track them, they generally will be identified by first names after their initial introductions in these pages.

THE NIXON ADMINISTRATION

WHITE HOUSE

President Richard M. Nixon
H. R. Haldeman, chief of staff
John Ehrlichman, domestic
  policy chief
Egil "Bud" Krogh Jr.,
  Ehrlichman's assistant

Henry A. Kissinger, national
  security chief
Tom Huston, staff assistant
John Dean, White House
  counsel

JUSTICE DEPARTMENT

John Mitchell, attorney general
Richard Kleindienst, deputy
  attorney general
William H. Rehnquist, chief
  legal counsel

J. Edgar Hoover, FBI director
William Sullivan, FBI
  intelligence chief

LEADERS OF THE 1971 SPRING OFFENSIVE

PEOPLE'S COALITION FOR PEACE & JUSTICE
Rennie Davis   Sidney Peck
David Dellinger   Jerry Coffin
John Froines

THE MAYDAY TRIBE / YIPPIES
Stew Albert   Jerry Rubin
Judy Gumbo   Leslie Bacon
Abbie Hoffman

VIETNAM VETERANS AGAINST THE WAR
John Kerry   Tim Butz
John O'Connor   Michael Phelan
Jack Mallory

POLICE AND COURTS OF WASHINGTON, D.C.

D.C. POLICE
Jerry V. Wilson, police chief   Gerald Caplan, counsel
Maurice "Cully" Cullinane,
assistant chief

LAWYERS
Barbara A. Bowman, director,   Michael Wald, public defender
Public Defender Service   Philip J. Hirschkop, civil
Norman Lefstein, deputy   liberties attorney
director, Public Defender
Service

D.C. JUDGES
Harold H. Greene, chief judge   Charles Halleck
William Bryant

MAJOR PROTESTS AGAINST AMERICA'S VIETNAM WAR

SPRING 1965
- First teach-in against the war, University of Michigan, Ann Arbor
- Rally in D.C. sponsored by Students for a Democratic Society (SDS)
- Vietnam Day teach-in, University of California, Berkeley

APRIL 1967
- Mass marches in New York City and San Francisco, sponsored by National Mobilization Committee to End the War in Vietnam (the Mobe)

OCTOBER 1967
- Mobe rally in D.C., with Yippies' attempt to "levitate" the Pentagon
- Stop the Draft Week in Oakland, California

AUGUST 1968
- Mobe and Yippie actions during the Democratic National Convention in Chicago

JANUARY 1969
- Counter-inaugural protest by the Mobe and others in Washington at Richard Nixon's first swearing-in

FALL 1969
- National Moratorium demonstrations, including rallies, work stoppages, and teach-ins, held October 15 and November 15

MAY 1970
- D.C. rally to protest war's expansion into Cambodia and mourn four students killed by National Guard at Kent State University in Ohio

MARCH THROUGH MAY 1971

- The Spring Offensive and Mayday, including protests by the People's Coalition for Peace and Justice, the Mayday Tribe, the National Peace Action Coalition (NPAC), and Vietnam Veterans Against the War (VVAW)

Prologue: Nixon's Insurrection City

AT DAYBREAK ON SATURDAY, MAY 1, 1971, TWO HELICOPTERS banked over the monuments of Washington, D.C., and hovered above the Potomac riverfront. The pilots relayed sobering news back to their superiors. It wasn't long before Jerry Vernon Wilson, the city's chief of police, left the downtown hotel room where he'd been sleeping all week. He headed to the Department of Justice for an emergency private meeting. There, he joined eleven men from Justice, the White House, the Pentagon, and the National Guard—the institutions most vested in preserving order on the streets of the capital.

For weeks, demonstrators had been flowing into Washington for marches, rallies, and sit-down protests, demanding an end to America's war in Vietnam. The nonstop action had exhausted the government men, eroded their patience and their confidence. Now they worried about what was coming next.

Down by the placid blue-tinged river, a ragtag encampment was growing fast. Tens of thousands of young people were turning West Potomac Park into the staging area for the most zealous of the protests. When the workweek got underway on Monday morning, May 3, the militants, who called themselves the Mayday Tribe, planned to stream out of the park into the city, using their bodies and their cars to block bridges, traffic circles, and the approaches to government office buildings. Deprive Washington of its workers, and the federal city would stall. Mayday's leaders hoped this unprecedented show of public disaffection would raise the "spectre of social chaos," knocking President Richard

M. Nixon off course and forcing him to bring all the troops home from Southeast Asia.

Nothing about the protest was secret. The group published its order of battle in a twenty-four-page tactical manual, distributed by the thousands and reprinted in underground newspapers. It displayed detailed maps and photographs of the targeted chokepoints, as well as tips for thwarting police. For months, posters with the Mayday motto had been pasted on walls and bulletin boards at hundreds of universities, coffeehouses, and bookstores across the country: "If the government won't stop the war, we'll stop the government."

Despite more than six years of petitions, speeches, teach-ins, door-to-door organizing, electioneering, campus uprisings, and enormous parades for peace, the war was grinding on. Not only had Nixon failed to end the conflict as he promised when he ran for president in 1968, but he had expanded it—in secret, at first—by sending bombers and troops into Vietnam's neighbors.

The U.S. invasion of Cambodia in 1970 had triggered a national student strike. Now Nixon's latest incursion, into Laos, fueled the series of protests that its leaders had labeled the Spring Offensive.

May 1971 marked exactly ten years since President John F. Kennedy had dispatched a few hundred soldiers and advisers to South Vietnam, to prop up a regime besieged by a guerrilla force allied with the communist North. Kennedy's successor, Lyndon B. Johnson, was initially skeptical of committing more resources to Indochina. "I don't see what we can ever hope to get out of this," LBJ, as he was known, privately told a key adviser. But one modest move in a Cold War chess match with the Soviet Union and China led to another, and then another. Each month, tens of thousands of men age eighteen to twenty-six were drafted into the army. By the time of Mayday, two million Americans had already served in uniform in Vietnam and returned. More than 275,000 U.S. troops still were deployed there. That was down from the peak reached under LBJ. But on Nixon's watch, dozens were still dying in the jungle every week. Total U.S. combat deaths had just ticked past 45,000. Many more came home bearing terrible scars on hearts, minds, and bodies. Hundreds of thousands of Vietnamese, Cambodians, and Laotians had lost their lives. American aircraft already had dropped more tons of explosives on Vietnam and its neighbors than had fallen on any place in history, and spewed more than nineteen million gallons of defoliants and herbicides over millions of acres of greenery, in a vain attempt to cripple the enemy by stripping away its cover.

The conflict, with its mysterious battle lines and muddled military and political goals, so dominated headlines, the nightly news on TV, and debate on campuses and at kitchen tables that people in their teens and twenties could hardly remember a time when it hadn't. The war had brought down LBJ and cost the Democrats the White House. The government's new programs to combat poverty and injustice at home were being starved as billions of dollars poured abroad. The war inflamed class, generational, and racial conflict that sometimes turned violent, even deadly. National Guardsmen had shot and killed four young people at Kent State University in Ohio during a demonstration against the 1970 Cambodia invasion. Police fired into a Jackson State dormitory in Mississippi; two students died. When a crowd of student protesters in New York City tried to lower an American flag, construction workers stormed in and beat them bloody with their hardhats. The most fanatical members of the campus-based movement known as the New Left had declared themselves revolutionary soldiers and disappeared underground. They began setting off bombs at a string of police stations, courthouses, banks, and at college buildings with connections to the military. Vietnam was a centrifugal force spinning the nation's self-image faster and faster, and pieces were flying off.

The organizers of Mayday wagered that huge numbers of people opposed to the war were ready to escalate their tactics. At first, as the weekend approached, their camp on the field by the river was thinly settled. It resembled the bedraggled remains of a Civil War regiment. A few hundred people slept there on the ground, wrapped in blankets or sleeping bags. Most were young men, bearded and shaggy-haired. The temperature sank into the forties at night and a cold breeze came off the river. Intermittent rain showers soaked their clothes and knapsacks. They reeked of smoke from wet firewood and marijuana. Some cobbled together lean-tos from tarps, rain ponchos, even American flags.

Informants walked among them — young police and federal agents, disguised in the worn green army-surplus field jackets favored by the peace movement, joining in the preliminary marches and the chants of "Stop the war!" and "Fuck the FBI!" They found the gathering less than impressive, predicting that in the end no more than five thousand hippies and radicals would show. One of Nixon's top officials dismissed the boasts of the protest leaders as "just a lot of hot air."

Yet by Saturday morning, as he stood in the conference room on the fourth floor of the Justice Department, Police Chief Jerry Wilson knew they'd misjudged Mayday. The incursion had swelled from a trickle to a flood. The helicopter surveillance confirmed that at least forty thousand people had arrived so far. Caravans of Volkswagen Beetles and microbuses continued to roll in from all over the country. Monday loomed as the largest act of mass civil disobedience the nation had ever seen, a coda to the most extraordinary season of dissent in Washington's history. Nixon's men were determined to make sure it failed. But how?

THE MAYDAY ENCAMPMENT rose on a couple of dusty playing fields, set roughly between the memorials to Abraham Lincoln and Thomas Jefferson. It was the western edge of the National Mall, the grassy expanse that over a matter of decades had emerged as a platform for Americans to air their grievances with the government, a role not quite anticipated by the founders.

To Pierre Charles L'Enfant, the artistic French engineer hired by President George Washington in 1791 to design a federal city from scratch, the grand "public walk" he imagined from the Capitol to the Potomac River would serve as a majestic inspiration for democratic values. Washington fired the testy Frenchman for scrapping with his colleagues before the plan could be executed. It would be nearly a century before L'Enfant's greenway was fully realized. Standing in the way were big patches of marshy land where two creeks emptied into the Potomac, flooding during high water and storms. The pools sometimes wouldn't dry up for months. Not an actual swamp in the tropical sense, but come the soggy choking heat of a mid-Atlantic summer, it could sure feel like one.*

---

* The mistaken idea that the whole of Washington, D.C., stands on reclaimed swampland persists to this day as a calumny against the city. This myth was stoked by wealthy eighteenth-century merchants and politicians to the north who hated the idea of building the new capital so far south. In fact, most of the federal district staked out by L'Enfant consisted of corn and tobacco fields and pastures, giving way to stands of huge tulip trees, oak, sycamore, and hickory.

As the city grew, parts of the riverfront turned into a steaming mess. Raw human waste from homes and shops, not least from the White House itself, less than a thousand yards away, dribbled into a wide canal. It had been built for navigation but became little more than an open sewer. The canal disgorged into the river. There, the grunge mixed with silt flowing downstream from where farmers were clearing the woods from the banks. Over the decades, the ugly weedy expanse only got larger, breeding malarial mosquitoes and spreading cholera. The winds off the river sent the acrid fumes wafting up through the city. "It is this cause more than all others," wrote one congressman from Ohio, "that compels the residents of Washington to flee from it during the months of heat, and causes well-informed persons all over the country to avoid it during that season as they would the pest-house."

The city's leaders resolved to get rid of these odiferous Potomac Flats. Congress in 1882 set in motion one of the largest public works projects of the time. The Army Corps of Engineers took on a thirty-year plan to dredge the channel and pile the mud up onto those flats. In the end, more than seven hundred new acres emerged, a permanent spot for recreation and quiet enjoyment. Best of all, the new dry land, divided into East Potomac and West Potomac parks, would fulfill L'Enfant's vision. The completed Mall would be a fitting tribute to America's soaring ambition — "the unexpectedly grand and new future opening before us as the leading nation in the progress of humanity, charity, and good will toward all others," declared the head of the agency that would eventually become the National Park Service.

The Lincoln and Jefferson memorials were erected. Groves of magnolia trees and shrubs planted along winding pathways and fountains and around a manmade lake (later transformed into the Tidal Basin) bloomed like an arboretum. The designers provided open fields too for baseball and polo, concerts and picnics. By the 1940s, a leading landscape architect pronounced it "the most beautiful place man has made in America."

The Congress and the White House, the monuments and the river were now all connected. L'Enfant had been right when he predicted, "The whole will acquire new sweetness." Something had emerged that was greater than its components. The National Mall felt like an entirely new kind of public space, both ceremonial and democratic, owned by no one but the citizens wandering through at any given moment.

Though it sat at the physical core of Washington, the Mall was nevertheless largely isolated from the business of the city. Not some well-worn European square, hemmed in tight by imposing stone buildings, not a manicured garden outside the palace of a prince, this was a big open vista in the heart of the republic. You could stand right in the middle, cheek practically grazing the white marble of the Washington Monument, and sweep your eyes from the tree-lined riverfront to the statues honoring those who had founded and sustained the place, then to the grounds of the president's home, and finally to the Capitol's bright dome. In a young nation you anoint hallowed ground where you can find it. The territory would come to be claimed not only by tourists but by the great social movements of the century.

Before, citizens who came en masse to Washington to appeal to the government, including the unemployed seeking relief and women demanding the right to vote, bickered with police and bureaucrats over access to streets and federal buildings. Now the First Amendment's abstract guarantees of assembly and expression seemed to materialize in the shape of the Mall. Veterans of World War I pitched their tents there to plead for their promised bonuses. People streamed in by the tens of thousands in the spring of 1939 to hear "America" ("My Country, 'Tis of Thee") sung by the renowned contralto Marian Anderson, decrying her exclusion from the whites-only hall of the Daughters of the American Revolution. A little more than two decades later, Martin Luther King Jr. gathered a quarter-million supporters of civil rights for black Americans and delivered his "I Have a Dream" speech.

Then came a protest movement without precedent. Beginning in the mid-1960s, increasingly large crowds arrived to proclaim their opposition to U.S. intervention in Vietnam. And in the spring of 1971 — which happened to be the numerical reverse of the year Washington the man got it all started — Washington the city would face ten tumultuous weeks, testing America's idea of itself as the "leading nation in the progress of humanity." The question at hand was whether the nation's power and prosperity were being misused, whether an empire uniquely built on democratic institutions and constitutional rights could self-correct when it veered terribly off course. In the midst of this struggle, people convinced of their rectitude would go to extremes.

It began with an explosion and ended with a mass arrest, the largest ever carried out in this country. More than twelve thousand people were taken into custody, a number that remains unsurpassed.

These events, and the stories behind them, have been largely forgotten, rendered obscure by the momentous scandals that immediately followed, for which they were both prologue and catalyst: a battle over leaked government secrets, corruption in the White House, and the first resignation of a president. Yet, as this book will show, the demonstrations against the Vietnam War in the spring of 1971 were not only the most extensive and provocative of the era we call the Sixties. They also bequeathed consequential changes to American law and politics, including the rules governing protests in the heart of the nation's capital, which remain in force today.

JERRY WILSON was six foot four, with the calm self-assurance of a big man. He had been running the police department for less than two years but had spent his entire adult life as a D.C. cop. When he arrived in Washington as a twenty-one-year-old fresh from small-town North Carolina, his drawl was so thick, it stood out even in a city still deeply rooted in the South. The other officers at the Seventh Precinct in the Georgetown neighborhood nicknamed him "Hogmaw," after a dish of roasted pork stomach — the stringiest, most backwoods food they could conjure. Jerry didn't mind the teasing. To tell the truth, he sort of enjoyed it.

Now the chief surveyed the men gathered to confront Mayday. He often liked to stand during this kind of meeting, with a good cop's poker face, a quiet towering presence in the corner. Of those in the room, nine were lawyers educated at the nation's top universities. Their résumés included stints in rough-and-tumble political campaigns. Two were army generals who'd commanded men in battle. For a few, career high points lay ahead: One would become the chief justice of the United States, another would come within a whisker of heading the FBI, and two would serve as federal judges. Three others faced a rougher future, behind bars.

And there was Jerry. He was now forty-three. He'd never been to college, let alone law school, and had no political experience to speak of. Yet no one around the table was better equipped to deal with Mayday. The chief had educated himself on D.C.'s streets during dozens of protests, whether polite marches, running skirmishes, or the burning and looting that followed the 1968 assassination of Martin Luther King Jr. How to keep your balance in that sweet spot between the rights of peaceful assembly and public order — that was something he'd studied up close. He understood the ebb and flow of a mass demonstration, the ever-shifting combustible edge between police and protesters.

Only Jerry wasn't in charge today. He answered to Richard G. Kleindienst, the number-two official at Justice. And to Kleindienst, this meeting was nothing less than the war council of a city and a government under attack.

A couple of days before, Kleindienst had been the official publicly belittling Mayday as "hot air." Now he acknowledged his error. "Everything is changed," he warned the others. Our preparations are weak, he said. We could be facing a full-scale citywide riot. Besides clogging traffic on the main arteries, the protesters could abandon cars on the four bridges over the Potomac and set them afire. A big enough crowd might crash its way through police lines and barricades and even the entrances to federal agencies.

Kleindienst's high forehead and inward-sloping eyebrows gave his face an impish, almost devilish, cast. He could deliver a bawdy joke one minute and a squall of rage the next. Back in his native Arizona, when he had worked for Barry Goldwater, LBJ's opponent in 1964, Kleindienst had been instrumental in making the phrase "law and order" a hallmark of Republican politics. Four years later he'd helped cement it as a centerpiece of Nixon's campaign. Here was a chance to make good on that promise. To protect the government, Kleindienst explained, the White House had already arranged for city officials to mobilize the National Guard under Jerry's command. Along with city police and officers from the Park Service and the Capitol, that would add up to a force of seven thousand. But Kleindienst wanted more. He looked over at the secretary of the army. How many troops were placed in or near Washington? About thirty-six hundred, came the answer. Not enough, Kleindienst said. He ordered another five thousand men flown in from North Carolina.

Jerry quickly grasped how intimidating the military presence would be. Troops from the Eighty-Second Airborne Division would be ferried to the National Mall in five Chinook helicopters, their twin rotors chopping above the monuments. Hundreds of men, with fixed bayonets, would line the bridges. There would be marines from the base at Quantico, in Virginia, and a battalion of army engineers. A column of vehicles from the Sixth Armored Cavalry at Fort Meade in Maryland would rumble through the streets. Kleindienst had even secured an army V-100, a huge tanklike vehicle with a turret and giant rubber tires that could run right over a car.

Kleindienst told his colleagues not to fret about needing any kind of executive order, such as a declaration of martial law. The president, he said, had already arranged things with the Pentagon.

Jerry had been making his own preparations for Mayday. Police stockpiled canisters of tear gas and pepper-fogger spray. They requisitioned more portable radios and instant cameras. Jerry canceled all leave for the force and scoped out potential holding areas, in case they had to make large numbers of arrests. He borrowed forty trucks from the National Guard and four big prisoner-of-war transports from the marines. But it was one thing to be prepared for intense police action. It was quite another to turn the city into an armed camp, as Kleindienst was doing.

In fact, Kleindienst and his boss, Attorney General John Mitchell, had been feeding the tension in Washington for weeks. At one point, after Mitchell had warned that some protest groups had vowed "to create violence," Jerry had his spokesman tell reporters that police had heard no such threats. Now the chief made another attempt to deflate the pressure. He pointed out that so far, during the string of recent demonstrations, his officers had taken more than a thousand people into custody and had encountered no serious problems. Yes, we expect many arrests on Monday, he said, but he doubted the Mayday Tribe would form a destructive mob. After all, they were unarmed and preached nonviolence. Only a small core of militants might cause trouble worse than sitting in the streets and waiting for a bust.

Jerry was hardly an apologist for the protesters. Shortly after taking over as chief, he had hurled one of the first canisters of tear gas at a crowd that refused to clear the steps outside Justice, an act that helped propel him onto the cover of *Time* magazine as America's emblematic big-city police chief. But unlike many of his colleagues, he didn't see demonstrators as unpatriotic. He kept it to himself that he had no love for this war. Some of Jerry's friends came to the marches. They weren't hippies or even left-wingers, just people sick of the conflict and what it was doing to the country.

The draft was at the heart of it all, Jerry maintained. The young protesters hated the draft even more than the war. He'd helped one friend get his son into the National Guard to avoid conscription. Another friend asked for a recommendation to place his boy in the army's finance office so he wouldn't see combat. Jerry thought the system, which gave enrolled undergraduates an automatic deferment, imprisoned young men in college — if you left school, and your birth date drew a bad number in the annual draft lottery, you'd be classified 1A, subject to instant induction. No wonder they were angry and scared. Thousands of draft resisters had fled to Canada; hundreds had gone to jail. Get rid of the draft, go to an enlistment-only military, Jerry believed, and the protests would stop.

So the chief wasn't especially surprised that so many kids made their way to the riverfront. Naturally it wasn't only about the politics — you had a dozen rock bands, even the Beach Boys, playing all day and night. It was springtime and the pink cherry blossoms had been painting a soft ring around the Tidal Basin. You could smoke some pot and probably get yourself laid. Hell, if he were young and not a cop, he might be there too, whether he cared about the war or not. He didn't want the police to tear things up without a very good reason. He sent memos to his officers, warning them to stay professional as they confronted the "many unusual circumstances that may arise" during the Mayday protests. He ordered them to be "patient, discreet and solicitous of the citizens of our own city and of the visitors to our city."

To Jerry, dealing with a day or two of sit-down protests, keeping the traffic flowing, those were solvable logistical challenges, not ideological ones. If someone purposely stalled an old junk car on a bridge, you wouldn't be able to get a tow truck through the jam. So maybe put a big crane on a barge, or get a helicopter with a tow cable, drop the car right into the Potomac. If hundreds of people, or more, refused to disperse and you had to arrest them, where would you put them after the jail cells were full? How would you feed them?

For Nixon and many of his closest advisers, though, Mayday and the protests building up to it presented a political crisis.

By the time of the Saturday meeting at Justice, the president already had left town. On short notice he'd boarded Air Force One on Friday morning to fly out to what had come to be known as his Western White House, in San Clemente, California. It was meant as a public display of indifference. But the president and his aides were anything but indifferent to the possibility that the antiwar movement was taking a more dangerous turn.

Nixon had taken office two years earlier, determined to wind down both the war and the domestic disorder it spawned. He yearned to devote his attention to what he believed was his calling, to reshape the Cold War world and earn an exalted place in history. Yet even as he reduced the number of U.S. soldiers on Vietnamese soil, his attacks on Vietnam's neighbors inflamed the protests again.

The president and Henry Kissinger, his chief foreign policy adviser, were gambling that breaching the borders to hit enemy bases and supply lines would force North Vietnam to negotiate what Nixon termed an "honorable" peace, one that could be sold to the U.S. public as a moral victory, or at least a stalemate, instead of a military defeat. If that could jell by the November 1972 election, Nixon's second term in the White House was all but assured.

But he was losing his grip on that plan, as polls showed opinion shifting in favor of immediate withdrawal. His standing among young people plummeted to a new low. They disrupted his inauguration and held dozens more demonstrations over the next eighteen months, including three huge marches outside the White House. No longer could Nixon visit a college campus without practically inciting a riot. Students at San Jose State had pummeled his limousine with rocks and eggs. He'd had to concoct a foreign trip to gracefully renege on his promise to speak at Ohio State University's commencement.

It wasn't just the demonstrations that rattled Nixon and his confidants. In 1970 radicals had bombed or tried to bomb thirty-two federal buildings. The Black Panther Party, as well known for its periodic violent confrontations with police as for its ambitious service work among the poor, had branches in multiple big cities. Even religious pacifists seemed to be turning more extreme. Federal authorities indicted a nun and three priests on the Catholic Left for merely discussing a fantastical plot to kidnap Kissinger and hold him as ransom for an end to the war.

During this period, the daily news summaries that landed on the president's desk "conveyed a sense of turmoil bordering on insurrection," Nixon would later recall. At press conferences, he and other government officials were asked quite seriously if the country was headed for a revolution. In early 1971, "the lowest point of my first term," he even speculated that the party might not nominate him for reelection.

The president's public response was to adopt a statesmanlike pose, promising to unify a fractured nation. Speaking to Congress in January, a few months before Mayday, he acknowledged the widespread sense of disintegration. "America has been going through a long nightmare of war and division, of crime and inflation. Even more deeply, we have gone through a long, dark night of the American spirit," the president said in his State of the Union address. "But now that night is ending. Now we must let our spirits soar again. Now we are ready for the lift of a driving dream."

In general, when he couldn't avoid discussing antiwar demonstrators in public, Nixon trod carefully. He was politely dismissive and patronizing, telling the press that while he thought the participants misunderstood U.S. foreign policy, he shared their goal of peace and recognized their right of dissent. He left the vitriol to others. His vice president, Spiro Agnew, lambasted campus activists and their sympathizers as "ideological eunuchs" and "an effete corps of impudent snobs" and "nattering nabobs of negativism." Attorney General John Mitchell suggested protesters were veering close to treason as tools of North Vietnam and the Vietcong, which was the nickname for the National Liberation Front, the communist guerrillas in the South.

In the privacy of his office, though, Nixon didn't hide his feelings. The demonstrators were "little bastards," "animals," "bums," "crummy-looking people, the lowest of the low," "the dirtiest damn people there are," "draft-dodgers, country-haters, or don't-cares." He considered a plan that would lift many legal restrictions on the FBI, the CIA, the National Security Agency, and military intelligence agencies to tap their phones and open their mail. He discussed getting "thugs" from conservative unions like the Teamsters, or pro-war veterans, to confront demonstrators and crack the kids' heads.

The events leading up to Mayday had only reinforced the view at the White House. First, a bomb went off in the U.S. Capitol. Then organizations representing college students and hard-left radicals, old peaceniks and young ex-soldiers, had managed to overcome infighting and descend together upon the city in a kind of chaotic choreography.

The initial arrivals, in mid-April, were more than a thousand U.S. military veterans of Vietnam. They came not to voice support for the war but to camp on the National Mall, march through the city, and return their combat ribbons and medals in anger and sorrow, hurling them onto the steps of the Capitol. The veterans stayed in town to join what probably was the largest march ever held in Washington up to that point, on Saturday, April 24. Sponsored by the coalition of antiwar groups, it drew hundreds of thousands of people. Unlike previous marches, which were overwhelmingly populated by college students, this one included throngs of older middle-class protesters, bringing home to Nixon's aides how deeply antiwar sentiment had spread beyond the core.

In the days that followed, thousands of people had roamed the streets, holding sit-ins and demonstrations outside the White House gates, inside congressional offices, and at the doors of federal buildings such as the Selective Service, which oversaw the draft. Guerrilla theater groups staged mock battles, ranging as far as the suburban home of the secretary of defense. On his porch they hung a Vietcong flag — a yellow star against a red-over-blue background. Among the hundreds arrested around the city during that week in April were veterans, Quakers, students, and mothers supported by welfare.

Private opinion polls showed that the sustained protests, especially those by Vietnam veterans, were stoking public opposition to Nixon's policies. And now Mayday approached — the most dangerous part of the offensive if you were in the White House, but the most thrilling if you were a militant.

As Kleindienst, Jerry, and the others met at Justice that Saturday morning, churches around the country were preparing to ring their bells in unison for an hour, starting at noon. The heads of twenty-seven national religious groups had called for the action, to mourn the dead and plea for an end to the killing. The bells might have been tolling for Nixon's men. A successful show of strength by the Mayday protesters, tying up the capital of the most powerful nation on the planet — that would only add fuel to talk that the government was on the run.

The president had made his wishes clear. That was why Kleindienst was pushing a military solution. The police chief made one last attempt to dissuade him. Let's just suppose the crowd is big enough to shut down the government, Jerry said. Wouldn't it be better for us, he gently suggested, if the militants could crow only that they had defeated the police, rather than the mighty U.S. military? An army official chimed in on Jerry's side. Why not wait a day, see if the troops were really necessary?

Also in the room was John Ehrlichman, the president's chief of domestic policy. He expressed astonishment at what Jerry was suggesting. Nixon wanted the streets kept open at all costs. The president didn't care if it took 100,000 troops. If this turns into a riot and we are caught short, Ehrlichman warned, "It will mean some asses." And, Kleindienst added darkly, "All those asses are in this room."

MARCH
1971

The Weather Underground Organization exploded a bomb inside the U.S. Capitol in the early morning of March 1, 1971.

1

This Is Real

THE TEN WEEKS THAT WOULD SHAKE WASHINGTON IN 1971 BE-gan with a telephone call to the U.S. Capitol early on the first day of March. The operator on the overnight shift remembered it as a man's voice, low and hard, coming not quite an hour after midnight. In thirty minutes, a bomb would go off. "Oh-one-thirty. This is real," the caller warned. "Evacuate the building immediately. This is in retaliation for the Laos decision."

It exploded one floor below the Senate Chamber.

At the time, as was the case in most government buildings, pretty much anyone could walk through the Capitol without showing even a driver's license or opening a bag. The bombers had wandered in with sticks of dynamite strapped to their bodies. They slipped into an un-marked marble-lined men's bathroom, hooked up a fuse attached to a stopwatch, and stuffed the bomb behind a five-foot-high partial wall.

The blast tore the wall apart, shattering the sinks and toilets into shrapnel. Shock waves blew the swinging doors off the entrance to the Senate barbershop down the hall. The doors crashed through a window and sailed into a courtyard. The force of the explosion cracked light fix-tures, plaster, and tile along the corridor. It reached as far as the Sen-ate dining room, where it knocked out panes in a stained-glass window depicting George Washington greeting two Revolutionary War heroes, the Marquis de Lafayette and Baron von Steuben. Each European lost his head. In the middle of the night those rooms were deserted, so there were no injuries.

No one had tried to destroy any part of the Capitol since 1915, when a former German language instructor at Harvard planted three sticks of dynamite and a timer inside the Senate's reception room, to express his strong desire that the United States stay out of World War I. (The device went off while everyone was gone for the July 4 weekend. Afterward, the forty-four-year-old bomber made his way to the Long Island home of J. Pierpont Morgan, the nation's most prominent banker, shot him in a failed assassination attempt, and when captured, leapt through a jailhouse window to his death.) Before that, you had to go back to the British burning the place during the War of 1812.

Despite the late hour, the *Washington Post* managed to get the bombing story onto the front page of the final edition.

At about ten in the morning of March 1, the phone rang with the news at a red-brick townhouse near Dupont Circle. This rented house on M Street served as one of the crash pads for the Mayday Tribe, the group organizing the final link in a chain of ambitious antiwar demonstrations that spring. For months, activists from disparate groups had been arriving and settling into temporary homes around town while planning their piece of the action. FBI and police agents struggled to keep track of who was sleeping where, what they were up to. People moved from place to place, depending on where they found their friends, lovers, and political soulmates.

The Mayday Tribe, in turn, had its own subgroups. One of these revolved around some of the original Yippies. The Yippies were flamboyant radicals with roots in Berkeley, California, who mixed intense left-wing politics, psychedelic drugs, and outrageous publicity stunts. This faction had pretty much taken over the M Street house, where they prepared a newspaper for the throngs they expected to show up in Washington in a matter of weeks.

Among them was a soft-spoken thirty-one-year-old man with a wrestler's build and a mass of blond curls. His name was Stewart Edward Albert. Also in residence was Stew's ex-girlfriend and fellow Yippie Judy Gumbo. There was a fire station across the road. The government men camped out there. They made no real attempt to hide their presence. The Yippies could plainly see a surveillance camera fixed in the upstairs window. Some of them would turn as they entered the house and make an exaggerated ironic bow toward the stakeout.

At first, Stew, Judy, and their friends celebrated the news of the bombing. It was another high-profile blow against the established order, a preface to the big demonstrations to come. Civil disobedience in a different form, as one put it later. No one had been hurt. They and their friends decided to taunt the FBI. They ran out into the middle of M Street, joined arms, and kicked out an unruly can-can. Later, when the heat was on her and Stew, Judy would maintain they were joyful because "we didn't do it, but we dug it."

Stew and Judy assumed they were staying in the same house again only temporarily. A few months back, when they were living together in New York, Judy, who was twenty-seven, fast-talking, and brainy, had broken off their romance after embracing the women's liberation movement. Stew was a male chauvinist pig, she'd decided, like so many of the radical men, railing against the corporate power structure but treating her like a clerk-typist or an invisible housekeeper instead of an activist with equal or more smarts and judgment. Many of the original New Left couples were splitting, and for the same reason. Judy had moved out of their windowless basement apartment in Greenwich Village, the one she had adored as their love nest, the one piled with cardboard boxes full of crafts to be sold at the civil-rights-movement shop upstairs. She set out for Boston to room with other women declaring their liberation.

Judy knew Stew still loved her and that he hoped they'd get back together. A part of her felt it too. She would replay their first meeting in her mind. It had been at a demonstration, of course. She'd just moved to Berkeley from her native Toronto, where she'd been raised in a Jewish family of hard-line pro-Soviets and had been working toward a Ph.D. in sociology. She needed to reset her life after catching her husband in bed with another woman. Brand-new to an adopted city, seeking out American radicals, Judy pulled on her most dazzling outfit: black fishnet stockings, a suede miniskirt, and high boots. She headed to a rally on the university's campus for the Oakland Seven — protesters who'd been arrested when a big crowd from Berkeley marched over the city line to block the doors at an army draft center. Judy spied the attractive, broad-shouldered blond guy. She boldly walked up and introduced herself. Stew marveled at the irresistible passion in this energetic Canadian girl, barely five feet tall, with wild curly brown hair down her back. As they chatted about the war and the draft, he reached out his little finger and, with a smile, touched the tip of her nose, a tender and erotic gesture she'd never forget.

By that time, in early 1968, Stew already was an established Berkeley activist. He had found his way to the San Francisco Bay Area a couple of years before Judy, embedding himself in the local political movements and the counterculture. He had become the lesser-known half of a team, a kind of straight man and consigliore to a showier personality, Jerry Rubin.

Now Stew was in Washington because of Judy. She'd left her Boston apartment and come to D.C. at the behest of the leaders of the Mayday protest. Besides the Mayday newspaper, they wanted her to help mass-produce a detailed manual of civil disobedience. After Judy arrived at M Street, she decided to invite Stew down from New York.

She would later tell the story like this: Her housemates had burned through all their potent marijuana. What was left was weak. None had a source in D.C. to get more, and they were wary about police surveillance. So she put in a call. "Stewie, we've run out of stuff," she told him, careful not to get more detailed on the line, which they had no doubt was wiretapped. Stew contacted one of the Manhattan lawyers who often defended radicals. According to Judy, the lawyer gave Stew a big plastic bag full of high-quality pot, saying it was his donation to the great cause of Mayday, and Stew shoved it into an army surplus bag. Then he bought a bus ticket to Washington.

Six days later, on the morning of the Capitol bombing, dancing in the street felt liberating. But the mood soon turned dark. Cops and the FBI were sure to go berserk now, shaking down all the houses that sheltered the movement. Maybe it made sense to leave town until things cooled a bit. They still had weeks before the Spring Offensive got underway. Judy, Stew, and a few others in the house started to get their stuff together, clean up, take showers. They weren't in a big hurry — Stew was lounging around practically naked on the living room couch — until another activist drove over to M Street and burst through the front door in a panic. She was frantic, sure she was being followed. It was time to clear out.

So Stew, Judy, and two guys from the house piled into Judy's car. Naturally, she had a Volkswagen Beetle, in royal blue. The little automobile with the air-cooled engine, and its boxy sibling, the VW microbus, had become the unofficial transport of the counterculture, the precise opposite of the big, powerful road beasts that the older generation loved. Judy was at the wheel. Stew, a city boy who never learned to drive, rode shotgun. Off they sped at about five o'clock, heading north, destination New York City.

They were driving in the dark through Pennsylvania when Judy glanced in the rear-view mirror. Blue lights flashed behind them. They hadn't outraced the bomb investigation after all.

THE AMERICAN ANTIWAR movement at the start of 1971 already was the largest and most effective the world had ever seen. Yet a weakness persisted at its core. While its leaders included many bright lights, no single person had stepped up the way Martin Luther King Jr. had for civil rights; no charismatic figure both inspired the nation at large and united the movement's often clashing 1930s-style radicals, back-to-the-land hippies, campus intellectuals, would-be revolutionaries, middle-class liberals, black-power evangelists. It was a strange brew, as complicated as America. And among the strangest elements were the Yippies.

The most intense wing of the antiwar movement had become known as the New Left, young radicals who rejected not only capitalism but also the orthodoxy of the Communist Party and other socialist groups active in the first half of the century. The Yippies constituted a tiny slice of the New Left. They arguably weren't even a real organization, existing mainly through the media attention garnered by their two best-known figures: Berkeley's Jerry Rubin and his East Coast counterpart, Abbie Hoffman. The Sixties launched both a political and cultural revolution for the young, but even in that cauldron, the Yippies didn't seem to have a natural constituency. Too freelance and too anti-intellectual for most of the serious radicals of SDS — Students for a Democratic Society, the country's largest left-wing campus group, with tens of thousands of members — they also came across as too political for many of the Summer of Love hippies and musicians whose countercultural epicenter was San Francisco's Haight-Ashbury neighborhood. And the Yippies were way too wild and disheveled for the taste of liberal Democrats.

Nevertheless the Yippies exerted an outsized influence. Their message — Stew, behind the scenes, was perhaps its main architect — found an audience among young people alienated from both mainstream politicians and the most rigid left-wing ideologues. They preached a free-wheeling approach to changing society by fusing the energy of the counterculture with the passion of the radicals. From the hippies they enthusiastically adopted LSD, the hallucinogenic drug also known as acid, which first became a mass phenomenon around San Francisco Bay. To the recipe of sex, drugs, and rock, they added politics, cherry-picking ideas from Marxist and other leftist theoreticians.

Part of the first generation to grow up with television, the Yippies leveraged their natural instincts about the medium. They seized the vacuum at the top of the movement, the lack of an obvious über-spokesperson. They reaped regular TV coverage and countless magazine stories. Rubin and Hoffman wrote bestsellers full of advice for personal and social rebellion, with attention-grabbing titles, such as *Do It!* and *Steal This Book.*

Stew Albert, too reserved and thoughtful to stand out on television, never became a household name, as Rubin and Hoffman did. Born in Brooklyn during the Great Depression to a lower-middle-class Jewish family and expecting to follow his father into a secure lifetime job in the civil service, Stew earned a degree in marketing at Pace College in Manhattan. But the Sixties were one of those eras when the great spinning gears seem to pause all at once, with something like a giant click. Into such gaps people can slip through to a path they couldn't otherwise have imagined. All they have to do is make themselves available to the times. Stew did so. As a college student he flew to Cuba to view the revolution there firsthand (prompting the FBI to open a file on him, which would grow fat over many decades). After graduating he wandered to San Francisco, where he hobnobbed with the Beat poets. He dropped acid on an African beach with the reigning guru of psychedelics. He took target practice with black revolutionaries. He ran, half seriously, for county sheriff. And he would help organize the most famous mass protests of the times. "I do not believe there is anyone else in the country," Stew would say much later, "who observed these events as closely as I did and yet manages to maintain a certain objective distance."

While the baby boomers dominated the ranks of the antiwar movement, the Yippie leaders, like many other prominent figures, belonged to the preceding generation. Rubin was a middle-class kid from Cincinnati who'd sported a bow tie in high school and briefly was a staff reporter for the local newspaper before moving to Berkeley. Of short stature and forever self-conscious about it, Rubin felt more secure around a big guy like Stew. Hoffman had been a teenage troublemaker in Worcester, Massachusetts. He graduated from Brandeis University, got a job as a psychologist at a state hospital, and then moved to New York City to get involved in the civil rights movement. The way another Yippie, the writer Paul Krassner, saw it, Hoffman was the right side of the brain, spontaneous and witty. Rubin was the left-brain person, calculating and intellectualizing. Over time they would clash over who was top dog and who could get the most publicity. Stew stood in the middle, a soft-spoken mediator like a "wise old rabbi." As such he was just as responsible for the show, both its wacky and serious sides.

The Yippies weren't the first self-styled Americans, nor would they be the last, to sell the idea that the past could be blotted out by the present, that old rules could be smashed without consequence. If acid was the rocket fuel of the counterculture, the Yippies were the acid of the New Left.

PLOT THE ANTIWAR movement as a fever chart, and you find Stew and his circle of friends at some of the sharpest spikes.

Begin the timeline in 1965. The intervention in Indochina had been relatively modest until March of that year, when LBJ decided to dispatch marines to the beaches of Cam Ranh Bay. Within two months, Jerry Rubin became the key organizer of a massive two-day "teach-in" about the war on the Berkeley campus of the University of California, serving up speakers, music, skits, and films. Its unexpected success — thousands of people showed up, at a time when most Americans had barely heard of Vietnam — earned Rubin a national reputation.

Like a similar teach-in at the University of Michigan in Ann Arbor, the nation's other chief incubator of campus activism, Berkeley's Vietnam Day offered a counterpoint to the government's claim that the United States was merely backing a legitimate democratic regime in South Vietnam against a communist invader, which, if victorious, would then knock down neighboring Asian nations like dominos and perhaps reach American shores.

Participants discussed Vietnam's history — its centuries-long struggle against occupations by the Chinese, the French, and the Japanese.

They learned that the intellectual leader of Vietnamese nationalism, Ho Chi Minh, had aided the Allies during World War II. He then sought American support to prevent France from reasserting colonial rule. The United States refused. Instead it futilely financed the French reoccupation and the subsequent war. The French were outmaneuvered and routed by Ho's fierce pro-communist forces in 1954. Under the terms of the peace treaty, Vietnam was divided at the seventeenth parallel. Ho's group took the North. Americans replaced the French in the South, where much of the population supported the pro-North guerrillas, the Vietcong, who with good reason considered the government a puppet regime of the United States.

Speaker after speaker made the point: the United States had no credible strategic or ethical grounds for trying to shoot, bomb, and burn into submission a small country of peasants.

LBJ could afford to ignore his critics as long as they remained a ragged patchwork of student, pacifist, and religious groups, concentrated on the coasts and the upper Midwest, many wary of one another's tactics and motives. His secretary of state, Dean Rusk, dismissed the teach-ins thusly: "I sometimes wonder at the gullibility of educated men." But over the next couple of years, prodded by a handful of experienced activists, antiwar groups began to pull together as a coalition, if an uneasy one. The strategy paid off. In April 1967, some three hundred thousand people had marched down Fifth Avenue in New York City. Tens of thousands paraded the same day in San Francisco. Martin Luther King Jr. explicitly linked the antiwar and civil rights movements. "If America's soul becomes totally poisoned," King preached, "part of the autopsy must read 'Vietnam.'" Together these developments were making it harder for politicians or journalists to maintain that such sentiment was on the fringe.

For their next step, the leaders of the coalition, newly named the National Mobilization Committee to End the War in Vietnam — the Mobe for short — decided to bring a huge crowd to Washington in the fall of 1967, to the doorstep of the people actually running the war. All they needed was a proven organizer.

Jerry Rubin had just lost a renegade bid for mayor of Berkeley, with Stew as his campaign manager. He was looking for a new cause. Despite the misgivings of the more traditional members of the Mobe, the coalition tapped Rubin. He moved to New York City and brought Stew along.

Soon they met another recent arrival, Abbie Hoffman. Seeking to bring excitement and attention to the movement (and, it must be said, to himself), Hoffman promoted a new brand of activism. He would mix the antics of the Diggers, a pre-hippie San Francisco grouping of anarchistic street actors and jokesters who staged spontaneous provocative events and gave away food, with the writings of Marshall McLuhan, a Canadian philosopher. McLuhan argued that electronic media offered more than information delivery, as books and newspapers did; the new inventions also changed human perception. Television could be a powerful new platform if you knew how to use it.

Hoffman and his new friends tested their ideas at the New York Stock Exchange. They posed as tourists and got onto the visitors' balcony, overlooking the trading floor. Hoffman carried a paper bag stuffed with a few hundred dollars — singles mostly, both real bills and pretend ones. The gang grabbed handfuls and tossed them down. They whooped as some traders lunged for the fluttering cash. Hoffman had alerted the news media in advance, and on the way out he and his friends burned some real money, for the benefit of reporters. The next morning, New York's *Daily News* ran a picture of Hoffman holding a flaming fiver, with Rubin gesticulating at it. You couldn't see Stew. The upraised arms of Rubin and Hoffman blocked his face. "Typical," Stew sighed to himself.

The publicity went national, supporting Hoffman's theory about outrageous acts. The trio and their friends vowed to apply the lessons to the upcoming demonstration in D.C., which Rubin was supposed to be directing as a traditional rally. They announced they would "exorcise the demons" from the Pentagon. Hoffman promised that protesters would not only encircle the building but also levitate it. "We're going to raise the Pentagon three hundred feet in the air!" he told reporters. Hoffman was aware that such stunts, tongue in cheek or not, alienated the straights. He would point out that lots of American colonists had been offended when patriots dumped tea into Boston Harbor.

Coming to New York, Stew had been excited at the prospect of working with David Dellinger and other antiwar leaders who'd earned widespread admiration in the movement. "Maybe a little might rub off," he thought. But many in the Mobe — which covered an enormous range of the American left, from liberal ban-the-bomb activists and San Francisco longshoremen to the National Lawyers Guild and the Socialist

Workers Party—weren't amused by the antics of Rubin's crowd, nor by their prolific pot-smoking and acid trips. (Leaders of one venerable group, the National Committee for a Sane Nuclear Policy, used to insist that its people wear suits, ties, and dresses to demonstrations.) The more traditional members balked at the radical and provocative articles appearing in the Mobe's newspaper, which Stew had taken over. They threatened to quit the whole enterprise unless Stew was yanked.

Despite the infighting, the Washington event was a success. More than a hundred thousand people rallied in West Potomac Park by the Lincoln Memorial that Saturday in October 1967. About half the assemblage then chose to march to the Pentagon, moving slowly out of the park and onto the bridge over the river. The novelist Norman Mailer, walking at the front, near Stew and Rubin, was reminded of the cover of the Beatles' new album, their foray into psychedelic rock. The marchers, Mailer would write, looked "like the legions of Sgt. Pepper's Band . . . assembled from all the intersections between history and the comic books, between legend and television, the Biblical archetypes and the movies."

The deliberately absurd talk of exorcism and levitation helped unnerve the authorities. Over a day and a night at the Pentagon, pitched clashes between the police and the most militant protesters left a slew of people bloodied. Nearly seven hundred were arrested, including Stew, Rubin, and Mailer, who would win the Pulitzer Prize for his account.

After they were bailed out, Stew and Rubin headed for the airport, where they happened to run into JFK's brother, Robert F. Kennedy, then a U.S. senator from New York. Earlier that fall, Kennedy had turned down pleas from the Democratic Party's liberal wing to challenge LBJ as an antiwar candidate. Stew and Rubin boasted about their role at the Pentagon. Kennedy wasn't impressed. He told the young men they wouldn't end the Vietnam War that way.

Maybe not, but soon enough, it would become clear how much the movement would encroach on presidential politics.

THE FORMAL BIRTH of the Yippies—to the extent that any formality was involved—came a couple of months later. It was the last day of 1967. Stew and Rubin, along with a few others of like sensibility, gathered at the apartment where Abbie Hoffman and his wife, Anita, were living, on the Lower East Side. On the agenda: how to carry forward the group's ideas in the form of a protest at the Democratic National Convention in Chicago, where LBJ was expected to accept the nomination for a second, and this time full, term and thus be able to continue waging his war.

They decided to mount a Festival of Life, some combination of a hippie gathering and a Vietnam teach-in — a contrast with what was sure to be the soul-deadening proceedings of the convention. There would be music, booths about dodging the draft, and lectures on the history of the war. They could bring forth Stew's "soulful socialism," a fusion of stoners and political radicals.

Newspapers would want to know who was sponsoring this extravaganza. Trying to come up with a name for their joint enterprise, the writer Paul Krassner slipped away from the pot-induced bedlam and wandered alone into the bedroom. He ran through some ideas in his head. Something short and punchy, like "kif," which he'd been hearing as a slang term for marijuana. Maybe a play on "hippie." Something like a shout of ecstasy, like "yippee!" That's it, he thought — YIP. Anita Hoffman took it a step further — let's tell reporters it's short for Youth International Party. On the way out, Krassner rubbed snow into Rubin's bushy hair in a kind of baptism.

Afterward Stew headed home to California to prepare for Chicago. That's when he met Judy for the first time, at the rally. He soon moved in with her, into the big old house where she was staying, up in the Berkeley Hills, on a rise dotted with giant pines, with views of San Francisco and the Bay. The fireplace downstairs, with cherubs carved around the mantle, became a gathering spot for luminaries of the Bay Area's left, a place where Stew, in particular, would build his reputation as a trusted intermediary among sometimes warring radical factions of the movement. "That was his job," Judy would explain later. "Going around, cooling things out."

One frequent visitor was Eldridge Cleaver, a leader of the Black Panther Party. The party had been founded a couple of years earlier in neighboring Oakland by Bobby Seale and Huey Newton, political activists who met while working in anti-poverty programs and came to embrace black empowerment, inspired in part by the writings of Asian and African revolutionaries. Their platform called for reparations for slavery and an exemption from military service for African Americans. The Panthers set up social programs, such as free breakfasts for poor school kids, but got more attention, particularly from the white news media, for establishing armed groups to shield black communities from harassment and violence by police. (Keeping a gun for protection wasn't a new idea among African Americans, many of whose parents and grandparents had to arm themselves against white terrorists. The original name of the new group had been the Black Panther Party for Self-Defense.)

At first the Panthers raised money for guns and ammunition by peddling the Chinese communist leader Mao Tse-tung's *Little Red Book* to students at Berkeley. The book, which presented Mao's theories of global mass revolution though pithy quotations such as "political power grows out of the barrel of a gun," was being embraced as a strategic and tactical manual by American radicals, white and black. Seale bought copies for twenty cents each across the bay in San Francisco and sold them for a buck to the kids on campus. The group's activities alarmed California lawmakers, who in the spring of 1967 passed the state's first law banning the open carry of loaded firearms, even as a clutch of Panthers, many of them armed, descended on the state capitol.

Cleaver, then thirty-two, had just released an electrifying prison memoir, *Soul on Ice,* chronicling his path from convicted rapist to incipient revolutionary. He would bring his young girlfriends to the Hippie Palace, as he dubbed Stew and Judy's house. Cleaver also gave Judy an enduring nickname. When they first met, he took to calling her "Mrs. Stew." One evening, as the three of them were riding around San Francisco in the Panther's yellow Pontiac, Judy finally told Cleaver how much she hated the name. So Cleaver came up with something else. "Gumbo," he said, laughing. Dig it: Stew and Gumbo. She found it kind of corny at first, but it stuck. From then on she would drop her birth surname, Clavir, and go by Judy Gumbo. Sometimes just Gumbo, which she used as her byline at the underground newspapers where she ended up working with Stew — the *Berkeley Barb* and the *Berkeley Tribe.*

THE MONTHS LEADING up to the Democratic National Convention in Chicago threatened to shove a teetering nation all the way into chaos. In January 1968, a couple of days after Stew met Judy, the Vietcong had shocked the world with the Tet Offensive, a coordinated invasion by tens of thousands of guerrillas and North Vietnamese regulars into more than a hundred cities and outposts, including Saigon, where they even managed to get inside the U.S. embassy compound. Although the attackers were beaten back by American and South Vietnamese troops and suffered devastating losses, the scope of the operation demolished the U.S. military's pretension that it had all but crushed the enemy. "The VC were everywhere all at once like spider cancer," wrote Michael Herr, a war correspondent for *Esquire* magazine, "and instead of losing the war in little pieces over years we lost it fast in under a week."

The political fallout was swift. Eugene McCarthy, a U.S. senator from Minnesota, had heeded the call from the Dump Johnson Democrats after Robert F. Kennedy had declined to run. McCarthy stunned the sitting president by garnering more than 40 percent of the vote in the New Hampshire primary.

Polls showed that half of Americans now disapproved of LBJ's Vietnam policies. The dean of television anchors, CBS's Walter Cronkite, visited Vietnam and informed his millions of viewers that the war was a "stalemate." Toward the end of March, LBJ's informal advisers, nicknamed the Wise Men, told the president that domestic opposition had grown so strong, it was tearing the country apart; he no longer had time to pursue or achieve any kind of military victory. It was commonly believed that it was mainly the young who opposed the war, out of fear, as Police Chief Jerry Wilson would say, that they might be drafted. That conclusion was misguided on two counts. While the draft was an important motivation, it wasn't the only one; most movement leaders, like Stew Albert, were older than twenty-six, the cutoff for conscription. Moreover, the war's unpopularity was widespread among all age groups. Polls showed that as a group, people over fifty were much more likely than the young to see the war as a mistake; the bulk of the marchers might have been college-age, but lots of their generational peers still supported U.S. policy.

Within five days, LBJ announced he wouldn't seek reelection. Less than a week after that, the assassination of Martin Luther King Jr. by a racist gunman in Memphis triggered devastating riots in dozens of American cities. Arson ignited ten blocks of Washington, D.C. Little more than two weeks later, the tide of student radicalism engulfed Columbia University, where protesters occupied four buildings and battled the police who tried to evict them.

Then in June, Robert F. Kennedy, who had decided to run for president after all, was shot and killed by an assassin on the night he won the California primary. That left McCarthy and LBJ's vice president, Hubert Humphrey, as the leading candidates for the Democratic nomination.

Suddenly the idea of all those politicians, students, and antiwar and civil rights activists converging on Chicago seemed much more fraught. Fearing violence, McCarthy appealed to his supporters to stay away from any protests at the convention. The Mobe pressed ahead anyway. And the Yippies doubled down. Rubin imagined half a million young people smoking pot, burning draft cards, dancing, and roaring through the streets. Stew thought that since their version of Marxism stemmed more from Groucho than Karl, the event ought to be wild, like *A Night at the Opera.*

And so it was. The Yippies tried to top one another, scaring the Chicago authorities and keeping themselves in the news. Krassner suggested they might put LSD into the city's water supply; another proclaimed that hundreds of "studly" Yippies would seduce the wives and daughters of convention delegates. As the events got underway, they procured a hog from a farm in the Illinois countryside. To mock the Democrats, they called a press conference to nominate "Pigasus" for president. Police impounded the animal and arrested the Yippies for disturbing the peace. In a rare bit of humor from the Chicago cops, one joked with them, "Boys, I have bad news for you. The pig squealed."

The fun part was short-lived. Jerry Rubin and Abbie Hoffman had grown increasingly competitive as to who was Top Yippie. They even argued angrily over what size pig to nominate. During one group meeting they practically came to blows. Stew sided with his longtime friend Rubin. Meantime, the Yippie throngs never really showed. Probably no more than five thousand outsiders came to Chicago.

Even without a major invasion of his city, it wasn't especially surprising that one of the most aggressive law-and-order mayors in the country, the jowly and humorless Democrat Richard Daley, who had recently ordered police to shoot looters in Chicago after King's assassination, would respond to the Yippie threats by denying parade permits, stationing guards at the water supplies, calling in thousands of troops, and jangling the nerves of his cops, who were already inclined toward contempt for the antiwarriors. While many officers tried to distinguish between peaceful and violent protesters, some cops were eager to teach a lesson to a generation they believed had flown off the rails. "These Yipps with their tough talk were making that very easy for some of the members," one said later. A confrontation seemed inevitable.

THE FIRST BLOOD shed in Chicago was Stew's. The Yippies and police clashed on the first night of the festival in Lincoln Park. Clubbed on the head, bleeding from his scalp, Stew found Hoffman. They embraced, crying and swearing at the police. The fighting was a prelude to five days of skirmishes around the city. As the cops grew more frustrated and abusive, the rhetoric of the protesters rose in militancy, as did their taunting and resistance.

Yippies weren't the only game in town. The biggest gathering of the week, some ten thousand people in Grant Park, was organized by the Mobe to take place as the Democratic delegates prepared to vote on their nominee. Police pushed into the rally, eventually triggering an intense clash that a national commission later labeled a law enforcement riot. Hundreds of blue-helmeted cops let loose their fury. Clubs swinging, they attacked thousands of protesters trapped by police lines on Michigan Avenue outside the Hilton hotel, where many Democratic convention delegates were staying. While the news cameras rolled, some cops yelled, "Kill, kill, kill," as they charged, beating people to clear the street and sidewalk. Tourists, onlookers, and reporters got clubbed too. Some crashed backward through the hotel's big plate-glass window. The crowd chanted, "The whole world is watching! The whole world is watching!"

Everyone had lost control of the events in Chicago, but the outcome was something like a Yippie acid dream — the revolution being televised, the participants also the audience, the images overtaking the narrative.

As the battles raged in the Chicago streets, a tumultuous convention rejected an antiwar plank for the party's platform. The next day, delegates handed Humphrey the Democratic nomination. He would go on to narrowly lose the general election to Richard Nixon.

A foundation of Nixon's campaign was the promise to restore law and order. The new president's choice for attorney general, John Mitchell, wasted no time. In early 1969, his Justice Department indicted eight people for conspiracy and incitement to riot in Chicago: the Yippies Rubin and Hoffman and, from the Mobe, David Dellinger, Rennie Davis, and Tom Hayden. Also charged were John Froines, an SDS activist with a doctorate in chemistry from Yale; a graduate student at Northwestern University named Lee Weiner; and Bobby Seale of the Black Panthers. They became known as the Chicago Seven, after Seale's case was separated.

Stew was named one of a dozen unindicted co-conspirators. Prosecutors apparently decided his work with the Berkeley underground press might give him a credible First Amendment defense to any charges related to the riot.

With the help of a paranoid and irascible trial judge, the Chicago Seven case would turn into a national circus and propel the defendants to celebrity status. Stew was forever disappointed that he hadn't been one of the headliners.

TWO YEARS LATER, two members of the Chicago Seven—David Tyre Dellinger, a longtime peace activist, and Rennard Cordon Davis, who had been a first-generation leader of Students for a Democratic Society and was known as Rennie—would become two of the main planners of the Mayday mass civil disobedience in Washington.

They promised their protest would be disruptive but nonviolent. Yet the shadow of Chicago loomed; many in the movement were skeptical that such a sizable Washington action could remain peaceful. That was why Rennie was dismayed when he took a courtesy call in February 1971 from the most radical splinter group in the New Left, the Weather Underground Organization. In support of the Spring Offensive, Rennie was informed, the group planned to kick off the festivities by bombing a high-profile target in Washington.

Rennie, twenty-nine years old, was raised in the Washington area and still lived there. His father had been a labor economist in the administration of President Harry Truman. Rennie spent his teenage years on his family's five-hundred-acre farm in Virginia's Blue Ridge. After being class president and valedictorian in high school, he headed to Oberlin College in Ohio. With a quick mind and a gift for extemporaneous oratory, he helped organize SDS in the mid-Sixties. He went on to run a short-lived SDS offshoot that sent white radicals into struggling urban neighborhoods to try to build an interracial movement of the poor. He set up antiwar coffeehouses outside military bases before joining David Dellinger and others in the Mobe. Leaders of the Old Left, who were often skeptical of young newcomers, respected him for his "practiced organizational talent," as one put it.

Rennie knew most members of the Weather Underground. He had worked with them before, when they were still in SDS. After Chicago, SDS disintegrated as its factions battled over the proper path to revolutionary change. The most militant cadres formed the Weather group. Like the Yippies, their relatively small numbers were out of proportion to the attention they received. Like the Yippies, they had grown impatient with tedious political organizing and picketing. But instead of theatrics, the Weather Underground had veered into guerrilla action. Their war was justified, they would argue, because the United States was only a pretend democracy, structured to oppress the poor and the powerless at home and abroad in order to protect the rich and powerful. What's more, the government had demonstrated that it would stop at nothing to crush dissent, not only at the Democratic convention but in gunfights with black militants; two Chicago-based Black Panthers, Fred Hampton, who was twenty-one, and Mark Clark, twenty-two, had been shot by police in their beds, an incident widely viewed as a cold-blooded execution. Isolated, intoxicated with self-importance, Weather members saw themselves as inspired by these revolutionary martyrs, as well as peasant guerrilla movements in Vietnam and Cuba. They felt kinship with John Brown, who had led the bloody 1859 raid on the U.S. armory at Harpers Ferry in hopes of triggering an uprising against slavery.

Many radicals who would never pick up a gun or a bomb viewed Weather sympathetically. They saw the leaders of the military and the FBI, not the guerrillas, as the real terrorists. There was a moral obligation to stand in the government's way. Yet few in the American left believed what Weather took as a matter of faith — that some well-placed explosions and other violent confrontations with state power could spark a revolution. (By most accounts, even the Vietnamese and Cubans didn't believe this.) They taught themselves how to make bombs with sticks of dynamite — "that most romantic of 19th century tools," as one wrote later. Since the fall of 1969 they had set off more than a dozen devices, in police cars and police stations, banks and courthouses, always to make a political point — to show blacks, prisoners, and the poor that they now had serious outlaw allies. Their continuing attacks triggered a frantic government manhunt and expanded surveillance of the entire

New Left. The fugitives depended heavily on aboveground backers — "such a network was crucial for everything from money to cars to addresses for receiving IDs," as one later acknowledged.

One underground Weather collective, based in New York, planned to go far beyond the group's previous actions. Its members assembled a bomb, packed with roofing nails, that was intended to blow up inside a room full of soldiers and their dates attending a dance at Fort Dix in New Jersey. Had they succeeded, they would have erased any argument against Weather being a purely terrorist organization.

Instead, on the day of the dance, March 6, 1970, it was the bomb makers who died. Somehow the device went off in their makeshift factory, in the basement of a townhouse in New York's Greenwich Village. Three people blew themselves to bits. At least two escaped, including Cathy Wilkerson, whose father owned the house, and Kathy Boudin, who had been taking a shower and staggered out of the rubble without clothes. They were taken in by neighbors (one was the wife of the actor Dustin Hoffman) and managed to disappear before the police arrived.

How much other members of the Weather Underground around the country knew about or supported the Fort Dix plan would never quite be resolved.* In any case, the horrific scene provoked self-examination among the survivors and the rest of Weather. From then on, "we were very careful to be sure we weren't going to hurt anybody," one claimed later.

RENNIE UNDERSTOOD ALL this history, and not only because he had crossed paths with Kathy Boudin and others in SDS. Rennie's youngest brother, John, who had helped Rennie organize the GI coffeehouses, was now working with the Weather Underground.

---

* Arthur Eckstein, in *Bad Moon Rising: How the Weather Underground Beat the FBI and Lost the Revolution* (New Haven: Yale 2016), cites evidence from interviews and FBI files to persuasively undermine the notion that the Townhouse Collective was a rogue operation. Eckstein argues that the Detroit Weather Collective coordinated with its New York City counterpart, placing two dynamite bombs meant to explode the same day as the one in Fort Dix. They were, however, disarmed, thanks to an informant's tip. One bomb was at Detroit's Thirteenth Police Precinct, and the other was in an alley between the offices of the Detroit Police Officers Association and a popular restaurant, where civilian casualties would have been a near certainty.

So Rennie tried to head off Weather's plan to bomb the U.S. Capitol. He cranked up his considerable persuasive power. As a teenager he was famous in his hometown for talking a judge out of giving him a speeding ticket by claiming he'd just been racing home to finish his homework. Rennie contacted his brother and others in Weather. A bombing now would undermine the careful preparations for the Spring Offensive, he argued. Rennie and his colleagues wanted to demonstrate the power of nonviolence to move the mass of antiwar sentiment from mere protest to resistance.

Weather wouldn't budge. The guerrillas believed the Capitol was the perfect target, "a monument to U.S. domination all over the planet." They gave code names to all their operations. This was "Big Top." As one wrote later, "Dynamite became ice cream or pickles. Much easier to say, 'I am taking three pounds of ice cream to the Big Top,' than, 'I am putting a three-pound bomb in the Capitol.'"

Rennie's arguments failed. "That was a nightmare for me," he recalled.

Big Top had become a project for two teams. The device would be placed by the first team, which published accounts would later identify as two women living deep within Weather. One was Boudin, a twenty-seven-year-old Bryn Mawr College graduate and the daughter of a prominent left-wing lawyer. The other was the charismatic Bernardine Dohrn, a twenty-nine-year-old graduate of the University of Chicago's law school whose looks, brains, and style had made her a romantic icon within the left. The second team was to scout the area and help find a place for the bomb. Team members posed as tourists and wandered through the Capitol for days, searching for the spot. They saw that visitors weren't frisked. There was free passage throughout the corridors. Doors to storerooms and offices often weren't locked. Automatic elevators and parking garages were basically unattended. There was no video surveillance.

A trashcan? A closet? A tunnel? Finally they found a spot. It was behind a five-foot-high wall in an unmarked first-floor bathroom. Full of dust, so it probably wasn't cleaned or checked regularly. They made a test call to the switchboard, to see how long it would take to evacuate the building at night. They concluded that only the night watchman remained in the building by midnight. They planned the bombing for February 27.

Dohrn and Boudin strapped the dynamite and timer to themselves, walked in, and assembled the device in the bathroom.

But as they lifted the bomb into its hiding place, it didn't sit securely. It fell to the bottom. After a sickening few seconds, they let out their breath. They left the building. The warning call came in to the switchboard at one in the morning. The Capitol police searched the building, found nothing.

And no bomb went off.

Dohrn and Boudin realized the bomb's fall must have detached its timer. So the call went out to get another explosive device, a small one that would detonate the whole bomb, like a starter motor. The next day, they (or perhaps other members of the team) returned and put the new mechanism in place. Again someone phoned the switchboard, as well as the *Washington Post:* "You may have other calls like this," said the voice, but take this one seriously.

Again the Capitol police searched as many rooms as they could in half an hour. One man looked into the bathroom, saw nothing, and moved on. Only seven minutes later, it blew.

The Weather Underground had mailed a letter to the newsrooms of the *New York Post* and the Associated Press, taking responsibility. Sent by special delivery, it carried the group's logo, a rainbow with a bolt of lightning. As always, brevity wasn't a strong point. (The manifesto that launched the Weatherman group, as it was first known, published in a journal called *New Left Notes* in June 1969, had sprawled to sixteen thousand words.) The writers now took five typed pages to elaborate on their motive: "The Nixon regime is now attempting the brutal conquest of yet another nation in Indochina. Lies about the war 'winding down' cannot hide the criminal invasion of Laos."

They suggested more bombs were on the way and again claimed solidarity with the Spring Offensive as well as real guerrilla uprisings. "All over the country," they wrote, "revolutionaries are getting ready for the Spring. Our plans can be as creative and indigenous as the bamboo booby traps of the Vietnamese."

The authorities had little reason to doubt that the Weather Underground was responsible. The question was, did anyone from the Mayday Tribe help?

• • •

LESS THAN TWENTY-FOUR hours after the bombing, a veritable convoy of state troopers stopped Stew, Judy, and two of their friends on Route 100 in southern Pennsylvania. One police car sliced in front of their car, to block their way. Judy hit the brakes. Over a loudspeaker came a voice: "Out of the car with your hands up." Several cars screeched to a stop and a dozen officers jumped out. Shotguns pointed out of the darkness. "Okay boys, you stay in here, I'm going to handle this," Judy boldly told the young men. But in a moment she knocked on the window and told them they had to step out as well.

It turned out the FBI had been following them for hours. Agents had waited outside when the travelers stopped, outside Baltimore, for dinner at the boyhood home of one passenger. He was Colin Neiburger, who had served six months in jail for his activities as an antiwar organizer in Ohio. (The FBI would search his parents' house the next day.) Assuming the position, Neiburger put his hands on the car, and one officer cocked a gun at Neiburger's head.

When asked, the FBI agent in charge told the four that they were being sought in connection with the Capitol attack. He said the agents had probable cause to believe that the car contained a knapsack used to transport explosives. The agents called for an army bomb-disposal unit to search the vehicle.

They stuck the three young men in the back of one police car and Judy in another, by herself. In the cruiser's rear-view mirror, she could see them search every inch of her VW. It felt like she sat in the cruiser for hours. They found nothing in Stew's green knapsack and nothing in the car but some stale peanut-butter sandwiches. In the end, one state trooper handed Judy a ticket for driving with a bald tire and let them go.

Stew later told reporters only the obvious: "They thought we blew up the Capitol, or they were going to frame us."

Three days later, the FBI nearly stumbled into capturing one of the Weather bombers — Bernardine Dohrn. She had gone straight back to her hiding place in the Bay Area. On the Thursday after the bombing, she and other members of the collective picked up some money wired to a Western Union office. An agent recognized them, but they sped away and later switched cars to elude the authorities. One of the drivers was Rennie's brother John. His were among the fingerprints the FBI later found in a San Francisco apartment where the band had been handling explosives.

As a fugitive, Dohrn, along with her colleagues, was already on the FBI's most-wanted list. But the bureau hadn't identified her as one of the Capitol bombers. Their focus remained on Washington, where they continued the hunt for links.

As FBI records would later show, the authorities thought they had several good reasons to suspect some organizers of Mayday. The bureau may have known about Rennie's brother. Furthermore, as would eventually come out, the police and the feds had placed illegal wiretaps and bugs in Mayday apartments and offices. Before the Spring Offensive, Attorney General John Mitchell had authorized electronic surveillance of the Mayday Tribe and the three other antiwar groups involved in the planning. In addition, one police informant was living with a couple of the women who ran the Mayday headquarters. Another undercover agent had dropped in on a Mayday house after the bombing, and though he found no evidence, he reported back his suspicion that the residents had been somehow involved.

The FBI shifted agents from all parts of the Washington field office to the case. They fanned out, tailing Mayday activists, knocking on the doors of their homes, trying to interrogate them as they entered and left the movement's headquarters. Once they stopped and searched a car full of antiwar Vietnam vets.

One team of agents took a stack of surveillance photographs of Mayday Tribe members and showed them around to anyone who'd signed the Capitol's visitor registry in the days leading up to the explosion.

A Capitol police officer who had been on duty at the rotunda on the Thursday before the bombing selected Stew's picture from among a half-dozen photos. He thought Stew could have been the young man who had inquired about touring the Capitol and asked if he could stash an olive-green canvas bag at the desk while he went sightseeing. The officer had declined to take the bag, sending the man, and the young woman who accompanied him, to the information desk. But others looking at the photo weren't sure; there could have been other blond hippies wandering through the halls that day. (Judy would later say Stew was never in the Capitol; the guard was either "set-up, a liar, or befuddled.")

One of the agents working the case was Thomas Strentz, normally part of the organized crime section. Strentz located an army major and his wife who had recently moved to the region and had been touring the

Capitol for the first time on the day before the bombing. The major and his wife separately pointed "in a heartbeat" to a picture of one woman in Stew and Judy's circle. The army couple said they recognized her as the person who had been pushing a baby carriage through the Capitol. They remembered, Strentz said later, because she was "rather portly and they could not figure out how she lugged that carriage up all those stairs."

The young woman in the photograph was Leslie Bacon. She was a tall, sweet-faced blonde, nineteen years old, from a well-to-do family in northern California. Her father owned a lumberyard. The eldest of eight children, Bacon went to Catholic school, dropped out of college, and eventually drifted to New York to work with the underground press. She made her way to Washington and now was booking musicians for the Spring Offensive.

Bacon had been at the house on M Street the day of the bombing, when Stew and Judy and the others jumped into the car and headed north. She elected to stay in town. She moved her stuff over to a green-painted brick row house where other Mayday activists had congregated. It was on Lanier Place, across from the one where Rennie Davis lived.

On the Saturday morning after the bombing, eight FBI agents stormed into the house and down the stairs, into the basement room where Bacon slept. They pulled her out of bed. They took her to police headquarters for questioning, and when she told them she knew nothing about the bombing, they released her. For the time being.

2

We Need Time

HE USUALLY KEPT THE GYM BAG AT HIS OFFICE ON THE SECOND floor of the West Wing. Most lunchtimes, if there wasn't a staff meeting, Egil Krogh Jr. would slip out of his suit, pull on his shorts and sneakers, and leave the White House. He'd head down to Seventeenth Street and begin his run. He did at least three miles, winding past the stately museums and the white monuments bright in the midday sun. If it felt right, he'd go all the way down to the river and circle around West Potomac Park. A jogging craze would seize the nation in a year or two, but in 1971 the sight of a grown man pumping his knees along the National Mall was still rare enough to make tourists stare.

The clean-cut, thirty-one-year-old lawyer hadn't run for fun or competition since his college days. Getting back to it felt natural, part of his birthright. His father had been track captain and an outstanding miler at the University of Chicago in the 1920s. The given name they shared, that of an ancient Norse warrior, a nod to their roots, was pronounced "eh-GEEL" but had been Americanized* to "Eggle" or sometimes "Eagle." Krogh the younger was nicknamed Bud practically at birth; his father thought it would be less of a burden for the child.

Bud believed these runs were saving his life. They were wringing out the tension of long days at his White House desk, not to mention working off the thirty extra pounds he'd laid on during his first couple of years in Washington. Before dawn he forced himself out of bed at his Virginia

---

* People would get the last name wrong too. Krogh rhymes with "rogue," not "crow."

studio apartment in time to make it across the river to the seven-thirty meeting of domestic policy advisers that convened most days in the Roosevelt Room, across the hall from the Oval Office. He rarely made it home before nine at night. The punishing schedule had pressured his marriage to the breaking point. He and his wife had recently separated. Their two young sons remained with her, at their home in the northwest part of the city. Bud often felt lonely.

The job weighed on him more than he'd imagined when, a year and a half earlier, the head of his Seattle law firm had invited him to pack his boxes and move east to join the new administration of Richard M. Nixon, as staff assistant to the counsel to the president. Meeting Nixon for the first time in New York City, as the president-elect assembled his team, Bud was nervous and couldn't stop staring at the man's oversized head. In the weeks to come he would often slip into giddiness about his future; once he and a colleague belted out show tunes while strolling down Fifth Avenue.

Not long after settling in to his new job, Bud wrote one of his old law professors that the honeymoon was over: "The problems are closing in with increasing pressure." To a Seattle friend he admitted, "The work gets heavier and heavier. I thought at the outset that I might get used to it, but the problems are always so new that you are going through continual periods of adjustment." He told a White House colleague that newcomers to Washington soon experienced "bruised heads, drained bodies, benumbed minds." To help him get through all the memos, reports, news articles, and studies piling up on his desk, Bud asked permission to take a class in the Evelyn Wood speed-reading system.

What burdened Bud were some of the biggest domestic challenges of the Nixon administration, handed down to him by his Seattle boss, who was now his White House boss: John Ehrlichman.

Ehrlichman, a land-use lawyer before he got involved in politics, was Nixon's top domestic aide and a member of the small inner circle, along with the president's chief of staff, H. R. Haldeman; the national security adviser, Henry Kissinger; and a handful of others. Ehrlichman was now in his mid-forties, a balding, dour-faced man with bushy eyebrows. He excelled at distilling complex information, but his propensity for exacting attention to detail and paperwork drove some of his colleagues crazy. He had been a friend of the Krogh family since Bud was ten years old.

When Bud's father died, Ehrlichman became a kind of surrogate father; he had helped Bud get into law school. Ehrlichman entrusted Bud early on in his job to develop policy ideas for some of the doozies on the administration's plate, including crime in the nation's capital and the illegal drug trade.

And, in part because Bud was one of the younger men on the staff, he also got stuck trying to figure out how the White House should cope with student unrest and the antiwar movement.

That was why, before he got a chance to go jogging on Monday, March 1, Bud pored over the intelligence memos and news stories about the bomb that blew overnight inside the U.S. Capitol. How should the White House respond?

FROM ALL APPEARANCES, Bud, who was the same age as the Yippie leaders, shared little with his generational peers on the picket lines. Earnest and even-tempered, he was raised a Midwestern Republican and a devout Christian Scientist, and he graduated from a college steeped in that faith. His official White House photograph shows a stiff, blandly handsome fellow with trimmed wavy hair; it could have been pasted in the dictionary next to the word "straight." He didn't drink or do drugs, in accordance with his religion and a promise he and his father had made to each other when Bud was eleven.

Most of Bud's colleagues found him to be unusually decent for a Washington type, practically a Boy Scout. (Playing off the name Egil, they sarcastically called him "Evil Krogh.") He might have been the hardest-working member of the group. On some mornings he'd show up with bloodshot eyes and rumpled suit, signs that he'd been up all night in his office, finishing an assignment. One time at New York's Kennedy Airport he spied a frazzled traveler, a teacher who had forgotten her passport and thus couldn't board a charter flight to London with her twenty-one students. Bud dialed up the State Department. He talked the staff into clearing her for the flight. Then he arranged for British authorities to bend the rules and grant her entry. The teacher's husband later wrote of his "boundless gratitude" to Bud: "It is unique in the world to find the highest authority of the land help one of its humblest citizens in her difficulties."

Still, while no dissenter himself, Bud had arrived in Washington with an open mind. As a navy intelligence officer in the Pacific, he had watched with detachment as young activists in Japan protested the U.S. nuclear submarines sailing into their ports. (While on leave in Tokyo and attending a Christian Science service, he met his future wife, Suzanne, a Florida native who was teaching in Japan at the time and thought he was "the best-looking man who had walked into church in months.")

He had grown accustomed to Vietnam War protests on the campus of his law school in Seattle. And, unlike most White House staffers, Bud had actually seen the messiness of the war up close. Not only had he decoded encrypted messages on the USS *Yorktown* during LBJ's military buildup, but he visited Vietnam when he was a law student. Bud traveled there with one of his professors, who theorized that redistributing land to peasants might keep them from joining up with the enemy.

In Saigon, Bud had met a Republican congressman from California, Pete McCloskey, who happened to be in Vietnam looking for answers too. McCloskey, a former marine, had won a special election by calling for a gradual withdrawal of U.S. forces, an unusual position for anyone in his party at the time. (Among those he defeated in the campaign was the former child movie star Shirley Temple Black, a Vietnam hawk.) Just back from the field, where he had visited his former unit, McCloskey told Bud he was even more discouraged about American tactics. We're destroying rural hamlets and creating more Vietcong every day, he said.

Stuck in the capital, Bud grew eager to see that countryside for himself. He knew Elizabeth Pond, a war correspondent for the *Christian Science Monitor* who had been a fellow undergraduate at Principia College in Illinois. Early in the morning on Christmas Day 1967 — about the same time the Yippies were cooking up their ideas for Chicago — Bud and Pond piled into a red Buick with a reporter from a British newspaper, a Vietnamese guide, and a driver. Passing through rolling hills and vast rubber plantations, they headed fifty miles east on the main highway to Xuan Loc.

Pond took Bud to the provincial hospital, a white one-story building staffed by Filipinos and the occasional American medic. Vietnamese children and adults with missing limbs and horrible wounds were crowded two or more to a bed. Grieving relatives stared. Bud spoke, through the translator, with one farmer. Surgeons had just amputated the leg of his twelve-year-old son, the farmer explained. The boy had wandered into a restricted area and was strafed by an American helicopter, which mistook him for Vietcong. Bud took a photograph of the farmer. When Bud got back to Seattle, he told students and professors he didn't think Washington fully realized the pain of the Vietnamese peasantry, nor did it understand the nature of that country's struggle for independence. He kept the photograph of the farmer so he wouldn't forget the agony frozen on the man's face. He hung it on the wall behind the easy chair in his office in the West Wing.

So Bud held at least some sympathy for people who criticized Nixon's policies, who acted out their dissent on the war and other matters. In D.C. he had made it a point to check out a demonstration against a new bridge and highway that would have sliced through the heart of the city. It troubled him when the cops battled with students blocking the bulldozers, when one kid's chin opened up as police dragged him away. "Nothing stirs animals more than the sight of blood," he warned his colleagues.

But by 1971 Bud had hardened his heart.

It wasn't just the Capitol bomb or the rash of other explosions claimed by the radical left. Bud had become caught up in a group of young Nixon aides who, vying for influence within a paranoid White House, had every incentive to heed the president's constant exhortations to show toughness. He had taken an object lesson from the man who'd preceded him as drug czar in the White House, a former football coach at the University of Oklahoma who had been admired but was too much of a nice guy to last in the job. As a result Bud grew "rather hard core because he found out that he had to be" to survive, one colleague observed. Bud applied his newfound toughness to a protracted bureaucratic battle with a hawkish colleague who wanted to wrest from him his control of intelligence about student radicals and antiwar protesters. Perhaps, he told Ehrlichman, the bomb at the Capitol presented more of an opportunity than a problem.

AS BUD WORKED on his memo about the bombing, the president was aloft, bound for Des Moines aboard Air Force One. The Capitol attack hadn't changed Nixon's plans for a quick day trip to the heartland to shore up political support. A few months earlier, Republicans had lost a slew of congressional seats and governorships in the 1970 midterm elections, despite Nixon's hope that his handling of the war would win over moderate voters. Now he put his mind to his next campaign, as he prepared to open the D.C. headquarters of the Committee for the Re-Election of the President. Next year promised to be a fierce fight. A Harris poll showed him three percentage points behind the presumed leader among the possible Democratic challengers, Senator Edmund Muskie of Maine.

Iowa was meant to be a milk run. Instead, when Nixon's entourage arrived at the state capitol that morning, they ran smack into a seething crowd. Among them were not only antiwarriors but union members and farmers angered by the administration's labor and agriculture policies. After Nixon spoke to the lawmakers inside, his aides tried to slip him out the back exit. The protesters spotted the motorcade and sprinted across the broad lawn, booing, chanting obscenities, and throwing snowballs and rocks. Even some hardhat construction workers, who had been a firm part of the president's base, brandished "Impeach Nixon" signs.

Nixon's foul mood deepened. Already he had been irritated that the White House response to the Washington bombing hadn't come quickly enough overnight to make the initial round of newspaper coverage. He made this clear to H. R. Haldeman, his forty-four-year-old chief of staff, a former advertising executive from Southern California. In his bearing and style (he wore a crewcut), Haldeman resembled a drill sergeant. He and Ehrlichman, who had been his college roommate, were not so affectionately called the "Prussian Guards" by other White House aides and reporters, because of their German surnames and their ferocious control over access to their boss.

By now, Haldeman had read the intelligence briefings. The bombing ratcheted up his concern about the upcoming spring protests. The Weather Underground "may very well have pulled this," he told the president. "All of it could very well be part of a general plan leading up to their April 24 [mass] demonstration and then their Mayday plan to close down Washington."

The American left and Nixon were longtime foes. He had embraced the enmity, indeed had made it a foundation of his political career. As a young congressman from California, he garnered a seat on the House Un-American Activities Committee, where he helped craft legislation that would have denied passports and federal jobs to members of groups the government considered linked to communists (the bill died in the Senate after sparking a protest march on Washington) and won fame for his pursuit of a State Department official accused of being a Soviet spy. Nixon thus helped lay the groundwork for the witch hunts of Senator Joseph McCarthy a few years later. In Nixon's own run for the Senate, in 1950, he proclaimed that the Soviets had given the American Communist Party "a virtual blueprint for revolution" and famously buried his opponent under insinuations she was a closet Red, or at least Pink. It would be a short hop to paint antiwar demonstrators as witting or unwitting agents of dark outside forces.

Beyond the reflexive anticommunism, something quite personal was at play. To a man like Nixon, who had clawed his way to power, born in a sparsely populated southern California farm town with a father who barely could support the family, who grieved along with his parents when two of his four brothers died of disease, the young people doing the protesting were themselves unworthy of respect, even reprehensible. Their youth was marked by privilege and hedonism, the opposite of his. Rather than working hard to build a future, planted in a chair in a college library for days and weeks on end as Nixon had done — his law school classmates had called him "iron-butt" — they cavorted on the campus lawns like sexual adventurers, fouling their young bodies and brains with dangerous chemicals, listening to incomprehensible songs. "You ever hear that music out there in the park?" he once asked his chief of staff incredulously, his tone enclosing the word "music" in invisible quotation marks. "Shouting 'Oooh, oooh'?"

Nixon's own undergraduate years coincided with the Great Depression. His family had moved from their failed citrus farm to the town of Whittier, twenty miles closer to Los Angeles, where his father opened a gas station with a little grocery store. An outstanding high school student, Nixon had been offered a scholarship to Harvard. His family couldn't afford the travel and living expenses, so he enrolled at Whittier College and lived at home. (Whittier had been founded by Quakers, and Nixon's mother was a committed Quaker, but Nixon would later move away from those pacifist roots when he declined a religious exemption in World War II and joined the navy.)

In college, his intelligence and fine judgment stood out, but those who knew him also recognized "an underlying unease and awkwardness," a girlfriend recalled later. He compensated for this with a drive for public recognition, maneuvering to be elected as student body president and pushing himself so hard, against type, to be a decent football player that the coach warned him not to risk more health troubles, as his family was already reeling from the tragedy of his older brother, Harold — described by a relative as the Nixons' favorite son, "a brighter, more handsome fellow" than Richard — who was dying of tuberculosis.

Nixon studied history and graduated summa cum laude, entering the law school at Duke University. He also excelled there. Yet upon graduation, the big New York law firms, which favored the Ivy League, turned him down. Nixon always would carry "certain resentments against the privileged," as a personal assistant once observed. At one point Nixon told Bud's boss, John Ehrlichman, that there were too many Ivy Leaguers in the administration and to hire no more of them for at least a year.

It certainly didn't help that some antiwar leaders came from well-to-do families and attended elite colleges. After meeting the Singing Cadets from Texas A&M, Nixon remarked to an aide that the school was larger than many of the Ivies combined: "And we've got to remember that just as the East spews out these revolutionaries and radicals and bastards that some of those big schools in the West are spewing out bright guys that are pretty good."

In his 1968 campaign he chose for a running mate Spiro Agnew, the overbearing Maryland governor who specialized in rhetorical takedowns of his enemies, particularly the New Left: "the cacophony of seditious drivel emanating from the best-publicized clowns in our society." In one Nixon campaign ad, the candidate's voiceover said, "I pledge to you we will have order in the United States," while scenes flashed by showing bloodied demonstrators, a burning building, and menacingly lit protesters holding up two fingers in a "V," the peace sign. In another spot, rock music and pictures of young people blared under Nixon's solemn words: "American youth today has its fringes."

Nixon and those close to him took great satisfaction in the Democratic Party's failure to recover from the chaos of its Chicago convention. Noted Ehrlichman, "That whole thing, with the Daley people and the police clubbing the hippies, and the fringes — that was a big net plus for us."

For his first campus speech as president, Nixon picked General Beadle State College in South Dakota, a place safely free of radicals. He delivered a hard-line sermon, declaring the United States faced "what may be the severest challenge of our history," a crisis of immorality that had spawned "drugs and crime, campus revolts, racial discord and draft resistance." However, Nixon told the crowd, they should not fret: "The nation has survived other attempts at insurrection. We can survive this one."

The president also noted, ominously, "We have a Constitution that sets certain limits on what government can do, but that allows wide discretion within those limits."

IN IOWA, NIXON arrived at the Hotel Fort Des Moines for a luncheon event. Reporters clustered outside the entrance with questions about the bombing. He had no news about the perpetrators, the president told them. But whoever they were, he said, the government would not allow "violent people" to keep citizens from freely roaming "these great public buildings."

The president went on to say that authorities had long received warnings that the Capitol or the White House could be targets. "Somebody," Nixon said, "has suggested it would be very easy for a visitor to come into the White House with a big bag or a shopping bag or something like that, or any receptacle which was not too obvious, go into a restroom, leave it there and the place would blow."

Somewhat incongruously, perhaps thinking of his reception outside the Iowa State Capitol, Nixon added, "They would like to keep the president in Washington rather than come out in the country. Well, it won't work."

PAINTING A CLEAR picture of the antiwar movement was always going to be a perilous enterprise for anyone working for Richard Nixon, a man whose incisive political instincts warred with his private demons.

Bud's job often took him to the depths of Nixon's id. He had investigated the security lapses at the inauguration in January 1969, when protesters got close enough to hurl eggs, rotten fruit, and bottles at the limousine taking the newly sworn president and his First Lady through the cheering crowds lining Pennsylvania Avenue. Secret Service agents batted away the projectiles with their bare hands, and one agent leapt atop the long trunk (an eerie echo of the scene of JFK's assassination less than six years earlier in Dallas) as the limo accelerated toward the safety of the White House gates. No doubt it triggered Nixon's bad memories of his visit to Venezuela as Dwight Eisenhower's vice president a decade earlier, when hundreds of people, angered by U.S. support for Latin American dictators, had rushed his car in Caracas, smashing its windows and rocking it back and forth as they chanted, "Nixon, go home!"

Bud's report to Nixon about the inauguration had described problems in radio communications, among other lapses. It came back to Bud with handwritten notations. The president didn't blame anyone in his entourage, but perhaps the demonstrators never should have been granted the right to gather in Washington in the first place. Permits, Nixon scribbled, "seem to aggravate the situation."

In the White House, it was easy to feel under siege, as the previous occupants had learned. LBJ's younger daughter, Luci, whose husband was serving in Vietnam, would lie in her bed at night and listen with rising anxiety to the chants drifting in from beyond the gates: "Hey, hey, LBJ, how many boys did you kill today?" When Nixon's people moved in, the Secret Service gave the newcomers a confidential history of protests outside the mansion. One section was titled "Potentially Explosive Situations at the White House." It warned that the president's safety could be in jeopardy in "the very obvious shift from non-violence to civil disobedience."

Nixon's most analytical assistant, Daniel Patrick Moynihan, a dapper, bow-tied professor brought in from Harvard to work on urban policy, had all but begged the new president to learn from his predecessor's political demise. Vietnam was a "disastrous mistake" because the war turned out to be unwinnable, Moynihan told Nixon privately, shortly before he took office. End it quickly. Don't turn this into Nixon's war. And don't feed the protests like LBJ did. "In a sense he was the first American President to be toppled by a mob," wrote Moynihan. "No matter that it was a mob of college professors, millionaires, flower children, and Radcliffe girls."

Nixon didn't take the advice. Having finally achieved his White House dream after humiliating losses when he ran for president in 1960 and for California governor in 1962, Nixon celebrated what he immodestly considered the "greatest comeback of all time." Now he yearned for recognition as "the man for the times," a figure of destiny like Winston Churchill in 1940, who had returned from the political wilderness to lead Britain through a terrible crisis. Nixon would reshape the Cold War world, open up lines to China, maneuver the Soviets into a safer corner. Securing a place in history was the sure-fire cure for self-doubt.

Evidence would later mount to support LBJ's suspicion that Nixon had worked a back channel to sabotage a possible peace settlement before the 1968 election, by promising the South Vietnamese they'd get a better deal under the Republicans.* Once in office, Nixon and Kissinger sought to close out the war on their own terms. Domestic opposition constrained their most robust military options. In the fall of 1969, the president seriously considered a Pentagon plan to invade North Vietnam, mine harbors, bomb dikes, and possibly even use tactical nuclear weapons. He dropped the idea, later citing the mass antiwar marches that year as the reason. Yet like their predecessors, Nixon and Kissinger would keep alive the fiction that a victory was still possible. Meanwhile they would withdraw in the least damaging way. They believed they could accomplish this by maintaining military pressure on the North Vietnamese and forcing the hand of Hanoi's negotiators in Paris, at the peace talks that had begun under LBJ.

In the long view, that would amount to an American defeat, but in the moment it could be packaged to voters as a respectable peace. That required South Vietnam to survive as an independent entity long enough for Nixon to win reelection in 1972 as the man who with honor ended LBJ's war. Kissinger had been suggesting privately for years that the only way out might be a "decent interval" between withdrawal and a likely communist takeover. The goal, he told a confidant, was to stage a great retreat, then emerge at the other end, still a great power. The fact that this strategy would entail more destruction, including the deaths of thousands more American troops and tens of thousands of Vietnamese, remained unspoken.

Bud understood that the president could work his miracle only if he kept "the nutty opposition isolated," as another aide suggested. He labored on what Nixon called a "game plan" for countering antiwar senti-

---

* For details on Nixon's scheming, see Jules Witcover, *The Resurrection of Richard Nixon* (New York: Putnam, 1970) and John A. Farrell, *Richard Nixon: The Life* (New York: Doubleday, 2017).

ment. "Generally we need to think through what specifically can be done to offset the fervor which is building up advocating a precipitous withdrawal," Bud wrote.

"As you know, we need time," he continued, "and we have to do everything possible to get it."

How to buy this time? For young aides to gain any clout or a political future in the White House, they had to craft proposals that would both protect the president's agenda and mesh with his deepest desires.

Bud had been a lawyer for only three months before coming to the White House. He told his wife that he felt out of his league every single day and worried about the impact of his work, whether it was up to the task. He wasn't alone in this feeling. Nixon's top advisers preferred a certain kind of young man for high-profile jobs as assistants — "intelligent, handsome, obedient and inexperienced," as a White House official outside the inner circle observed. Another apt description of such people, he noted, was "subservient and pliant sycophants." Nixon himself suggested it would be good politics for the administration to "get the word out" that so many of his aides were in their twenties and thirties.

Since the younger men rarely got into a room with Nixon, they often found the president hard to read. In fact, Nixon cultivated a certain inscrutability. He encouraged his closest aides to describe him as an iceberg: you only saw the tip, with the real power beneath the surface.

That only made it harder for Bud and his colleagues to interpret mixed signals from the president. While Nixon made stern pronouncements about lawlessness and moral turpitude on the campuses, he also directed his aides to research the causes of the youth rebellion and solicited ideas for winning over less radical students. He made honest requests for all of the "good, recent literature" on campus unrest.

So Bud and others faced a dilemma. Did you appeal to Nixon's vindictive side or his analytical side? At first, Bud took seriously Nixon's directives to study the antiwar movement. He sought out student leaders and called for "liberal and radical thinking" to understand the campuses. He clipped an article from the *Boston Globe* about the first student commencement speech ever permitted by the leaders of Wellesley College, whose students were all women. This graduating senior predicted that her generation would inspire a new kind of social action: "To practice politics as the art of making possible what appears to be impossible." The graduates gave the speech a seven-minute standing ovation. Bud drew a circle around the speaker's remarks. Her name: Hillary Rodham.

Such research wasn't likely to sway the president. Yet somewhere deep in his nature, Nixon grudgingly admired the preternatural public-relations skills of his nemesis from 1960, John F. Kennedy. Once, JFK had sent urns of hot coffee out to thousands of college students who were picketing on the White House sidewalk in support of nuclear disarmament. At the time it was the largest protest Washington had ever seen.

While Nixon could not meet a contentious situation so smoothly and graciously, he decided to try his own dramatic gesture of reconciliation. It would develop into one of the oddest moments in the history of the modern presidency.

3

The Hot Buttons

IT HAD HAPPENED IN MAY 1970, A YEAR BEFORE THE SPRING OF-fensive. The preceding month had offered some relief to a country riven by years of war, crime, and urban decay. First, the safe return of the Apollo 13 astronauts from the brink of a horrible death in space buoyed American spirits — it was a triumph of courage and ingenuity. Then, on April 22, millions of people celebrated the first Earth Day, the hopeful beginning of a new movement to protect the environment.

On the last day of the month, Nixon snapped everyone's head back around. He announced that he had ordered thousands of U.S. and South Vietnamese troops into Cambodia to hit Vietcong command and supply centers.

The enemy sanctuaries had long been a source of frustration to U.S. generals, and Nixon and Kissinger had made them a strategic focus almost as soon as they took power, secretly sending bombers over the Cambodian border. (Infuriated when the *New York Times* found out, the president and Kissinger ordered wiretaps on reporters and administration officials to hunt down the leaker.) But this was now a major territorial expansion of the war, a full invasion to "go to the heart of the trouble," as Nixon put it.

The president knew he risked not only military failure but also the fury of many within his administration. Likewise, after a lull in demonstrations against the war, protests were bound to re-ignite. Under acute stress, Nixon fortified himself with late-night drinking binges, long rambling conversations with Kissinger, and multiple viewings of the movie

Patton, in which George C. Scott portrayed the iconoclastic World War II general.

Nixon went on TV to explain his move. He told viewers he would rather do the right thing and be a one-term president than "see this nation accept the first defeat in its proud one-hundred-ninety-year history." He attempted to front-run the expected campus revolts by denouncing "mindless attacks" on institutions such as universities. "We live in an age of anarchy," Nixon proclaimed. The next morning, in an off-the-cuff remark at the Pentagon overheard by reporters, the president denounced "these bums, you know, blowing up the campuses."

As the president feared, campuses did blow, with more intensity than ever, as national discourse again reached a boiling point. Hundreds of thousands of students marched through their colleges and cities, occupied buildings, abandoned classes, and called for a nationwide strike. Antiwar activists traded rhetorical and sometimes physical blows with college administrators, politicians, and those on the front lines of preserving order. Something had to give.

On Friday, May 1, the day after Nixon's speech, militant students swarmed out of Kent State University in Ohio and rampaged in anger through the city, drawing police into street fights. Saturday night, the campus headquarters of the army's Reserve Officers' Training Corps went up in flames. Ohio's governor, James A. Rhodes, calling protesters "the worst type of people we harbor in America, worse than the brownshirts and the communist element," ordered the National Guard onto the university grounds.

That Monday, May 4, a series of small skirmishes between the troops and the Kent State students crossed a red line. Guardsmen, under some combination of confusion, fear, anger, or orders — the truth remains elusive after a half-century — kneeled and fired, sending a fuselage of more than sixty bullets toward the crowd of students. Thirteen youngsters were hit. Four died. Informed by his chief of staff, Nixon responded in shock: "Is this because of me, of Cambodia?"

The killings horrified the country.* Suddenly it was no longer possi-

---

* Less than two weeks later, police called to quell rowdy students at Jackson State College fired into a dormitory and killed two young people. The incident didn't receive the same national attention as the one at Kent State, which led to charges

ble to dismiss as paranoid fantasy the New Left's warning that the government might resort to deadly force to repress dissidents. In its public statements, the administration at first seemed to blame the students. Nixon's press secretary said the deaths show that "when dissent turns to violence it invites tragedy." The unforgettable photograph of an anguished girl kneeling over one of the dead appeared on the front page of nearly every daily newspaper in the country, to be enshrined as evidence of the nation's unraveling. The pressure on Nixon became even more agonizing. A telegram arrived, signed by thirty-nine college presidents: "We implore you to consider the incalculable dangers of an unprecedented alienation of America's youth." They urged Nixon to "take immediate action to demonstrate unequivocally your determination to end the war quickly." Editorial pages condemned the atmosphere that had led to the killings. Said the *New Yorker* magazine, "The two hundred year old American system came under its most serious attack in modern times, not from the poor, the blacks, or the students but from the White House." Rennie Davis told a crowd at American University, "The blood is on the hand of Nixon." More than five hundred U.S. campuses would shut down early for the semester. Antiwar leaders rushed to put together a rally in Washington for the following Saturday, likely the fastest-ever organization of such a big national protest.

On Friday, May 8, the day before the demonstration, explosions or fires hit more than a dozen campuses. At Colorado State University in Fort Collins, the student body president sat on the curb in tears as Old Main, the original college building, dating from 1879, burned down.

Meanwhile, tens of thousands of young protesters streamed into Washington by car and bus for the big rally. As night fell, those who hadn't made other arrangements laid out their bedrolls on the grass of the National Mall and along the monuments. Many sacked out at the Lincoln Memorial, on its cold floor of pink Tennessee marble. Buses circled the presidential mansion. It was "a very strange feeling as the White House and DC batten down for another siege," Haldeman wrote in his diary. Like a biblical plague on the city, millions of cicadas had just emerged after spending their seventeen-year life cycle underground.

---

of racism in the media and the government, and among the public. The Ohio students were white, and the Mississippi dead were black.

Their incessant chirping merged into one piercing, never-ending note, an assault on the ears and nerves. Bud found himself wondering what was going to give way next. Kissinger thought "the very fabric of government was falling apart."

Nixon's aides were increasingly worried about his mental and physical state. He was exhausted and his speech was rambling. So angered was he by his cabinet's lack of support for sending troops to Cambodia — and a letter of open criticism made public by his secretary of the interior — that he ordered the beloved White House tennis court removed. The president believed that the goal of the left "is to panic us, so we must not fall into their trap." Some aides counseled a spirit of conciliation toward students, but others, including Kissinger, advised Nixon to "hit them hard." That evening, a reporter asked Nixon if the country "is headed for revolution" or "an era of repression." Another inquired as to whether he felt lonely and isolated.

While the protesters slept or prepared for the rally, Nixon made almost fifty phone calls past midnight, seeking reassurance from aides, friends, and political allies, before finally getting into bed at a quarter past two. Less than two hours later he was up again. He wandered into the sitting room named after Lincoln and, still in pajamas, cued up some Rachmaninoff on the turntable and settled into his favorite brown easy chair. He gazed out the window at the knots of protesters at the park known as the Ellipse. Then he got his personal assistant, Manolo Sanchez, out of bed. Born in Cuba, Sanchez was a relatively new U.S. citizen.

He asked Sanchez, "Have you ever been to the Lincoln Memorial at night?"

AT THAT MOMENT, Bud Krogh stood in the Secret Service command post at the White House. As many as a hundred thousand angry people were on their way to D.C., intelligence sources had suggested. Bud had pulled overnight duty to keep an eye on things. To protect the president, buses from the police department, the school district, and the transit company surrounded the White House on all four sides.

This cordon had been Bud's idea. He had hatched it six months earlier. That was when the first big peace marches during the Nixon administration took place, in October and November 1969, the president's first year in office. The protests had been called by the moderate forces in the antiwar movement, including veterans of the McCarthy campaign who had helped drive LBJ from the White House. They urged people to hit the streets for a monthly "Moratorium" on business as usual until the government stopped the war. The White House feared that enraged young people might storm the fences, forcing troops to fire tear gas, or even bullets. "We all felt threatened," one of Bud's colleagues acknowledged. Bud had always loved westerns, especially those starring John Wayne, in which the settlers circled their wagons when attacked by Indian warriors. Buses could serve that same purpose, Bud figured.

During the October 1969 Moratorium the largest turnout had been in Boston. Hundreds of other cities, campuses, and high schools hosted good-sized crowds. Some soldiers in Vietnam wore black armbands in support. A Rhodes scholar named Bill Clinton led a protest at the University of Oxford. *Life* magazine's editors called the Moratorium "the largest demonstration of dissent ever seen in this country." That distinction lasted only a month. Organizers decided that the next Moratorium would be focused on Washington. On November 15, the crowd "turned out to be huge," as Haldeman wrote in his diary, after he took Bud and a couple of others up in a helicopter to check it out. They found it "weird" to look down and see the White House like an island, walled off by the solid barricade of Bud's buses. "Official estimate was 250,000. By our photo count it was 325,000."

Now, in May 1970, in the wake of Cambodia and Kent State, the buses were back. It had been a hot Friday for May, well into the eighties, and the warm air still enveloped the city. In the darkness Bud walked the perimeter, making sure the buses were "chock a block" against one another, with no gaps for anyone to slip through. He wandered over to check the Old Executive Office Building next door, where army transport vehicles filled the courtyard. The soldiers they'd carried now lined the hallways, sitting with their backs to the walls, trying to catch a little sleep before —who knows?—being summoned to fight a mob storming the White House. Nixon's aides had wanted enough troops around to avoid what they had taken to calling "Custerism," meaning too few forces to beat back an assault.

About four-thirty in the morning, Nixon called down for a driver. He and Sanchez were heading to the Lincoln Memorial. The president instructed that no one else was to know—not in the White House, certainly not among the press. As the president later recalled, he had never seen the Secret Service so petrified.

One astonished agent got on the radio. Using the code name for Nixon, he exclaimed, "Searchlight is on the lawn!" It crackled over the speaker in the command post.

Bud couldn't believe his ears. He quickly dialed his boss to wake him with the news flash. "Get over there right now," Ehrlichman barked. Bud sprinted through the grounds, arriving by the Rose Garden just in time to see the taillights of Nixon's limo disappear through the southwest gate. Hearing where the president was going, Bud quickly commandeered another White House sedan, a black Mercury. Follow the president, he ordered the driver. Bud tried to suppress his panic. Other presidents had no doubt slipped out of the White House on private errands, but none had confronted thousands of young people furious that four of their peers had been shot dead, protesting that same president's hated war.

Clusters of kids dotted the grounds and the broad marble stairs leading to the columned memorial. Bud's car braked to a stop on the street below, right behind Nixon's limousine. Bud peered inside. The back seat was empty. The president and Sanchez — along with Nixon's personal doctor and the four Secret Service agents who had managed to tag along — already had climbed to the chamber that hosted the giant seated statue of Lincoln. Bud raced up the fifty-eight steps.

At the top the scene was surreal. A few people, at first no more than a dozen, had noticed the president and his nervous little entourage, and had begun to mill around him. Half of them had never been to Washington before. No doubt most of them had been roused from sleep, or were stoned, or both. Bud warily studied their faces. There was more amazement than anger. Many of these protesters had driven all night to add their voices to a chorus they hoped would be big and loud enough to rattle Nixon, to break through the walls that kept him sequestered, and now instead they could reach this unreachable figure with an outstretched hand, with a whisper. He stood there, practically alone.

Though not an unhealthy man, the president, then fifty-seven years old, rarely looked hale, and this night his exhaustion was obvious. In the reflected beams of the monument's floodlights, Bud could see the dark bags under his eyes, the toll of his lack of sleep, his worry, his bouts of drinking. The students stared at the president and then glanced wide-eyed at one another, sharing the unspoken thought that this is really him, not some look-alike, not some amateur impersonator in a bizarre publicity stunt.

This crossed Bud's mind: if anything bad happens, if any bystander tries something now, I'll be spending the rest of my life testifying before investigative committees.

For more than half an hour, Nixon, facing the Lincoln statue, rambled from subject to subject in a virtual monologue. He said he understood that "most of you think I'm an S.O.B." but that he shared their goals for Vietnam — "to stop the killing." His listeners mostly stood in unsmiling silence. Jon Shure, a nineteen-year-old Cornell student, had driven down for his first antiwar protest, so shaken was he by the Kent State killings. Yet, standing just five feet from Nixon, "I couldn't muster the feeling to say something bad to the president's face," he recalled.

Nixon spoke to them of Churchill, saying the British leader had seemed like a bellicose madman in the 1930s but in hindsight was correct about the Nazi threat. The implication was that Nixon would be proved right too. He appealed to them to travel the world while they were young, to see other cultures, and to appreciate America even as they understood the suffering of blacks, Mexican Americans, and Native Americans. He even hinted slyly at his still-secret initiative to reopen ties to China, saying it was his fond hope that the students would get to know the Chinese people in their lifetime. He said he had bold plans to preserve the natural environment, pointing to his effort to open to surfers a beautiful stretch of military-owned beach in California.

Still, he said, ending the war, cleaning up the environment is "not going to solve the spiritual hunger which we all have." Nixon, as he set down several days later in a recorded memo, was trying to convey to the students the "depth and mystery of life," to lift them out of their "intellectual wasteland." He decided the students were quiet because they were "somewhat overawed and of course surprised." But even Nixon could tell he wasn't selling it. The students were in no mood for a philosophical discussion or a travelogue. "We're not interested in what Prague looks like. We're interested in what kind of life we can build in the United States," said one. Another declared, "I hope you realize that we're willing to die for what we believe in."

To Bud, Nixon came across like a man making an honorable gesture, "trying very hard to reach out," genuinely attempting to cross a probably unbridgeable gap.

More people drifted over. Nixon's retinue grew increasingly agitated. Sanchez had been trying everything to get Nixon to leave, even lying that there was an urgent call for him on the car phone. Finally, as sunrise was beginning to light the Mall's monuments in a pink glow, the president agreed to head back down the steps. A few youngsters heckled him. On his way to the car, he asked some students where they went to school and then commented on their college football team.

Settling with relief into the Mercury, Bud figured the excursion was over. Back to the White House. But no. The little convoy sped right past. They were heading for Capitol Hill, the next stop on the president's tour.

Inside the Capitol, practically deserted at dawn, Nixon made Sanchez sit in the chair belonging to the Speaker of the House and pretend to give a speech. The president stopped to tell a cleaning woman that his mother had been "a saint." He rattled the locked door of the Senate Chamber. Then, like a college kid after a night of carousing, Nixon insisted on taking Bud and the others out for breakfast. They drove to the Mayflower Hotel, where the café workers were just opening up. Nixon scarfed down corned beef hash and poached eggs. It was his first restaurant meal as president. He beamed when the waitresses told him the Cambodia invasion had been a great idea.

Energized, Nixon wasn't quite done with his royal night out. He wanted to walk the five blocks home. Bud swallowed hard, took Nixon's arm, and steered him firmly to the limo. There was no pedestrian entry today at the White House, he explained. It had been fortified for the antiwar rally that was due to begin in just a few hours. Bud got into the car with Nixon.

They had left the White House in the dark of night. Now the sun was up. As they approached, Nixon at last understood why he couldn't return on foot. "Whose idea," he grumbled, "are all these goddam buses?"

PERHAPS, SETTING OUT in the dark of night, Nixon had in mind his famous Checkers speech of 1952. Accused of campaign finance violations, he had saved his spot on the Republican ticket with Dwight D. Eisenhower by pioneering the idea of appealing directly to voters via television. (In the most-remembered part, Nixon said the only political gift he'd ever accepted had been a cocker spaniel puppy named Checkers, which he endearingly vowed to keep for the sake of his daughters.) Or the time he tried to reach the kids and soften his image during the 1968 campaign with a cameo on *Rowan & Martin's Laugh-In,* the wildly popular TV variety show that embraced the counterculture. He had appeared for only a few seconds, to repeat the show's catch phrase: "Sock it to *me?*" The directors ran through six takes to get it less, well, Nixonian. (Coincidence or not, shortly before Nixon invited Sanchez to visit the Lincoln Memorial, the president had called long-distance to California to chat with the *Laugh-In* producer who'd arranged the bit.)

The Lincoln Memorial trip wasn't a public relations success. Some news coverage veered close to ridicule. Reporters hadn't gotten to the scene until well after Nixon left; when they interviewed students, there was little mention of the president's monologue. All Nixon wanted to discuss was surfing and football, one complained to the press. John Ehrlichman, Bud's boss, who hadn't been present that night, read the papers and lamented, "It's too bad all he could talk about was sports."

Deeply frustrated, the president hunkered down in the White House as the march got underway later in the day. More than a hundred thousand people paraded through Washington, denouncing his invasion of Cambodia. As Kissinger later noted, "The tidal wave of media and student criticism powerfully affected the Congress." Lawmakers would prohibit sending U.S. forces stationed in Vietnam over any more borders.

So much for Nixon's analytical side. It sank into the depths. The vindictive Nixon was back.

In the subsequent weeks, he contemplated vetoing legislation giving eighteen-year-olds the right to cast ballots in national elections. Politically, the best course would be to kill the bill before they could vote against him in 1972. Nixon ultimately signed it only because, as he told his aides, he feared how the kids would react. "You do have an obligation not to have the goddam country blow up," he said.

The president also summoned leaders of the intelligence community to the White House on June 5 to discuss how to sharpen penetration of the antiwar movement and how to look harder for its possible links to foreign powers. And Nixon brought along with him a young aide named Tom Huston, who had been jockeying for a year to get into the room.

Huston was a thin and morose-looking twenty-seven-year-old, a whip-smart former army captain who proudly considered his politics well to the right of Nixon's. Where Bud was conciliatory and well-mannered, Huston was unapologetically abrasive. His road to the White House had begun at law school in Indiana, where he had become national chairman of Young Americans for Freedom, a conservative campus group that predated SDS and longed to be as consequential. Listed as one of *Esquire* magazine's one hundred influential Republicans, Huston was asked to name the party's best hope for the presidency in 1968. His answer: Nixon. When the magazine came out, Nixon invited him to his New York law office to chat. The two hit it off. Nixon later had him brought onto the White House research and speechwriting staff.

No photos of Vietnamese peasants for Huston's office. He hung on his wall a portrait of John C. Calhoun, the nineteenth-century South Carolinian who served as vice president and whose work to preserve slavery helped lead to the Civil War.

Huston arrived with certitude about the mortal dangers of the New Left. He bragged that he'd known the SDS founders before they'd even formed the radical group. He assured his bosses, "These fellows are careful students and skilled practitioners in the art of revolution . . . You don't win their confidence by talking with them." Instead, Huston firmly believed, they had to be undermined from within, infiltrated by undercover agents, their phone calls and correspondence monitored. The American people, he would say, "are unwilling to admit the possibility that 'their children' could wish to destroy their country."

While Huston focused on his initial White House job, which was to help produce the president's daily news summaries, he also sowed the administration with theories and dire predictions about the militants. He warned Nixon that the White House was "the most logical target" for an attack by left-wing terrorists, perhaps by someone posing as a tourist. It wouldn't be difficult "for a 23 year old beauty to place her handbag with 5 sticks of dynamite in the ladies room of the Residence while going through on a White House tour," Huston said. After the Capitol bombing, Nixon remembered that prediction and parroted Huston when he spoke to reporters in Iowa. Later, Nixon would observe, with some admiration, "Everything he wrote was inflammatory."

• • •

BUD'S TROUBLES with Huston had begun brewing during his first summer on the job. At Nixon's insistence, Bud researched whether foreign powers had helped finance the antiwar movement. Nixon didn't care that the FBI and CIA had already told LBJ that there was no evidence for this. Representatives of the New Left continued to make pilgrimages to Hanoi and Havana. There had to be something there besides moral support. (Most career agents, in fact, thought the very idea was foolish. They believed that the movement's leaders, who often came from the middle and upper classes, didn't need outside help to survive; they were "credit-card revolutionaries.") But in June 1969 Bud asked the intelligence agencies to take yet another look.

The answer came back the same: the groups appeared to be paying bills not with secret support from abroad but in the old-fashioned way — collecting dues, selling literature, soliciting donations from wealthy liberals. Full-time organizers were hardly rolling in money; they were getting paid no more than twenty-five dollars a week. Passing Bud's work to Nixon, Ehrlichman massaged the language a bit for his audience: the intelligence community "does not have specific information or 'ironclad proof' that Red China or Cuba is funding campus disorders," he wrote.

But Nixon wouldn't let go. He decided Bud and Ehrlichman weren't being aggressive enough. "Give Huston the job of developing hard evidence of this probable support activity," he told Ehrlichman, "or if not Huston someone with his toughness and brains."

Toughness being the highest Nixon compliment, Huston was empowered. As he would later acknowledge, he understood Nixon's "dark side," as well as "certain hot buttons, and if you inadvertently trip that wire, it was going to set off an explosive reaction."

Huston couldn't drum up any evidence of outside funding either, but he told the president that didn't matter: "Other weapons in the revolutionary arsenal are as powerful as money; for example, the 'thoughts' of [the Chinese leader] Mao Tse-tung are mental missiles launched against the minds of thousands of young Americans and can prove as fatal as bullets." He said groups that originally advocated for social reforms "have been transformed into hard-core revolutionary movements dedicated to the total destruction of our democratic traditions and our society," and since those are also the objectives of "international Communists" it is "inevitable that they will join forces in common cause." Huston fancied himself an expert on gathering intelligence. He would soon install a special scrambler telephone in his office to speak with his contacts at the FBI and other agencies. When he wasn't using the phone, he kept it locked in a safe.

HUSTON'S RISING STOCK threatened Bud's position in Nixon's hierarchy. Bud had managed to beat back Huston's first attempt to take over the national security portfolio; Bud had told his bosses that while Huston was a "genius" at stirring up action against militant groups, he was also "uncompromising, acerbic and at times paranoid" and shouldn't be given the job that rightly was Bud's. Maybe Huston would be a better fit at Justice instead of the White House, Bud suggested innocently — adding in longhand to his boss at the bottom of the memo, "assume it goes no further." Bud sought to burnish his own credentials for toughness by declaring that the administration's goal should be "isolation of the Peace Now nuts."

But by now the fallout from Cambodia and Kent State had raised the bar even higher. Within the administration, sympathy faded for the four dead in Ohio. The FBI director, J. Edgar Hoover, told Bud that in his view the students "invited and got what they deserved." A crackdown on the New Left gained traction, moving Huston closer to the heart of the action.

Nixon called the intelligence chiefs together in June 1970. His talking points came almost verbatim from Huston: "Certainly hundreds, perhaps thousands of Americans — mostly under 30 — are determined to destroy our society ... They are reaching out for the support — ideological and otherwise — of foreign powers and they are developing their own brand of indigenous revolutionary activism which is as dangerous as anything which they could import from Cuba, China, or the Soviet Union."

A few weeks later, on June 25, the heads of the FBI, the CIA, the National Security Agency, and military intelligence signed an agreement to work together secretly to gather information on the people in the antiwar movement.

Huston made his move. Working closely with the FBI's number-three official, William Sullivan, who ran the bureau's domestic intelligence operations, he cherry-picked the most extreme options that had been discussed and turned them into recommended action items for presidential approval. They included authority to break into homes of "urgent and high-priority internal security targets," to monitor international calls and letters from U.S. citizens, to intensify electronic surveillance of dissenters, and to step up spying on college campuses.

Yes, break-ins and reading someone's mail were illegal, Huston acknowledged. He brushed off that small problem. The benefits outweighed the risks. For good measure, Huston also declared himself the "exclusive" contact point in the White House for internal security.

On July 14, 1970, Haldeman told Huston that the options — which would become known infamously as the Huston Plan — had been approved by the president.

Huston was overjoyed. But he had made one big miscalculation. He had been trying to bypass and sideline Sullivan's boss, J. Edgar Hoover. The FBI director had long made it clear he considered Huston a pissant. In private he referred to him as "that snot-nosed kid." He liked to jab at Huston in public, pretending to forget his name, calling him "Mr. Hoffman" at meetings. Hoover had no intention of having the White House or anyone else tell him how to do his job. In the report he'd sent to the president, Huston had ignored the caveats and footnotes that Hoover had inserted into an early draft. He demeaned Hoover to the president, writing that the director had been "bullheaded as hell" and was "getting old and worried about his legend."

When Hoover finally saw the Huston Plan, he "went through the ceiling." The director marched over to Attorney General John Mitchell, who hadn't seen it. Mitchell couldn't believe that the president was going to leave a paper trail ordering illegal break-ins and surveillance. He talked to Nixon.

On July 27, Nixon made it known to Huston that he was revoking the approval. Huston had already made four copies of his memorandum and sent them by courier to the intelligence chiefs. He had to go down to the White House situation room, where the couriers came and went, and sheepishly ask them to retrieve all the copies.

Huston had lost. He would be sidelined, and embittered, for the rest of his time at the White House. For Bud, though, the damage was done; he would never fully revert to his pre-Huston state of mind.

Here was the irony: most, if not all, of the things Huston was recommending were already going on, without explicit sanction.

BY MID-FEBRUARY 1971, Nixon's sense of himself as a historic figure was fully commixed with his paranoia. He ordered the secret installation of a voice-activated taping system in his offices, "just to be sure that we can correct the record," he noted, in one of the first recorded conversations. Almost no one on his staff knew they were being taped.*

The previous spring's invasion of Cambodia hadn't accomplished the goals of crippling the enemy's resources in South Vietnam or forcing Hanoi to sue for peace. Nevertheless, on the same theory — keeping up the military and diplomatic pressure — Nixon and Kissinger at the end of January had crossed another border, into Laos, where the enemy also had sanctuary. Per the congressional prohibition, no U.S. ground troops were dispatched this time. Instead, some seventeen thousand South Vietnamese, backed by U.S. air strikes and artillery barrages, were to drive west and cut the main North Vietnamese supply route, the Ho Chi Minh Trail; capture and destroy their base in the Laotian town of Tchepone; and then withdraw.

Two days after the taping system was installed, the president and Kissinger discussed the war in the Oval Office. The two of them optimistically put the odds at fifty-fifty that the Laos move would bend the North Vietnamese by the summer. Peace talks in Paris had long been at an impasse. Hanoi insisted that no deal could be made until the United States agreed to a firm date for unconditional and unilateral withdrawal and the end of its client regime in the South, while the Americans had demanded that the North first commit to a mutual withdrawal and the return of all prisoners of war. "For us the objective of all these things is to get out of there," Nixon said. "We can't lose. We can lose an election, but we're not going to lose this war, Henry. That's my view. Do you agree with it?"

That same day, an intelligence report from the Justice Department warned, "It can be anticipated that military action in Laos or Cambodia

---

* U.S. presidents from Franklin D. Roosevelt through LBJ had secret White House taping systems, but until Nixon's the machines had to be turned on and off manually and thus recorded only a fraction of the conversations.

will give new impetus, purpose and unity, to the anti-war movement." The report predicted that "escalation of violence may occur as a result of demonstrations surrounding the Laos and Cambodia situation."

Such warnings were turning the attention of the president's top aides to the Spring Offensive, including the plan for mass civil disobedience. A confidential report to Bud and others pointed out that "a relatively small number of individuals could seriously disrupt the flow of traffic into the Washington area."

A few days later, Haldeman told the president, "They've been trying to put this plan together to [block the streets] on May First."

"Are they going to do that or not?" Nixon asked.

"Well I don't know," Haldeman said. "One faction has said they'll do it and another faction has said they won't."

Less than a week later came the explosion at the Capitol. It seemed to confirm that the warnings about violence were no mere threats.

As a newly styled hard-liner, Bud suggested in a memo to his boss that the bombing could be a blessing in disguise. The upcoming protests loomed at the same time that support for the war "from middle-of-the-road Americans may be getting softer," he noted. Furthermore, he said, public opinion of the government's pursuit of radicals was weakening, thanks to a general feeling that J. Edgar Hoover was a "doddering old man."

The bombing could be just the antidote they needed, a way to shut down the doves. "A bomb detonating in the breast of the Senate is as close as one can get to the heart of super-liberal thought in this government," he wrote. He recommended that Nixon condemn the bombing and tie it firmly to everything the administration had been doing to counter dissent. It is, Bud said, "a chance for us to point out that we have not been tough for nothing."

A WEEK AFTER the bombing, in early March 1971, much of the country was transfixed by the Fight of the Century — a battle between two undefeated heavyweights, Muhammad Ali and Joe Frazier, for the boxing title. That was the hour when a band of eight antiwar activists from the Philadelphia area chose to break into a local FBI office.

The files they stole in the town of Media, Pennsylvania, would show that, contrary to public opinion, the FBI hadn't been soft on radicals.

The documents would lay bare two years of activities even Tom Huston didn't know about—an initiative by FBI agents to undermine the New Left through illegal break-ins, wiretapping, and dirty tricks. The code name in FBI-speak, COINTELPRO, was short for "counterintelligence program." Within weeks, the first public notice of the cloak-and-dagger activities would be printed in the newspapers.

At the same time, an even more consequential government secret was about to rise from the depths.

The day after the Capitol bombing, a former marine turned defense analyst now living in Cambridge, Massachusetts, had placed a fateful telephone call. He had been wrestling with his conscience and his definition of patriotism. He finally decided it was time to make public a government study that contained explosive revelations about politicians and generals who misread Vietnam and hid the truths of the war; about the resilience of the enemy and the ineffectiveness of the bombing; about the selfishness and duplicity of leaders who had prolonged a conflict while knowing victory wasn't possible.

The analyst's name was Daniel Ellsberg. He had been one of thirty-six people who worked for two years on the seven-thousand-page secret history, which had been ordered by LBJ's defense secretary, Robert S. McNamara, and had been completed just after Nixon took office. Few had read the whole thing. Ellsberg was one who had. He had been working under government contract at the RAND Corporation, a nonprofit think tank in California that specialized in national security matters, and, with the help of a colleague and his family, he had secretly photocopied much of the report.

Ellsberg had disclosed his actions to a few liberal U.S. senators and for months tried to persuade them to hold hearings on the report, or to at least make its findings public in the congressional record. But the politicians feared the consequences of releasing a classified Pentagon document.

So on the Sunday after the Capitol bombing, Ellsberg followed advice he had been given by friends. He contacted Neil Sheehan, a reporter for the *New York Times,* whom Ellsberg had known well when both of them worked in Saigon. Sheehan invited Ellsberg to his Washington apartment. Ellsberg didn't bring the report, but the two stayed up all night talking.

Rumors of the secret report had been floating around the capital for months. Within a week, a writer for the *Boston Globe*, Thomas Oliphant, was able to nail down the fact that the report existed, though he didn't know its contents. His story was headlined "Only 3 Have Read Secret Indochina Report; All Urge Swift Pullout." Soon enough, Ellsberg's history would get a nickname: the Pentagon Papers.

4

A Mighty Waters

AS BUD KROGH TRIED ON HIS NEW ROLE AS A CRITIC OF NEW Left activists, and as Tom Huston plotted against them, the heart of the peace movement was beating five blocks from the White House, inside a well-worn, eleven-story office building.

The drab neoclassical tower on Vermont Avenue Northwest had barely been updated in the fifty years since it went up at the corner of L Street. One by one, its tenants had decamped for more modern accommodations. "Rent slashed!" the landlord advertised. "Suites for $65 a month!"

That was why the groups planning the Spring Offensive could afford to move in. Day and night, their staff and volunteers ignored the creaky elevator and clomped up and down the narrow stairs connecting the three floors they'd taken over. On eight you could find the National Peace Action Coalition and the Vietnam Veterans Against the War. The ninth floor housed the People's Coalition for Peace and Justice. One floor up, on ten, was the Mayday Tribe. They jammed makeshift desks into untidy rooms, slapped posters on the walls. Phones jangled amid the clack of typewriters and mimeograph machines. In early 1971, 1029 Vermont Avenue was the most important nexus of antiwar energy in America.

Like atoms in close proximity, the Vermont Avenue groups could exert just enough force on one another to pull in the same direction, if only temporarily. Wary of one another's motives and beliefs, they had now united, thanks to their fury at Nixon's incursion into Laos as well as their growing sense that the Spring Offensive could be wider, deeper, and longer-lasting than any single action by the American left. Perhaps it was the last best chance to stop the war.

Over the years, legions of people had led or pushed the movement along the crooked road to this place, within sight of the summit. But no single person deserved more credit than David Tyre Dellinger.

If only he could hold it together for a couple more months.

ON THE FIRST DAY of March, when he awoke to news of the Capitol bombing, David Dellinger had to wonder if the blast would unravel his latest artful compromise. Only a day earlier, all the main players in the Spring Offensive had finally pledged to work together on its largest single event — a peaceful mass march through the heart of Washington, on Saturday, April 24.

The agreement was a testament to Dave's legendary fortitude. Over many decades, he had stood countless times in front of tedious, never-ending political meetings. He had a knack for earning the trust of all sides and calming the rhetorical wars. "You could work with Dave, you could talk with Dave, he's a normal guy," recalled a Vietnam veteran who spent time at the Vermont Avenue building. "Dave was probably the most liked, the most respected by those of us who weren't on the inside of all this."

At fifty-five, Dave saw himself as the older brother of the antiwar movement. Standing amid twenty-somethings, with their untamed hair and eclectic clothes, he resembled a careless college professor, usually spruced up for public appearances in a tie and an oversized sports coat. Once a gifted athlete, he remained a large if not especially imposing man, a bit paunchy. His receding hairline plunged precipitously into long sideburns.

For all of his years in the trenches, Dave was little known outside pacifist circles in the Northeast. Then the Nixon administration took office and promptly turned him into a celebrity. U.S. prosecutors had indicted him, along with seven others, for conspiracy and incitement to riot during the Democratic National Convention in Chicago. The case went on the docket as *United States of America v. David T. Dellinger et al.* He faced at least ten years in jail.

For decades he had spoken to modestly sized rallies and small college groups. He lived by certain rules: Never say no to an invitation to join a protest. Never cancel a meeting, no matter how few people show up. Now he was flying around the country, making speeches that sometimes drew thousands of cheering students. When he recently earned a fee of one thousand dollars for an appearance at Syracuse University, the FBI duly noted it in his file. For while the average American had no idea who Dave was, the government certainly did.

Federal agents had been tracking him since before World War II, when he went to prison for refusing to register for the draft. They followed his work in the ban-the-bomb movement and against the Vietnam War, which included several visits to Hanoi to view the effects of American bombardment. ("It's all so terribly real over here — not a matter of abstract politics," Dave wrote home.) The FBI noted that on one trip he had even met with the North Vietnamese leader Ho Chi Minh.

J. Edgar Hoover had branded Dave a "key activist" and ordered the FBI office in Newark — near where Dave lived with his wife and five children in a four-family commune they called St. Francis Acres — to keep a special eye on him. He was one target of the FBI's COINTELPRO program to neutralize the New Left, which was about to become public knowledge, thanks to the break-in at the bureau's office near Philadelphia. Agents came up with schemes they thought would undermine his position, including concocting anonymous letters and literature claiming he was gay.

In the White House, Tom Huston had singled out Dave in his report to Nixon about foreign influence in the U.S. left. He denounced Dave's "intimate" relationship with the North Vietnamese: "They insisted upon his presence in Paris before they would even discuss the promised release of three American prisoners of war."

As an orator Dave lacked the natural eloquence and confidence of some movement leaders. TV news producers gravitated toward more "colorful and symbolic" figures, like the Yippies. Dave's voice, accented with vestiges of his patrician Massachusetts boyhood, came out a little high-pitched for his size and, like his bearing, a little thin. As an organizer his attention to detail often suffered from a tendency to be distracted. Rather, his authority flowed from the apparent purity of his pacifism and the surrender of his personal life to the cause, not to mention the long list of donors he'd assembled over the decades.

One on one, Dave would impress people who were unsure about jumping in. A young man from Kansas wrote that meeting him "dissolved a few preconceived fears about the movement or movement people."

Yet this personal history and his "Gandhi-like serenity," as the angel-voiced folksinger Judy Collins described it, didn't translate into Martin Luther King Jr.–like prominence. Had he been equipped for such a role, Dave would have insisted it was against his principles. A movement had to grow from below. It had to be built on the sacrifice and the commitment of its masses, not the charisma of a leader.

Dave was fond of quoting a leader of the Socialist Party of America, Eugene Debs: "I would not be a Moses to lead you into the Promised Land, because if I could lead you into it, someone else could lead you out of it."

DAVE HAD BEEN deeply involved in the strategic debate that gripped the antiwar movement almost from inception: if a democratically elected government goes rogue, if you no longer trust politicians of any stripe to do the right thing, what's the most effective way to force change?

After you've signed petitions, door-belled for insurgent candidates, boycotted military suppliers, carried a million protest signs, helped turn public opinion against an indefensible war, and the war continues anyway — do you keep marching? Do you turn to civil disobedience? If so, which rules and laws do you disobey? Do you burn your draft cards, refuse to serve, and go to jail, flee to Canada? Is stopping the killing the only goal, or do you attack conditions and institutions that made the war possible, even inevitable?

Within the Spring Offensive schedule, the main force behind the April mass march was the National Peace Action Coalition, or NPAC. Its rank and file included many flavors of leftists. But its leaders largely came from the Socialist Workers Party, a venerable group that barely survived the splintering demise of the Old Left after World War II. Now the party had earned itself a second act. It had done this by making Vietnam its central issue and by offering the movement some desperately needed know-how in the nuts and bolts of organizing.

Although NPAC wasn't formally an arm of the Socialist Workers Party, people at the top tended to follow its rigid philosophy. This, within the topsy-turvy politics of the New Left, made it a conservative force — even though, as an inheritor of the Trotskyist brand of Marxism, its ultimate goal was supposed to be worldwide revolutionary change. The party line went something like this: The only strategy that made sense was to assemble the widest possible coalition of students, workers, radicals, and liberals to parade in the streets, to show strength on the single issue of ending the war. Anything else, like provocative slogans about social issues such as racism, was a distraction. Spontaneous actions or sit-ins were counterproductive; they scared off potential recruits such as middle-class people with kids.

Dave belonged to the People's Coalition for Peace and Justice, the rival faction on the ninth floor, which saw things in another way. He shared its leadership with a few others, notably his fellow Chicago Seven defendant Rennie Davis. The group was pushing a People's Peace Treaty, which had been signed by Vietnamese student groups as well as the U.S. National Student Association. It called for immediate withdrawal of U.S. troops from Vietnam, a return of all prisoners of war, and democratic elections for a new government in South Vietnam, which would include on the ballot the National Liberation Front — the communist guerrilla movement otherwise known as the Vietcong. But the People's Coalition also demanded social justice at home, including a guaranteed national income of $6,500, which NPAC's leaders thought was just muddling the message.

Rennie also led the sister organization of the People's Coalition, which occupied the tenth floor at 1029 Vermont Avenue. Called the Mayday Tribe, it was focused on plans for the blockade of Washington traffic. Over time the People's Coalition essentially would absorb the much smaller Mayday group. Together they contained the more freewheeling components of the New Left.

That was exactly what worried NPAC's leaders. While the People's Coalition — the Dave-and-Rennie bloc — comprised many student groups, union organizers, and longtime pacifists, its loosey-goosey tent also beckoned to unpredictable types such as the Yippies, whose lack of discipline, NPAC believed, could lead to trouble. They never quite bought it when those folks preached nonviolence. They didn't consider it out of the question that the Yippies had something to do with the bombings around the country. They were reluctant to welcome them into the April 24 parade.

NPAC and the People's Coalition originally cohabited under the broad umbrella of the coalition known as the Mobe.* But a year ear-

---

* The coalition had survived several bumps and reorganizations over the years,

lier, at the May 1970 protests against the invasion of Cambodia and the Kent State killings, the two sides had split in bitterness over civil disobedience. Parade marshals organized by NPAC had muscled away demonstrators trying to stage a massive sit-in at the White House. Dave considered that weekend one of the big missed opportunities of the antiwar movement. That feeling was a big reason why he was now working with Rennie to try mass action again in 1971.

Rennie regarded NPAC members as robotic. "It was a part of this goody-two-shoes control mentality still existing, with its roots in the Fifties," he said. And it was true that NPAC could be paranoid. There was, for example, the matter of the front door. One activist with friends in both camps was dismayed to visit Vermont Avenue and find the NPAC entrance reinforced with a layer of galvanized iron, complete with brackets for two-by-fours that could be wedged in to hold off a battering ram. They claimed to be protecting the office against an FBI raid, but the visiting activist thought the real reason was to keep out the riff-raff. His heart sank at "the state of disunity that the anti–Vietnam War movement had reached."

COMPARED WITH his fellow organizers, Dave's personal road to Mayday had begun much earlier and was replete with more lessons learned.

He might be shouting outside the White House gates now, but as a boy Dave was an invited luncheon guest. In his hometown north of Boston, his father had been a pillar of the Republican Party, a big bear of a man and Ivy League lawyer who counted Calvin Coolidge among his cronies. When Coolidge ascended to the presidency, he entertained the father and his sons at the executive mansion.

The elder Dellinger was proud when Dave followed him to Yale, excelled at economics, served as president of the cross-country team, and earned a fellowship to Oxford. But then his son veered off the path. Dave would say his dedication to nonviolence arrived one day out of a sense of shame. It happened after Yale lost a football game to Georgia. A near-

---

and in the process had changed its name from the National Mobe to the New Mobe. After the 1970 split, the Davis-Dellinger faction was briefly known as the National Coalition Against War, Racism, and Repression, before the name changed again, to the People's Coalition for Peace and Justice.

riot ensued. Dave knocked a local kid unconscious. Remorse flooded in: "I dropped to my knees, lifted his head and inert upper body and cradled him until he came to."

After he graduated in the 1930s, Dave drove an ambulance for the anti-fascist side in the Spanish Civil War. As the enemy advanced in Madrid, he came close to picking up a gun. But he didn't — "the hardest decision I ever made in my life." Upon his return, he enrolled in a seminary. While there, he decided it would compromise his pacifism to cooperate with the military draft instituted by President Franklin D. Roosevelt. People studying for the ministry were exempt from service but still had to register. Dave persuaded nineteen other students to join him in refusing to sign up.

He called his father, who tried to talk him out of a move that would send him to jail and possibly ruin his life. "If you hang up I will kill myself immediately," he told his son.

Dave was expelled and sentenced to a year in prison. Upon release, he once again refused to report for the draft. That earned him two more years behind bars. After promising his family he wouldn't go on a hunger strike, he did so anyway. His father wrote him in jail that he was "near the breaking point."

> You evidently think you should do everything you think is right, regardless of the effect it might have on the rest of us, whether we be wife, parents, brothers or sisters. I am sure you do not comprehend how much suffering and misery you are causing us . . . It does seem to me that you owe a duty to your God and to the cause you are trying to serve by not ruining your health or dying by your own determined stand. Even though you think that some of the prison rules are unjust you do not set a good example by being just as extreme. There must be some point that is right and just between the two . . . PLEASE, PLEASE, PLEASE, PLEASE end it tomorrow . . ."

Dave stuck with the hunger strike for sixty-five days, until the administration agreed to some improvements in prison conditions.

After his release, Dave learned to be a printer and started several short-lived magazines. (Eventually one of them, *Liberation*, would gain traction and influence, attract dozens of progressive writers, and publish for twenty years. Dave's cofounder was one of his mentors, the Dutch-born clergyman and activist A. J. Muste, who would become the first chairman of the Mobe.) Dave would, by and large, stick to the editorial stance of these publications for the rest of his life. He considered himself a radical pacifist. He embraced socialist and anarchist themes without joining any party, or any group with a rigid ideology. Injustice, Dave would argue, had to be attacked on many fronts at once, through a "nonviolent war carried on by methods worthy of the ideals we seek to serve."

There was a Christian cast to his philosophy. Dave's friend Staughton Lynd called it "the vision of love as an agent for fundamental social change." Later, Dave would characterize the tactics he supported as "Gandhi and guerrilla." He saw it as a synthesis of persuasion and disruption, a combination of direct action with the mass civil disobedience that helped India defeat colonial rule. "We can expect to face tear gas, clubs and bullets," Dave wrote. "But we must refuse to hate, punish or kill in return."

His personal pacifism had to be absolute, even if it caused him serious injury. Which is exactly what it did one day in 1951, after the United States had entered the Korean War. Dave helped lead a small march in New York City against American involvement. The protesters moved along the sidewalks from Harlem to Times Square. An enraged passerby, whose son had just died in Korea, began shouting and swinging his fist at some of those watching. Dave came over, and when the man refused to calm down, he put his arms by his sides and said, "Go ahead and hit me if it will make you feel better." The man did, knocking Dave to the ground and then kicking at his head.

Dave's jaw was broken. Worse, his right eye was permanently damaged. It would cause him periodic pain and trouble for the rest of his life.

In the mid-Sixties, Vietnam drew him back into active protest.

His first arrest of the era came in the summer of 1965 in Washington. Neo-Nazis hurled red paint all over Dave and his companions as they marched at the head of a column. When the marchers arrived at the Capitol, some 350 people were taken into custody for trespassing, at the time D.C.'s largest mass arrest ever. The same day, LBJ insisted to reporters that the war was going well. The president added, "I would warn any would-be hopeful enemy of the United States that he must not make the miscalculation others have done in the past, to believe this country is divided."

Dave got forty-five days in jail. As was his general custom, he wouldn't allow anyone to free him on bond; it would be wrong to rely on a privilege that others arrested with him couldn't afford. He admired the pioneering alto-sax player Charlie Parker, who preached that you had to live jazz to play it right. "That's what I believe about politics," Dave once explained. "If you don't live it in your own life it won't come out of your horn."

Dave initially shied away from a leading role in the numerous antiwar conferences, where warring factions prepared to fight to the death for their own strategies and tactics. But he saw the need and stepped in.*

"There was never a meeting where I wasn't at one point in utter despair, when I concluded the whole thing was going to fly apart," he later recalled. At one such session, the steering committee for a New York march wrangled bitterly for hours over whether to stick the word "Now" at the end of its official slogan, "Stop the War in Vietnam." After the raucous debate, the vote was deadlocked at seventeen and a half votes for each side, with one delegation split. As chairman, Dave had to break the tie. (He voted yes.) After another particularly painful session, a leading labor and civil rights organizer buttonholed Dave outside the doors. "What a zoo!" he said. "I don't understand how you do it."

Through trial and error Dave found one sure-fire tactic: bring into play what he would later call the "pressure of events." He would wait until the last hour of a meeting — when the room rental was about to expire. "We have to leave in an hour, and two hundred GI's are coming home dead every day, and we have an obligation to them," he would say, arguing they should agree to hold the demonstration and work out the points of disagreement later.

---

* Dellinger was not alone among earlier generations of activists to strive for coalition in the antiwar movement. Among others were Douglas Dowd, a Cornell University economics professor; Fred Halstead, a labor organizer and the 1968 presidential candidate of the Socialist Workers Party; Brad Lyttle, a longtime Chicago activist; Sidney Peck, a sociology professor at Western Reserve University in Cleveland; Benjamin Spock, a pediatrician who wrote a best-selling guide to child-rearing in 1946 before joining the movement against nuclear arms; and Cora Weiss, a New York peace activist and leader of Women Strike for Peace.

The same practical thinking informed his dealings with the younger, more militant types who began swamping the staid pacifist organizations that had long dominated the left. In 1967, Dave decided to welcome the edgier antiwar elements — including former SDS members and radical Berkeley types like Jerry Rubin and Stew Albert — into the planning for the Pentagon protest. Dave admitted to some ambivalence. He trusted their sincerity and dedication despite a lifestyle that seemed alien. The things they did, he said, "enchanted all kinds of young people and either horrified or were begrudgingly accepted by a lot of old people." Rubin was "a bit insane, you know," he once said. "But this is a time for mad men." Without their energy, Dave felt, the movement could die or break apart, like the split in the civil rights ranks between integrationists and black nationalists. "Think of Dave as a master politician," the Sixties historian Todd Gitlin would say later, "trying to assemble a winning coalition."

After Chicago, Dave admitted he wasn't sure how he felt about working with the Yippies again. Yet he believed that, like scientists, a social organization had to experiment with different approaches. The movement, he later told the writer Tom Wells, should be "a mighty waters of many streams."

DAVE HAD CROSSED paths with the former SDS organizer Rennie Davis a few times. But it was during the 1967 protest in Washington that they truly connected, walking together on the bridge over the river to the Pentagon. Each had separately visited Hanoi, where Rennie had fled into an air-raid shelter during a U.S. bombing run and decided then and there to devote himself to stopping the war. They cast their eyes forward, to the Democratic National Convention coming up the following summer in Chicago. They teamed up with another SDS founder, Tom Hayden. They agreed to organize a Chicago protest separate from the Yippie Festival of Life.

Visiting planning meetings around the country, Dave made the case for nonviolence. Some movement leaders feared Chicago would be "a massacre." Even members of Dave's coalition were skeptical. They almost always posed two questions to him: "One, is there any chance that the police won't create a bloodbath, and two, are you sure that Tom and Rennie don't want one?" Hayden might not have yearned for blood, but he did hope for a confrontation, on the theory that it would highlight or exacerbate the divisions in the country. If the movement could, as he told a fellow organizer, "arouse the sleeping dogs on the Right," it would push the leaders to end the war more quickly.

Fear of violence kept most activists away. Even Rennie had considered staying home. With good reason, as it turned out, because police did create a bloodbath. Rennie was among hundreds aggressively beaten by the Chicago cops at the bandshell in Grant Park; he crawled away and passed out, and his wounds were so bad, he had to have thirteen stitches in his scalp. He was later indicted along with Dave and the others.

As Stew Albert would note, given Dave's age, the other members of the conspiracy felt a little bit like kids who'd just gotten Daddy in trouble.

The five-month trial in federal court in Chicago began in the fall of 1969, during Nixon's first year in office. It had been one of the more remarkable spectacles in American jurisprudence, a stage for playing out the pains of a hopelessly fractured nation. From the start, the seventy-three-year-old presiding judge, Julius Hoffman, made no effort to hide his disdain for the accused or their lawyers. In turn they mocked him with the name of a cartoon character, "Mr. Magoo," sometimes refusing to stand when he entered the room, blowing kisses, and raising their fists at the jurors. Many proceedings sank into shouting matches and absurdities. When the folksinger Judy Collins testified, the defense attorney asked her to reprise the ballad she sang at a pre-Chicago Yippie press conference, "Where Have All the Flowers Gone?" Told by the judge to stop, she kept on singing; he ordered the bailiff to clamp his hand over her mouth.

One of the defendants, Bobby Seale of the Black Panthers, demanded the right to represent himself, flying into hostile exchanges with the judge, whom he variously called a pig, a racist, and a fascist. At his wit's end, the judge issued the bizarre order that Seale be bound and gagged while sitting in the courtroom. It would become another of the enduring images of the era, a scene akin to some racist medieval inquisition. The judge ultimately declared Seale's case a mistrial and sent him to jail for contempt. The Chicago Eight became the Chicago Seven.

During most of the proceedings, the other defendants were free on bail. Hailing from different factions of the antiwar movement, they had plenty of time to bond and to borrow one another's ideas. Dave grew closest to Rennie, who would later describe them as "joined at the hip." The accused and their lawyers would often smoke pot as they went over their legal strategies. The Yippies and their friends would take LSD. They urged Dave to try it. Abbie Hoffman, no stranger to tripping, stepped in. "Dave doesn't need to take LSD," Hoffman scolded the others. "He already has enough visions. He got them on those hunger strikes in prison."

In his final summation to the jury, the prosecutor, U.S. attorney Thomas A. Foran, said the Chicago Seven were "evil men" who want to "stand on the rubble of our destroyed system of government." He scoffed at comparisons that some witnesses had made between the defendants and Martin Luther King Jr., Gandhi, Jesus, and Robert F. Kennedy: "Can you imagine any of those figures supporting liars and obscene haters like these men?" Dellinger's daughter Natasha retorted from the first row: "I can imagine it because it's true!"

The trial and the related appeals dragged on for months. "The winter days blurred into each other," Tom Hayden would write. "As the trial unfolded, Dave had gradually lost his patience. Either from despair or a Quaker sense of direct action, he began reacting vocally, often eloquently, at outrages in the courtroom." On Valentine's Day in 1970, Judge Hoffman prepared to sentence Dave to nearly two and a half years on thirty-one counts of contempt, for his outbursts. Dave stood to make a statement. When he began to explain that his protests were motivated by Vietnam and racism, the judge ordered him to sit back down. He refused.

"You want us to be like good Germans supporting the evils of our decade, and then when we refused to be good Germans and came to Chicago and demonstrated, now you want us to be like good Jews, going quietly and politely to the concentration camps while you and this court suppress freedom and the truth," Dave said. "I am an old man and I am just speaking feebly and not too well, but I reflect the spirit that will echo throughout the world."

The furious judge ordered marshals to remove Dave. As they took hold of him, he kept on speaking, and his two teenage daughters, who were sitting among the spectators, began screaming at the marshals to leave their father alone. Several rushed over and seized the two girls, who fell to the floor between the benches. Among those in the courtroom was John C. Tucker, a Chicago attorney who was advising the defense. He sat stunned as Dellinger "somehow shucked two marshals off his back" and, with two fellow defendants close behind, plunged into the crowd:

> More marshals joined the fray. A spectator leapt over two rows of benches onto the back of one of the marshals. Everyone — the audience, the press, the defendants and their lawyers — was screaming or shouting or sobbing. [The defense lawyer] Bill Kunstler broke down completely . . . Tears streaming down his face, he collapsed on the lectern . . . the marshals finally succeeded in dragging Michelle and Natasha Dellinger out of the courtroom, along with a dozen or so other supporters of the defendants. Jerry Rubin shouted "Heil Hitler!" at Judge Hoffman again and again. David Dellinger was dragged back to his seat, and suddenly the courtroom was eerily quiet. Dellinger spoke one last time, his voice breaking the silence. "Well, you preserved law and order here, Judge. The day will come when you take every one of us."

Later, at a gathering of defendants and their friends, they kidded Dave. What's up with a pacifist getting into it with federal marshals? Dave replied that at the right place and time, a shoving match could be a form of nonviolence. Feeling a bit giddy and uncharacteristically macho, he joked that if he ever had to, he could take on any of the defendants, except probably Bobby Seale. Looking around the room, his eyes alighted on the Yippie Stew Albert, a former weight lifter. "I'm not sure about Stew," he admitted.

The jury in February 1970 had cleared all seven Chicago defendants of conspiracy, but it found Dave, Rennie, and three others — Abbie Hoffman, Jerry Rubin, and Tom Hayden — guilty of crossing state lines to foment a riot. They remained free while a higher court considered the case. Their appeal wouldn't be decided for two more years.

DAVE AND RENNIE had landed on the FBI's top-ten list of "leading New Left revolutionaries." (One of Dave's sons, with his encouragement, changed his name to avoid notoriety.) But neither the increased federal attention nor the Chicago trial dampened their enthusiasm for another run at a big demonstration.

A few months after their sentencing came Cambodia and Kent State. This is when Rennie began pressing for a major act of civil disobedience in Washington for the following spring, in 1971. He initially worked on the idea with an activist named Arthur Waskow, an ordained rabbi with the left-wing Institute for Policy Studies in D.C. Waskow believed that mass nonviolence was "by all odds the correct tactic for the present moment of American history." Their first stop was an antiwar conference in Milwaukee at the end of June 1970. He and Waskow pitched their plan, "A Proposal for the Formation of Liberation Collectives and Brigades and for the Disruption/Liberation of Washington." It would include blocking bridges and highways to the Pentagon and the CIA. They would combine civil-rights-style sit-ins with a tactic rooted in anarchist philosophy — dividing a big protest into small *grupos de afinidad,* or affinity groups, mobile and able to elude police.

They failed to win a consensus in Milwaukee. In a second try, the Mayday plan fell four votes short at a Minnesota conference of the National Student Association. It wasn't that people opposed the idea, Rennie felt, but just that they thought it was an impossible organizing challenge, that "we would just humiliate ourselves if we tried to go down that road."

Discouraged, Rennie consulted with Dave and others. He decided to press ahead, to prove he could whip up support for the idea. "I was one of the Chicago Seven, and the Chicago Seven were rock stars," he recalled. On his campaign trail, Rennie could be a convincing advocate, able to project both passion and an inner calm. While those close to Rennie found him hard to read, in a large group he came across as confident and relatable. "It was really a testimonial to the power of oratory," Rennie recalled. "People were moved . . . It wasn't so much me, it was just everybody was ready for it."

Rennie got a friend to donate $50,000 in seed money. (Rennie says it was a New York woman who wanted to remain anonymous and still does.) Several wealthy individuals contributed to Mayday, including Larry Canada, an activist who had studied at Indiana University and had married into Eli Lilly pharmaceutical money. Canada would later tell the FBI he donated $100,000 in all to Mayday. Rennie used the cash to set up a small office in the Vermont Avenue building in Washington. While the office staff began corresponding by mail with activists around the country to coordinate the action, Rennie took off to campuses in person, sometimes accompanied by John Froines, one of the acquitted Chicago defendants.

One of the first stops for Rennie and Froines was Syracuse University, on October 26, 1970. It was a Monday night, and the organizers had warned them not to expect a big turnout. But when they walked into the big chapel in the heart of the campus, they saw pews packed to overflowing. Rennie got especially wound up, railing against the use of the defoliant Agent Orange in Vietnam and how kids would be born deformed, he said, because their fathers were exposed. At the end he improvised a catch phrase: "If the government won't stop the war," he said, "then we will stop the government." There was a pause, and then applause began, growing bigger and stronger, a thousand people leaping to their feet, standing on chairs and roaring, just pandemonium. Froines marveled as the slogan "really brought the house down." With excitement, Rennie thought, *The time is right, this will work!*

Between the fall of 1970 and the following April, Rennie and Froines split up and made dozens of speeches, and the FBI tracked nearly every one. As Rennie barnstormed along, he refined the pitch. During a Halloween rally in El Paso, at the University of Texas, he urged students to organize themselves into small collectives, buy old cars, drive them to Washington, and arrange for them to break down on the roads leading to the Pentagon and other government offices. As few as a hundred stalled cars could shut down access to the Pentagon. "We're going to paralyze the government," Rennie told the crowd. "This planet is going to shake to let Vietnam live." He cemented his image as a spokesman for the antiwar groups, writing an op-ed for the *New York Times* in which he bemoaned the "national ignorance of Vietnamese history" and declared the movement was negotiating its own peace treaty with Hanoi.

Dave soon joined in, making his own rounds of the colleges. Without institutional support, they operated like a startup, recruiting talent where they could find it. The president of the student body at Boston University got a call one day from Rennie, inviting him to D.C. for an interview. When the student climbed the stairs to Rennie's apartment, he saw Dave sitting in an easy chair, smoking a Cuban cigar with a glass of cognac by his side, looking to the kid like nothing less than the godfather of the movement. The older man questioned the student closely about his experience in protests and civil disobedience. "Are you sure you're ready to make this commitment?" Dave asked him.

The plan was taking shape, but Rennie and Dave still needed to legitimize it with approval from some organization. As late as January 1971, undercover FBI agents reported with satisfaction that Rennie couldn't get an endorsement from even the remainder of his People's Coalition. "Lack of unity" over civil disobedience "was much in evidence," said the intelligence report, which reached the White House.

Then Nixon provided Rennie and Dave with just what they needed. Shortly before another National Student Association conference, this one in Ann Arbor, Michigan, in early February, the president announced the invasion of Laos. By acclamation, the delegates endorsed Rennie's call for a week of "intensive direct action" in May 1971. The government would have until then to ratify the People's Peace Treaty or face the shutdown.

That was a triumph for Rennie. But the rift within the movement remained. It wasn't just members of the Socialist Workers Party who were suspicious of Mayday, fearing it could turn violent and provoke Nixon, possibly leading to another Kent State. It was obvious from "Davis' actions and statements" that the People's Coalition "has no control of him," the FBI reported to the White House.

Meanwhile NPAC's plan for the April 24 mass march was drawing more and more sponsors. By February more than four hundred groups and individuals had signed on. But still not the People's Coalition. Reluctant to play second fiddle to the leaders of the more autocratic group, Rennie and Dave were still talking about possibly holding their own separate mass march. Many activists fell into despair about the split, fearing it would undermine the spring plans at just the time when unity was critical. In an open letter to both sides, one New York group asked, "What madness has brought this upon our movement?"

On February 27, Dave met with Rennie and the NPAC leaders at the Hamilton Hotel in Washington. Afterward, they all announced that the People's Coalition would join the April 24 parade. Dave had pulled off a feat. A coherent Spring Offensive was locked into place. Activists in all factions rejoiced.

Hours later the Weather Underground planted the bomb in the Capitol.

• • •

FIVE DAYS AFTER the explosion, when the FBI stormed the row house across the street from Rennie's apartment and grabbed Leslie Bacon for questioning, Rennie had every reason to think he might be next. The day before they seized Bacon, two agents had confronted Rennie outside the Vermont Avenue Mayday office, pushed him up against a car parked in the alley, and questioned him about the bombing for about ten minutes. Rennie had been telling reporters he was "absolutely not involved" in the bombing in any way; he hadn't mentioned that he'd known about it in advance.

The feds let him go, but the government was well aware he had known the guerrillas before they went underground, and agents may have suspected Rennie's brother had thrown in his lot with Weather. That same day, a couple of FBI men hustled Larry Canada, the friend of Rennie's who had helped finance Mayday, into his own car. They drove him around town for forty-five minutes, trying to persuade him to give up information in exchange for a $10,000 reward.

Rennie focused on the logistics for the upcoming demonstrations in D.C. The schedule had fallen into place. First, in mid-April, would be the Vietnam Veterans Against the War. Then the big march on Saturday, April 24. On subsequent days the People's Coalition would lobby and picket around Washington in favor of the People's Peace Treaty. Then the weekend after that — Saturday, May 1, and Sunday, May 2 — there would be a festival and rock show to charge everyone up for the mass civil disobedience that would tie up the Monday-morning rush hour on May 3.

Rennie's next order of business was to figure out where people could sleep on that first weekend in May. For a while, he and his colleagues debated a wild-eyed idea to hold the rock show out on a Virginia farm and then march miles into the city to build momentum and attract attention. But they eventually decided to seek a permit to camp in Rock Creek Park, a meandering stretch of woods along the main stream winding from Maryland down into northwest Washington and emptying into the Potomac. The Mayday Tribe's Tactical Manual* had called on everyone

---

* The manual was largely produced by another of Rennie's associates, Jerry Coffin of the War Resisters League, which considered itself the nation's oldest secular pacifist organization.

to gather there. But there was a big problem. The government refused to grant a permit for Rock Creek Park, stating that it would be impossible to manage and control a crowd in such a sprawling landscape. Rennie had tried to bluff the government by saying everyone would camp there anyway, knowing that if the People's Coalition didn't obtain permission, there could be clashes with police before the actual civil disobedience had even started.

Then one of the activists in the Vermont Avenue building came to Rennie with an idea. Why not hold the gathering down by the river, at West Potomac Park? It's an open space, farther from the heart of town, and the government might be more likely to allow the Mayday Tribe to claim it. Avoiding another Chicago was still on Rennie's mind. He agreed.

Still, no one knew for sure how many people might show up for Mayday, which was a little more than a month away. Dave kept trying to stir interest around the country. At the end of March, he made an appearance at New York University, calling on the students to take this next step despite their "tiredness," their frustration that previous demonstrations hadn't ended the war. Since 1965, more than 40,000 American soldiers and hundreds of thousands of Vietnamese soldiers, guerrillas, and civilians had died; 350,000 civilians had been wounded; bombs and artillery had destroyed hundreds of hamlets in the South and civilian targets, including hospitals, in the North; and nearly a third of South Vietnam's sixteen million people had become refugees.

"Yes, it is a protracted struggle. Yes, it is a disappointment. People go to jail, march, refuse to pay taxes" and the war goes on, Dave told them. "But the truth is, we have no choice."

They were listening to him. But Dave didn't know whether they were hearing him. Would they come to Washington?

5

The Pivot Point

NOT FOR THE FIRST TIME, J. EDGAR HOOVER, THE DIRECTOR OF the Federal Bureau of Investigation, had reason to be furious with Washington's police chief, Jerry Wilson.

True, relations between the two men had never been warm. When Jerry ascended to the top job, he had been in no hurry to make the traditional pilgrimage to Hoover's office. New chiefs in D.C. were supposed to kiss the ring, show respect to a man born in the nineteenth century who had built the FBI from scratch, who was the only director the bureau had ever had.

Jerry had sought no such audience. He didn't especially admire Hoover's imperious style. The months went by. Hoover noticed. Then the special agent in charge of the FBI's Washington field office invited the police chief to lunch: Please, as a favor to me, go see the director. So Jerry headed across town to FBI headquarters and listened patiently to Hoover's war stories. Hoover even tried to impress him with lurid details from the bureau's secret tapes of the late Martin Luther King Jr.'s extramarital activities.

Nothing about the meeting changed Jerry's opinion of Hoover. It wasn't just temperament that separated them. When they posed for the obligatory handshake picture, Hoover, who was maybe five foot seven, had to stand on a box next to the balding chief with prominent ears, who otherwise would have towered a full head above him. FBI lore had it that Hoover disliked having tall men around because of just such possible comparisons.

So there was little basis for trust after the explosion at the Capitol on the first day of March in 1971.

The FBI should have been well positioned to find the bombers. Notwithstanding the view of some people in the White House, the director hadn't been complacent about the radical left. His agents had been swarming over the movement, particularly its more extreme members, for years. "We used the same general investigative techniques against the New Left we had used successfully against the Communist party: wiretapping, informants, hidden microphones — the lot," as William Sullivan, the bureau's director of domestic intelligence, would note with pride.

But in the matter of the Capitol bombing, it seemed that the Metropolitan Police Department possessed some firsthand intelligence the bureau didn't have.

The police had embedded at least two people inside the Spring Offensive. Just hours after the blast, one of the undercover agents had checked out one of the houses used by the organizers. He reported back to his bosses his opinion, admittedly based on hearsay, that the residents could have been involved. The department did hand that tidbit and others to the FBI. It was one of the reasons the bureau put out the all-points bulletin, which, less than twenty-four hours later, snared the Mayday Tribe's Yippie contingent — Stew Albert, Judy Gumbo, and their friends — on a Pennsylvania highway.

Afterward, the FBI asked Jerry Wilson for direct contact with the sources of the police department's information. The chief declined.

The cops running Jerry's intelligence bureau figured it would blow the operation, or at least their control of it, if they gave up their informants and their methods to the feds. And they needed their own people inside the movement to figure out how to prepare for the spring protests.

Hoover was acutely tuned to any note of disrespect. And this was the second affront in a row from his hometown force. Just two weeks earlier, he had been enraged by a *Washington Post* story about the city's police recruits. The latest crop to come out of the academy reflected Jerry's determination to remake the force. No longer could a white department be effective in a city that was majority black. Jerry, who had only a high-school diploma himself, also wanted better-educated cops. So about half of the 375 graduates were African American, and at least two dozen had college degrees, some from top schools.

If Jerry had intended for the new recruits to broaden the department's worldview, he got quick results. For their graduation ceremony, the cadets selected a twenty-three-year-old graduate of Yale to address the class. He seized the moment to deliver a call for more progressive American law enforcement. He suggested that police engage with critics from the community and not be as thin-skinned as, for example, the director of the FBI. He slammed the Nixon administration's new D.C. crime bill, which gave the cops controversial powers, such as authorization to break down a door without first identifying themselves. That would only exacerbate distrust of the police. Some officials, he added, "wish to see their own peculiar view of America pushed onto everyone else."

Reporters were taking it all down. The head of the academy, who had been fiddling with his closing remarks and not paying attention to the young cadet's words, got up and addressed the audience of new police and their families: "I assure you this officer is representative of the type of officer we're trying to bring to you."

Representative, eh? Fine, Hoover would punish the department accordingly. He decreed Washington police ineligible for the special three-week training program the FBI academy offered to select officers. In Hoover's view, this excluded Jerry's force from one of the most prestigious honors in all of policing. Jerry saw it differently: big deal. He never found the program that appealing or useful in the first place.

Hoover wasn't done. A few days later, Jerry was meeting in his office with one of his deputies when another officer rushed over. "There's two FBI agents want to see you, right now," he informed the chief. Jerry waved him off. I'm in the middle of a conversation, he said.

After Jerry finally deigned to greet the agitated agents, they explained their purpose: Hoover wanted a formal apology for the cadet's remarks. And to make it easy for the chief, they'd taken the liberty of drafting the letter themselves. Jerry only had to sign it. Looking on, Jerry's deputy felt embarrassed for the FBI men. Hoover had long ago lost track of what was important.

Jerry thought the whole thing was ridiculous and told the FBI emissaries exactly that. Since when does the FBI director think a rookie who hadn't been a single day on the street speaks for the department?

For the sake of peace, he agreed to make the act of contrition. But, he added, I write my own letters, and he sent the agents on their way. Eventually Hoover got his written apology—but not before he had to complain once more to the White House about the slight.

And still it seems Hoover wasn't finished. The cadet who gave the graduation speech, a Manhattan native named Joseph B. Green, soon noticed that some of his mail, including the pink envelopes his mother used for her letters to him, arrived at his front door dog-eared, inside plastic sleeves, and marked "damaged in transit." After he alerted his bosses, the tampering stopped.

Beyond the bureaucratic bickering between the chief and Hoover was something much more toxic: Jerry was being mentioned in Washington circles as a possible successor to the seventy-six-year-old head of the FBI.

Hoover had already fended off suggestions from three presidents that he step down, but the Nixon White House noted his increasing unpopularity in opinion polls. The president hoped to replace him before the 1972 election, maybe getting him to retire on his next birthday.

The national reputation of the Washington police chief, on the other hand, had been steaming fast in the other direction. The previous summer, a portrait of Jerry's stoic face had been emblazoned on the cover of *Time* magazine as the quintessential big-city cop. It described the chief as displaying competence and compassion as he confronted crime and civil disorder. Soon after that, Jerry became the first cop to receive the annual brotherhood award from the National Conference of Christians and Jews, which among other things had been impressed by the chief's performance during three mass marches against the Vietnam War, all of which had gone off without widespread violence by the participants or the police, unlike similar situations in Chicago or in Kent, Ohio.

Of Hoover, Jerry would say one day: "He died hating me."

HAVING YOUR WORK second-guessed—that was built into the job of running a big police force. But it wasn't just the FBI on Jerry Wilson's back. Washington was a special case, a federal city without self-rule.*

---

* Congress would finally give D.C. residents the right to elect their own mayor and city council in 1973.

The White House handpicked the city's leaders. Congress doled out the money. The Justice Department oversaw the capital's security. Public safety on federal property and parkland fell to the Department of the Interior. No other top cops, not even the ones in New York City or Los Angeles or Chicago, had to contend with so many politicians, bureaucrats, and big shots at so many levels, lots of whom thought they knew better than you did.

Take what had happened just after Richard Nixon moved into the White House.

At the time, Jerry was still assistant police chief. Nixon's narrow victory over Hubert Humphrey in 1968 owed much to his vow to make American streets safe again. The biggest national disgrace, Nixon had suggested, was the deteriorating safety of Washington's streets, a terrifying place where permissive Democrats allowed "marauders and criminals" to run free.

Nixon hadn't invented law and order as a national campaign issue. It had been forged into the Republican platform four years earlier by the party's then nominee, Senator Barry Goldwater, who railed against rising crime in cities like the capital. Nixon adopted the theme to peel support from Democrats among rural and suburban whites, many of whom were frightened by violent scenes in black urban neighborhoods and disgusted by students who seized college buildings. Crime and protest twirled together like a double helix, the code underlying the troubled times. It was cynical politics, a barely concealed nod at racial prejudice, a hammer to drive deeper the wedge between generations.

But it was also a fact that, in Washington, fear was more than a product of political messaging. Much of the capital felt like a war zone. Scorched buildings and vacant storefronts had stood untouched for two years, monuments to the black community's rage over the King assassination. ("I *hate* those moldering ruins," Daniel Patrick Moynihan, the Harvard professor Nixon appointed to oversee urban affairs, told a colleague, after a field trip to the lingering destruction along D.C.'s Seventh Street. "Like so much dried vomit of a sick culture.") Moreover, the five days of rioting, arson, and looting accelerated the flight of businesses and middle-class residents of all races to the Maryland and Virginia suburbs. If you drove into town now from the north toward the

White House, you'd cruise by block after block of crumbling, boarded-up row houses.

Violence had been on the rise for more than a dozen years. The drumbeat of crime news fed the feeling that the old order was breaking down. Thanks in part to a surge in heroin addiction, D.C. was now more dangerous than any city its size. Murders had tripled in just a decade. Robberies spiked so sharply that churches were hiring armed guards for bingo nights and their Sunday collections. On one typical Tuesday, the police blotter recorded more than two dozen holdups, the targets including retail shops as well as people just walking on the street or sitting inside their homes or cars. The various assailants brandished knives, handguns, and sawed-off shotguns. That same day, two women were raped in their homes and another was abducted by three men and assaulted outside an elementary school. Police seemed increasingly ill-equipped to respond to the wave, not least because the force remained overwhelmingly white in a city with a population that was more than 70 percent black.

The lawyer who had helped develop the law-and-order message for Goldwater was a Republican activist from the senator's home state of Arizona named Richard Kleindienst. After LBJ crushed Goldwater, painting him as a warmonger, Kleindienst connected with Nixon, and then worked ferociously to help him land the Republican nomination for 1968. Upon taking office, Nixon rewarded him with the job of deputy U.S. attorney general, the second-highest rank in the Justice Department.

At his confirmation hearing, Kleindienst promised a panel of senators that the new administration would immediately flood D.C. with two thousand new police officers. That would represent an increase of some 70 percent in a city that already had one of the highest ratios of cops to citizens, and spent more per capita on law enforcement than any comparable place.

Jerry did plan to hire several hundred more cops. But two thousand? He figured Kleindienst just pulled a big number out of his hat to dazzle the lawmakers. When a reporter asked about it a few days later, Jerry expressed restrained enthusiasm. That wouldn't be my top priority, he said. He added that probably the biggest thing Nixon could do right off the bat to fight crime was to bring the district's antiquated court system into the modern age, unclogging the bottlenecks that kept the bad guys out of jail.

After the interview ran in the newspaper, the phone rang at police headquarters. Would Jerry please drop over to the Justice Department? He was ushered into the office of Kleindienst's boss — John Mitchell, Nixon's new attorney general. Mitchell calmly explained that he was sure Jerry actually thought it was a wonderful idea to hire two thousand officers. Without quite saying so, the attorney general made clear that if he happened to be wrong about Jerry's opinion, it would be a simple thing for the expanding police force to be reduced by one assistant chief.

Jerry understood. He'd have no future if the White House thought he was too independent. He was a more deeply ambitious man than he appeared to be. He adjusted. A few months after Mitchell called him on the carpet, Jerry had been elevated to the top job.

And still the back-seat drivers proliferated. Even those who championed individual rights against the power of the state now found themselves prepared to restore safety and order by trading away some freedom and justice, although not necessarily their own. The most prominent private citizens in the city decided to appeal directly to the new administration for drastic action, some even raising the possibility of militarizing the capital by deploying the National Guard to patrol the streets. (Even a hard-liner like John Mitchell thought that was a "crazy" idea from "frightened liberal cohorts.") Among them was Edward Bennett Williams, the leading criminal defense lawyer and part owner of the Washington Redskins. Another was Katharine Graham, publisher of the *Washington Post.*

They sought out Moynihan, the main Democrat in Nixon's circle. The elite group gathered one fall day in the elegant wood-paneled conference room of the American Security and Trust Company, directly across Pennsylvania Avenue from the Treasury Department. They told Moynihan that nothing they had done as business owners or private citizens seemed to be slowing the city's decline. They were close to giving up, perhaps to follow their customers to the suburbs. Williams said he was "embarrassed for my profession" by the breakdown in the criminal justice system, the long delays in prosecution and trials that were allowing dangerous suspects to stay out on bail.

When it came to the size of the police force, Williams echoed Klein-dienst's comments to Congress months earlier, saying the city needed "not one thousand, but two thousand more" officers. Williams complained that Police Chief Wilson "does not seem to think he needs help."

TO MOST D.C. COPS, Jerry's ascent was a puzzle. He owed it to a fortuitous move by President Lyndon B. Johnson late in his term. LBJ might have crushed Goldwater on election day, but the Republican's attack on crime in Washington hit home. So the president had ordered a wholesale reconstruction of the police force. In the chain of events that followed, Jerry was plucked from the budget office and put in charge of field operations — essentially running the department day in and day out.

Thus far Jerry had spent almost all of his twenty years on the force handling finance and crime statistics, often a solitary endeavor. The department was his life — his wife, with whom he had two young boys, was a former police stenographer. Yet Jerry never did what his colleagues considered real police work — never worked as detective, labored on the vice squad, or patrolled the tough neighborhoods like the rest of the grunts. They grumbled about it in the precinct houses. "The department was going nuts," recalled Maurice Cullinane, an officer who would later become one of Jerry's top lieutenants. "Who was this tall boy coming down the hall? Nobody knew who Jerry Wilson was! He did not know fifty people in the department, and I honestly believe he didn't know twenty."

But he impressed the White House. To Bud Krogh, who was the liaison between the department and Nixon's men, Jerry was a theoretician about crime at a time when just such a thinker was needed. Cullinane shortly came to realize that Jerry's low-key manner and molasses-thick drawl could make you miss just how bright he was, why he was so indispensable. He warned his colleagues: don't try to trade tractors with this country boy.

Jerry had arrived in D.C. in 1949, determined not to follow his parents into the cotton mills in his North Carolina hometown of Belmont, near Charlotte. He had been only fourteen when he enlisted in the navy during World War II; having reached his full height of six foot four, he was able to lie convincingly about his age. One day near the end of the war, Jerry, only seventeen and already a gun captain, fired his three-inch gun at a Japanese kamikaze that was careering toward a destroyer in his flotilla. The plane was hit, exploding harmlessly into the Pacific. The destroyer had been firing its bigger guns too, and Jerry had no way to know for sure who let off the true shot. Later in life, though, after a couple of Southern Comforts, he would convince himself his gun had won the day. He read somewhere that those who cheated death were entitled to write their own stories.

His first assignment in D.C. was in the Georgetown neighborhood. To his surprise, Jerry, whose mother had always promised to take the hickory switch to any of her children who used the N-word, found the city even more segregated than back home, where poor and working-class blacks and whites lived in close proximity, with more daily interaction. In Washington, racism was baked into the institutions. While the majority of the population was black and growing, there was an unspoken rule, Jerry soon learned, that the police force itself could be no more than 15 percent black. White and black officers weren't assigned together to squad cars. When the Secret Service requested help protecting motorcades or events involving President Harry Truman, and then Dwight D. Eisenhower, police headquarters would send a teletype to the precinct captains asking for personnel. The message included this warning: "Send white officers only."

Policing hadn't changed much in decades. All the power in a street encounter belonged to the cops. Many officers believed that standing on the dangerous front lines, protecting good citizens from harm, exempted them from accountability. As long as anyone could remember, for example, a patrolman could haul people down to the station on mere suspicion, on the thinnest of pretexts, and hold them incognito for a good long while. It was a formal D.C. police process called an "arrest for investigation." The street cops were supposed to run all such busts through a lieutenant, but, as always, things got sloppy. Suspects were held for hours or longer. Few of them ever got charged with a crime. This was a notorious practice in black neighborhoods, but Jerry never heard anyone in the city's white establishment complain, since it almost never happened to them.

Racial tensions in the department persisted well into the Sixties and indirectly helped propel Jerry to the top ranks. In early 1968, a carful of cops from the Sixth Precinct, heading home late one night after ending their shifts with whiskies and beers in the locker room, no doubt airing their grievances about the country's direction, drove past the home of James M. Nabrit Jr., the president of Howard University, one of the nation's most prestigious historically black colleges. Nabrit was a lawyer who had handled prominent civil rights cases. The cops slowed down, fired off several shots in the direction of the house, and sped away. No one was hit, but unfortunately for the shooters, Nabrit's private security guards got their car's tag number.

The police chief at the time, John B. Layton, tried to cover up the incident. By then LBJ had installed a czar to clean up the police department and identify younger, more open-minded officers. The czar, an ex–New York policeman named Patrick V. Murphy, had recognized Jerry's quiet intelligence and savvy. Jerry no doubt recognized the career benefit of bonding with Murphy. When Murphy exposed the cover-up, he forced the chief to accept Jerry as the head of field operations, over objections that Jerry was too young, too ignorant of the streets, too much of a loner.

Murphy let Jerry know that if he were to take over as chief someday he'd have to learn more about gritty police work. Don't be an office man, get your own squad car, and get out there, he said.

Barely a month after settling into the job, Jerry was glad he had taken Murphy's advice. He was at his home across from American University on Thursday, April 4, 1968, when, shortly after seven p.m., Murphy phoned him with news: Martin Luther King Jr. had been shot by an assassin in Memphis. Jerry got into a car and was driving up to the heart of black Washington, at Fourteenth and U Streets, when the radio crackled with the news that King had died. Angry crowds began to gather. A light drizzle came down. I wish, Jerry thought to himself, that it would start raining like hell.

More than twenty thousand people would hit the streets. Jerry didn't feel completely unprepared. He'd attended a national conference of police officials in Memphis to compare notes on urban disorder. There had been plenty to learn from others' mistakes.

The United States had already suffered three straight summers of the worst racial mass violence in at least half a century. More than a hundred separate riots had hit dozens of cities. It started with the uprising in the Watts section of Los Angeles in 1965, triggered by a drunk-driving arrest, where thirty-four people died and about a thousand were injured.

The summer of 1967 had been the bloodiest. In Detroit, scores of African Americans were killed and thousands were arrested, held in a big outdoor prison, all because cops had raided a rowdy homecoming party for a black Vietnam veteran. A similar riot in Newark left more than two dozen dead and hundreds injured. Racism and social inequality were the main causes, but a contributing factor was the destabilizing influence of the Vietnam War, said the New York mayor, John Lindsay, vice chairman of the national commission later set up to investigate the disorder.

Jerry had sent his chief of special operations to cities with outbreaks of violence, to observe and report back on what went wrong and what went right. His main takeaway wasn't exactly rocket science: be careful about firing your guns. Cops in places like Newark were indiscriminate. So Jerry wrote a riot plan, saying that police were not to shoot looters in Washington.

For three days, Washington burned. More than a thousand fires were set, some as close as ten blocks from the White House, and rioters smashed hundreds of shop windows. More than a thousand people were hurt. But, unlike the situation in Newark, D.C. cops chased suspected looters instead of gunning them down. They busted those caught with a lot of stuff; for others, they'd often just take back the merchandise and send the kids home. Late in the afternoon on the second day of the riots, LBJ had authorized a military presence. The army eventually sent fifteen thousand troops and guardsmen, most with unloaded guns, to restore peace. It was thought to be the largest military contingent to occupy any American city since the Civil War. The same day, the city set a 5:30 p.m. curfew to keep people off the streets at night.

In the end, thirteen people died, most in fires. Two looters had been shot dead. Murphy called it "truly miraculous" that the toll wasn't higher. Jerry shared in the accolades.

When Jerry was growing up in the 1930s, he had witnessed brutal clashes between labor organizers and the hired guns of textile barons in his North Carolina hometown. His father, a mill worker, slept for years with a shotgun stashed under his bed. The whole country then seemed on the brink of radical change, just as it would in the Sixties. Looking back much later, Jerry would decide that police were "the bearings at the pivot point of history." The way they handled things in the heat of events, he thought, could help transform a potential revolution into a peaceful evolution. His philosophy would be tested soon enough.

JOHN LAYTON WAS out early in Nixon's first term. Jerry Wilson became the new chief. He dealt with the big Moratorium marches in the fall of 1969, winning praise for the relative lack of injuries or damage. But the pace of protests through Washington streets kept quickening, until they averaged more than one per day. Most were small, and Jerry kept things under control. Except for one time, when he managed to infuriate not only the protesters and their sympathizers, but also his own men.

The incident unfolded on a Thursday afternoon in mid-February 1970, during a rare Washington snowfall, the day after the verdict in the five-month-long conspiracy trial of the Chicago Seven. David Dellinger, Rennie Davis, and three others — Jerry Rubin, Abbie Hoffman, and Tom Hayden — had just been convicted of crossing state lines to incite a riot. A few thousand people, mostly students from George Washington, Georgetown, and American universities, massed near the GW campus and headed for the Watergate, the swank hotel, office, and apartment complex not yet associated with national scandal. It was emerging as the favored residence of the Republican arrivistes (as well as, fatefully, the headquarters of the Democratic National Committee). Among those living there was Attorney General John Mitchell, who had pressed for the Chicago indictments.

The marchers chanted, "Two, four, six, eight — Liberate the Watergate!" Wilson's white-helmeted civil-disturbance unit stopped them, triggering a stampede back toward campus. The police continued the chase, firing tear gas at the kids, some of whom turned and threw snowballs or rocks as they ran a half mile through the streets toward George Washington University. Cops on motorcycles plowed their machines right into the crowd. Squad members and undercover officers grabbed students and bystanders, sometimes punching them down or cracking them on the head with a nightstick. Even Philip Hirschkop, the local civil liberties lawyer who had long been the main emissary of Washington peace groups in their permit negotiations with the police and had represented many famed activists in court, was swept up. "You pigs!" students screamed from the windows of Thurston Hall, the nine-story women's dorm on F Street, as they watched police clubbing and arresting their classmates. They threw whatever they could find, even the occasional clock radio that woke them for class, out at the cops. Of the 150 or so people arrested, more than 90 percent were taken away without any paperwork. The injuries included one broken collarbone.

Jerry knew it was really his fault. He'd grown a bit complacent after his successes at the 1969 marches. He should have stopped his men from chasing the kids down. Now the campus was inflamed, the faculty furious that police had invaded the heart of the university and had behaved like the Chicago cops in 1968. GWU's president, Lloyd Elliott, no friend of the New Left, visited police headquarters to complain to Jerry, suggesting that he come down to the university to explain himself.

The chief accepted. "We've handled a lot of demonstrations and this is the worst we've ever come out," Jerry told four hundred students in the university's auditorium. "Motorcycle men should never go up on sidewalks." He said, "It will not happen again," and promised that from now on police would go by the book, using the more orderly arrest procedures that had been recommended by a city commission following the riots after King's death. Some students called out "Bullshit!" and told him he was being naive, that the civil disturbance cops took out their anger on the kids as soon as the chief's back was turned.

It was exceedingly rare for a police chief to admit a mistake. Yet Jerry's appearance hardly won him friends among the students, and it enraged his rank and file. The Washington Patrolmen's Association condemned the chief, saying he shouldn't apologize, nor criticize the tough job the cops had to do while he stayed comfortably behind the lines.

Now it was Jerry's turn to be angry. He typed out a seven-page letter to the union and fired off copies to the newspapers. He'd been on the streets for every disturbance, not sitting in some quiet office, directing traffic. "I don't stand behind my men. I stand in front of them," the chief wrote. "You know very well that I have had as many invectives and rocks thrown in my proximity as any 20 of those 200 men who unanimously voted to deplore my actions. I have done this so that I will know what goes on. I sincerely believe that if a chief of police wants to have the credibility in the government and the community to effectively support his men, then he must have the guts to recognize when things are done imperfectly and to stand up and say: 'We must improve.'"

It may not have made his cops happy, but it sure bolstered his national image.

NOW, IN MARCH 1971, Jerry's intelligence division warned him that the biggest challenge was on the horizon. The Spring Offensive promised more than two straight weeks of protests all over town, with multiple factions taking part and employing varied tactics.

It wasn't a secret that the police were monitoring radical groups on and off campus. Jerry had told a government commission that while he thought it was "somewhat unethical" to infiltrate student organizations, it was necessary. Otherwise, he said, police could be caught unprepared and make things worse. Excepting the Weather Underground and the Black Panthers, the New Left was pretty much an open book, so it wasn't hard to get into their meetings. Many young police officers welcomed the assignment to go undercover and play at being hippies for a while.

Nevertheless, Jerry and his officers sometimes found it hard to fathom the dynamics of the movement. For a while it had seemed like a bunch of separate elements — the hippies, the women, the blacks. Now all of a sudden they seemed to be acting together, and through some mysterious process they could summon a protest at the drop of a hat. "The thing that surprised me the most," said one of Jerry's deputies, "was that it almost seemed like someone would say, 'I'll meet you down at 14th and Washington Drive' and these Volkswagen buses would just arrive held together by tar tape."

Trying to get a handle on the Spring Offensive, the police covered the waterfront. They tracked flyers on the street, attended meetings on all the campuses in town. They checked on the members of the editorial staff of college newspapers, like the GW *Hatchet,* which they reported was "becoming increasingly more radical." They observed the Washington office of the Black Panthers, noting that a "Negro/Female from New York" had joined. They reported on a meeting of the Metropolitan Abortion Alliance, which is "composed chiefly of girls from Women's Liberation, Young Socialist Alliance and Planned Parenthood." They even tracked ticket sales for a concert by the Four Tops at the D.C. Armory.

But most of the focus was turning toward the Mayday action. The undercover reports were getting quite detailed about the plans by the group headed by David Dellinger and Rennie Davis to stop traffic on Monday, the third of May.

"The people involved will work and act not as an atomized mass of thousands of lonely individuals under the command of an executive committee, but as a multitude of collectives, each of which has decided how to carry out its own commitments," agents reported. "Some collectives may decide to act in the classic Gandhian style, to fill the jails; others may seek to remain sufficiently mobile as to avoid arrest."

Some of the intelligence coming back, from what the police unit claimed was a "very reliable source," contended that the Mayday group also planned "acts of violence," arson, and kidnapping. Jerry was dubious about that, but it certainly cranked up the concern of the authorities. In mid-March, he was called to a meeting at city hall, in the office of the deputy mayor, where city and police and government officials discussed security for the Spring Offensive. It was decided that Jerry would have full command.

But there would be other tests, initially from a little-known group calling itself Vietnam Veterans Against the War. Wilson's intelligence department reported that the group planned to have as many as five thousand vets, dressed in fatigues, camping at the foot of the Capitol as a base for lobbying to end the war. Trouble was, they had no permit to be there, and the government didn't seem inclined to give them one. Another headache was brewing.

6

This Is 36

RIGHT FROM THE GET-GO OF AMERICAN INTERVENTION IN Indochina, no publication seized the attention of GIs better than *Playboy.* The house ads in the men's magazine — posing the question "What sort of man reads *Playboy?*" — depicted well-groomed fellows with sleek briefcases and expensive watches. But more than one soldier thought the typical reader could be found "in Vietnam, about nineteen, twenty years old. He sits just off a jungle trail."

In the mid-Sixties, when it was only a decade old but growing fast, *Playboy* had offered a special promotion. Buy a lifetime subscription, for what was then a tidy sum of $150, and you'd get your first issue delivered in person by one of the young women working in its nightclubs. A lieutenant serving in Vietnam with the 173rd Airborne, idling in the hospital with a shoulder wound, passed the hat around his platoon. He sent in the money and alerted newspapers about the stunt. And so *Playboy* flew its nineteen-year-old Playmate of the Year across the Pacific Ocean to drop off his copy. Some five thousand cheering guys greeted her at the airport in Saigon.

The magazine debuted just as the behavioral norms of the 1950s had begun to fray. It tested the loosening rules and attitudes about sex and nudity, such as when one cover promised pictures of the actress Jane Fonda "in the buff." *Playboy* bought them from a photographer who had furtively climbed into the rafters on the set for her 1966 French film *The Game Is Over.*

By 1971, *Playboy* was making regular nods to the counterculture, with edgy articles about drugs, rock, and the environmental movement. Even the woman who posed for the centerfold in the issue dated February (which went into the mail at the end of December 1970) was described as a "nonconformist" — though one who nevertheless "prefers the hearth to the barricades."

That same issue carried a striking full-page advertisement on page sixty-five. It showed a flag-draped coffin, lit against a black background. Underneath it were these words:

> In the last ten years, over 335,000 of our buddies have been killed or wounded in Vietnam. And more are being killed and wounded every day. We don't think it's worth it.

At the bottom was a membership form to clip and mail to a group few Americans had yet heard about: Vietnam Veterans Against the War.

VVAW's organizers weren't prepared for the response. Envelopes stuffed with the forms poured by the thousands into their New York headquarters. With one stroke, the group had tapped into the boiling discontent among troops and veterans. In a matter of weeks the VVAW was transformed into one of the most important actors in the antiwar movement.

A full-page ad in *Playboy* would have been a big expense for the VVAW. As one White House aide asked his colleagues, "Where does this money come from?" It was said that the magazine's founder and publisher, Hugh Hefner, donated the space in sympathy with the cause. At least, that was the story told for years. Only insiders knew of the link between the ad and the surreptitious photos *Playboy* had published of Jane Fonda five years earlier.

Fonda had filed a lawsuit seeking $17.5 million in damages from the magazine for violating her privacy. By the time *Playboy* agreed to settle, she had moved on from her ingénue roles. She had become an evangelist in the antiwar movement. The thirty-three-year-old actress was particularly focused on GIs and, with her Hollywood friends, led by the actor Donald Sutherland, was working up a radical version of the USO shows that toured to entertain the troops. They called theirs FTA, for "Fuck the Army." (Hearing of this, Nixon instructed that Fonda be kept away from military bases. "This must not be approved," he scrawled on his daily news summary.)

As part of her confidential settlement with the magazine, Fonda told the vets, she had demanded the VVAW be given a full-page ad for free.

Without Fonda, without the lawsuit and the *Playboy* ad, it was unlikely that hundreds of angry and bitter ex-warriors would now be packing for Washington to mount their part of the Spring Offensive.

THE WAR HAD become almost as divisive inside the military as it was in civilian life. Hundreds of thousands of young Americans who had volunteered or been drafted to Vietnam fought bravely in punishing conditions and under challenging rules of engagement, trying to keep themselves and their buddies alive. Most probably at first bought into the official reason for their presence in Southeast Asia — an honorable crusade to contain the spread of communism. In 1969 the army had estimated that there were fewer than three hundred "known and suspected dissenters" among its troops. A vast understatement, to be sure, but in any case, two years later doubts about the mission had taken hold deep into the ranks. Among other things, the cynicism fed growing friction between black soldiers and white officers. Not only was the Vietnam War the first major conflict the United States had fought with a fully integrated army, but, especially early in the war, African Americans numbered disproportionately among draftees and those killed in action.

Forty army officers training in jungle warfare in the Panama Canal Zone wrote an open letter to Nixon. Even if the war could be won, it was apparent that the American people weren't prepared to pay the price. As a result, they wrote, "We are asked to lead others who are unconvinced into a war in which few of us really believe."

Morale, and the readiness of the troops, was "lower and worse" than perhaps at any time in history, a retired marine colonel acknowledged in the *Armed Forces Journal.* "There's never been a more unpopular war," he wrote, "and it's had its effects."

Like their generational brethren back home, but even more in need of psychic escape, U.S. soldiers in the field had turned to recreational drugs, which were widely available, cheap, and very potent. Bud Krogh, the Nixon aide who counted stemming the illegal trade in narcotics among his many Washington responsibilities, had made his second visit to Vietnam in the summer of 1970 to look into the matter. The extent of the drug culture stunned him. At a firebase called Charlie 2, Bud found a group of soldiers sitting behind a tank, smoking pot.

"Hi," he said. "I'm Bud Krogh from the White House."

One of them took a big toke and looked him over. "Yeah, man, and I'm from Mars."

Bud asked what kind of drugs could be obtained easily. The soldier responded, "Well, what kind of shit do you want?"

Upon his return, Bud reported that marijuana was the main event ("going rate: 20 superb joints 50¢") and that the army leaders were clueless. "The brass doesn't know what it is, what it does or how to cope with it," he noted. More worrying was the rising popularity of high-quality heroin; four soldiers had died of overdoses in the week before Bud's visit.

Their low spirits made GIs a "tempting vineyard" for antiwar organizers, Bud told his bosses. "It is not inconceivable that we could have a 'symbolic mutiny' or other equally damaging event," he wrote. And even worse was the growing number of actual mutinies — the attacks known as "fragging," in which enlisted men went after their officers, often because they had been ordered into a risky mission they thought was pointless. One general confided to Bud that in the first half of 1970 there had been "83 instances of GI's trying to kill their sergeants or lieutenants."

If the American public saw the whole picture, it wouldn't help the Nixon administration. The reputation of the armed forces already was deteriorating. There was, for example, the upcoming court-martial of Lieutenant William Calley, an army platoon leader who stood accused of massacring dozens of Vietnamese men, women, children, and babies in a hamlet called My Lai. The case, exposed by the investigative reporter Seymour Hersh after an army cover-up, raised broader questions about the conduct of troops trying to sweep the Vietcong out of the countryside. Then there had been the separate revelation that the South Vietnamese government, with American complicity, was torturing political prisoners on Con Son Island, where some 400 people were crammed in tiny "tiger cages."

In light of all that, Bud had told his military contacts in Vietnam to keep quiet about the epidemic of drug use, especially when members of Congress came to visit. Congress had generally granted LBJ and Nixon whatever funding they requested for the war, but the mood had been shifting. Lawmakers had already banned sending U.S. ground forces into

Cambodia. And although the Senate had recently rejected a proposal to force a U.S. withdrawal by the end of 1970, another vote was likely. "We pointed out that My Lai, Con Son and the drug abuse were the type of issues which 'radical liberals' would publicize in their efforts to end the war," Bud explained to his boss.

IN EARLY 1971 the staff members at the VVAW's main office in New York City sorted through the mail generated by the *Playboy* ad. For those still on active duty, they would send membership cards back to their units. Some envelopes would be returned unopened and marked "Deceased."

The forms from veterans around the country were grouped by state, then shipped off to satellite offices so activists could make contact and keep growing the organization.

It wasn't the first attempt to build the VVAW into a genuine force. The group had been founded in 1967, when Jan Barry Crumb, a former army radio technician who did a tour early in the U.S. intervention, decided to join the big peace demonstration in New York City that spring. David Dellinger had been a key organizer of the parade, and he had also been one of the first to broach the idea of soldiers joining the movement. "In a sensible world," he had written, "it would be obvious that there is a natural alliance of sympathy and common interest between the men whose lives and limbs are threatened in a dishonest and unnecessary war and those who are trying to bring that war to an end."

The words on the banner Crumb marched under — "Vietnam veterans against the war" — attracted a handful of other ex-warriors. That summer Crumb gathered a small band of them in the kitchen of his apartment on the Lower East Side (not far from where the Yippies were cooking up their big Pentagon action for that fall). They formally launched the group and made Crumb the president. But the following year many grew discouraged by the violent clashes at the Democratic National Convention. The organization dissipated and became insolvent.

In the fall of 1970, the group was springing back to life. One reason was the attention and financial support from Fonda. Another was an injection of new leadership, including the new executive secretary — a tall, goateed former air force sergeant named Al Hubbard, the only African American to hold a senior role in the group. Hubbard became the

VVAW's most recognizable national spokesman, while the membership remained overwhelmingly white; the most militant black veterans gravitated toward civil rights groups or the Black Panthers.

Hubbard nudged his VVAW colleagues to stir things up and begin building a truly national organization. Taking a page from the Yippies, he and the other leaders decided to mount a spectacle during the Labor Day weekend. They held a march from Morristown, New Jersey, to Valley Forge in Pennsylvania, the route where George Washington took his revolutionary army over its most difficult winter. The VVAW held educational skits along the way, mimicking the search-and-destroy missions they'd carried out in Vietnam.

Notable at the Valley Forge events was the speaker the leaders recruited, after seeing him on a TV talk show. He was a tall former navy lieutenant, a winner of the Silver Star, with craggy features. He had already made a short-lived bid for the Democratic nomination for Congress from his Boston district. His name was John Kerry. He would soon supplant Hubbard as the public face of the VVAW.

THE VVAW MEMBERSHIP forms had asked only for addresses, not telephone numbers. Which is why a stocky twenty-seven-year-old veteran named John O'Connor had been driving his bright-red 1970 Mustang around the Washington region, knocking on the doors of guys who'd sent them in.

While John was ex–air force, he hadn't served in Vietnam. He'd been stationed in Germany as a medic. After his service he returned to his hometown, Rochester, New York, where he'd grown up in a big Irish working-class family. He tried to make ends meet as a part-time bartender.

In late 1970 he decided to relocate to the D.C. area, where his sister lived. He began exploring the antiwar movement. Wandering over to the annual ceremonial lighting of the White House Christmas tree, John had met some veterans holding protest signs. Before you knew it, he was walking into the VVAW's Washington office. The local leader was an ex-army engineer named Michael Phelan. Phelan asked, John, you have a car? I need somebody with a car. With the stack of membership forms, they set off to recruit new volunteers.

One day they knocked on the door of Jack Mallory, a former army

captain who had volunteered to serve in Vietnam because he was thinking about a military career and "had a feeling it was the historical event
of my lifetime." After his service Mallory moved back to the Washington
area where he was raised. Trying to work off the bad memories of the
war, he hadn't been doing much except going on strenuous daily bicycle
rides along the canal path next to the Potomac River. Getting involved in
something with a mission sounded like a good move.

John O'Connor, Phelan, and Mallory, along with another air force veteran of Vietnam named Tim Butz, would become the core of the Washington office.

In the meantime, the VVAW's leaders decided in early 1971 to stage
another public event. They called it the Winter Soldier Investigation,
playing off the famous propaganda pamphlet by Tom Paine, who decried
the colonists who abandoned George Washington's revolutionary army
in its hour of need as "summer soldiers and sunshine patriots." Winter
Soldier had two objectives. One was to provide a time and place for vets
to safely air their personal horrors of war. Many had returned in tough
mental shape, suffering silently from a malady that hadn't yet come to be
called post-traumatic stress disorder. "We didn't tell each other war stories," Mallory said later. "We didn't talk about *not* talking to each other."

The other objective was to give the press and the public a better idea
of conditions on the ground in Vietnam, including atrocities that some
vets considered war crimes. The three-day event began on the last day
of January, in the conference rooms of a Howard Johnson's motel outside Detroit. Jane Fonda helped pay for the meeting with proceeds from
her campus appearances. Dozens of presenters gave firsthand accounts,
to drive home the point that Lieutenant Calley's massacre was only the
most infamous of the terrible acts being committed in America's name.

Jack Mallory was one of the speakers. He described mistreatment of
Vietnamese civilians by his unit, the Eleventh Armored Cavalry Division. Some troops violated enemy graves and used skulls as candlehold-
ers. The U.S. military, he testified, regarded the Vietnamese "much as
America regards her own minorities — a pat on the head for a trick, a
kick in the ass for an imagined fault, and invisible the rest of the time."

To the dismay of the VVAW leaders, the national news media largely
ignored Winter Soldier. John Kerry despaired that "America was asleep
. . . here were these guys spilling their hearts out, and not many peo-

ple were listening." A few weeks later, the organizers held a contentious meeting to discuss their next steps. As Jan Barry Crumb would recall, it was Kerry who crystallized the goal: we have to do something else to make Americans understand how the soldiers of this war feel about it. Let's march to Washington, he said. Let's take this to Congress.

KERRY ENVISIONED SOMETHING like a lobbying campaign. Many other VVAW activists, influenced by the rest of the Spring Offensive, wanted something more intense — a veterans' base camp on the National Mall, a confrontation with the Pentagon.

Kerry began spending more time in Washington. John O'Connor and the other vets could see he was a different kind of animal. Kerry carried himself with poise and could command instant respect and attention from establishment politicians and reporters. The VVAW crew joked among themselves that he "looked like a Lincoln and talked like a Kennedy."

A good many in the rank and file of the antiwar group didn't see Kerry that way, however. They came from working-class homes and had been grunts, not officers. They regarded Kerry with some suspicion. His very respectable Boston family had sent him to a prestigious New England preparatory school. He had graduated from Yale. He had recently married into a wealthy New York dynasty, the Thornes. Already he had taken a run at a congressional campaign, and though he dropped out of the primary, no one around him doubted he had his eye on the White House, even if he didn't say so out loud, as he once had to his navy shipmates. What was a guy like that doing here?

But as far as John O'Connor was concerned, Kerry was the real thing — a war hero, a serious man with strong beliefs. He thought it was somewhat silly for people to grumble that Kerry was just a self-promoter who came across well on TV, that he was trying to capitalize on the movement to fuel a political career. Maybe he was using the VVAW, but it was using him too. And for an aspiring politician, he was taking a gamble — no one could say whether his being out there against the war would help his career or cripple it.

As for John O'Connor, he soon found himself embedded even more firmly within the Washington area's leftist groups, not just the VVAW. He was one of the more organized and reliable of the volunteers. He was generally more sober; while he pounded back beers with the others, he always declined to join them in smoking marijuana. So the vets asked him to manage the clerical end of things.

At the time the vets group didn't have its own office in Washington. John worked from a spare desk inside another peace organization's headquarters. He was sitting there one day when an activist from NPAC, the group planning the big April 24 march in the middle of the Spring Offensive, walked in with a problem. His car, which was towing a U-Haul trailer, had stalled down on the street in the thick of rush hour. John went out to look. All it needed was some transmission fluid. John got it moving and parked it safely, and the NPAC activist was impressed. His group was moving into a shabby but cheap building nearby. They could pay for an office manager. Did John possibly want the job?

Sure he did. So John began his stint at 1029 Vermont Avenue, setting up the NPAC office. As far as his new bosses were concerned, he could continue doing his volunteer work for the veterans as well.

Before long, the groups led by Rennie Davis and Dave Dellinger would also move into the building. It became a leftist beehive. The vets sometimes felt that the younger activists didn't quite get them, didn't understand that they came to their protest from a different perspective. "Don't you just love the Vietnamese?" gushed a young flower child to one of John's veteran colleagues, Tim Butz, an Omaha native who had enlisted in the air force and spent eighteen months in Indochina. Butz gave her a hard look. "No, I don't love them," he said. "They tried to kill me."

Despite the occasional tension, John was now in a terrific position to help all the elements of the Spring Offensive. He wasn't an ideologue; he was friendly to everyone, a self-effacing guy, a charming Irishman, considered competent and professional. He would answer the phones, get leaflets and signs printed, take care of business, coordinate between groups.

John O'Connor would do all these things with gusto and without complaint. Because John was secretly an intelligence officer in the Washington police department.

HE HADN'T JOINED the air force out of any big desire to wage a patriotic fight. Like a lot of guys he knew, John O'Connor just needed something to do after high school, and "three hots and a cot," as the promise went, looked pretty good to him. While in Germany, he hadn't paid much attention to the protests. At a foreign base you didn't have a lot of access to news that the military didn't produce itself. The brass would sometimes send everyone down to the cafeteria at night to see Vietnam propaganda films. Bombs would drop in the jungle, the cause was just. Rah-rah and all that, John thought to himself.

When he got home and watched the news, saw hard-hat construction workers beating on college kids, things looked a little more complicated.

He got a job bartending part-time. On his break one day, he sat at the bar, leafing through the Rochester newspaper. There was a big ad showing two D.C. cops getting out of their spanking new cruiser, with the U.S. Capitol gleaming in the background. Join the D.C. police! Chief Jerry Wilson was adding hundreds to the force.

John dialed the number in the ad. Before he knew it, his Mustang was on the road to Washington. He pulled into the D.C. strip mall where the police had their recruiting office. Standing in the orientation line, he noticed he was a bit older than the others. A couple of officers from the intelligence division noticed that too. They realized that, as an out-of-towner, John knew no one here, and no one knew him.

They pulled him out of the line and asked if he wanted to go undercover. Strictly undercover, they said—no badge, no gun. How long, asked John, thinking they'd say a couple of weeks. No, they said, a year, maybe two.

John wouldn't even have to go to the police academy right away. In fact it would be better not to, so he could avoid picking up any telltale cop behaviors. Grow your beard, grow your hair, try to blend in. John asked, And do what exactly?

Just tell us what's going on, wander around, collect leaflets, see if you can work your way into some meetings, let us know if there's any trouble coming our way.

John's sister lived nearby in suburban Virginia. He went over and told her he wasn't sure he wanted to be a rat, to pass on information that could get someone in big trouble.

So don't, she said. Don't hurt anybody. Be a good rat.

And so John said yes.

JOHN WAS FAR from the only person secretly monitoring the antiwar movement and leftist groups in Washington. Police Chief Jerry Wilson had greatly expanded his intelligence division. Besides several other undercover agents, the unit in 1971 had seventeen investigators and more than twenty paid informants. Some enrolled at department expense in the local universities.

Washington wasn't unusual in that way. Most big-city police departments operated "red squads," holdovers from the communism scares of the 1950s. A hippie who had volunteered as the Yippie Jerry Rubin's bodyguard during the 1968 convention protests showed up on the witness stand of the Chicago Seven trial and outed himself as a local undercover cop.

At the same time, federal authorities were all over the movement too. In violation of their charters, the CIA and the NSA ran surveillance not only overseas but within U.S. borders, relying on a list of some ten thousand U.S. leftists handed over by the Justice Department. One part of this, known as Operation Chaos, had begun under LBJ and was expanded during the Nixon administration.

The military also contributed. A few months after Nixon took over as president, the army's intelligence command directed agents to collect information on "Anti-War/Anti-Draft Activities, Militant Organizations, Extremists in the Armed Forces, Demonstrations, Rallies, Parades, Marches, Conventions, Conferences, Picketing Activities, Strikes, and Labor Disturbances." As the Spring Offensive approached, Congress was investigating this spying (prompted by yet another exposé from Seymour Hersh, the reporter who'd uncovered the My Lai massacre). It turned out that army and navy agents had posed as newsmen to interview and photograph New Left leaders. Others had been embedded with the protesters at the 1968 convention, officials admitted: "Agent personnel, consisting of Negro teams and hippie teams, joined with potentially violent elements across the country and traveled with them to Chicago."

The activities of the FBI, which included break-ins, use of listening devices, and other actions that J. Edgar Hoover kept secret from even the White House, also were seeping into the daylight. Senator Edmund Muskie of Maine was about to reveal that agents had spied on him and other participants during the first Earth Day celebration the previous year. A newspaper reported that the FBI leased 450 lines from the Chesapeake and Potomac Telephone Company to handle all its wiretaps in

Washington. (The Vermont Avenue building was a particularly ripe target. A repairman who unlatched the phone box in the basement told John and his buddies that he'd never seen such a snake pit of cables.)

And in March, a reporter named Betty Medsger opened her mail at the *Washington Post* and found secret FBI documents about the New Left. They were sent to her by the people who broke into the field office outside Philadelphia, a small band calling themselves the Citizens' Committee to Investigate the FBI. (It would be decades before the eight burglars, led by a Haverford College physics professor, revealed their identities to Medsger.) Her first story on the cache of papers quoted an FBI memo that suggested agents should step up their interviews with dissenters "for plenty of reasons, chief of which it will enhance the paranoia endemic in these circles and will further serve to get the point across there is an FBI agent behind every mailbox."

In one of the synchronicities of the era, the agent in charge of that Pennsylvania FBI outpost was the same man who led the posse that stopped Stew and Judy's Volkswagen the night after the Capitol bombing. Hoover, furious at the burglary that exposed his secret activities, eventually would punish the agent for the security lapse, suspending him without pay and shipping him off to another state.

ACTIVISTS MIGHT NOT yet have been aware of the enormous reach of such spying, but it was hardly a secret that they were being watched and monitored, or that the most eager volunteers might not be exactly who they appeared to be. (One of the stolen FBI memos acknowledged that informants sometimes "got carried away during a demonstration, assaulted police, etc.") That was why, when John O'Connor walked into the VVAW office for the first time, he was frightened. His bosses at police headquarters warned him that these were dangerous people, with dangerous ideas. They must be so, or they wouldn't be under surveillance by the FBI. Moreover, John had zero experience lying about who he was, or what he was doing. They'd see right through him.

But he steeled himself, took a deep breath, and walked in.

To John's surprise, the vets had been friendly and welcoming. They turned out not to be scary revolutionaries or boring political drones. They were regular guys, really smart and fun-loving. He quickly became a comrade. Soon it hardly felt like pretending. He had been naive about

Sixties culture, and now he enjoyed getting educated. It wasn't all about the war and the movement. The vets gave him practical advice too, like how it was wrong to call women "girls" or "chicks" if you wanted to make any progress with them.

Once a day, John would excuse himself from whatever he was doing and find a pay telephone. If they were at a movie — the guys liked to get high and watch Dracula matinees at the cheap theater in Georgetown — he'd slip out to the lobby. He'd dial the intelligence office of the police.

When someone answered, he'd give his code name: "This is 36."

Usually he'd follow up with "All is quiet." Sometimes he'd get the call to drive his Mustang down to the river, by West Potomac Park next to the Lincoln Memorial. There was a small Park Police building there. In the parking lot, where they thought it was safe, his boss would hand him his pay in cash. Once in a while, in between the meetings, he'd let the office know he'd left something for them in the trunk of his Mustang — usually some movement literature or schedules — so they could use their duplicate set of car keys to retrieve it when the coast was clear.

If his handlers went off the rails in denigrating the antiwar folks, John would say, you guys aren't all right on this. If they complained he was getting too close to his targets, he'd say, Hey, I'm an Indian in Indian territory. I've got to act like an Indian. None of the vets suspected John was a cop, not even when visitors noticed he refused a joint and wondered, out loud, why.

When the Mayday Tribe moved into an office upstairs from the vets, John was his usual friendly self. One time a group of them came down for a favor. They'd just rented an apartment on Lanier Place, and it was pretty filthy. They knew John was in charge of office equipment. Could they borrow some cleaning supplies to make the place habitable? John apologized, saying he didn't have anything available right then.

Early in the morning of March 1, John's police bosses rousted him out of bed with a phone call. They explained that the Capitol had just been bombed. They sent him to the bus station to see if anyone he knew was trying to hightail it out of town. Then they asked if there was any way he could check the Yippies at the Lanier Street apartment, where one of the residents was Leslie Bacon, suspected by the feds of having knowledge of the bombing.

Sure, John said. I've got an idea how to do it.

He grabbed a mop and some supplies and knocked on the door. Here you go, John said. I thought I'd bring these by for you. The residents invited him in and after a bit asked what he thought of the Capitol bomb. John told them, it was such a dumb thing to do, it couldn't be a movement group. Probably it was set by government provocateurs, he suggested.

When John left, he went to a pay phone. Oh yeah, I think they must have been involved, he told his bosses. They seemed so proud at first, and then so crestfallen when I criticized it.

BY MID-MARCH, the Vietnam Veterans Against the War decided on their plan for the Spring Offensive. John Kerry described it to reporters on Capitol Hill. For five days, he said, former GIs wearing jungle fatigues would set up camp "as close to the Capitol as possible." They would lobby legislators to end the war, and would reenact the search-and-destroy tactics the Americans employed in the jungle. Most dramatically, Kerry announced, the vets would turn in their combat medals, in protest, to a joint session of Congress.

Providing Kerry with some weighty support at the news conference was a former commandant of the U.S. Marine Corps, David M. Shoup. The sixty-six-year-old retired general, a recipient of the Medal of Honor for his bravery in the Pacific during World War II, had been saying for years that there was no reason for the United States to intervene in Vietnam, which should be allowed to determine its own destiny. For the VVAW, he said now, "I wholeheartedly support their hopes and dreams and share their universal hunger for peace."

Thousands of disgruntled American ex-soldiers would arrive in the capital two weeks afterward, just in time for a subtle change in the Vietnam debate. It was no longer only about geopolitics, but how the United States was actually waging the war on the ground. This shift was crystallized by the court-martial of Lieutenant William Calley for the My Lai massacre.

The Calley case divided the country, and not always along the usual fault lines. Was Calley a unique monster, or a patsy for higher-ups? Was he a scapegoat being used to deflect criticism of U.S. atrocities? Were his actions worse than dropping napalm on defenseless villages?

On March 29, the army court-martial found Calley guilty of murder.

APRIL
1971

Embittered GIs who served in the Vietnam War return their ribbons and medals to Congress.

7

The Courage Part

Thursday, April 1, to Thursday, April 15

IN THE HOURS AFTER LIEUTENANT WILLIAM CALLEY WAS SEN-
tenced to life in prison for murdering twenty-two South Vietnamese
peasants, President Nixon was at his Western White House, beside the
California coast in San Clemente, trying to decide what to do about it.

Nixon didn't doubt that Calley committed the killings. But when it
came to punishment, he drew a contrast between Calley and another
man recently found guilty of a string of lurid slayings — Charles Manson,
the vicious, spaced-out Southern California cult leader who orchestrated
the deaths of seven people, including the actress Sharon Tate. The president didn't think Calley should be treated like that species of criminal.

Furthermore, Nixon calculated that an act of compassion would be
good politics because the Calley case was scrambling the national debate
in worrisome ways.

Tens of thousands of people, both for and against the war, had been
firing off telegrams and burning up the phone lines at the White House
and Congress, denouncing the sentence as too harsh. From the right
Calley looked like a scapegoat for the muddled mission of the U.S. military, from the left, the fall guy for America's moral lapse in Southeast
Asia. A sympathetic country song titled "The Battle Hymn of Lieutenant
Calley" had just been released. It would sell more than a million copies
in its first few weeks.

One Georgia congressman, a conservative Democrat who had long
backed the war, heard from so many constituents that he rose on the

House floor to call for ending the draft, because "our people are more divided than at any time in the last one hundred years." The head of the Senate Foreign Relations Committee publicly asked why, if the military believed a war crime was committed, the only person brought to justice was a platoon leader, while his higher-ups, all the way to the White House, went free.

Nixon made his decision. Just after noon on April 1, he picked up the phone. He reached the chairman of the Joint Chiefs of Staff, Admiral Thomas H. Moorer. Release Calley from the stockade, the president ordered. Let him live under house arrest until his appeals are exhausted. When Nixon hung up, he turned with satisfaction to his chief of staff and said, "That's the one place where they say 'Yes, sir' instead of 'Yes, but.'"

Looming in the air was Nixon's next address to the nation about Vietnam. It was less than a week away. He hoped to seize the high ground ahead of the new season of Washington demonstrations. For the first time, the protests would include thousands of people who had actually fought in the war. Some of them planned to discuss the atrocities they'd witnessed, to claim that Calley's massacre was no anomaly. It was dawning on the president and his men — including Bud Krogh — that this could develop into a serious public relations challenge. Allowing the reaction to Calley's punishment to fester could complicate things even more for Nixon and his grand strategy.

And Nixon had been refining that strategy for months. Speaking privately in March with his national security adviser, Henry Kissinger, the president had mused about his latest poker round with the North Vietnamese. With the Cambodia and Laos invasions, he was trying to force them to "look at their hole card" and decide they had no choice but to negotiate on Nixon's terms. Meantime, he could draw down the number of American troops just enough to blunt opposition at home without crippling the army's ability to fight. Keep arming the South Vietnamese while bombing the North. Ignore demands from campus and congressional liberals to set a hard deadline for withdrawal, which would just give away the main bargaining chip. The plan could work, Kissinger agreed, "If our domestic situation holds reasonably well."

That was the trick — to push the edge of the war hard enough to keep the enemy off balance, but not so far as to trigger anguish and massive protests at home.

But now it was clear that the attack on Laos was failing miserably on both counts. Despite heavy artillery and bombing by U.S. planes, the enemy was driving the South Vietnamese back across their own border. The North Vietnamese killed or wounded nearly half of the retreating army, and they shot down 168 U.S. helicopters, leaving nearly a hundred Americans dead or missing in action, the worst spate of air-crew deaths in the entire war. Adding to the tragedy, four photojournalists working for American outlets were killed while covering the invasion. And the antiwar movement, which had finally seemed to die down into embers a year after the invasion of Cambodia, flamed again.

A FEW DAYS after making his decision about Calley, Nixon flew back to Washington. He got his hair trimmed and then spent all day April 7 in his hideaway office in the Old Executive Office Building, refining his television address.

He delivered it that evening from the Oval Office. Nixon hit back at critics who claimed Laos had been a failure. Although the South Vietnamese suffered heavy casualties, he insisted the outcome was much worse for the North Vietnamese. In fact, he argued, the performance of the South's military proved that that his strategy of turning the war over to them — a process he called Vietnamization — had been a success. And as a result, he would withdraw another hundred thousand U.S. troops by December. While "American involvement in Vietnam is coming to an end," he said, announcing a final date would only "serve the enemy's purpose."

One of the groups planning the Spring Offensive — the People's Coalition for Peace and Justice, whose leaders included Rennie Davis and David Dellinger — sent a letter to CBS, demanding the right to respond to Nixon's speech under the fairness doctrine. The TV network declined. But, as was traditional, the Democrats were given time, and the party's two leading candidates for the 1972 presidential nomination, Senators Edmund Muskie of Maine and George McGovern of South Dakota, made their case for a complete pullout by the end of the year. "Whatever you or I or any of us now think about the war," Muskie said, "I believe we all agree on one terrible price it is making us pay. It is the price of division, fear, and hatred in America."

Two days after the speech, the private White House polls were in.

Haldeman, the chief of staff, walked into the Oval Office to brief Nixon. At first the president seemed to be bracing himself. He knew public confidence had tanked when he announced the Laos action in January. Now he quickly brightened. The portion of the public disapproving of his Vietnam policies had fallen by six percentage points — from 46 percent down to 40. As he often did when getting good news, or reinforcement of his worst instincts, he began to drum his fingers in kind of a marching beat on his big mahogany desk — *bumbumbumbumbumBUM*. He boasted to Haldeman, "You know when you really stop to think of it, though, a speech that turns that many people . . . that turns around approval/disapproval of the war is very significant, don't you think so? That's what we did with one speech!"

Any turnaround, though, could be fickle, especially with the demonstrations about to get underway. Haldeman reassured the president, based on the intelligence he was getting, that the events wouldn't draw as many protesters as came to D.C. after the Kent State killings in 1970. Nixon wasn't so certain. Antiwar leaders still had a little time to get their act together, and "it may be that they'll have huge numbers," he said, noting that previous D.C. marches were "organized awful well."

The White House press secretary, Ron Ziegler, who had joined the meeting, opined that even if there were big crowds, it didn't necessarily mean they were angry about the war or politics. A lot were coming "just for kicks, for fun," Ziegler said, just as he himself had gone down to the California beaches for spring break.

Haldeman joked, "If we went out and shot four kids on a campus somewhere you'd have a pretty big demonstration."

THE POLLS NOTWITHSTANDING, antiwar sentiment didn't seem to be fading on the streets. Quite the opposite: it annoyed the president almost every time he or his top people ventured out. On an official visit to Williamsburg, Virginia, the president smiled when a young teenager approached him, but the boy then asked, "Mr. President, how does it feel to be a war criminal?" It still pained Nixon that he'd missed his younger daughter's graduation from Smith College the previous year. Julie had told him the campus was just too volatile. "I truly think the day will be a disaster if he comes," she wrote one of her father's top aides.

With Easter weekend approaching, the Nixons made plans to go to

Camp David in western Maryland. Then on Sunday, they would head twenty miles farther on, to Gettysburg. They would celebrate Easter at the Eisenhower family's church, with the namesake of the presidential mountain retreat, David Eisenhower. David was not only the grandson of the man Nixon served as vice president, but also Nixon's son-in-law.

But just before leaving Washington, Nixon scotched the Gettysburg idea. He was angry about what had happened when he and the family tried to slip quietly into Good Friday services at the church across the square from the White House. When the president arrived, "a half-dozen minister types" were waiting at the entrance, shouting, "Peace now!" They were still out there when the Nixons left the service. They chanted "something about Christ died to save men's lives," the chief of staff recorded in his diary. Gettysburg would probably attract even more protesters. Instead, on Easter Sunday the Nixons and Eisenhowers all went unannounced to a small Methodist church near Camp David.

When Nixon got back to Washington, the Monday news summary on his desk noted that a speech in California by the deputy secretary of defense, David Packard (cofounder of the technology giant Hewlett-Packard), had to be moved at the last minute, to avoid a clutch of anti-war protesters. When Packard got to deliver his remarks, the summary reported, "Packard sharply blasted radicals like Jane Fonda who 'want to destroy everything our country stands for . . . Don't let them do it.' He told business leaders of need for strong US defense which combined with RN accomplishments has made the president 'the most respected and influential leader in the world.'"

In the margin Nixon wrote, "Excellent — thank him for RN."

The same summary referenced a TV talk show where an aide said the president has "intelligence and discipline" and is "open and flexible," adding that it would be impossible for any president to be popular in such challenging times. "Good job," Nixon scrawled.

On the night of April 12, Nixon had dinner with Kissinger in the Lincoln Room. The two of them were cooking up the surprise that had been on Nixon's mind. If their diplomatic coup worked, they could reshape the debate not only about Vietnam but also America's place in the world.

Two days earlier, the U.S. Ping-Pong team had landed in the capital of China for a weeklong visit. It was the first sign of a thaw in bilateral relations since the communist revolution in 1949. Nixon had long been weighing the idea of opening up ties to China as a way to tip America's rival superpower, the Soviet Union, off balance. He and Kissinger had revived nuclear arms control talks with the Soviets,* and now they were secretly making contact with the Chinese leaders, something even the State Department didn't know was happening. If all went well, he might even travel there himself before too long.

"We're fighting a delaying action," Nixon said, and Kissinger replied, "If we can get three months, we can change this course."

The president's spirits were buoyed. The following evening he went down to the bowling alley and nailed a score of 229, a personal best.

PERHAPS NIXON WAS heading for a world-shaking diplomatic and political triumph. He talked about it constantly with Kissinger. "Let's face it, in the long run this is so historic. Jesus, this is a hell of a move," he said in one of their many phone calls.

But that wouldn't be enough. The president's other obsession was fixing his personal image. He chafed at the widely held perception that he was shifty and socially awkward. At the same time he didn't want people to know how much this notion bothered him. He instructed his men to make it clear that "RN is less affected by press criticism and opinion than any president in recent memory." How to make the public see him as he wanted to be seen? "We need a little more poetry," he once told his aides. For presidents, he said, "it's not about what they do but how they do it." The public should know about the real Nixon — "hard work, how he works, his guts, restoration of dignity, the family, church, square."

He revisited the problem in a conversation with Kissinger in the Old Executive Office Building on the morning of April 15, contrasting his image with the growing public deification of the late President Kennedy. Regular folks thought JFK was "warm, sweet and nice to people" when he was actually "cold, impersonal, he treated his staff like dogs," Nixon fulminated. It was a myth, he added, and "we have created no mythol-

---

* In late April Kissinger reported the Soviets had bought into a joint commitment to move ahead. See Patrick J. Garrity and Erin R. Mahan, essay, "Nixon and Arms Control," Presidential Recordings Program, Miller Center, University of Virginia.

ogy." Nixon thought of himself as showing "sheer unadulterated guts and boldness that stand alone. And coolness under fire." In fact, guts was his most important attribute. In a plaintive voice he asked Kissinger, "For Christ's sake can't we get across the courage part? Courage, boldness, guts? . . . What the hell is the matter with our staff? What is the matter with our cabinet?"

In one unintentionally revealing memo, Nixon urged his personal secretary, Rose Mary Woods, to spread the word about his outstanding work and leisure habits: He didn't waste time playing golf, took only five minutes for breakfast, five minutes for lunch, eschewed social calls, and gave up the social cocktail hour. He liked classical music but couldn't have it on while he was reading. "I do not enjoy fishing myself," he told her, "but I do enjoy being on a boat and watching other people fish."

For the president's aides, the issue was political rather than psychological. The "focal point," one noted, had to be the following summer of 1972, when the reelection campaign would really crank up. "Primarily," the aide wrote, "we are concerned with the manner in which the president is to be perceived by the public by that date." One way for Nixon to "show the human, sentimental, or color aspects of himself" might be to set up "unplanned activities" such as going out shopping for neckties. They arranged for a leading women's magazine, *McCall's,* to photograph the president and his wife for a warm cover story that would be titled "The Nixons Nobody Knows — A Surprisingly Private View of a Public Marriage."

Neckwear and puff pieces weren't likely to change anyone's perception. Nixon truly was a prig. His helicopter pilot couldn't believe how different he was from LBJ, who knew how to close up shop, relax, and socialize. Now it was like a study hall inside the chopper. Nixon would sit reading, drafting notes, or gazing alone out the window. The onboard bar gathered dust. Nixon confined his drinking to after hours.*

Bud Krogh recognized the trouble with Nixon's "manner and tone." The president, Bud told his bosses, "is criticized as being remote, cold, an unemotional manager and not caring enough about individuals, and

---

* Nixon knew well that he couldn't hold his liquor. After a few drinks he'd become maudlin and slur his speech.

I know there has been a substantial effort of late to generate a warmer, more compassionate human being."

WHATEVER WARMTH and compassion the president could muster wasn't coming through in his discussions of the upcoming demonstrations. "The people that lead this are left-wing sons of bitches," Nixon declared in private. "They're not patriots. I'll lay you money, in that group that's down here, you won't find 1 in 100 that ever served in Vietnam. Little bastards are draft dodgers, country-haters, or don't-cares."

The first of the little bastards, the veterans, were to begin arriving in Washington within days. No one was sure how many would come, but regardless of the number, they wanted to pitch their tents and sleep on the National Mall for five days. So far, the Park Service had denied them a permit. One of the local lawyers who volunteered to help the vets had gotten a message to Bud: if thousands of former Vietnam soldiers showed up in the nation's capital with sleeping bags and no place to bed down, "trouble will be inevitable."

Nixon was concerned about the potential for the vets to sway people who were still supporting his policies. Already restless were the hundreds of families of American prisoners of war held in North Vietnam (among them was a future U.S. senator, John McCain), who saw little progress made on bringing their men home. A key Republican senator told the president the families were like a "tinder box that is about to explode." Haldeman noted after one meeting with Nixon, "We can't afford to let them come unglued at this point."

Nixon got regular briefings from Haldeman as he mulled over whether to stay in the White House or get out of town again. The chief of staff told Nixon that the veterans were supposed to start showing up on Sunday, April 19. Two weeks after that, "the ones who want to bring the government to a halt" were to arrive. "Rennie Davis is involved," Haldeman added.

In between would be the parade on Saturday, April 24, "the big march, where they're now talking about attracting half a million, the biggest in history."

"You ought to go to Camp David that night, though. The 23rd. Get out of here for the 24th," Haldeman said, recalling how the president had hunkered down uncomfortably behind the ring of buses and troops during the mass marches in 1969 and 1970.

"Oh yes, I'll be outta here," said the president.

Good, said Haldeman. "I think that thinking you had to sit in the White House while all this was going on was wrong."

AS THE PROTESTS APPROACHED, Bud stepped up his quest for a theory of the student revolt that made sense, that could generate ideas for quieting things down. His own boys were still little, but those in the White House who had kids in college or high school had to contend with the generation gap themselves. The children of his boss, John Ehrlichman, had been showing up at demonstrations; Ehrlichman sat them down with Kissinger to try to talk some sense into their heads.

Bud studied a Sunday think piece in the *Washington Post* that claimed the "turmoil of youth today" stemmed from a clash between two developments in their lifetimes, the utopian vision of childhood joy and the growing bureaucratic nature of the state. "The troops of the revolution," it said, "are not the toiling masses of the Marxist prophecy but naked children of nature dancing to the tune of primitive drums." Bud circled the line that "the revolution is taking place . . . in a subculture of upper middle class youth."

As he tried to piece together a more rounded view of the opposition to Nixon, Bud also began to wonder if the administration's heavy-handed tactics might backfire and turn off middle-of-the-road voters. The Friday before the vets were set to arrive in town, the newspapers were full of the latest outrage highlighted by the Democrats — Senator Edmund Muskie's discovery that the FBI had spied on the inaugural Earth Day festivities the previous year. Reports of surveillance, bugging, and FBI misdeeds, as uncovered by the burglars outside Philadelphia, were piling up, Bud told his bosses.

"Liberals," Bud pointed out, "will continue to hammer away at the suggestion that the Administration is repressive." Bud wondered if Nixon could "quell the current excitement" by condemning "needless government snooping" and publicly repudiating such tactics as "too nosey." Once again, he risked looking naive compared to his competitors within the White House.

8

Move On Over

Thursday, April 1, to Thursday, April 15

WHEN THE STATE TROOPERS SET FREE JUDY GUMBO AND HER friends that March night on a Pennsylvania highway, she had driven her blue Volkswagen Beetle back to Boston. On the way up she dropped her ex-boyfriend, Stew Albert, at his Manhattan home. Maybe he wasn't completely an ex, given that they'd slept together again in D.C., albeit only once.

The authorities had found nothing suspicious in Judy's car. But they were still testing their theory that the pair had something to do with the U.S. Capitol bombing, even if the device itself had been set by members of the Weather Underground.

Physical evidence wasn't getting the authorities anywhere. They'd figured out the explosive material was dynamite but had no luck finding the source. In the wreckage of the Capitol's bathroom, agents picked out the remains of a Westclox pocket watch used as the bomb's timer. Forget trying to trace it — investigators reported to J. Edgar Hoover's office that thousands of such watches had been sold around D.C. since the beginning of 1970.

Agents attempted to get some information from Stew. A little more than a week after the bombing, they had tracked him to the apartment on Riverside Drive in Manhattan where he was staying. Two agents knocked on his door. Stew told them he'd be glad to be interviewed but needed some coffee. So he took them down to a place on Broadway, only to disappoint them with his denials.

The night of the highway stop, the FBI had been worried that Stew and Judy and their friends might just keep cruising north and flee into Canada. After all, it was Judy's native country. She had been born as Judith Lee Clavir in Toronto, to parents active in the Canadian Communist Party. Her father was the first importer of Soviet films to North America. That background was red meat for the FBI. They had posted agents at the border crossings.

But it turned out to be a waste of effort. Judy, they eventually determined, was still living in Boston, where she had moved the year before the Spring Offensive, drawn by the region's reputation as the heart of the so-called second wave of American feminism.

Though accustomed to speaking and writing what was on her mind, Judy, like most of the female members of SDS and the Yippies, nevertheless found herself stuck behind the men in the movement. They took on quotidian tasks while the guys got cheered at campus rallies and basked in national publicity. This had long been the case. An organizing project in inner-city Chicago spawned from SDS in 1964 listed among its summer staff needs "a girl to handle office work."

So Judy struck out on her own, away from Stew's shadow. In the spring of 1970, she helped organize what she called a Yippie women's delegation to visit Hanoi, along with Jerry Rubin's partner, Nancy Kurshon, and Geni Plamondon of the White Panther Party, a Detroit-based radical group. Observing the resolve of the North Vietnamese, Judy "could not help but sop it up like a sponge," vowing to become a stronger leader.

It had taken a while for Judy to decide that a struggle for the rights of women needed its own separate path, aside from the larger aims of the New Left. Many antiwar women had come to believe that sexual freedom was perpetuating the ability of hippie and radical men to control their relationships. And Judy always regretted that she'd decided to "stand by my man" and turn down a chance to join the famous protest that thrust the existence of a women's liberation movement into the public eye. That was the apocryphal "bra-burning" — which wasn't actually a bra-burning at all — at the Miss America beauty pageant in Atlantic City in 1968. One of that protest's organizers recalled "huge arguments" with the Yippie men, who thought the Miss America protest would just distract radical women from planning for the Chicago demonstrations, which were to begin a few weeks before the pageant. (The fuse lit by the

Atlantic City action would burn extremely slowly; exactly fifty years later the Miss America pageant ditched the swimsuit portion of the competition.) Now antiwar women were dissolving their work and romantic ties to focus on feminist issues.

In Boston, women-only collectives had been springing up all over town. Some were built around single goals like women's health, women's literature — even do-it-yourself auto repair. An International Women's Day event drew thousands of women to the Boston Common in 1970.

A handful of the collectives quickly shifted far left: in October of that year, in what they proclaimed as a blow against Harvard University's work for the government, the previously unknown Proud Eagle Tribe, which described itself in a communiqué as a group of revolutionary women, had slipped a pipe bomb into a desk drawer at the school's Center for International Affairs. (A Cambridge police sergeant said he thought the claim was a feint because the device just seemed too sophisticated to have been built by a woman.) The nighttime explosion caused no injuries. The bombers weren't caught, but the Proud Eagle Tribe would later reveal itself as the Women's Brigade of the Weather Underground. The same day as the Harvard attack, the brigade's leader, the former SDS activist Bernardine Dohrn, was added to the FBI's most-wanted list. Five months later she would be one of the people to plant the bomb in the Capitol.

So the FBI field office in Boston had been quite busy.

In April 1971, not long after Judy had returned to the city, an FBI agent, dressed down in a polo shirt to blend in, drove over to her apartment building on a dead-end street at the edge of the Back Bay.

He knocked on one of the doors. The occupant was an idealistic young man who formerly had volunteered with VISTA, the domestic version of the Peace Corps, and now taught English as a second language to the city's new Spanish-speaking residents. He lived alone with his cat. The agent confided they were in the middle of a top-secret investigation, hinting it had something to do with organized crime and heroin trafficking. Would he mind doing a solid for his country by moving himself to the YMCA for a few days, at government expense, of course, so the bureau could take over his place and do some important surveillance?

He agreed, without realizing the FBI wanted his place because it shared a common wall with the apartment next door, which Judy Gumbo rented with a couple of roommates. The apartment had a separate entrance, and the teacher had never met Judy or anyone who lived with her. The FBI was convinced that one of the roommates was a member of the Weather Underground.

THE FEDS HAD so far failed to document their suspicions about links between the Yippies and Weather. The two groups certainly made no effort to hide their mutual admiration. Judy had proclaimed that she "dug" the Capitol bombing. Colin Neiburger, one of the men driving with Judy and Stew when they were stopped after the bombing, had been an early member of Weather but left when its members went underground. Nevertheless, he acknowledged later, "quite a number of the people that I was with were pro-Weather." Meanwhile, Bernardine Dohrn, spokeswoman for the guerrillas, had sought to erase the widely held belief that political and cultural radicals were deeply at odds: "Freaks are revolutionaries and revolutionaries are freaks," she declared in a communiqué. LSD was already commonly used in its collectives, and now Weather members started dressing more like hippies. They even "changed our diets to center on brown rice, tofu and vegetables, and fruit and yogurt," as another fugitive recalled.

Jerry Rubin dedicated one of his books to the guerrillas, reproducing Dohrn's FBI most-wanted poster on the inside cover. Abbie Hoffman would later brag that the Yippies "had the closest association" with Weather of any aboveground group, and that he and his wife met regularly with the fugitives, sometimes in disguise. Though claiming to disagree with Weather's "polemics" and some of their tactics, "I saw great value in their myth and was part of their support system," Hoffman would write.

Stew had also edged closer to Weather's ideas after the Chicago protests. His blossoming friendship in Berkeley with Eldridge Cleaver and other Black Panthers convinced him that white militants needed to learn self-defense and "revolutionary first aid." In the fall of 1968, Stew, Judy, Jerry Rubin, and a few friends joined about twenty Panthers at a firing range with shotguns and AR-15 semiautomatic rifles. Stew's account of the outing in the *Berkeley Barb*, written in his increasingly overwrought language, opined that while guns were "ugly," they were necessary to overthrow the system that produced them. "We will have to swim to our humanity through rivers of tragic blood," he wrote. "This fact is not something to relish, but to prepare for."

At the time Stew was rooming with one of the Chicago Seven, Tom Hayden, who had been a key founder of Students for a Democratic Society after being beaten and jailed while working for civil rights in the South. Chicago had stoked Hayden's militancy too. He criticized David Dellinger's pacifism, saying the "fear of violence must be overcome." Hayden worried that a repressive police state was forming in the United States, and thus he should "explore the shrouded world beyond everyday life and law." Along with Cleaver, Hayden and Stew organized what they called the International Liberation School, "to educate and train potential revolutionaries," as Judy Gumbo put it. Once, while they practiced karate, Hayden got so mad at Stew for pounding him in the ribs, he kicked him in the foot, breaking Stew's toe.

According to an account Stew wrote later but kept private, he and Hayden got their hands on two boxes of dynamite. It's unclear where they obtained the explosives, or why. Worried about their house being monitored, they decided to store the sticks with someone above suspicion. Carrying the crates, they strolled nonchalantly down a Berkeley street to an acquaintance's house and stashed them in her basement.

Stew never discussed the dynamite or its fate. Nor did Hayden, who would soon move on to denounce violence and seek respectability in California politics. There's no evidence that federal agents ever learned about the dynamite, nor that anyone linked to Stew or the Yippies ever used it.

In the fall of 1970, Stew had played a role in one of Weather's more unusual actions: the California prison breakout of the LSD guru Timothy Leary, who had been sentenced to ten years for possession of marijuana.

Weather arranged for the forty-nine-year-old drug apostle to slip away from his minimum-security prison near San Luis Obispo by climbing a roof, shinnying up a telephone pole, and working his way along a cable that stretched over the wall. Using $17,000 raised from Leary's acid-loving friends, Weather members met him with a getaway car, gave him a disguise, and transported him north, near Seattle. He shaved his head, donned glasses, and dyed his sideburns gray. (Leary and his liberators ventured out unrecognized one night to see the movie *Woodstock*.) Once upon a time, Leary had preached gentle disconnection from society through chemistry, coining the mantra, "Turn on, tune in, drop out." Now, grateful to his guerrilla friends, he issued quite a different piece of advice from his hiding place: "Total war is upon us. Fight to live or you'll die."

By then, Stew's friend Eldridge Cleaver had jumped bail on a firearms charge and fled the country. He was living in Algeria under the auspices of that country's socialist government. Unlike most leaders of the Black Panthers, who disagreed with Weather's tactics and theories, Cleaver was a supporter of the underground. Weather got fake IDs and passports for Leary and his wife and, at the guerrillas' request, Stew persuaded Cleaver to welcome the Learys in Algiers. Stew flew over himself. At one point he sat on the African beach, tripping on acid with the man who had helped turn on a generation.

"For a while, there was a sort of Yippie–Weather Underground alliance," explained another activist who had a foot in each camp, "and it would have been difficult for an outside observer to say for certain where the Yippies ended and where the Weather Underground began."

ONCE THEY SET up their equipment in Boston in April 1971, the FBI agents listened in for a few days to conversations in Judy's apartment. From all accounts they got nothing useful.

By the second week of the month, Judy was on her way back to D.C. On the morning of April 10 she and her friends readied a big banner. Painting in purple letters, they identified themselves as the Janis Joplin Brigade, after the soulful twenty-seven-year-old rock star who had overdosed on heroin six months earlier in a Hollywood hotel. Joplin's death came barely two weeks after another iconic musician, Jimi Hendrix, died in London after downing barbiturates. Hendrix too was twenty-seven. And so was Judy.

Judy and her group took their banner and joined about five hundred women who met in front of the Department of Justice. They set out for the Pentagon, walking three and a half miles alongside the National Mall and then across the Potomac. They waved Vietcong flags. They sang songs of women's liberation, including this chorus, to the tune of "The Battle Hymn of the Republic":

Move on over or we'll move on over you
Move on over or we'll move on over you
Move on over or we'll move on over you,
For women's time has come!

Late in the day they rallied on the Pentagon steps, stretching out scarves between them to encircle as much of the building as possible. The vibe was joyful. Up on the second story of the Pentagon, someone had pasted a message in large letters stretched over a few windows: "Hi, Mom!" It was the first time, as one speaker said, that women of the left marched on the military headquarters on their own, not as "auxiliaries" in a procession led by men.

That was true but incomplete. Women had massed in Washington protests for decades. In the first wave of feminism, some five thousand marched for voting rights the day before Woodrow Wilson was sworn in as president in 1913. (It would take seven more years before the Constitution was amended to grant them the right to cast ballots.) And women played a significant role in the nuclear disarmament and early antiwar movements. One of the first contacts between Vietnam peace activists and the Hanoi government had come in July 1965, when ten members of the group Women Strike for Peace flew to a meeting in Indonesia. In early 1966, some fifteen hundred members of the same group picketed in front of the White House to protest LBJ's resumption of bombing after a month's pause. And in early 1968, thousands of women calling themselves the Jeannette Rankin Brigade (after the first woman elected to Congress) marched, through a snowstorm, against the war.

As in the larger society, women inside left-wing organizations still wrestled with how to shape their new roles. Those with more radical agendas often unnerved their older sisters, who came of age in the 1950s and traced their rising consciousness to writings such as *The Feminine Mystique* by Betty Friedan and *The Second Sex* by Simone de Beauvoir. The younger crowd tended to look to thinkers like Kate Millett, whose *Sexual Politics* inspired them to take action to upend male-dominated institutions.

At first, the reaction of men in the movement to the women's focus had been patronizing and crass. During the protests at Nixon's inauguration in 1969, a female SDS leader had been booed and shouted down when she tried to make a speech about feminism; some yelled verbal assaults like "take her off the stage and fuck her." (The women never forgave the leader of the counter-inaugural, David Dellinger, for both failing to defend them and ordering them to leave the stage so the fracas would stop.)

The tension between sexual liberation and feminism persisted. This generation was the first to reach adolescence when birth control pills were almost as easily obtained as aspirin, and when sexually transmitted disease could be cured with a quick spate of antibiotics. Alongside drugs and rock music, the counterculture enshrined "free love." Early on in the movement, sexuality was used as a lure; young men were urged to resist the draft with the slogan "Girls say Yes! to guys who say No!" Then women took back control. "Free dope, free food and free sex are all promised in the same breath as if a woman was some kind of survival commodity," one woman activist complained to Stew Albert. Within groups like SDS and the Weather Underground, women as well as men bashed monogamy as bourgeois and counterproductive to group solidarity. Sexual freedom would build the strong men and women of the future.

But the transformation wouldn't be so easy. In 1970 a leader of the Miss America protest had penned an influential call to arms. She declared that the women's movement no longer wanted men around. "White males are most responsible for the destruction of human life and environment on the planet today. Yet who is controlling the supposed revolution to change all that? White males," she wrote. "We are rising with a fury older and potentially greater than any force in history, and this time we will be free or no one will survive."

By then, Judy had weighed in too. "Capitalist ideology and practice puts women in an oppressed, slave situation," she wrote in the *Berkeley Barb* underground paper, where she was a regular contributor. "Our minds have been fucked over for 2000 years to accept our position and like it" but "it is important that we overcome our fear of fighting and learn to defend ourselves adequately and by any means necessary." And she quoted her friend, the Black Panther leader Eldridge Cleaver, as suggesting she overcome her reluctance to "kill for women's liberation." (She would later chalk that statement up to youthful exuberance, saying that she only ever really believed in fighting for self-defense.)

The role of women remained a salient issue among the groups in Washington preparing for the spring events in 1971. John O'Connor, the undercover D.C. cop who had infiltrated the Vermont Avenue building, noticed right away that almost all the people doing the grunt work there were female — answering phones, stuffing envelopes with flyers, nego- tiating with prickly musicians to come to the rallies. The men were the media stars.

This also played out in the group house where John lived with lead- ers of the Vietnam Veterans Against the War. Their female roommates frequently called all-hands meetings to complain they were sick of doing all the cooking and cleaning. He and the other guys would dread these sessions, where invariably the woman leading the talk would sit in the one overstuffed living room chair, with her lieutenants perched on the arms. The men were appropriately shamed, and the housework situation would get better afterwards. But usually just for a few days.

The dynamic wasn't unusual for leftist collectives. Another police informant told his bosses that the group he was trying to infiltrate, which published Washington's underground newspaper, the *Quicksilver Times*, also struggled to overcome male chauvinism. Its members were trying to ensure that men and women "assist in all aspects of the com- mune," he wrote. For that reason, the informant said, he refused to live there himself.

EVEN IN ITS nascent form, feminism was one more wedge, along with sex, drugs, and rock, stretching the chasm between the young and the establishment in Washington. Under pressure, some institutions took baby steps. In the days before the Spring Offensive, the Senate moved to allow female pages for the first time, despite "some shuddering in the cloakrooms," but said they would have to dress like boys, in black pant- suits. Meanwhile the air force came under fire for its longtime rule that, unlike men, women had to submit photographs with their enlistment applications — a full-length front view, a full-length profile view, and two close-ups. We are not looking for "physical beauty, per se, but a healthy personable appearance," explained a spokesman.

Jerry Wilson had been hiring many more women as police officers, but the rank and file dragged their feet on his plans to put them in patrol cars instead of just keeping them behind the lines. The men dispatching the units by radio would add a "W" to the car number if a woman was riding inside, as in "22-W." The code alerted others on patrol to steer away from working with them. Jerry put an end to that. He also quashed a prototype for a separate policewoman's badge. Sending women out on the streets meant they'd need uniforms. Jerry overruled the idea of pastel-colored outfits as something airline stewardesses would wear. He couldn't imagine an officer chasing a burglar down an alley in that. He ordered a standard skirt and blouse with a military cut. After some women officers complained of getting cold in the winter, he agreed they could wear slacks. The male cops discussed widely among themselves whether that would attract lesbians to the force.

Meantime, the White House was making its own nod toward gender equality. Nixon agreed to hire a woman into the administration to recruit females for good-paying government jobs. Yet the cultural dissonance between the Nixons and the youthful armies heading for Washington could be downright comical. A few days after Judy's Pentagon march, the newspapers were full of the president's proud announcement that his elder daughter, Tricia, would soon be married on the grounds of the White House. Tricia told reporters she'd been practicing making bacon, one of the favorite foods of her fiancé, Edward Cox, a Harvard law student who had been her escort at the Debutante Ball in New York. "It's so easy to burn or to undercook," Tricia lamented. "To do it just right, and not have it greasy, is real gourmet cooking."

Tricia's bridal-shower presents from the women of the White House press corps would include a bacon flattener and an anti-splatter device; one of the more iconoclastic scribes gifted her a tool kit instead.

TO WASHINGTON'S LARGEST news organizations — the *Washington Post*, the *Washington Evening Star*, the TV stations — the women's march on the Pentagon was just another unremarkable protest, worthy of a short article deep inside the paper at best. But the underground *Quicksilver Times* treated it for what it was, the kickoff of an unusual month of protests.

On its April 14 cover, *Quicksilver* displayed a big photograph of Judy and a fellow marcher at the Pentagon. "It is right," the newspaper said, "that the women had the first action for the Spring Offensive."

Judy liked the picture. It was a flattering, tight shot of the two of them smiling and gazing forward with hope and confidence. Okay, maybe it did remind her a bit of something by a Soviet realist painter. (It wouldn't quell the FBI's suspicions about Judy to note that the second woman was Linda Evans, a member of the Weather group. When Evans had been indicted the previous year for her activities with Weather, Judy and a co-author had written that "it's up to us, to hide, protect and cherish our sisters who have been forced underground.")

Like the dozens of alternative publications that had sprung up in college towns and big cities over the past decade, aided by the advent of cheaper offset printing, *Quicksilver* operated on a shoestring budget. About every ten days it published another issue, running off some twenty thousand copies. The fractious *Quicksilver* editorial collective filled a rundown house near Dupont Circle, barely scraping together enough money for the next stack of newsprint. Much of the staff survived by joining the hawkers who bought copies for a dime from the collective and sold them on street corners for the cover price of a quarter. You weren't going to get rich, but it maybe kept you in brown rice for the month. In fact, *Quicksilver* sometimes offered recipes for eating cheap with the counterculture's favorite staple.

Each edition was generally an untidy mix of reports on local activist groups, revolutionary poetry, music ads, and funky cartoons, with classified ads serving as a counterculture bulletin board. ("Mary R. and Sharon D: please call Bill or Tom. We need stuff from bus" . . . "2 chicks, 1 pregnant, looking for room and board in a commune.") *Quicksilver* eschewed straight reporting for stories that at their best might be considered advocacy journalism, at worst propaganda.

In the same issue that had Judy on the front was a no-holds-barred call to arms from the Mayday Tribe.

For seven years now . . . we have met, discussed, analyzed, lectured, published, lobbied, paraded, sat-in, burned draft cards, stopped troop trains, refused induction, marched, trashed, burned and bombed buildings, destroyed induction centers. Yet the war has gotten steadily worse —for the Vietnamese, and, in a very different way, for us. And on May 3, we will enter some 26 roads and bridges in the Washington area, in rush hour traffic, to stop the government. The largest coalition of forces ever to be put together for a national action has been assembled, including not only thousands of Vietnam veterans, women, student, clergy and pacifist groups, Third World organizations, Welfare rights organizations and Farm workers organizations. May 3 should bring the largest attempt at mass non-violent disruption ever attempted in this country's history.

The inside pages reproduced the Mayday Tactical Manual, the Tribe's guide for the traffic blockade, listing nearly two dozen spots targeted for civil disobedience, along with a map marking their locations. One faction explained that it had chosen the Fourteenth Street Bridge over the Potomac as its focus because "it is probably the major traffic artery used by government employees from Virginia heading for the Justice Department . . . and for a number of other government agencies" but did not risk inconveniencing the city's black neighborhoods.

But that was still some weeks away. The issue also carried a more urgent call, from the Vietnam Veterans Against the War, who said they were on their way to Washington to raise their voices. "Never before in the history of our country," it read, "have veterans demonstrated against a war that is still being waged."

Those who have been to Vietnam and back, said the piece, "must tell the whole story . . . we feel that these men and their families can make a unique impact to set the momentum for the Spring Offensive."

In a few days, they would know just how big an impact it would be.

9

Fringe Group

FORMER SOLDIERS FROM AROUND THE COUNTRY HEADED TO Washington on Sunday, April 18. The leaders of the D.C. branch of Vietnam Veterans Against the War — Jack Mallory, Tim Butz, Mike Phelan, and John O'Connor — battled a case of nerves. Their advance work was over, but would it pay off? They killed some time that morning with a game of hearts around a table at the group's Vermont Avenue office. Finally they put down the cards, and John drove them over to West Potomac Park in his red Mustang.

Their protest would set the tone for the Spring Offensive. It would kick off seventeen straight days of nearly nonstop action in Washington.

The vets would own the streets for the first week. The Saturday after that, April 24, would bring the massive march and rally at the Capitol, sponsored by the big coalition of antiwar groups. In the following days, the more radical wing of the movement, led by Rennie Davis and Dave Dellinger, would take over. It would stage events around town all week, leading up to a rock concert and rally on the weekend of May 1. Finally, on Monday, May 3, would come the mass civil disobedience aimed at clogging the capital's streets and bridges.

On his way to the park to register the incoming vets, John couldn't avoid rooting for a huge turnout — even if that would cause trouble for his bosses on the police force.

He had worked as hard as anyone else to set up the protest, to visit and recruit the guys who'd sent in the *Playboy* coupons. Since the beginning of the year, the VVAW's national membership list had ballooned to more than twenty thousand. Still, no one knew if more than a handful would actually show. The organization was far from flush, despite John Kerry's last-minute scramble for donations from a few wealthy liberals. A lot of veterans around the country wouldn't be able to make it without help in paying for gas or bus tickets. That's what the White House was counting on. The vets' plans are "not mobilizing very well as of now," Haldeman told Nixon optimistically.

And at first it seemed Haldeman might be right. Only a few groups were trickling in down by the Potomac, their faces "a little harder, a little more mature" than the kind of antiwar protesters Washington was accustomed to seeing. But as the afternoon turned to evening, the pace quickened. By five o'clock, John had taken down four hundred names at the registration table, and people were still lining up.

Like the larger movement, the VVAW was an alliance of disparate ideologies. The organizers had hoisted an American flag by the tent that served as the headquarters. More militant arrivals objected loudly that the flag made the encampment look too much like an official military base, an endorsement of the powers that be. Down it went.

Where everyone would sleep — that became a problem. The vets had planned to pitch their tents within spitting distance of the Capitol. But the Park Service, at the direction of Nixon's lawyers, turned down their application for a permit to set up at the head of the National Mall. The vets appealed to the courts, but a federal judge on Saturday had upheld the denial. The First Amendment, the judge said, didn't include the right to sleep where you assembled.

So on Sunday night, with a brisk wind blowing in from the river, John and his fellow vets told everybody to bed down for the night right there in West Potomac Park. They had no permit for that spot either, but it was at the opposite, less visible end of the capital's greenway, and they figured no one was going to care enough to force a bunch of former warriors out of their billets in the middle of the night.

And they were right. The vets kept coming, and no one tried to stop them. There would be well over a thousand by morning. Not the five thousand John and others had hoped for, but enough to make some waves in town. They were as diverse as a basic training company, one reporter found — "college graduates and high school dropouts, goldbricks and platoon leaders, black and white southerners, young men from the cities and from the farms, potheads and Dr. Pepper addicts, OCS material and candidates for the stockade."

NO ONE WAS sure how the nation would react to the veterans. The White House decided to take no chances. Nixon handed the problem to a trusted member of his legal team. Charles Colson, thirty-nine years old, was a Washington lawyer long active in Republican politics. Originally brought aboard to act as the administration's liaison to right-leaning interest groups, he had evolved into something of a mobile hit man, winning the president's admiration for his "instinct for the political jugular." Many of his colleagues considered him an "evil genius" with a gift for stoking Nixon's dark side. They already were joking about his "Department of Dirty Tricks." Soon enough Nixon and his inner circle would tap Colson's creative ideas to undermine opponents in the 1972 campaign, with devastating results for the president.

One of the actions that John Kerry had promised during the protest was especially worrisome to the White House, whose aides were acutely aware of the power of symbols at a time when so many Americans felt unmoored. The vets said they would return their combat medals, and one possibility was that they would show up outside the White House to do it. They promised to hurl the decorations over the fence if no one was there to accept them.

Nixon's aides first thought it would be best to have an official representative of the Pentagon take delivery. Then there was talk of bringing in some pro-Nixon wounded veterans to greet the protesters. But they thought better of it, concerned that might look like an official ceremony. Just before the vets were due to arrive, Colson told his colleagues the updated plan was for a "low-level White House clerk or messenger to accept them in the routine fashion — just as any other package or piece of mail would be received." Colson, however, admitted he was still a bit worried this could backfire, making the White House appear to be "downgrading the importance of the medals."

Colson didn't know yet that the same debate was being played out inside the Vietnam Veterans Against the War. When it was finally resolved, the medals would take on far more significance than even the

Nixon men anticipated. Their return would, as they feared, become an enduring symbol of rancor over the war.

As the vets gathered at West Potomac Park, Nixon spent Sunday at the White House. He welcomed a visit from Joe Frazier, the heavyweight who had just beaten Muhammad Ali for the title. Nixon gave Frazier and his family a tour. The boxer said later that the president was friendly but "didn't seem to know a lot" of the mansion's history.

In the evening, Nixon and his wife hosted a performance by the Singing Cadets of Texas A&M University. The male choral group was on a road trip after a national TV debut on *The Ed Sullivan Show*. Nixon enjoyed meeting some clean-cut college students, who told him, in the president's recounting, "We're behind you in your policy, we're all with you and that kind of thing."

Not far away, at the National Theatre, another touring company was in town, but staging the cultural antithesis of the Texas troupe. It was *Hair,* "the American Tribal Love-Rock Musical." The president had once considered attending a performance just so he could storm out dramatically in protest of its nudity, obscene language, and songs about drugs. His aides convinced him that wouldn't be a good idea.

Before they left the White House, the boys from Texas serenaded Nixon with their hit single: *"No man is an island, no man stands alone."*

THE VVAW'S INCURSION into Washington, which the group named Operation Dewey Canyon III, after the U.S. invasions of Laos, got off to a difficult start.

At sunrise on Monday, the vets crawled out of their sleeping bags by the Potomac. Before eight, with the mist still rising off the water, more than a thousand of them filed onto the broad sidewalk of the bridge across the river, heading for Arlington National Cemetery. At the head were several Gold Star mothers, whose sons had died in Vietnam, accompanied by widows of fallen soldiers. Next came wounded warriors from nearby veterans' hospitals. Some hobbled along on crutches. A few amputees rode in wheelchairs. Behind them stretched a long line, overwhelmingly male and white, more than a few men with long hair and beards, some with headbands, wearing battle fatigues, helmets, and boots. Combat ribbons and medals dangled from their shirts.

Their plan was to lay wreaths at the Tomb of the Unknown Soldier and say a few words over the graves. They approached the entrance with anticipation. Tim Butz, one of the Washington organizers standing among them, said: "This, I think, is the beginning of a not-so-silent spring."

Then they saw that the tall iron gates were locked.

The superintendent of the cemetery had ordered them closed. Political demonstrations weren't permitted on that sacred ground, he told them. Nor would the Gold Star mothers be permitted inside to visit their sons' graves.

The column halted at the barrier. The vets were incredulous. First, their camping permit had been denied. Then it had taken forever to get permission to meet their congressional representatives on the steps of the Capitol. Now they effectively were being told the only way into Arlington was to die first.

The cemetery superintendent later claimed that it had been his idea alone to lock the gates. In fact, the order came from Richard Kleindienst, the deputy attorney general. "Groups will not enter Arlington," he had decreed secretly during the previous week. In addition, Colson, the White House lawyer, had dashed off a memo to his bosses, expressing frustration that the government allowed the ex-soldiers into town at all. Colson was searching for ways to show that they were "a fringe group" and "a pretty shoddy bunch" that didn't represent true veterans. "There just must be more that we can be doing," Colson had written.

The closure infuriated the vets. One hurled his plastic replica M-16 rifle at the cemetery gate, where it shattered. A Gold Star mother wept. Attending his first demonstration, in a wheelchair, was First Lieutenant James Dehlin, a twenty-year-old from Michigan who had lost both legs when he stepped on a land mine in Vietnam. "It seems like they could let us in to pay tribute to our brothers," Dehlin told reporters. John Kerry was there too. "It is absolutely incredible that the American government closes the gates to this cemetery where our brothers lie," Kerry said.

The ranks erupted in strident debate over whether to ram the fence, or maybe scale it. In preparing for the Spring Offensive, the vets had vowed not to use force. "We have come to Washington to show the American people that the Vietnam War is totally wrong," read one of their leaflets. "And we have to do it with nonviolent action or we will have missed the point entirely." They had even published a special note to the Washington police, promising to be law-abiding. Barely an hour into their first action, this promise was being tested. Newspaper reporters were on the scene, and so far they were recording the vets as the aggrieved party. An assault on the gates might change that.

Most of the VVAW leaders pleaded for calm. Jan Crumb, who had first organized the vets back in 1967, was among them. So were John Kerry and Jack Mallory. Charging the gates would only undermine their cause, Mallory argued, as he circulated through the crowd trying to avert what he feared would be a "horrible" outcome.

Cooler heads won the day. The vets headed back over the bridge peacefully, if more embittered. In an orderly column they tramped through Washington's streets toward the U.S. Capitol, for a midday meeting with antiwar members of Congress.

Along the way, they filed past the white-columned Constitution Hall, the city's largest auditorium, built and owned by the Daughters of the American Revolution. The hidebound organization had just convened its Eightieth Continental Congress. Later in the day, Nixon was to address the assembly, which hadn't hosted a presidential speech since the last time a Republican was in the White House. Outside the hall, DAR delegates lined up in their conservative dress and eyed the veterans sourly. Their mouths fell agape as the scruffy throng chanted, "One, two, three, four, we don't want your fucking war!" Some vets tried to hand out leaflets explaining their purpose. A few delegates talked back.

"Son, I don't think what you're doing is good for the troops," one woman scolded a marcher.

"Lady," he replied, "we *are* the troops."

When the vets reached the Capitol, around noon, they rallied on the steps. Demonstrators generally weren't permitted on the Capitol grounds unless they were considered guests of members of Congress. Soon enough, on Mayday, this would become a major issue. The vets had been invited by two sympathetic lawmakers, Democrat Bella Abzug from New York and Republican Pete McCloskey, the ex-marine from California who promised to work to stop the war by the end of 1971.

McCloskey was the congressman who had met Bud Krogh in Saigon years earlier. Just before the Spring Offensive got started, McCloskey, in a speech on the House floor, raised the question of whether Richard Nixon could be impeached for waging a war against the wishes of the citizens and their representatives. He cited the argument made in 1787 by Edmund Randolph of Virginia, a delegate to the Constitutional Convention: "The Executive will have great opportunities of abusing his power; particularly in time of war, when the military force, and in some respects the public money, will be in his hands. Should no regular punishment be provided, it will be irregularly inflicted by tumults and insurrections." (Hearing about McCloskey's speech, Nixon demanded that his chief of staff explain "what action has been taken on him?" and, told there was nothing, had his aides quietly arrange for a petition to circulate in the congressman's home district, calling for his resignation.)

Some vets applauded Abzug and McCloskey. But the left-wing contingent shouted that even December would be too late for a U.S. withdrawal: "We want the end, now!"

THE VETERANS SPENT an afternoon lobbying their senators and representatives. Then they defiantly moved their camp from the river to a spot on the Mall, less than a ten-minute walk from the Capitol steps. It was a grassy quadrangle between Third and Fourth streets, exactly where the Park Service had refused to allow them to settle down. No one knew if police would try to kick them off.

They walked amid the ghosts of another throng of ex-soldiers who mounted a Washington protest, which had ended in disaster. It happened in the summer of 1932, during the deepest trough of the Great Depression, the last time the country had seemed so hopelessly divided. Thousands of men who'd served in World War I demanded early payment of their promised government bonuses. They built a shantytown by the river. Two ex-soldiers died in clashes with police. President Herbert Hoover then called in an army regiment of five hundred men. They were under the command of a fifty-two-year-old general named Douglas MacArthur, who promised to halt the "revolution" by a group he considered nothing more than a mob threatening to take over the government. His troops cleared the camp using horses and tanks, burned the tents and lean-tos, and then chased the Bonus Army out of town. Many Americans were outraged to see men who'd risked their lives pursued like vermin by their own military.

At the end of Monday the Vietnam vets got some good news: a three-judge panel of the U.S. Court of Appeals had deliberated only thirty minutes before lifting the injunction against their campsite. The judges practically mocked the arguments of Justice Department lawyers, representing the Park Service, who claimed the Mall camp would create "a situation of potential violence and disorder" as well as a dangerous precedent of allowing protesters so close to the heart of the government. One judge pointed out that the Boy Scout Jamboree and other groups had slept in nearby parks before. The vets could stay, but only if they promised not to build campfires or dig deep holes for their tents.

The fight, though, was not over. The government refused to back down. One reason was the upcoming Mayday protests. If the administration let the vets onto the Mall, how would they justify refusing permits to David Dellinger and Rennie Davis? So the Justice lawyers took the matter of the injunction to the Supreme Court.

Nixon, a student of history, was conflicted. He didn't want a repeat of the Bonus March. "Poor old Hoover," he told his aides. "They never forgave him." Nevertheless, the president didn't stand in the way of the Justice Department's appeal.

It was the latest hot-button issue tossed on the high court's doorstep by a nation divided against itself. As the Spring Offensive got underway, the justices were preparing to announce that they had granted a hearing in a case brought by a Texas woman against her state's law banning abortion. It was known as *Roe v. Wade.* The morning of the vets' march to Arlington, the court, led by Chief Justice Warren Burger, a Nixon appointee, had shocked Southern conservatives with a unanimous decision upholding the use of busing to desegregate public schools.

Right after issuing that ruling, the justices heard arguments on another case spawned by the unpopular war. This one involved the world-famous boxer whom Joe Frazier had just knocked down in the Fight of the Century. Muhammad Ali had been convicted a few years earlier of draft evasion. Ali, who had joined the Nation of Islam, an African American Muslim movement, applied for status as a conscientious objector on religious grounds, one of more than seventy-two thousand men who sought such an exemption from combat during the Vietnam era. The army turned him down, saying his adopted faith didn't reject all forms of violence and that a draftee couldn't be selective about when to fight. As the vets rambled through the city on Monday, the U.S. solicitor general, Erwin Griswold, told the justices that Ali's bid should be rejected because his opposition to serving in Vietnam was based on politics and race. "The petitioner just doesn't want to fight the white man's war, and I can understand that," Griswold had said. "But that's not the same thing as being a pacifist."

The Ali matter wouldn't be decided for weeks. On the question of the vets and the Mall, the chief justice indicated he would rule the next day.

Meantime, on Monday night, Nixon went over to Constitution Hall. His speech to the Daughters of the American Revolution, outlining his intention to reorganize government in his second term, struck some odd chords. The "long train of abuses and usurpations" that led the American colonists to rebel against England, he said, could be applied today as "a not very exaggerated description" of the federal bureaucracy. He called for a "peaceful revolution which returns power to the American people." The four thousand delegates cheered wildly.

BY TUESDAY MORNING, some of Nixon's private disparagement of the vets had begun to leak out, specifically his doubts that many of them had actually served in the war. When the story made its way to their encampment, the infuriated veterans collected their discharge papers, their DD214s, and passed them to an Associated Press reporter, who confirmed that almost all of those in the Mall camp were ex-Vietnam fighters.

A contingent of about three hundred vets decided to make another run at Arlington Cemetery, led by Al Hubbard, the VVAW's executive secretary. This time the entrance was wide open. In a tableau of anguish, the marchers got on their knees or raised their fists as their comrades lay wreaths under a flowering crabapple tree. The cemetery's superintendent said he simply hadn't realized at first that their intentions were so peaceful. But there could be little doubt that the bad publicity generated by Monday's locked gates had changed his mind, or that someone from above had changed it for him.

The rest of the vets headed back to the Capitol. Some let loose with guerrilla theatrics to reenact the "search and destroy" missions they'd carried out in Vietnam. They chased victims, shot them with toy guns, or pretended to brutalize them. In the Senate, the Foreign Relations Committee opened new hearings on the war. More than a hundred vets sat in the gallery. They broke into thunderous applause and shouted,

"Right on, brother!" when George McGovern, the South Dakota senator whose bill would set a December 31 deadline for withdrawing all troops, proclaimed that "the very soul of this nation demands" an end to the war. The same day, Mike Mansfield of Montana, the Senate's majority leader, informed his colleagues what he'd just heard about an army lieutenant he'd nominated years earlier to West Point. The young soldier had been killed by his own men in Vietnam, "fragged to death as he lay sleeping in his billet." The number of such attacks was soaring, Mansfield said. He then read out loud a letter from the lieutenant's mother, begging for an end to the draft.

The growing desperation in Congress over Vietnam and its warriors opened up the possibility of a bridge between the left wing of the Democratic Party and the antiwar veterans. John Kerry, lanky and shaggy-haired, clean-shaven and telegenic, was uniquely suited to become the front man in this effort.

One of the congressional liberals courted by Kerry was Philip Hart, the soft-spoken senior senator from Michigan. A World War II veteran of D-Day, Hart helped lead the fight for civil rights legislation during the LBJ years. His white-streaked beard stood out among his clean-shaven brethren in the Senate. (His children had made him promise to grow it if he won reelection in 1970.) Hart's wife, Jane Briggs Hart, who once was arrested as she demonstrated outside the Pentagon, suggested to her husband that they hold a mixer and fundraiser for the Vietnam vets at their home. And so they invited lawmakers and the group's regional leaders, including Kerry and Jack Mallory, to a party on Tuesday night.

During the festivities, the vets got the news that Chief Justice Burger had ruled in favor of the Justice Department's emergency petition to remove the vets from the Mall. He had given them until 4 p.m. on Wednesday to clear out.

The vets were crushed, and angry. Standing in the Harts' back garden, one former special forces soldier who had won the Bronze and Silver stars told the head of the Foreign Relations Committee, Senator J. William Fulbright of Arkansas, a Democrat who had long been one of the most outspoken congressional critics of the war: "Those guys on the Mall have logged a thousand years in Vietnam . . . We think that's worth five days of a piece of grass here in Washington."

Mallory couldn't believe it either. He thought of the vets sleeping on the cold earth while he and the other regional coordinators snacked on finger food and sipped wine at a senator's lovely home. He stared at the "cases and cases" of wine and hard liquor at the party. No point letting it go to waste. Mallory and a friend grabbed a couple of crates. They already were loading them into a car to take back to the Mall before Kerry caught on. He rushed out after them, in high dudgeon.

"Are you crazy?" Kerry asked. He said he'd worked hard to cultivate these people, and now the vets were stealing their booze. Put it back, he ordered.

Mallory did, sheepishly. Kerry was clearly in charge now. During the cocktail party, Kerry had garnered an invitation to testify later in the week before Fulbright's committee, and he didn't want the more free-wheeling vets to mess it up. And Kerry already had reason to be wary of Mallory. Trying to manage all the sudden demands on his time, Kerry had asked Mallory to stand in for him at a meeting of a Capitol Hill liberal interest group. When Mallory got there, the members turned out to be a bunch of suits, Johnny-come-latelies to the antiwar movement. Mallory had lectured them accordingly. Later, Kerry dressed Mallory down, complaining that he had needlessly insulted potential allies.

As the party at the Harts' house petered out, the campers on the Mall heard the bad news about the Supreme Court decision. The vets' lawyer — Ramsey Clark, who had been U.S. attorney general under LBJ but now worked for the other side — came down to give them the details. At the mention of Burger's name, the vets booed and began chanting, "We won't go!" One asked Clark if he thought they'd be dragged off by the police the next day. Probably yes, Clark admitted. Another camper passed the former attorney general a bottle of white wine. He took a big swig.

Observing all this, John O'Connor couldn't believe the government was giving the vets an ultimatum. He wondered how the White House could be so screwed up. He slipped away from the action to make his daily "36" call to his police handlers. "This place is jumping," confided the frazzled detective at the other end. He told John he'd been in the room earlier in the day when the police chief, Jerry Wilson, took a call from the Justice Department on his hot line. The chief had turned red in the face and told his caller that none of his cops were moving in on crippled veterans, whether they were camping illegally or not. The chief, he told John, nearly broke the phone when he slammed it down.

At the White House, Nixon had dinner, then went bowling alone for an hour.

A COUPLE OF DAYS earlier, Bud had met with other aides to discuss how to handle public statements during the Spring Offensive. They wanted to maintain the fiction that the White House wasn't paying much attention, so they concluded that they would present D.C.'s mayor, Walter Washington, as the main government spokesman since, as one aide wrote in a memo to his bosses, the mayor "has a good image and will cooperate with us — as he has in the past." (Nixon was considering putting the mayor in the cabinet in the second term — saying privately he could be a "good Negro for HUD.") Nixon's aides also decided that Jerry would oversee all law enforcement, even the parts of town, like the Mall, normally under the purview of the Park Service.

On Wednesday morning, Jerry was summoned to an emergency meeting at Justice. Going in, he knew there was no way the vets would obey the order to vacate the Mall. The federal officials gathered in the conference room mulled over what to do in that case. Can we make a move? Can we arrest them?

Jerry realized how bad it would look on TV to see the U.S. government dragging away its former soldiers. Yet he kept his mouth shut. He was a technician, not a policy maker. He wasn't about to tell John Mitchell in public that he was wrong. Jerry didn't say it out loud, but he decided that no matter what happened, he wouldn't be grabbing guys who had risked their lives for their country, who were doing nothing wrong.

He thought to himself, you grow up and you believe that people above you can't be dumber than you are. Then you become chief of police and you find out they certainly can be.

On Wednesday the full Supreme Court affirmed Burger's eviction order. But, like Jerry, the White House was growing uncomfortable with the prospect of a confrontation. "I trust we are not going to use force to throw them out," one of Nixon's speechwriters told a colleague. The "crazies" coming next week would be a better enemy: "If we want a confrontation, let's have it with them — not with the new Bonus Army." So Nixon's aides told the Justice Department to find a face-saving compromise.

First the government offered to move the vets to another campsite. One possible spot was a field outside the football stadium; another was

Bolling Air Force Base. The vets declined. Both of those places sounded like detention camps.

But Clark did accept another deal. The vets could stay on the Mall around the clock; they just couldn't sleep there. They could bed down instead at sympathetic venues like churches or the offices of liberal lawmakers, and then return to camp when they were rested. They would be kicked out if they were seen "sleeping, lying in on or under bedrolls, making any fire, erecting any shelter, tent . . . doing any digging or earthbreaking or carrying on any cooking activities."

Clark announced the compromise early Wednesday evening. John Kerry spoke in favor, as did several other leaders. The militants objected. They decided to put it to a vote. The vets retreated into their regional groupings to debate and count up the yeas and nays. One by one, a representative from each state climbed the makeshift plywood stage to announce the tally. It ran close until the very end. The final vote came out, 480 to 400, to defy the government. They would sleep on the Mall. If arrested, they would march off to the paddy wagons, hands clasped behind their heads and singing the national anthem. As one former navy corpsman explained, the threat from Justice was nothing compared to the need to stop the war. He said, "I'm going to stay because I'm paying dues for the guys who can't talk — for the guys over in Arlington under those cheap headstones."

The night turned cold and wet. With the wind chill it would feel like thirty-five degrees on the Mall. As the hours ticked by, the vets huddled in their tents or sat under ponchos as they waited to see what the government would do. In the Oval Office, Nixon's men chuckled about the weather. "I'm glad" it's going to rain, Attorney General John Mitchell said, and Haldeman agreed: "That'll fix the veterans. Their sleeping bags will leak and their girls will get damp." Nixon added, "They really are a gruesome-looking bunch of people."

But the controversy was beginning to work in the vets' favor. The TV networks showed substantial footage of the protest. Supporters began streaming down to the Mall in solidarity, including many Capitol Hill aides. Lawmakers stopped by too, including the surviving brother of the Kennedy clan, the Massachusetts senator Ted Kennedy, who sat in a tent while someone played guitar. He sang along with some protest songs. When that night's performance of *Hair* ended at the National

Theatre, cast members came down and performed "Age of Aquarius" for the troops.

This was not turning out well for the White House. So privately, while his Justice Department vowed to enforce the eviction, Nixon decreed that the vets could stay put. "The policy — which the VVAW are totally unaware of — is that there will be no arrests made of VVAW who violate the order and it has been clearly and unequivocally given to the appropriate authorities," a White House aide noted. The president directly told the attorney general, "Be sure, John, there are not going to be any policemen ride in there." For insurance, Nixon had Bud's boss, John Ehrlichman, put in a call to the police chief. Said Ehrlichman, "The president asked me to call you and tell you that he does not, under any circumstances, want any of those veterans arrested."

Ehrlichman's call was redundant. Jerry had already sent one of his most trusted deputies, Maurice Cullinane, down to the Mall to ensure there was no trouble, that no renegade city or park police would do something stupid. "Cully," the chief had said, "make sure nobody locks them up." Standing there in the dark, on the edge of the encampment, Cullinane could see these guys weren't the bums that Nixon had described, but rather people who'd suffered, some grievously, for their country, in a war they believed was wrong. As far as he was concerned, they could camp anywhere they wanted. If they camped right inside his own office, that would have been fine with Cully.

THE RAIN BLEW away by dawn Thursday. "This capital never looked more beautiful in perfect spring weather nor was it ever more troubled, confused and torn by the divisions that wrack the country," wrote one columnist. "Between the Daughters of the American Revolution, sternly opposed to every revolution since 1776; the Vietnam Veterans Against the War, today's revolution; and masses of tourists, it is enough to send the police right up the wall."

By now it was clear to the vets that no one was coming to arrest them. They were jubilant. Some decided to press the victory. Shortly before nine in the morning, more than a hundred of them headed over to the Supreme Court. They aimed to protest Burger's eviction order and to demand that the court rule on the constitutionality of the war.

The vets blocked the Court's white marble steps shoulder to shoulder, six men deep (only two women were among them), brandishing toy rifles and American flags. Burger told the federal marshals that he wanted them arrested. The cops removed them politely. One twenty-year-old protester, in a wheelchair, his legs missing, insisted on being taken. "I want to go with my brothers," he cried. But Jerry, now on the scene, refused. "I just won't do it," Jerry said. The vets were initially charged with intent to obstruct justice, but this would later be reduced to disorderly conduct. Other vets panhandled and sold peace buttons to raise the ten-dollar collateral, and the prisoners were all released four hours later. Kerry thought it was an unfortunate sideshow. "If all our guys get arrested, the camp will split up," he said.

Meantime, the administration kept running into trouble for the way it was handling the vets. The federal judge who issued the original injunction against the Mall campsite, George L. Hart Jr., looked out on the vets from the courthouse window and grew furious to see his order "flagrantly" violated while the government did nothing to enforce it. He pounded out an angry note to the attorney general: "I deem the present situation to be absolutely intolerable." L. Patrick Gray, a Justice lawyer, had to inform the court that the government had changed its mind. Gray had already been publicly embarrassed earlier in the legal fight when he passed on an erroneous report from an FBI informant that the vets had hoisted the Vietcong flag over their tents. It turned out to be the flag of the state of California.

Now Gray told Hart that the Justice Department didn't mind if they camped because "these men are men who have served their country honorably."

The judge practically went berserk, and Gray's face turned red under the scolding. "The judiciary has been degraded by this whole affair," said Hart. "I don't think it could have been handled worse." Gray, who would later become FBI director and preside over the bureau's investigation into the Watergate scandal, knew the judge was right, and he thought about resigning.

Hart was just "a bad guy," Haldeman reassured the president. But the worst was far from over for the administration, and the Spring Offensive had barely begun.

10

The Last Man

Thursday, April 22, to Friday, April 23

THE ARRESTS AT THE SUPREME COURT GAVE RICHARD NIXON exactly what he didn't want — the whole nation seeing a bunch of ex-soldiers being run off government property on his watch. The increasingly media-savvy vets marched to the paddy wagons with hands clasped behind their heads like prisoners of war. Layer on the images of their parades and their street theater and their defiant bivouac on the Mall, and the administration was getting "pretty chopped up" every night on network television news. Nixon's analysis of public opinion aligned with the Yippies: it was all about what people saw on TV.

Early Thursday afternoon, Nixon's chief of staff, a former advertising executive who knew well the media business, came to the Oval Office to chew it over with the president. The vets may be "the rattiest-looking people in the world," Haldeman told Nixon, but "they're getting a hell of a play, which is too damn bad, because it's so totally out of proportion." The only silver lining was that the press hadn't quite cottoned on to just how badly Justice and the White House had bungled the mess over the camping permit.

"God knows," the president said, "what effect all this has on the country."

He didn't have to wait long to find out. A poll commissioned by the White House found that an astonishing 77 percent of the country had heard or read about the week's events. And while a plurality of those surveyed said they disapproved of the protest, the vets were garnering a far more positive rating than the typical demonstrators. Worse, the president's credibility rating dropped by three percentage points overnight, while the bump in approval for his Vietnam policy, which he celebrated after his Laos speech, had vanished. "The only conclusion can be that the veterans' deal, and the coverage of it, is the cause," Haldeman recorded in his diary.

The success of the protest hardened the attitudes of the president's men, including Henry Kissinger, the national security adviser. "I'm sure a significant percentage are phonies [who] get five minutes on national television every night," Kissinger scoffed.

"Yeah," said Nixon.

Haldeman complained that there were "about six paraplegics" in the crowd and the press was writing "nauseating stories" about them. "God, everything you read would make you think all those guys out there had no legs!" he said. Perhaps they could "crank up the vice president again" and have him try to take the focus off the vets, blame the whole thing on TV and the newspapers.

Suddenly they had a public relations disaster on their hands, with the two most emotion-packed segments of the veterans' visit about to begin.

ON THURSDAY AFTERNOON, John Kerry strode into a Senate committee room in his clean green fatigues to make one of the most consequential speeches of the antiwar movement.

In the thirty-six hours since the Capitol Hill mixer, where the chairman of the Foreign Relations panel got the idea to invite Kerry to testify, the ex-navy lieutenant had spent all his spare moments on preparation, "burning with this anger" about the war. He stayed all night at the VVAW office in the Vermont Avenue building. While some of the vets napped on the couches, Kerry took the stump speech he'd been testing and massaging at rallies for months and poured into it everything he had — his Ivy League erudition, the raw, smoky memories of battle, the hair-raising tales that fellow veterans had offered up at the Howard Johnson's in Detroit, and the ups and downs of the week in Washington.

With the TV cameras whirring, Kerry folded his frame into one of the big brown leather chairs at the witness table, looking up at the senators arrayed on their curved dais. A tall man always appears more imposing in such a position, especially one with striking looks — a long, chiseled chin — and the credibility of the twenty-seven-year-old was beyond doubt. He had left the service with three Purple Hearts. He commanded a swift boat, one of the patrol crafts sent up the waterways of the Mekong Delta to "prove to the Vietcong that they didn't own the rivers," as Kerry had put it. The fifty-foot aluminum ships, powered by two big diesel engines that could be heard for miles, ventured up treacherous jungle channels so narrow, there was barely room to turn. The boats had one of the highest casualty rates of any unit in the war. Kerry earned his Silver Star when his boat was ambushed in February 1969. He beached the craft and leapt onto the bank, chased the enemy on foot into the trees, and killed a Vietcong soldier who was preparing to shoot a rocket-propelled grenade at his crew.

Kerry acted heroically in that moment to be sure, but that didn't mean the overall mission made any sense. To Kerry and most of his fellow officers and crewmen, by his account, it didn't. What was the United States really doing in Indochina? On the ground, prevailing arguments rang hollow — that Americans should die in Vietnam to stop the spread of communism there or to preserve a friendly regime in Saigon. The warriors could see firsthand that those on the other side were more nationalists than clients of Beijing or Moscow, and that South Vietnam's own soldiers and citizens had little affection for their government.

There was no doubt Kerry's appearance in Congress that day served his personal goals as well as those of the Spring Offensive. He knew he'd been granted a solid launching pad for the career in public service he'd already mapped. Yet whatever self-interest was present took nothing away from his twenty-minute speech, which certainly ranked among the most remarkable political and historical arguments heard in Congress about an ongoing war.

Kerry told the senators he'd been up most of the night as the vets debated whether to obey the Supreme Court ban on sleeping on the Mall, yet he showed little sign of fatigue. He began by discussing how, before they came to Washington, the embittered Vietnam vets had borne witness in Detroit to the horrors they'd seen or perpetrated, atrocities "committed on a day to day basis with the full awareness of officers at all levels of command."

He warned that "the country doesn't know it yet but it has created a monster," millions of men who, after risking death for "the biggest nothing in history," have come home "with a sense of anger and a sense of betrayal which no one has yet grasped."

Kerry said it was "criminal hypocrisy" to claim, as Nixon did, that American soldiers perished for a cause that included preserving freedom at home. The real reason was to avoid admitting what the whole world already knew, that Vietnam was a terrible mistake. "Someone has to die so that President Nixon won't be — and these are his words — 'the first President to lose a war.' We are asking Americans to think about that because, how do you ask a man to be the last man to die in Vietnam? How do you ask a man to be the last man to die for a mistake?"

In closing, Kerry noted the reaction of the Nixon White House to the veterans' arrival in Washington. Through "blindness and fear," he said, "they have attempted to disown us and the sacrifice we made for this country." He concluded:

We wish that a merciful God could wipe away our own memories of that service as easily as this administration has wiped their memories of us. But all that they have done and all that they can do by this denial is to make more clear than ever our own determination to undertake one last mission, to search out and destroy the last vestige of this barbarous war, to pacify our own hearts, to conquer the hate and the fear that have driven this country these last ten years and more and so when, in thirty years from now, our brothers go down the street without a leg, without an arm or a face, and small boys ask why, we will be able to say "Vietnam" — and not mean a desert, not a filthy obscene memory, but mean instead the place where America finally turned, and where soldiers like us helped it in the turning.

More than a hundred vets had followed Kerry into the standing-room-only chamber. They exploded into applause, cheers, and whistles. The senators appeared mesmerized. "I can't imagine anyone communicating more eloquently than you did," Fulbright told Kerry. "You said you'd been awake all night. I can see that you spent that time very well indeed."

• • •

"HOW CAN YOU ask a man to be the last man to die for a mistake?" Kerry's words echoed through the ranks of the protesters, the office canyons of Washington, and the West Wing. That same afternoon, the White House made a futile attempt to draw attention away from the vets. Nixon held a ceremony for three Medal of Honor recipients who'd died in Vietnam protecting their comrades. The press largely ignored it. Kerry, in contrast, would get extended time on all three television networks that night. Excerpts from his speech would be reprinted in the *Washington Post.*

After Kerry had spoken, the vets returned to the Mall, where they got the good news that the judge who'd originally issued the injunction against their campsite had rescinded it, and had even raked the government's lawyers over the coals. No one would mess with their camp after all. It was time to celebrate.

Soon an emergency communiqué landed on Bud Krogh's desk in the West Wing. The Secret Service, which had placed three informants posing as vets into the camp (they had at one point been passing out antiwar leaflets in front of the White House), warned that a new spontaneous demonstration was brewing. The vets planned to leave their tents at eight o'clock and march single-file in a candlelight procession around federal Washington. First they would swing past the Capitol and then come down the sidewalk of Pennsylvania Avenue, right past the White House, where Richard Nixon was dining with his daughter Tricia. The trouble was, the sidewalk in front of the White House was supposed to be off limits this whole week. Furthermore, the vets had no permit for the march.

There were about a thousand veterans. Many supporters showed up too, doubling their ranks, until the line stretched along ten blocks. At the front the vets carried a sixteen-foot-wide American flag upside-down, the signal of distress. The marchers held lit candles punched through the bottom of paper cups. Some wrapped themselves in blankets or quilts against the cold wind, which occasionally extinguished the flames. "Come in, sister, join us," a vet told a sixty-four-year-old tourist from California who had ventured out to see the White House at night. She stepped into the line and took a candle. Kerry was there, of course. So was his mother, down from Massachusetts. She rated the actions of her son's group as "extremely impressive."

With the fight about the campsite over, Police Chief Jerry Wilson had been taking a breather at home. Then his phone rang again. The call came from Bud's office. Get down to the White House right now.

The sidewalks around the executive mansion were supposed to be the province of the U.S. Park Police. But members of that force had a reputation for dealing with protesters in ways that ended up all over the newspapers. So the White House had, before the demonstrations, given Jerry full authority in order "to avoid the problems that have arisen in the past."

As he grabbed his things, Jerry thought to himself, whatever happens, no more arresting soldiers, if it could possibly be avoided. When he arrived at the scene, he gathered a half dozen park police officers and explained that a column of Vietnam vets was coming their way. We're going to stand on the sidewalk at the corner of the White House fence, Jerry said, and tell them they have to go across to the other side of Pennsylvania Avenue. The other cops nodded.

But, Jerry added, should they want to push through us, we're going to fall back and let them go. And if any of you can't eat shit with me, Jerry went on, you go stand somewhere else. I'll find some replacements.

The cops didn't look happy, but they said they understood.

Before long the column showed up, walking on the sidewalk past the Treasury Department. They halted at the line of police. The vet at the front was, like Jerry, a six-foot-four ex-navy man. The two stood toe-to-toe and eye-to-eye.

Sorry, Jerry said, you guys can't walk on this side of the street. So the tall guy went back to his men and returned with a compromise. How about if the column goes across the street like you ask, but I walk alone, just me, past the White House, just to make a point?

That was fine with Jerry. Even then, he thought much later, John Kerry proved to be a born diplomat.

BY FRIDAY MORNING, Nixon had seen the coverage of Kerry's Senate speech. "He was extremely effective," admitted the president. Haldeman agreed, saying that Kerry "did a hell of a great job," adding, certainly to Nixon's annoyance, "he looks like a Kennedy and he talks like a Kennedy" and would no doubt be running for public office soon. (One

Nixon aide, misreading the situation, suggested later they might be able to persuade Kerry to join the Republican Party.)

Nixon grew more agitated about the press coverage as the morning wore on. The China story got one day, Nixon said. An economy story got one day. "And then for one full week they run these veterans. For one full goddam week!" There had been one ray of light for the president and his men: they had fed a juicy scoop to *NBC Nightly News:* Al Hubbard, the VVAW executive secretary, had been lying about his rank in the air force, claiming to have been a captain when he never rose above sergeant. The story didn't seem to be gaining much traction, though, and a sense of desperation pervaded the White House.

Just before noon on Friday, Nixon met with Kissinger, his national security adviser and main co-strategist on the war, who was preparing to head to Paris where, separate from the stalled peace talks, he would hold his eighth clandestine session with the chief representative from Hanoi, Xuan Thuy.

Kissinger would later refer to the spring of 1971 as awakening "that uneasily dormant beast of public protest — our nightmare, our challenge and, in a weird way, our spur." The protests certainly contributed to the decision made that season by Kissinger and Nixon to soften at last their secret negotiating position in Paris. Under the new proposal, the administration still wouldn't agree to a cease-fire or a firm date for an American withdrawal without the guaranteed preservation, at least temporarily, of the existing regime in Saigon. But the United States would give in on some key points, mostly notably agreeing that even as the U.S. forces pulled out, Hanoi could keep troops in South Vietnam as long as it pulled others out of Cambodia and Laos.

They would try to convince the North Vietnamese this was their "final" offer. To press the point, Kissinger nudged Nixon to revive what the president had long called his "Madman Theory." The idea was to frighten the enemy into thinking Nixon was so frustrated, he would do anything to end the war. Kissinger suggested he could get Xuan into a private, five-minute chat:

"If I tell him, 'Now look, this president is extremely tough. You've been wrong every time. If you think you're going to defeat him, if you don't accept this, he will stop at nothing.'"

"That's right," Nixon replied.

"And imply that you might do it —"

"That's right," said Nixon.

"— use nuclear weapons."

Nixon said, "And then you could say . . . 'I cannot control him.' Put it that way."

"Yeah," said Kissinger. Trying to get Nixon to clearly state it, he repeated, "And imply that you might use nuclear weapons."

"'Yes sir, he will. I just want you to know he is not going to cave.'"

Kissinger added, "If they then charge us with it, I'll deny it."

"Oh, sure," said the president.

Whatever language Kissinger used in Paris, Hanoi didn't back down. A firm American withdrawal date had to come first, with no conditions, and the South Vietnamese leaders had to be removed immediately.

FOR ALL HIS SUCCESS in the Senate hearing on Thursday, John Kerry had been losing one battle inside the ranks. It involved the dramatic closing act for Operation Dewey Canyon. The vets were to return their combat medals to the government. The gesture would be both a catharsis and a kind of atonement. The question was, how to do it?

The original plan had been to take the medals right to Nixon. If no one accepted them formally at the White House, the vets would stuff them in one of the black rubber "body bags" used for corpses in Vietnam and throw it right over the wrought-iron fence.

It wouldn't have been the first time combat decorations were tossed onto the White House lawn. The undercover cop, John O'Connor, had participated in a preview. One of the other vets in the Washington office had lofted his combat ribbons over the fence in protest of one of Nixon's previous actions. A foreign television crew heard about it and asked the vet to reenact it for their audience. John's veteran friend realized he had no more ribbons. So he and John went over to Sunny's Surplus, an army-navy store that was a downtown D.C. fixture, and bought a handful.

The White House aide in charge of dampening the veterans' political impact was Charles Colson. So far his efforts to undermine the protesters and their relationship with the Democrats hadn't borne much fruit. He'd ordered a crate of oranges sent to their encampment under the name of the Democrats' most likely 1972 candidate, Senator Edmund Muskie of Maine. Colson had hoped this might tarnish Muskie among those who thought the protest was unpatriotic. He leaked the delivery of oranges to the press. But the veterans had earned too much public support for that scheme to work.

In the end Colson was spared the decision of how to handle the returned combat medals. The vets decided to bring them to Congress instead of the White House. Kerry's idea was to set up a big table outside the Capitol, have the former soldiers approach one by one, unpin their hardware, and place it with dignity on a white tablecloth. He thought it would be the kind of gesture that the "part of America that was not with us could understand," he said later. But that was ruled way too tame by the more radical factions. They wanted something more reflective of their anger, and in the final vote their view prevailed. They would throw their decorations away, right onto the steps of the Capitol.

Some had brought their medals and ribbons with them to Washington. Many hadn't, and John O'Connor told them he knew where they could procure some. He even mentioned to Kerry and others that it might not be a bad idea for those veterans who came with their own stuff to get their hands on some surplus instead. Sure, they're angry today, but in ten years they're going to want those things for their children. Soon the rumor went around that Sunny's had been sold out. You had to drive out to surplus stores in Virginia to find ribbons.

ON FRIDAY MORNING, whether holding their own decorations or surplus ones, hundreds of vets began trekking to the Capitol. The line stretched nearly a half mile, all the way back to the campsite. When those in the front arrived at the west entrance, they realized they were blocked from getting to the steep white steps. The authorities had erected a six-foot wire fence with wood supports to prevent unauthorized access to the building. The purpose was to control the enormous crowds expected the next day, Saturday, when the antiwar coalitions were mounting their giant march. But to some veterans it looked like another insult — like the locked gates at Arlington — and it stoked their anger. A fence might keep them off the steps, but the steps certainly could be reached with a firm throw.

The first shower of medals sailed over the fence and landed in the plaza below the entrance a little before 11:30 a.m. For the next two hours, the pile grew. The vets had set up a microphone by the fence. One by one, they said their piece and then threw their symbols of honorable service. They looked by turns defiant, angry, and sorrowful — sometimes all three at once.

First up was Jack Smith, a former marine from Connecticut. "We now strip ourselves of these medals of courage and heroism," he said. "We cast these away as a symbol of dishonor, shame and inhumanity." Hundreds of spectators, many of them congressional aides, were standing on the terrace halfway up the steps. They cheered.

Many vets were overcome as they reached the mike. Ronald Ferrizzi, a former infantryman from Pennsylvania, carefully recited the names of three fallen friends. His voice shook as he tossed a Silver Star and other medals, and then, sobbing, he embraced others from his state delegation, repeating, "I'm all right, I'm all right." Rusty Sachs of Boston, a former marine captain, couldn't stop the tears for a long time after throwing his medals over. "It was very, very, very heavy," he said. "This was the final act of contempt for the way the executive branch is forcing us to wage war."

Kerry, perhaps showing his ambivalence, was one of the last in line. His stash contained some of his own ribbons, as well as ribbons and medals he'd been given by comrades who couldn't make it to Washington. He lobbed rather than hurled them. He didn't show the anger many others did. He was calm, saying he wasn't acting to oppose anyone, but rather to wake the country up.

The pile grew larger and larger. It happened to be at the base of the statue of John Marshall, the chief justice who had cemented the role and authority of the Supreme Court in the nineteenth century. Meanwhile, the current Supreme Court held its first private vote on the conscientious objector case of the boxer Muhammad Ali. The justices decided, five votes to three, that Ali wasn't a true conscientious objector and thus should be convicted. (However, after much internal debate, they reconsidered, and in June they would rule, eight to none, in Ali's favor.)

After everyone had left the Capitol and went back to break camp, a few vets, including John O'Connor, tried to make sure the medals weren't randomly grabbed as souvenirs by tourists. On the Mall, before they headed for home, the vets planted a fifteen-foot American elm they bought from the National Park Service.

DEWEY CANYON WAS OVER. From an unpromising beginning it had turned into a wild success. Nixon would spend the next few days with his aides trying to figure out how to counter it. At one point he called his friend the evangelist Billy Graham, who told the president to get ten thousand of "our" vets to march in support of his policies.

In the end, Nixon's only hope was that the rest of the Spring Offensive would wipe the vets from America's infamous short-term memory. The big peace march was right around the corner. "On Saturday anyway," Nixon said, "that demonstration will engulf this one."

11

The Saturday March

Saturday, April 24

THE FENCE THAT THE VIETNAM VETERANS TOOK AS AN INSULT
was in fact evidence of a victory for dissenters. The vets had prevailed in
their fight to sleep on the National Mall, and now this barrier outside the
U.S. Capitol signaled how much the Spring Offensive was breaking down
the rules restricting demonstrations in Washington.

For nearly a century, the property outside the building where members of Congress did business had been off limits to dissenters — the very
citizens who had sent the politicians there. Seeking to preserve "quiet
and dignity," lawmakers in 1882 made it "forbidden to parade, stand, or
move in processions or assemblages" or display any flags or signs on the
grounds of the Capitol.

Fittingly, the leader of the maiden mass march on Washington was
the first to be convicted of violating this law. He was a forty-year-old
Ohio businessman named Jacob Coxey, who lost his fortune in the Panic
of 1893. Coxey's radical idea for ending the economic depression was for
Congress to fund a huge national road-building project to create millions of jobs. He rallied hundreds of the unemployed, an army of the
wretched, and led them on a five-week trek from his hometown, Massil-
lon. When the column reached D.C. on May 1, 1894, Coxey crossed the
Capitol lawn. He tried to mount the steps to explain his infrastructure
proposal. Police clubbed the crowd off the property. Coxey and his lieutenants went to jail for twenty days.

By the 1940s, Congress had gotten even more specific: organizations petitioning the government had to break into groups, each no larger than five people, if they wanted to approach the Capitol, and each group of five had to keep a distance of at least a hundred feet from the next. Exceptions remained rare. Police in the summer of 1959 turned away hundreds of D.C. residents who wanted to rally for the right to elect their own mayor and city council.

The Spring Offensive was different. By bringing many organizations to D.C. in 1971, the antiwar movement was throwing the government off balance, testing the limits. Permit applications were piling up. The vets wanted the Mall and a ceremony at the Capitol steps. The Mayday Tribe asked permission to erect tents throughout sprawling Rock Creek Park. And organizers of the big Saturday coalition march sought approval to gather on the Ellipse between the Mall and the White House.

Before the Vietnam veterans had arrived in town, White House aides gathered to prepare for the onslaught. Bud Krogh was among them. He tried to warn his bosses not to create a public dust-up that would only build sympathy for the protesters. In the end they all agreed that one of the administration's goals for the spring had to be "minimizing adverse PR for government in dealing with demonstrators, re location of rallies, routes, housing, etc."

That mission, of course, had been bobbled when it came to the vets. But, surprising the peace coalition, Nixon's men agreed to a permit for the Saturday march. Not on the Ellipse — which they thought would be too close to the White House for security purposes — but rather at the Capitol. In his capacity as president of the Senate, Vice President Spiro Agnew, a sworn enemy of the antiwarriors, sent a letter to Philip Hirschkop, the lawyer for the organizers, who had been negotiating all of the logistics. Agnew agreed to waive the ban at the Capitol, with the understanding that the crowd would number about fifty thousand people. A temporary fence would go up to control the west entrance, to protect the landscaping and contain the crowd on the far side of the Capitol steps.

By this time, though, the organizers knew something the White House didn't. The crowd was certainly going to be much bigger, perhaps bigger than at any march in Washington history.

The march had been drawing more and more support from organizations around the country. Good planning was one reason. Not only had the left wing of the movement finally come into the tent — the People's Coalition for Peace and Justice, led by David Dellinger and Rennie Davis—but moderates had been signing up. Eight U.S. senators, seventeen House members, the governor of Massachusetts, and the mayor of New York City had endorsed the march, as had several organizations of active-duty GIs and officers, and many labor and church groups.

Two other factors were adding fuel. One was the extensive news coverage of the Vietnam veterans' activities, particularly John Kerry's testimony and the medal-return ceremony. These events had tuned in more of the public to the movement than had any previous protest, with the possible exception of the Moratorium march in November 1969. "The peace movement has many martyrs, but few heroes, and the veterans, who held the Mall for four nights against a stony-hearted government, had given it a victory that already has become a legend," wrote the *Washington Star* columnist Mary McGrory.

The second factor was the overheated rhetoric of hard-liners in Washington, which had the opposite of its intended effect. Their tough talk angered people and motivated those who had wavered about coming to D.C. Among the fear-mongers were two congressmen from the Midwest, who took to the floor of the House to rail against the march, saying its leaders were "under substantial communist influence." A spokesman for Jerry Wilson's police department said the cops had heard nothing to suggest the protest would be anything but peaceful, but John Mitchell promptly contradicted him. At a press conference the attorney general warned that "some of the people who are coming to Washington are saying they are going to create violence."

At the same time, the FBI's secret counterintelligence program also worked to find ways to "ridicule and disrupt" the organizers of the march, including the "emerging homosexual groups who are becoming more militant daily." Agents in the New York field office created a leaflet to mail anonymously to "selected individuals" involved in the Spring Offensive, to stir up trouble between factions. The agents warned J. Edgar Hoover's office that it was "written in the jargon of the New Left, necessitating the use of a certain amount of profanity." Hoover approved the scheme, provided that the agents used untraceable paper and "all efforts [would be] made to protect Bureau as source of leaflets."

Mitchell was drawing his opinions about the march indirectly from government informants, who were feeding the Justice Department's frequent intelligence reports. Some of these informants were, wittingly or not, passing increasingly improbable tidbits to their handlers. For example, they reported that Yippies might rush the stage during the rally while members of Congress were speaking, and beat them down for being "sell-outs."

The gap kept widening between the administration and the media about the Spring Offensive. The day before the march, Secretary of State William Rogers told reporters that neither the Saturday event nor the rest of the protests would have any effect: "I'm not sure anything that can be said can change many minds." Rogers added, "I have no doubt the president is getting us out" of the war, and couldn't go any faster. A *Washington Post* editorial criticized the administration's stance, saying that the president "has conspicuously and contemptuously turned a deaf ear to the protesters; the Department of Justice has consistently looked upon them as radicals and traitors, has goaded and frustrated and discouraged them as though every effort to exercise the constitutional right of the people peaceably to assemble and to petition the government for a redress of grievances were a subversive act."

JUST A COUPLE of weeks earlier, Nixon had considered sticking around and calling a press conference the morning of April 24, the day of the march. He expressed doubt that the protest would be large or important enough to overshadow anything he said. "Even though they are here, would that be the news?" he asked his chief of staff. "Demonstrations are routine." Nixon grumbled about "all that concern about a bunch of people in Washington" and briefly mused upon taking out his boat to go "cruising on the river" while the protesters shouted their slogans. But in the end he agreed. "I'll be outta here," Nixon said. "I think we'll just go to Camp David."

Before leaving on Friday, the day before the march, he again complained to his aides that the protests were essentially a creation of the media. TV "has zeroed in on these people," Nixon said. "It'll zero in on the demonstrations Saturday. And then they'll try to play with the next two weeks. They're stringing it out, and it's highly unconscionable reporting on the part of television."

Kissinger agreed it was deliberate. News people, he said, "want to destroy you and they want us to lose in Vietnam." As far as the New Left was concerned, the war wasn't even the real issue, Kissinger insisted. "They want to break confidence in the government," he said. "They don't give a damn about Vietnam, because as soon as Vietnam is finished, I will guarantee the radicals will be all over us" for other things.

Let them try, Nixon replied. "They know that they never will influence me."

Then Kissinger pressed perhaps too far, suggesting obliquely that Nixon hadn't been tough enough on the radicals. "I am wondering, Mr. President . . . whether one isn't on the wrong wicket, batting back the balls they throw? Whether one shouldn't accuse them of turning the thing over to the Communists?"

He had hit one of Nixon's hot buttons, and the president was stung. He said, "I think I have been on the offensive as much as I can be."

Then Nixon added, "Or should I do more? I can hit them harder."

Kissinger was playing both sides, being careful to cultivate a public image of sympathy to dissent. He occasionally met with pacifists and student groups. He felt privately that the "self-righteousness and brutality" of the militants was "repellent" but professed to feel somewhat guilty that "my generation had failed them by encouraging self-indulgence and neglecting to provide roots."

The evening before the march, Kissinger even took a call from the poet Allen Ginsberg, a star of the Beat generation and a friend of the Yippies. Ginsberg suggested that Nixon, Kissinger, and the head of the CIA meet with Rennie Davis, David Dellinger, and others in early May. "I gather you don't know how to get out of the war," the poet told Kissinger. "They have some ideas. They have been to Hanoi." When Kissinger almost seemed to be taking the idea seriously, Ginsberg added: "It would be even more useful if we could do it naked on television."

The White House had already noted that the Yippies took pleasure in poking fun at the president's national security adviser. Aides passed around a college newspaper article quoting Abbie Hoffman's promise to "take Henry Kissinger out for a midnight snack" when he came to D.C. for the Mayday protests.

While Kissinger spoke with Ginsberg, Nixon was heading out of town. He had boarded a helicopter to have dinner with his daughter Julie and her husband, David Eisenhower, in Virginia Beach, where Eisenhower was stationed at the naval base. Later that night the president flew to Camp David, where he would spend the weekend.

Signs of the march's gathering momentum had been showing up all day. At lunchtime, some two thousand employees of the National Institutes of Health rallied in support on their wooded campus in Bethesda, north of the city. Some scientists leaned out their laboratory windows and sang along with Pete Seeger as the troubadour did an intense rendition of "This Land Is Your Land." That evening, while Nixon was traveling, more than three thousand people filed into the Washington National Cathedral. A group of active-duty military, the Concerned Officers Movement, had advertised a two-hour memorial for those killed on all sides in Southeast Asia. "It's terrible to think our sons died in vain," one Gold Star mother told the congregation. "But perhaps if their deaths have awakened America, they will not have died in vain." William Sloane Coffin, the Yale University chaplain, also took the lectern. "The war is a lie," Coffin said. "For years we have been told we are helping a foreign nation repel an attack. But the veterans coming back tell us that we are waging war against the South Vietnamese people." Peter Yarrow, of the folk group Peter, Paul, and Mary, sang, "And if you take my hand my son, all will be well when the day is done."

When it was his turn to speak, Robert F. Drinan of Massachusetts, one of the first-term antiwar Democrats in Congress, praised the full Spring Offensive. Drinan, who was also a Jesuit priest, likened it to the seminal events of the movement for civil rights. His hope, he said, was that "these demonstrations are the Selma of the war."

AT TEN O'CLOCK on a clear and sunny Saturday morning, the marchers convened. It had been exactly a decade since JFK sent the first U.S. advisers to Indochina. This would be the seventh mass parade against the war since 1965, and would prove to be almost certainly the largest of the seven, and thus the largest assembly of dissenters the nation had ever seen.

The main sponsoring organization, the National Peace Action Coalition, and its erstwhile competitor, the People's Coalition, had been wrestling over details for weeks. They bickered about the order of speakers, control of the sound system, and how donations would be collected from the crowd. They didn't let up even as the march got underway.

Yet almost none of the hundreds of thousands of participants knew much about the battles within the movement. Few, if any, could have explained the philosophical differences between the groups. And even if they could, fewer still would have cared. They came because they were frustrated with Nixon and because the march was shaping up to be the largest event against the war in its history.

This was the secret truth of organizing. It was less about winning ideological debate points than about building support around a big idea — in other words, not so different from mainline politics as the radicals might believe. You kept planning and sweating all the details, trusting that you'd be ready when the right moment arrived in time and space. The size of the crowd validated the work of David Dellinger, who had spent so much of his life willing to throw almost anything on the table to keep people from flying off in different directions.

In the original plan for Saturday, the demonstrators streaming into the city would come together at the Ellipse, the circular greenscape between the White House and the Washington Monument. Then at noon they would all march east, down Pennsylvania Avenue to the Capitol, for the big rally.

But it was clear from the start this wasn't going to work as planned; the crowd was just too big. Thousands of parade marshals had been recruited, and they began to herd the marchers off the Ellipse and onto the parade route a couple of hours early.

And still people kept coming. All morning long, they packed into the city. Cars jammed every highway. One toll plaza on the interstate counted 347 chartered buses going by. Typical were the four buses from the state university in Edinboro, Pennsylvania, filled with students who paid ten dollars for the round trip, rode all night, and arrived just after dawn. Even at 11 a.m., cars and vans and buses coming from Boston, New York, and Philadelphia were still stuck in a three-mile backup at the entrance to the Baltimore Harbor tunnel, forty miles from Washington.

As the marchers set off down Pennsylvania Avenue, they were supposed to leave one traffic lane open. That plan was quickly abandoned, and still there wasn't enough room. Police agreed to let the marchers use

Constitution Avenue as well. And yet the human columns were so huge, they couldn't move faster than a snail's pace.

A holiday atmosphere prevailed. People sang, clapped, and chanted. They carried pennants and balloons and American flags, some held upside-down. Vietcong flags popped up here and there. The sheer variety of marchers exceeded anything seen before. There were thousands upon thousands of young people, but also many middle-aged folks, including union members displaying their affiliation, like the eight hundred members of District 65 of the Distributive Workers of America. The United Auto Workers chapter in Cleveland dispatched buses to an antiwar protest for the first time. Soldiers out of uniform brandished the names of their bases. There was a gray-haired band of brothers from the Abraham Lincoln Brigade, who had fought in the Spanish Civil War. Banners identified groups including federal employees against the war, gay liberation organizations, and "Business Executives Move for Vietnam Peace." Almost every tree and statue on the route sported a protester or two or three, seeking a better view. Many marchers had ignored obstacles to make their trip. A second-grade teacher from New Jersey refused to change his plans after he broke his leg at home. He struggled along on crutches. "I'll be over this in a couple of weeks, but there are some fellows in Vietnam who will never recover," he said.

To assess the crowd, the *Washington Post* put seventeen people on the streets with survey forms. Their unscientific sample found that two-thirds had traveled more than two hundred miles, that more than a third were newcomers to demonstrations, that men outnumbered women by two to one. Eighty-four percent of the people in the *Post*'s sample were younger than thirty. Nearly half were students. Fifty-five percent identified themselves as liberals, and another 23 percent said they were radicals.

The march, like most of the antiwar movement, was primarily white. The *Post* found that only 5 percent were people of color. "Black people are just too busy trying to survive to march up and down Pennsylvania Avenue," explained one young African American Vietnam vet.

When the front of the parade reached the west face of the Capitol, people quickly filled up the plaza in front. The throngs spilled back onto the Mall. Agnew's temporary fence, the one that had enraged the veterans the day before, didn't survive for long.

From the speakers' platform at the Capitol steps, Representative Bella Abzug, a New York Democrat, surveyed the enormous turnout. "Well," she said as she stepped to the microphone, "it looks like everybody's here today — except Richard Nixon."

Peter, Paul, and Mary sang their cover of Bob Dylan's "Blowin' in the Wind," reminding the crowd that they had first performed it in Washington at Martin Luther King Jr.'s 1963 March for Jobs and Freedom. His widow, Coretta Scott King, exhorted the crowd to "declare the war is over."

David Dellinger, the man largely responsible for bringing the coalition together on this day, also spoke, though he appeared weak and exhausted from the effort. He told the crowd the peace movement should "leave the violence to the government." John Kerry, fresh from his historic Senate testimony, also took the microphone: "This is not the struggle of one month, or one year or one war. It's a contribution we must make for the rest of our lives." The most enthusiastic response of the day was triggered by the San Francisco rock group Country Joe and the Fish, who got much of the crowd singing along to their jaunty anthem, "I-Feel-Like-I'm-Fixin'-to-Die Rag."

And it's one-two-three, what are we fighting for?
Don't ask me, I don't give a damn, next stop is Vietnam.

POLICE CHIEF JERRY WILSON had been out on the streets since 5:30 a.m. He monitored the march and the rally all day, but there was no way the police could control such a large crowd by themselves, which was why the organizers had put some two thousand trained marshals on the street. Despite a few incidents here and there, the day was remarkably peaceful. John Mitchell's warning about devious communist plans for violence faded away.

One of the jobs left to the police was also one of Jerry's least favorite: making an official estimate of the size of the crowd.

It was more than a matter of academic interest. This had always been a challenging duty, because of the politics involved. The organizers always overestimated; the administration always tried to undercount. The number influenced the amount of news coverage and the bragging rights and the momentum.

For example, back in November of 1969, Nixon's men hadn't wanted to acknowledge the scope of the Washington Moratorium march, the first really large protest on their watch. At the end of that day, the Justice Department's point man on the protests, a lawyer named John Dean, had called in Jerry and his police counsel, Gerald Caplan, so they could settle on an official number. During the permit negotiations with the Moratorium organizers, "we promised an apolitical, good faith estimate, though we understood that the Nixon administration wanted a low estimate," Caplan recalled. Jerry had seen the 1969 crowd with his own eyes from a helicopter and had conferred with his police counters on the ground. He and his lawyer told Dean that there were at least 325,000 people in the parade. The government had no intention of confirming such a big success for the antiwar movement. During the day, the Pentagon had put out a crowd estimate of 119,000. Maybe that would be a hard sell, but Dean "argued that only about 250,000 protesters participated." The White House ultimately put out Dean's number. Even Nixon's own chief of staff acknowledged in his diary that it was wrong.

Jerry's desire to be fair and truthful back then had irked the White House. "What is he trying to tell us?" Bud Krogh's boss asked. Six months later, Nixon's aides were still stewing about it, so Bud had Jerry write a response to the criticism. The chief typed it out himself "to insure that the information is shared only by me and others at your discretion." He laid out his reasons for the higher count and wrote, "I think you will agree" that the official count was too conservative. But the dispute put Jerry on notice.

Even at its lowest estimate, the 1969 march was the largest protest in Washington to date, exceeding the turnout at Martin Luther King Jr.'s March on Washington for Jobs and Freedom six years earlier.

Now, few observing the April 1971 march doubted it was even larger, the biggest yet. The *Washington Post*'s observers on the street counted 110,000 by early afternoon in just one section of the parade, those coming off the Ellipse toward Pennsylvania Avenue. Add a probably similar number who took the Constitution Avenue route, plus all the others who kept arriving all day and never passed through the Ellipse at all, and you likely approached 400,000.

But the official estimate would be less than half of that. The president, while publicly pretending not to care, was monitoring the event closely from Camp David. He phoned his chief of staff six times, emphasizing he wanted the demonstration "downplayed as much as possible." He made additional calls to other aides watching the march.

The pressure fell on Jerry. The police put out an official estimate of 200,000. Even that wasn't low enough for the White House. At 11 p.m., a police spokesman called the newspapers to say the department was revising the number down to 175,000, after receiving "final reports" from the field.

That night, thousands stayed around for an all-night rock concert on the grounds of the Washington Monument. Later, euphoric protesters driving back north mounted a spontaneous blockade of the New Jersey Turnpike in both directions, just north of the Delaware Memorial Bridge. They stopped their vehicles and sat on the roadway for four hours, singing, chanting, and building a bonfire in the middle of the asphalt. "Get the boys out of Vietnam and we'll give you back the Turnpike," one young woman from Connecticut told police.

Regardless of the official estimates, Nixon didn't kid himself about the size of Saturday's turnout. He privately attributed the enormous crowd to the fact that it was a "pretty day," which encouraged people who hardly cared about the war to get outside. "All the jackasses were down here and screwing around," he explained.

THROUGHOUT THAT SATURDAY, the Mayday Tribe had been active. Organizers wandered through the crowds, handing out literature and asking people to stay for the rest of the week's activities.

The government, trying to avoid another fiasco like the one with the vets, had finally decided to grant the Mayday crowd its permit. Not in Rock Creek Park, which Rennie Davis had first proposed, but at West Potomac Park. That was where the Vietnam vets had originally come to town. It was also the spot where John O'Connor, the undercover police officer working with the vets, had been secretly meeting his police handlers. John's bosses thought it would be a lot easier to control the Mayday kids if they were grouped together on the open fields by the river rather than scattered through the woods of Rock Creek. So John had gone to Rennie and lobbied for the change.

At first Rennie protested. We've already printed up thousands of Mayday manuals telling people to come to Rock Creek Park, he reminded

John. Right, John said, but we already have experience at West Potomac Park with the vets, and we're more likely to get a permit there. John was impressed by Rennie's willingness to change his mind.

So the Mayday lawyers switched their request to West Potomac Park. The government acquiesced. Rennie was surprised. He had to admit to himself he didn't think they'd get a permit at all. He thought things might end up like Chicago, with police trying to roust them out of the parks.

Now they could settle in without worrying about a raid on their camp.

12

What's the Harm?

BY SUNDAY MORNING ONLY THE MOST MILITANT OF THE ANTI-warriors were still in town. They were the ones who boasted they weren't just weekend marchers but were prepared to put their bodies on the line. Some had taken to disparaging the many years of parading with "babies and balloons," which had failed to move the needle far enough.

Many were new converts. They had come down for the Saturday rally not intending to stick around, but found themselves caught in the intensity of the unusual spring in the nation's capital.

Down at West Potomac Park, the newcomers had wilder hair than their Vietnam vet predecessors and more cultural luggage, such as recreational drugs, guitars, and flutes. They also had notably more difficulty keeping their campfires lit during the cool evenings. Sometimes they scavenged firewood from nearby construction fences. The early arrivals got fed by the Raintree Tribe, a couple dozen youngsters who lived on a commune founded in Indiana by Larry Canada, the friend of Rennie's who, along with his heiress wife, had helped finance Mayday. Canada was footing the bill for the food, supplemented by donations from sympathetic church congregations. Still, everyone ate a lot of oatmeal.

The Mayday organizers had given the settlement the hopeful nickname of Algonquin Peace City, in honor of the original Native American inhabitants and the atmosphere they hoped would prevail. They emblazoned the cover of their Mayday Tactical Manual with a drawing of an Algonquin warrior.

Mass civil disobedience was still a week away. But the Spring Offensive schedule called for some kind of action almost every day by the Mayday group and others. Police Chief Jerry Wilson had the feeling he was playing a game of whack-a-mole. At noon on Sunday, a large cluster of Quaker families gathered in front of the White House for a pray-in. They ignored warnings that they were flouting the rules of dissent around the White House, which dictated that no more than one hundred people could assemble. Jerry's officers tried to get the young parents to walk away so their children and babies wouldn't go to jail, but in the end some 150 protesters were arrested.

The principle of nonviolent but more disruptive protest had gained traction among even some moderates in the movement. More than half of the Saturday marchers surveyed by newspaper reporters said they approved of a Mayday-like action. "We can't seem to reach them any other way," a New York stockbroker said of the Nixon administration. "If millions of people came here and stopped the wheels, that would be the only way to stop the obstinate people."

Of course the Mayday Tribe would make a lot of commuters angry by trying to close down the city. But some non-radicals on the left were coming around to the idea that the peace movement and the country had little to lose. "Unless tens of thousands of people come here and go to jail, it won't work completely, but to the extent it does, sticky, painful mess that it is, it will kick [Nixon] into shortening the war and saving the lives of American men, to use one of his favorite phrases," wrote the *Washington Post* columnist Nicholas von Hoffman. "Object if you must, but what else are they to do? Give up?"

Von Hoffman added, "If May Day fails, if it's smashed or it peters out because not enough old marchers turn up for it, what's the harm?"

Plenty of liberals, though, did see the potential for harm. The previous week, Rennie Davis and others in favor of Mayday had been invited on a public television show to debate Democrats including Philip Hart, the U.S. senator whose cocktail party booze had been the target of the aborted raid by the Vietnam veterans.

Moderating the debate was a Massachusetts politician, Michael Dukakis, who within a few years would be elected governor and later become an unsuccessful Democratic nominee for the presidency. He told the audience that the conflict between the Nixon administration's policy on Vietnam and the will of the majority to end the war "has become the prime fact of American political life today." He posed a question: should people opposing the war answer the call for massive civil disobedience?

IT WAS FAR from the first time a version of that question had surfaced in U.S. history. While the best-known manifestation of large-scale pacifist resistance might be Mohandas Gandhi's nonviolent revolution, which hastened the end of British rule in India in the 1940s, in fact civil disobedience was arguably an American invention. By many accounts Gandhi borrowed the idea from Henry David Thoreau, the nineteenth-century New England philosopher who spent a night in jail for refusing to pay taxes in order to protest slavery and the Mexican-American War.* His 1849 essay, "Resistance to Civil Government" (later retitled "On the Duty of Civil Disobedience"), became a foundational text. Thoreau and others, including a young Abraham Lincoln, considered that war a land grab unworthy of a new democracy and an evil attempt to expand human bondage to new lands.

Roots of the American tradition go even deeper. In colonial Massachusetts Bay, Quakers who publicly practiced their religion in defiance of a kind of one-party rule by the Puritans endured jail, banishment, and in some cases the death penalty. The Quakers went on to practice an unswerving pacifism, even through the American Revolution and Civil War. Later, opponents of slavery, racial segregation, and nuclear arms all employed forms of civil disobedience to call attention to their causes.

Like the anti–Vietnam War coalition, those previous movements often split along lines of militancy about which acts of civil disobedience were proper. Purists might argue that the purpose was to stage a public event against a specific injustice — such as segregated lunch counters — passively accept the consequential arrests, and go to jail to gain attention through a kind of martyrdom. Many in the movement took this path, burning their draft cards or refusing to pay taxes.

Others, including David Dellinger, came to believe that moving from mere protest to resistance meant confronting power in a broader way,

---

* Amy Greenberg, in *A Wicked War: Polk, Clay, Lincoln, and the 1846 U.S. Invasion of Mexico* (New York: Knopf 2012), documents the breadth, depth, and efficacy of the American antiwar movement against the Mexican conflict.

through a symbolic violation rather than only breaking the actual law you opposed. That could involve trespassing or blocking traffic on private or government property. It gave dissenters an option beyond passive demonstrations, but stopped short of violence. Mass civil disobedience could be more effective and ethical. "It's possible to use force, it's necessary to use force if you're going to have an impact," he said. "But there's a difference between force and violence, they can and must be separated."

The debate sometimes perplexed the rank and file. A group of leftist videographers worried in print that the concept wasn't clear enough for Mayday: "The theme of Non-Violent Civil Disobedience was confusing to many people, does it mean sitting down and passively absorbing punishment from the police, does it allow for self-defense or offensive non-violent actions, such as barricading streets, trashing, or violence against property???"

IN THE PUBLIC DEBATE ON TV, Hart acknowledged that civil disobedience was occasionally "appropriate and useful." But the Mayday Tribe, he said, would only frighten away many Americans already on their side and thus undermine efforts in Congress to end the bloodshed. Agreeing with Hart was a Democratic activist named Allard Lowenstein, who had been instrumental in Eugene McCarthy's presidential campaign, which contributed to LBJ's abdication. Lowenstein maintained that the electoral process was the only way to change the system. Political reformists would have stopped the war by now, he contended, if they hadn't been paralyzed by the assassinations of Martin Luther King Jr. and Robert F. Kennedy. To Lowenstein, the question of whether to employ civil disobedience rested only on its efficacy. He said it would not work this time. Rather, it would play into the hands of Nixon's men, who wanted to portray all their opponents as extremist.

On the other side of the debate, the radical lawyer William Kunstler, who had represented Rennie Davis and David Dellinger and their fellow defendants in the Chicago Seven trial, argued that the failure of the government to stop the war was a crisis that called for extreme measures. Mayday would be effective, he said, and yes, it would be disruptive, but by its nature civil disobedience, from the Boston Tea Party to the Selma March, always infringes on someone else's convenience.

Howard Zinn, a leftist historian who taught at Boston University, pointed out that civil disobedience had been very effective when employed by antislavery forces, by labor unions, and by the civil rights movement. "Throughout American history, the political leaders have always exhorted the American people to be nice and quiet and leave things to them. But when very serious evils confronted the American people, they had to go beyond the congressmen and senators, and they had to commit civil disobedience and they had even to break the law," Zinn said.

For Rennie, there was only one important question on the table: "How can we move this government?" He called the lack of support from liberals for more intensive protest "one of the great tragedies of this decade."

THE INTERNAL DEBATE over tactics might have intrigued Bud Krogh, but not Nixon's inner circle. The Spring Offensive had already cost them political points. They were determined to chalk up a victory in the next and final round.

Although the White House men had taken to calling the Mayday Tribe "the violent group," and John Mitchell branded its members as "terrorists," there was no evidence, beyond the whispers from some sketchy informants, of violent actions on the agenda. No one had been talking about putting anything on intersections and bridges other than themselves and the occasional stalled car. Nixon and many of his aides, though, had come to endorse the view of the New Left offered by Tom Huston and by the FBI. Any differences between, say, the Weather Underground, the Yippies, the Mayday Tribe, and even the Vietnam vets were just a matter of degree. Just look at the Capitol bombing. The FBI was about to make a major arrest related to that case.

Brooding at Camp David during the weekend of the April 24 march, the president had been obsessed with developing "a counterattack." He wanted his aides to get out the word that television had covered the vets "in a totally unfair way" and to "be sure we're alert to handling the violent demonstrations when they come up." The president's idea for Mayday was to make a show of tolerance at first, then come down hard when the protest got out of hand, as surely it must. His chief of staff described Nixon's attitude: "We should let the nuts sort of hang themselves."

Outwardly, Nixon's pretense continued — that the demonstrations had no effect on him or his policies. When a caucus of Republican senators suggested a special meeting with the president to address the topic, Nixon refused. In addition, the issue "should not be raised" at the regular weekly policy meeting between the White House and the GOP lawmakers, the chief of staff noted: "If it is, P will not speak to the subject."

On Sunday evening, April 25, the president and his family prepared to leave Camp David and return to Washington. Nixon strolled to the helicopter with his Irish setter, King Timahoe. The second the leash was unfastened, the dog made a break for it. He sprinted for the hilly Maryland forest and disappeared into the trees. The family had to fly back without the animal while the Secret Service hunted him down. In truth, the dog and the president had no relationship. His actual master was Nixon's personal assistant, Manolo Sanchez. They had to bribe King Timahoe with biscuits to get him to sit by the president for pictures in the Oval Office.

NIXON WAS BACK in the White House on Monday, as the Mayday people began making their presence felt in official Washington.

That morning, one band of protesters drove out to the suburban home of the secretary of defense, Melvin Laird. They staged a mock jungle battle on his lawn, with those playing GIs shouting the racial epithet "Gooks! Gooks!" at the pretend enemy. They hung a Vietcong flag on Laird's porch. The secretary may have been home, but he didn't come outside. The next day Laird sought to undercut the movement's momentum by promising to slash the maximum number of men drafted each month from fifteen thousand down to ten thousand, which he said would be the lowest level of the war.

There was action on Capitol Hill too, where no security gates yet existed to control public access to congressional office buildings. Squads of "soldiers" roamed the halls, pursuing groups of wailing female demonstrators who wore burlap sacks, spewed fake blood from their mouths, and screamed, "God have mercy; don't kill my baby!" The display sent one middle-aged Senate staff member running back to her desk in tears. Protesters pushed their way into a dozen offices, including that of the Senate's leading conservative, Barry Goldwater of Arizona. He called guards to clear the room and then decided to close his office for the rest of the tumultuous week. Goldwater blasted the protesters as "crude, foul-mouthed and completely irresponsible. I resent the news media referring to this kind of visitation as 'lobbying for peace.'"

Trying to keep the protesters at bay, the Capitol Police blocked one entrance to the Senate. The young people ran around the corner. "Don't let them in!" the hapless cops shouted as they gave chase. They did get in, and made their way to the visitors' gallery while the Senate was in session, creating a ruckus. Nine people were arrested and marched out to a police van. They pounded defiantly on the inside of the vehicle while their compatriots outside raised clenched fists.

At the Department of Justice, the chief of analysis summarized the daily intelligence coming in from informants. He told his bosses that by Monday night "there were approximately eight hundred persons present, mostly males, in West Potomac Park." A police cruiser swung by the park and observed "hundreds of tents with 'hippie' type people milling around the area in large and small groups. Registration tags of many out-of-state autos parked around the campsite indicated that the occupants represented a cross section of the entire United States who would now unite with and strengthen" the early arrivals.

In the evening, Rennie addressed the campers by the river. He told them the stakes were high. They were responsible "for the entire peace movement. Everybody is watching us." The Washington spring remained unusually cool; temperatures were down in the forties and many shivered under blankets as they listened.

RENNIE WAS DIVIDING his time between West Potomac Park, the Vermont Avenue offices, and his apartment in the Adams-Morgan neighborhood, near the National Zoo. But his Mayday partner, David Dellinger, was suddenly nowhere to be seen. He had disappeared on the cusp of perhaps his greatest feat of organization.

Dave had been suffering from wear and tear. He'd been on the road nearly every week for months. Besides shuttling regularly between his New York office and the Washington headquarters, he'd continued to hit campuses around the country all month to build support for Mayday. In the days before he addressed the April 24 march, he had visited DeKalb, Illinois; Cleveland, Ohio; and Syracuse, New York. The pressure of constant travel, the fundraising, the diplomacy required to hold the coalition together — all that was taking its toll. There was added strain on his marriage of nearly thirty years to Elizabeth Peterson, a minister's daughter. His personal financial condition, always precarious, had grown worse. He fell behind in tuition payments for his son, who had followed him to Yale. His daughter wrote to ask if he could possibly come up with some cash to help her pay for adult education classes.

On Monday Dave was supposed to be off again, to St. Olaf College in Minnesota. But he canceled. Instead, telling almost no one, he checked into Georgetown University Hospital.

His eye was causing him severe pain. It was the legacy of the beating he'd suffered in the summer of 1951 from a bystander at a rally against the Korean War in Times Square. He had been legally blind on his right side for years. This time doctors worried he might lose his vision completely. To ease the agony they injected morphine in his eye.

His close friends were alarmed when they heard about his health troubles, both for his sake and Mayday's. "I saw you on TV during the April 24 rally and felt you were not well," wrote one longtime colleague. "Even tho we all believe the Peace Movement has no leaders I for one know where much of my personal inspiration has come from. When all is lost, quiet, repressed, your steadfastness has been my beacon."

DAVE REMAINED OFF-SCENE, but the long debate over the nature of nonviolent resistance continued to haunt the Spring Offensive. As his friend Staughton Lynd had suggested a few years earlier, the true test for pacifists comes when their movement fails to get results and the establishment hardens against them. At that point, it becomes seductive to justify violence.

Dave had raised the question during one of his recent barnstorming trips to campuses: "Sometimes the people who are most shocked and struck by the depth of the problem go off in frustration and bitterness and into a course that I, at least, think of as counter-productive — they start talking about picking up the gun or trashing windows or armed civil war." At another rally he declared, "The actions this spring are more powerful than the bomb that exploded in the Capitol — they shall express the power of the people, rather than the illusory power of dynamite."

He didn't mention how much his position was informed by personal knowledge. A year earlier, Dave had been in deep debate on this point with a member of the Weather Underground, Terry Robbins. When they came to an impasse, Dave later recalled, Robbins "shyly kissed me on the cheek." Dave was sickened when he later heard that Robbins was one of the people blown to bits in the group's Greenwich Village bomb factory.

A day after Dave entered the hospital, the FBI in Washington stepped up its pursuit of those it suspected had knowledge of the Capitol bombing claimed by Weather.

Among the places the organizers slept in Washington was a three-story green brick row house on Lanier Place, across the street from Rennie's apartment. The owner rented it to the group for $350 a month. The spartan rooms, decorated by little more than posters celebrating Mayday and the revolutions in Cuba and Vietnam, could accommodate at least ten people.

Just before noon on Tuesday, April 27, FBI agents tore off the screen door on the front entrance. They rushed in and fanned out to search the place for Leslie Bacon, the nineteen-year-old California woman who moved in activist circles with the Berkeley Yippies Stew Albert and Judy Gumbo.

Weeks after the FBI had briefly taken Bacon into custody in March to ask her about the Capitol attack, and released her when she insisted she knew nothing, Nixon had been briefed on the investigation into the bombing. Thanks to an informant, "they think they know who did that," John Ehrlichman told the president. In the briefing, he mixed up members of the Weather Underground with the leaders of Mayday.

The feds alleged that Bacon had "personal knowledge of the circumstances and the persons responsible for" the Capitol bombing, which made her a "necessary and material witness." In court filings and internal memos, the Justice Department would cite information from at least one informant, from wiretaps, which would prove to be illegal, and from the FBI's survey of possible witnesses. Later, they would also accuse her of assisting in a previous Weather incident, an attempted bombing of a bank on East 91st Street in New York. Bacon would admit to a grand jury that she had helped to scope out the target for that plot but said she dropped out of the plan long before it was executed. She would continue to deny knowing anything about the Capitol attack.

John O'Connor, the undercover D.C. police officer working with the

Vietnam vets, had limited contact with the Mayday group. But the police had another person embedded with them. Ann Kolego was such an effective informant, she had been named a "special employee" of Jerry Wilson's department. Her cover was "to act a little goofy," which explains why her movement comrades knew her as "Crazy Annie."

Kolego, who had previously helped the police monitor activists at the Democratic National Convention in Chicago in 1968, managed to move in as a roommate with two of the people who ran the Mayday office on Vermont Avenue. With the assistance of the CIA and the Secret Service, the police employed a surveillance method that agents had used to listen in on diplomats from the Soviet bloc staying in hotel rooms in the West. The cops gave the CIA two household lamps. The agency's Office of Security installed secret transmitters inside. There was one problem — the D.C. police had a longstanding written policy against "the use of wiretapping or 'bugging' equipment by members of the Force." Police Chief Jerry Wilson took care of that. At the end of March, he rescinded his predecessors' orders. Kolego then placed the lamps at the home she shared with her movement colleagues.

Armed with their shards of hearsay and snatches of conversation, but no direct evidence, the agents busted into the Lanier Place house. Bacon wasn't there. One of her nine roommates said she was working at the Mayday office on Vermont Avenue. As soon as the agents were gone, Bacon's friends alerted her. She quickly dialed her lawyer, who told her to lie low until he could arrange a proper surrender.

Bacon figured she had time to go back to her house at Lanier Place to collect some things. As she was packing, four gray sedans pulled up outside. The agents spilled out. Someone in the house ran to warn her: "Leslie, get the fuck out, the FBI is here again!" Bacon bounded up the stairs and then slipped onto the roof through an access door. The FBI men hustled up and captured her just before she could leap to another building. "We picked up that object we were looking for," one agent announced triumphantly into his radio mike.

Bacon was held in lieu of $100,000 bond and within a couple of days was flown to Seattle, where a grand jury had already been empaneled to investigate American radicals. She would be held for more than two months. Among the other Mayday activists who would soon be subpoe-

naed in her case were Stew Albert, Judy Gumbo, and the two young men
who'd been riding with them in Judy's Volkswagen in Pennsylvania.

JUST AS HE had been out of town for the big Saturday march, Nixon
was planning to be gone during the Mayday protests. He would retreat to his Western White House. He invited along his two best pals —
Charles "Bebe" Rebozo, a Florida businessman, and Robert Abplanalp,
a New York entrepreneur who had grown rich by inventing the modern
aerosol valve and who often hosted the president at his private island in
the Bahamas.

Nixon was trying to look beyond the perilous week. He pushed his
China initiative ahead. On Wednesday morning he held a long meeting
with Kissinger and Haldeman to discuss a secret note from the Chinese
prime minister, Chou En-lai, which had been delivered by Pakistan's am-
bassador in Washington. Chou was responding to Nixon's initial note
in December. The Chinese official wrote that restoration of relations
would require "direct discussions between high-level responsible persons of the two countries." The president and his men decided the next
step would have to be a clandestine visit to China by a trusted emissary.
Ultimately that would be Kissinger.

As for the upcoming protests, the president told his personal secretary, Rose Mary Woods, he was tired of "these bearded weirdos." And
she agreed, saying the campers at the park would be better off "if parents or the Communist Party or somebody weren't giving them money
to keep them going."

The rest of Nixon's men were occupied with how to keep order on
Mayday. Bud Krogh was no longer the sole White House point man on
the matter. He had bequeathed much of the job to another young aide
— a blond, bespectacled lawyer whom Bud himself had recruited to the
White House — so he could put more time into his other projects, particularly the fight against drug trafficking and addiction.

This new man covering the protest was John Dean, who came over
from the Justice Department. He had impressed Bud over the past two
years with the way he handled negotiations between Justice and antiwar
groups on the details of demonstration permits — parade routes, medical tents, and security arrangements. Dean's main job at Justice involved
the department's dealings with Congress. As far as Dean was concerned,

he'd been tapped for demonstration duty because, to his buttoned-up, crewcut bosses at Justice, his ever-so-slightly-longer haircut made him more relatable to the protesters.

At first Dean had been wary about moving to the White House. Nixon's West Wing had a reputation for rigid hierarchy and infighting. One sunny afternoon, Bud took Dean out to his favorite bench on the Mall to talk him into it. Bud was unaware of an asterisk on Dean's record — that Dean had gotten into a dispute over an alleged conflict of interest and had been fired from his law firm before joining Justice. When the formal offer from the White House came down, Dean couldn't refuse a job with the title of counsel to the president, one that would no doubt open doors someday to a lucrative private career. It's just too good for the résumé, he thought. While Bud considered Dean a smart guy — "He's terrific conceptually," he told an assistant — not everyone shared his enthusiasm. Dean is a "very smooth, cool, calculated, tough and probably very self-centered individual," one White House official said in a memo. "I have a real hang-up with the degree of commitment that he would have to the President — something that I feel that the person who is Counsel to the President should have. Maybe it is his arrogance — I am not sure." Another aide thought Bud was demonstrating a pattern of poor judgment, falling for what he saw as Dean's transparent effort to land just such a job.

Dean didn't lack for self-confidence. Having gone to law school at Georgetown and served briefly as an aide on Capitol Hill, he believed he knew the town better than anyone in the president's circle, except for the president. ("I was often stunned at how they didn't understand how the city really worked. That's one of the reasons they got into the trouble they got into," he would observe years later.) Dean envisioned an expanded role for the counsel's office, akin to a small firm within the White House, serving both the staff and the president. He became an empire builder, seeking to grow his staff and their office space.

Dean and Bud remained friendly though not close. They went sailing once on Dean's boat in the Chesapeake Bay. Both were single — Bud separated, Dean divorced — and drove cool bachelor cars, a white BMW 2002 for Bud and a maroon Porsche 911 for Dean. Slicker than the straight-laced Bud, Dean was more apt to bend the rules. When a woman he wanted to date declined to give him her unlisted phone number, Dean used the White House operator system to track her down. He got reprimanded by his bosses for refusing to wear a flag lapel pin at the office. And Dean didn't always fit in with his peers either. While Bud socialized with a group of young White House aides who gathered periodically at a Georgetown bar for gossip and mutual support, Dean (along with Charles Colson) had been secretly blackballed from the sessions.

Like Bud, Dean sought Nixon's approval, joining the competition that would soon enough destroy so many of the president's aides. "I could play the admiring staffer in my own way," he later admitted. To his second wife, Maureen, he would fantasize that if things went well there could be an ambassadorship to a small country in his future. Bud began to worry that Dean might fall under the hard-line influence of the archconservative Tom Huston, who had been assigned to Dean's staff, and might help Huston push the president to take harsher measures against his critics.

On Wednesday, while Nixon focused on China, Dean surveyed federal agencies on how they planned to deal with the coming disruption. The consensus, he reported to his colleagues, was that the government would conduct "business as usual" all week. Furthermore, he said, officials in federal offices were not to hold "rap sessions" with demonstrators, or even allow them inside their buildings.

Dean laid out some additional proposals for undermining the traffic blockade the protesters planned for the following Monday, May 3. Could they get the city to impose a curfew? Could they ask Congress to pass an emergency law making it a felony to stop traffic in D.C.? Could they seek an injunction against the demonstrators? Bud, recalling the debacle over the Vietnam vets and their Mall campsite, scribbled next to the latter idea, "Tried this. Credibility shot."

On Dean's first day at the White House, Bud had given him a tour and showed him the secret tunnel that ran into the basement from the Treasury Department next door. Bud explained it would bring troops to the White House if a protest went off the rails. So far, the plan for Mayday called for Police Chief Jerry Wilson to handle any trouble with his four thousand police officers. The only certain role for the military would be having the air force fly over the city and take aerial photos for a crowd count.

But the use of troops wasn't ruled out, not by a long shot. Late on

Wednesday afternoon, Kleindienst, the deputy attorney general, met with military brass to discuss ways, as a confidential army memo describing the meeting put it, "to combat dissent in Washington." Among other things Kleindienst said he would look into was whether a deployment of troops would violate an 1878 law intended to prevent the military from being used for civilian law enforcement. Kleindienst seemed certain he could secure a legal opinion from the Justice Department that endorsed the president's authority to call in the armed forces if he thought it necessary. That decision, Kleindienst said, would be "predicated on the evaluation of the threat" during the weekend before Mayday.

13

Public Defenders

THE CHIEF JUDGE OF THE D.C. SUPERIOR COURT WATCHED WITH trepidation as the rising tide of the Spring Offensive crept closer. While police had busted hundreds in the first couple weeks of action, the arrests had mostly been scattered and hadn't placed an undue burden on his three dozen judges. Now the protests were getting more intense. Arrests were beginning to add up.

And there might be a huge wave on Mayday.

Judge Harold H. Greene was a bespectacled man of short stature and thinning hair in his late forties, whose soft-spoken voice never completely shed the inflections of his native Germany. He brought some unique qualities to the challenge ahead. He was no stranger to the tension between individual liberty and the power of the state; his was among the Jewish families who had escaped the Nazis. In America he graduated first in his law-school class and went to work for the Justice Department under the Kennedy administration. There he played a crucial role in drafting the landmark civil rights laws of the 1960s, after which Kennedy's successor, LBJ, appointed him to the bench.

Greene had been named chief judge in D.C. in 1966. Two years later, when the assassination of Martin Luther King Jr. set Washington ablaze, he could see the flames from the window of his chambers. Some six thousand people were arrested in those riots, but Greene refused to cut corners, like courts in other cities trying to quell civil disorders; there, suspects were hustled through arraignment in clumps, as many as fifty at a time. Greene ordered judges to consider each case on its merits and kept the courtrooms open around the clock for days. "A mass arrest situation, like no other we are likely to be confronted with, is a test of our commitment to the rule of law," Greene explained. The courts, rather than participate in the "symbolic burning of individual rights, should be islands of calm in the midst of the hysteria."

Greene added, "Whenever American institutions have provided a hysterical response to an emergency situation, we have come later to regret it."

NOW ANOTHER EMERGENCY situation was upon Greene. In the run-up to the coming week's traffic blockade, portions of the Mayday Tribe were hitting one government agency a day with a demonstration. On Wednesday night, April 28, Greene's docket was loaded to bursting with 260 defendants who had been detained that morning after lying down in front of the headquarters of the Selective Service, the agency in charge of the military draft.

In large part they owed their presence in court to a change in policy made by Police Chief Jerry Wilson. It had long been standard procedure to allow people booked on minor charges to pay ten dollars in collateral at the station house and go free until a trial date. They wouldn't even be fingerprinted or photographed. If they failed to appear for trial, they would simply forfeit the money. The idea was to keep small stuff—like people picked up for being drunk and disorderly—from clogging an already overburdened judicial system.

But Nixon's men saw the collateral policy as a revolving door that could allow thousands of protesters to break the law and immediately return to the streets to cause more trouble. They pressured the chief to rethink the system.

Jerry might not have been happy about it, but he agreed anyway. On Wednesday he told his station clerks to stop accepting collateral, meaning the detainees had to be held in the lockups until they could be arraigned. Lawyers for the demonstrators, who had dispensed advice based on prior practices, were furious. One accused the police of breaking faith with the organizers and "precipitating another Chicago."

To handle the load and prepare for more arrests, Greene, as he had during the King riots, put the court on a twenty-four-hour schedule for the duration — three shifts of four judges each. The defendants were to be represented by a group called Georgetown Legal Interns, five volunteers from the law school with experience in handling matters related to political demonstrations.

Those arrangements were made before Jerry's policy change sent the flood of clients their way. On Wednesday, the young lawyers were quickly overwhelmed. Adding to the confusion, each judge had his own idea about how high to set bail, meaning some defendants got out quickly while others charged with the same offense would languish in jail.

The chaos and uncertainty were too much for the small band of Georgetown volunteers. They decided there was no way to provide an adequate defense, and they refused to handle any more cases. And they walked right out of court.

Suddenly Greene had dozens and dozens of defendants behind bars without any representation. He knew of only one way to get large numbers of attorneys familiar with the system quickly down to the courthouse. At nine o'clock that night, he told his chief clerk to get Barbara Bowman on the phone.

WHEN THE CALL CAME, Barbara Allen Bowman was getting ready for her weekly commute from Washington to New Haven, where she was teaching a course at Yale Law School. If she got a window seat on her flight each Thursday from National Airport, she could survey a city laid out like some kind of architectural model, white buildings and monuments in a neat row, the parallel lines of the National Mall stretching from the river to the Capitol, the broad avenues sliding away gracefully, diagonals that disappeared in the haze of the horizon. From that distance there was no sign of the messy turmoil of life outside the clean geometry, the other Washington that Barbara confronted every day as head of the District of Columbia's Public Defender Service.

At the age of thirty-three, Barbara was an anomaly. Just a decade out of Yale Law herself, she was now running one of the largest agencies in the United States that was dedicated to providing representation to people who couldn't afford their own lawyers. She had close to a hundred people working for her, almost all of them men, in a cramped warren of offices a couple of blocks from the courthouse. All their indigent clients came from the city's mostly black residential neighborhoods, plagued with poverty and crime.

Perhaps 4 percent of all the nation's lawyers in 1971 were female. While elite schools had graduated small numbers of women for decades, hardly any had made partner at a major law firm. Most were shuffled to sedate fields like real estate or probate law, or even into jobs as legal secretaries or librarians. Those turned down as inadequate by the big firms included the future Supreme Court justices Sandra Day O'Connor and Ruth Bader Ginsburg, as well as the future attorney general Janet Reno.

Among those women of Barbara's generation who did attend law school, few chose to practice criminal law. As much as she relished the rough-and-tumble of criminal trials — in fact had never wanted to do anything else since she was a kid — that wasn't what Barbara was teaching at Yale. It had happened like this: A delegation of that university's female law students had twisted their dean's arm to create a new course on women and the law. They heard about Barbara and came down to Washington to meet her. They took her measure. Then they went home and demanded that Yale bring Barbara to teach.

Barbara wished she could have turned them down. Her life and work were complicated enough and, despite the fact that she had given a similar class at Georgetown University, this wasn't really her area. But how could she refuse these young women? Barbara could see they were nothing like what she and her classmates had been.

It wasn't that they were smarter. Barbara was a brilliant student. She attended the University of Pennsylvania's then separate College for Women on a full scholarship and graduated as valedictorian in 1960. In her commencement speech, she called her Cold War generation "the confused, other-directed apathetic victims of possible annihilation" who as yet "haven't found any new insights to replace the old ones."

She became one of thirteen women accepted to Yale Law that year. Like all coeds, Barbara unquestioningly wore garter belts or girdles, skirts and stockings to class, and rented a room off campus; the elegant suites attached to the classroom building, complete with fireplaces, all went to young men.

Her male classmates occasionally remarked that she had better excel because "you're taking a man's place." She did. She won the all-important moot court competition, a first for a woman at Yale. Shortish in stature, with a head of tight dark-brown curls, prominent eyebrows, and expressive eyes, she was already splendid on her feet, even though she had to argue the side of the red-baiting House Un-American Activities Committee in a First Amendment case. (She bested a fellow student named Eleanor Holmes, who would become her roommate and lifelong friend, as well as a towering figure in civil rights and women's rights, and eventually, as Eleanor Holmes Norton, D.C.'s delegate to Congress.)

While Barbara would wind up near the top of the class of about two hundred students, during her three years at Yale she never dared venture inside one single professor's office — all of them were male, and most conducted themselves like monarchs. For the entire first year she never volunteered to speak in class without being called upon. She couldn't get over the fear she'd ask a dumb question and thus make all women look bad.

This new generation of women, though, had nothing *but* questions. They blew into the Ivy League like a gale force, planning to use their degrees to fight against poverty and injustice, for the rights of blacks and peace activists, but above all for the rights of women. They wanted to know: "Where are women's legal issues in these courses? Why aren't there any women teaching here?" They scared Barbara to death, using curse words all the time. They scared her, but she thought they were wonderful.

Barbara had long resisted being cast as a role model or a pioneer for women, feeling it would somehow diminish what she'd accomplished. Popular culture reinforced her view. The glib shorthand for feminists was still "bra-burners." One newspaper profile of Barbara described her as "hardly the classic women's lib type. She is feminine, soft-spoken and seemed to be wearing all her underwear."

But now something big was happening, and it felt like her duty to join in.

COMING OF AGE, Barbara had been concerned about poverty, not gender. The justice system needed to protect the weak and vulnerable. Growing up in a three-story Victorian house outside D.C., she inherited this mission from her father, also a defense lawyer, though sometimes a struggling one. He liked to say his job was to comfort the afflicted and afflict the comfortable. Barbara drew moral force from her mother too, a deeply Christian woman who prayed for her husband to stop drinking.

After law school Barbara had returned to Washington in 1963 to take a clerkship with a federal judge. All the talk in the hallways was about the big civil rights march coming up in August on the National Mall. One of the organizers was her Yale roommate Eleanor Holmes, and among the speakers was to be the charismatic preacher from Atlanta, Martin Luther King Jr. The other clerks planned to watch from the courthouse windows, but Barbara wanted to join in.

Her colleagues warned her it might be too dangerous. The civil rights leader Medgar Evers had just been assassinated in Mississippi, and police in the South had long been attacking demonstrations with dogs, clubs, and fire hoses. But Barbara went anyway. She marched down the Mall in a red-and-white-striped skirt and a white blouse, the first time she'd ever been among such an overwhelmingly black crowd. It felt exhilarating, more like a joyous Sunday School picnic than a protest.

Along with hundreds of thousands of people, she was lifted up by King's "I Have a Dream" speech and came away even more determined to defend the oppressed. But when her clerkship ended, the only good job she could find was with the private law practice of Edward Bennett Williams, whom she had met once when he visited Yale.

Already a legendary criminal lawyer, Williams — tall and magnetic, with wavy reddish hair — was well on his way to becoming one of Washington's most respected and prominent citizens, a mover and shaker, trusted adviser to millionaires, senators, and presidents. But in those days his clients still came largely came from the underworld. As he grew more respectable, Williams didn't want to devote as much time cozying up to gamblers, pornographers, and Mafia lowlifes, so he frequently left customer service to junior associates like Barbara. As part of her job she would fly around the country on first-class tickets, visiting bookies in places like Las Vegas and Houston. She once escorted a serial bank robber to a session with a truth-serum doctor. She regularly kept one of Washington's gambling kingpins out of jail. She went to boxing matches; she loved running into her shady clients, who would throw their arms around her and introduce their hotshot young lawyer to all their cronies.

After a couple of years Barbara had grown restless. Williams wouldn't let her run her own cases. The people who hired his firm, he told her, would never accept a woman as a trial lead. At the same time she longed for a more deserving clientele. And increasingly she would clash with the emotional Williams. She once watched in terror as his face flushed red with rage because she took a pro bono case representing antiwar pick- eters without telling him first. Williams, while having no problem rep- resenting Mafia chieftains, corrupt politicians, or union bosses, never wanted to take on political activists.

It was clearly time to move on. There was an opening at the place where she really wanted to work. She happily left behind Williams's cushy office near Farragut Square, with its fat paycheck and luxury travel, for a rundown Washington legal aid office above a dive bar, where drunks passed out on the heating grate outside.

Finally she could handle her own cases. Nervous on the morning of her first trial, Barbara got out of bed and promptly threw up. She was defending a kid caught red-handed, walking down the sidewalk with a transmission from a stolen silver Jaguar. But she had learned a lot watch- ing Williams take care of moneyed clients. There was no reason poor people shouldn't get the same kind of defense.

The prosecutor wouldn't offer a plea deal. He looked at Barbara, a thin, nervous girl, twenty-eight years old. She was already a curiosity in the courthouse. Who leaves a job with the most prestigious criminal firm in the city for this?

Her young client had no prior convictions, and she maintained that since the cops couldn't find the tools he supposedly used to dismantle the engine, no one could be sure he was guilty. At the back of the oth- erwise deserted wood-paneled courtroom sat an old client, a gambling kingpin — a fan who came down just to watch her performance.

Barbara was baffled to see the seats fill up as she gave the jury her closing argument. The judge hearing the case, William Bryant, who had been a partner in the city's most prominent African American law firm, called Barbara over to the bench to explain. Word had circulated around the courthouse; people think this must be a really huge trial if the king- pin is watching.

Much later the gambler was captured on an FBI wiretap marveling that the defendant "had the transmission on his shoulder, and she got him off!"

. . .

NOW IN APRIL 1971, Barbara had a decision to make. After hearing from Judge Greene that Wednesday night, she hung up the phone and explained to her colleagues what they were being asked to do — to handle the defense of hundreds or possibly thousands of antiwar protesters. They debated whether to accept. Should they take on such people, when the agency had been established with public funds to serve the poor of Washington?

True, with its size and scope, the D.C. Public Defender Service was blazing a trail for courts in the rest of the country. But it had been around for less than a year in its present form. Maybe they shouldn't give their critics any reason to snuff out the experiment.

The agency owed its existence to a happy historical accident, a collision of two opposing forces. The first was a revolution in criminal justice at the hands of the Supreme Court. Under Chief Justice Earl Warren, a string of important rulings had been reshaping the practices of police officers and the rights of suspects. In 1957, the court unanimously overturned the conviction of Andrew Mallory, a nineteen-year-old who had been sentenced to death for rape in D.C. His lawyer was William Bryant, the same man who would become a judge and preside over Barbara's first trial. The justices agreed with Bryant that the confession given by the defendant was unconstitutional because he had been locked up for many hours without a formal charge, subjecting him to mistreatment by police eager to extract an admission.

Another momentous decision came down just as Barbara was finishing up law school in 1963. In *Gideon v. Wainwright,* the justices held that a Florida man convicted of breaking into a poolroom was improperly denied a court-appointed lawyer. When the states failed to provide poor people with representation, the court said, it turned the guarantee of a fair trial into a hollow promise. (These cases were followed by the *Escobedo* and *Miranda* decisions, which, respectively, ruled that police couldn't question suspects without giving them a right to consult a lawyer and that suspects must be fully apprised of their constitutional rights when arrested.)

In D.C., the import of *Gideon* had been clear. The courts had to provide for the poor. But how? All the city had was a small legal aid agency with six lawyers to represent indigent clients.

Then came the second opposing force. When Richard Nixon won the presidency, he had to follow through on a promise to break D.C.'s crime wave. He had been among the politicians, cops, and right-wing groups encouraging a backlash against Warren's decisions, which, they argued, put handcuffs on the police. Rural highways were dotted with billboards reading "Impeach Earl Warren."

The first daily news summary to land on his desk in January 1969 steeled Nixon's determination. It listed recent acts of violence in the city, including a purse-snatcher who had thrown an eighty-one-year-old woman down a flight of stairs. The president scribbled a note on it: "We are going to make a major effort to reduce crime in nation—starting with DC!!" Weeks after that, while Nixon and his entourage were jetting across the Atlantic on a victory lap, meeting with European leaders and the pope, a burglar broke into the Watergate apartment of his longtime private secretary, Rose Mary Woods, and made off with more than $5,000 worth of jewelry. "This brings the problem of crime very close to home," the White House press secretary told reporters.

So, early on, the Nixon administration sent a package of anti-crime measures for D.C. to the Democratic Congress. It called for pretrial, preventive detention of suspects for up to two months, at a judge's discretion. It gave police the right to go through a door without identifying themselves, the so-called no-knock rule. It allowed prosecutors to charge sixteen-year-olds as adults, provided for mandatory and longer sentences for some crimes, and greatly expanded the authority for police wiretapping.

Police Chief Jerry Wilson confided to his White House liaison, Bud Krogh, that he thought the bill was mainly political window dressing for Nixon, more than anything that would really help fight D.C. crime. Bud didn't disagree. Others slammed the proposal in public. The Senate's leading constitutional expert, the North Carolina Democrat Sam Ervin, pointed out that one reason American colonists rebelled was because the king tried to impose no-knock warrants upon the people of Boston. He called Nixon's bill "literally a garbage pail of some of the most repressive, nearsighted, intolerant, unfair and vindictive legislation that the Senate has ever been presented." One former aide wrote the president to say that even some business executives believed the administration "is intent upon the diminishment of civil liberties in the nation, and has already to some extent succeeded."

Those voices would drown in political realities. The nation's "epidemic of fear," as a House sponsor of the bill called it, made voters likely to punish anyone opposing a tool to restore order. One of Ervin's fellow Democrats put it this way: "No Senator can possibly accept the kind of appalling statistics that we have had in the District and around the country without feeling that we have to act . . . We have to do whatever it takes, pay that price, even though the price may be the surrendering of some of our liberties."

One section of the law called for reorganizing and expanding the antiquated D.C. court system. That opened up the opportunity for Barbara and her deputy at the little legal aid agency to pitch Congress on a hugely expanded operation, which they renamed the Public Defender Service. The bill passed. The big infusion of money allowed them to hire forty new lawyers, ten investigators, and a half-dozen social workers, plus lots of support staff.

Filling the jobs turned out to be no problem. Applications flooded in. As Barbara would soon discover on her return to Yale, the sensibilities of the Sixties had transformed many top law schools. Suddenly they were churning out people whose ambition was not a cossetted corporate job but a spot in the trenches, fighting injustice. (At the time such a choice didn't mean giving up as much in starting salary as it would in later years.) The portion of Yale's graduating law-school class going into private practice dropped from 41 percent to 31 percent. The best and brightest pursued public-interest careers rather than prestigious Wall Street firms. "The people who weren't successful in law school had to go to Sullivan & Cromwell," recalled one Yale graduate who joined Barbara. Newly minted lawyers who landed the nation's most sought-after clerkships, on the Supreme Court, applied to the Public Defender when their tours were up. Barbara had to turn some away.

So, as it turned out, Judge Greene was calling on some of the best-educated and most charged-up young lawyers in the country to deal with what no one yet knew would become one of the most intense courtroom battles in the history of the city of Washington.

BARBARA DIDN'T HAVE a natural inclination to turn her agency into a legal shop for antiwar protesters. Her lawyers certainly didn't need any new work. Their cases already consumed them. With the fate of dozens of impoverished clients on their shoulders at any given time, they worked late into the nights and on weekends. "Filing a motion, finding a witness, or stopping by the jail for a chat on a Sunday afternoon could mean the difference between victory or defeat, between freedom and prison," as Barbara would say.

Many of her lawyers felt as she did, driven by what she called a repressed rage at a system stacked against the poor and black. They loved being members of a kind of Justice League, putting their passions into the right place at exactly the right time, as cataclysmic changes rocked society and the law. Most of them were in their twenties and thirties, and they socialized together, often slept together. Before she ascended to the top job, Barbara had married the man who originally hired her at legal aid, a star defense attorney named Addison Bowman. He had since moved on to a teaching post at Georgetown Law.

Her devotion to the job inevitably pressured their marriage. Another source of tension had come when Addie, as he was known, took one particular case. Nine Catholic leftists had broken into the D.C. outpost of Dow Chemical, destroying files and wrecking office equipment to protest the company's manufacture of napalm, the flammable chemical being dropped by U.S. forces in Vietnam. Barbara had been perturbed when her husband joined the defense because it seemed like the wrong use of his talents; the white antiwar people had a lot more options than the poor people of Washington. She was annoyed to see his trial strategy concerning the "D.C. Nine" discussed amid clouds of marijuana smoke. Addie was on the way to transforming himself from public defender to movement lawyer, growing his hair long and donning black turtleneck sweaters. Eventually he got arrested himself for civil disobedience at the White House.

While the case of the D.C. Nine was being heard, Barbara was across the courthouse, representing a client accused of first-degree murder. She won her case; Addie lost his. It would prove to be the beginning of the end for them.

Nevertheless, things seemed different to her in the spring of 1971. Some of her lawyers resisted jumping in. Barbara could be a bit dictatorial, she'd later admit. Abruptly she cut off debate. "We're doing it," she told them.

Barbara let Judge Greene know they would move ahead. Then she led the public defenders down to the courthouse, where they worked for six hours processing the 260 protesters arrested at the Selective Service. About half of them were arraigned, with some able to post bond, before everyone ran out of steam and went home to catch a few hours' sleep.

14

Barricades

BY MIDWEEK NIXON'S MEN WERE DEEP INTO THEIR OWN AR-rangements for Mayday. As they conferred on all the options, John Dean, one of the White House lawyers, had jotted down an important question: "Should the president be in White House on May 3rd?" Nixon hadn't been sure what to do, how best to signal his pretense of indifference, even though he had gone so far as to put details of Mayday into his personal calendar. "John, P plans keep changing," one aide wrote to Dean in exasperation.

In the end, they all agreed he should again get out of town before the weekend. Instead of Camp David, where he had holed up during the April 24 march, he'd go to California and meet up with his cronies, Rebozo and Abplanalp. They would play some golf and watch some movies. On the way to his San Clemente compound, the president would swing twenty-five miles south to visit Camp Pendleton, to welcome the First Marine Division home from Vietnam. That would, he hoped, remind the country that he was winding down the war, even as legions of the impatient and the unwashed clogged the streets of the capital.

The president made one other attempt to deflate any excitement over the protest. He called a televised press conference for Thursday night. The day before the appearance, he put off some other business to prepare. He pestered his chief of staff, phoning Haldeman six times, the last call coming close to midnight. The next morning he picked up again, obsessing over the mechanics. Should he use a podium or a raised platform?

Go with makeup or not? Blast the demonstrators or act detached? For sure he couldn't pretend to understand their motives, to praise them even faintly. "In my case it would just sound hypocritical as hell," Nixon said.

When he walked into the East Room of the White House to face the reporters, many of whom he correctly believed were sympathetic to the protests, the first question was "Do the antiwar demonstrations . . . influence in any way your Indochina policy?"

This gave Nixon his opening. He stated that he intended to stay the course of gradual troop withdrawals, and at the same time professed to respect the opposition. "I would not want to leave the impression that those who came to demonstrate were not listened to," Nixon said, adding wryly, "It is rather hard *not* to hear them, as a matter of fact."

Later in the session, though, he revisited the subject with a harder edge. He allowed that Americans who'd been watching television news over the past couple of weeks might believe that Washington was "somewhat in a state of siege." He wanted to "correct" that impression. "Let me just make one thing very clear," Nixon said. "The Congress is not intimidated, the president is not intimidated, this government is going to go forward." What's more, he promised, "those who come and break the law will be prosecuted to the full extent of the law."

As Nixon packed for San Clemente, the Pentagon confirmed that the number of Americans who had died in combat since the start of the war in Vietnam had just passed the 45,000 mark.

DOWN BY THE RIVER, the Mayday Tribe piped Nixon's press conference through loudspeakers set up on a flatbed truck. The crowd, numbering now about two thousand, booed the president. When it was over, Rennie Davis climbed the platform to again encourage peace and cooperation in the camp, to exhort his listeners to try to live like the Vietnamese. They were "a precious, gentle people who have a lot of lessons for us here in this park."

The big field had been filling up all week. It was now clear the encampment would be larger than the settlement erected there by the Poor People's Campaign in 1968. That had been a gathering of more than two thousand blacks, whites, Mexican Americans, and Native Americans who had marched to D.C. seeking better jobs, schools, and housing. The architect of the campaign had been Martin Luther King Jr., and after his assassination his colleagues decided to carry on. Like the Mayday group, the Poor People's Campaign had also secured a permit for West Potomac Park; they had erected tents, wooden shacks, and lean-tos and had given a name to their shantytown — Resurrection City. But when they overstayed their permit, police forced them out, often roughly, and demolished their shelters.

That recent history wasn't far from the minds of the Mayday leaders. For now, things felt celebratory, with Frisbees flying, dogs fetching, and a rising sense of mission. Each evening there were more campfires. Parking spots became scarce as the Volkswagens rolled in from all over the country. Newcomers had to hunt harder for open patches for their tents. Nearby liquor stores were running out of Boone's Farm Apple Wine, the best-selling cheap alcoholic beverage in the country, a counterculture favorite that could add a sweet overlay to the buzz from pot or hallucinogens. There was no way for Park Police to manage the sheer scope and variety of highs, so they studiously ignored it all.

The atmosphere remained anarchic; anyone with something to say could stroll up to the mike, though they had to squeeze their spiels between the parade of jets roaring overhead from Washington National Airport just across the river. One member of the Raintree Tribe, the group doling out the meals, got up to announce that "people might as well get used to the fact that there aren't steak and eggs. Vegetables and rice is a perfectly okay diet." A young mother asked the crowd, "Has anyone seen a five-year-old boy with bare feet called Adam?"

When no one was making announcements from the stage, rock songs blared from the main speakers as well as from the tents, where campers turned up their radios or clicked compact cassettes, the latest portable music technology, into their tape players. Drugs and music enhanced each other. Psychotropic substances awoke some kind of internal tuning fork that resonated best with the tones of an electric guitar. Rock was the soundtrack of the war too. GIs stationed in Vietnam were buying hundreds of thousands of cassette players.

There were plenty of impromptu live performances at the camp. One young guitarist put his own words to a Bob Dylan song:

Hey government employees, don't you even care?
Better take the day off Monday, you ain't goin' nowhere.

At one end of the field, a group of movie and video enthusiasts set up a truck with a makeshift screen. In the early morning hours of Friday, they showed some inspirational films. One was *The Battle of Algiers*, a chronicle of an urban guerrilla uprising against French colonialism. Government officials had long worried that the movie provided a tactical blueprint for U.S. radicals like the Black Panthers and the Weather Underground. Some White House aides had gone to see it in Georgetown right after the fugitives' bomb factory blew up in Greenwich Village; one subsequently wrote to Bud Krogh, suggesting tighter security for White House tours, given that the film depicted how easy it was for "well-dressed Arab women carrying handbags" to plant explosives.

At West Potomac Park, the protesters also screened footage of an American uprising. This was a homemade documentary of the 1969 clash between the authorities and the counterculture over a patch of land owned by the University of California in Berkeley. It had been the most violent Bay Area confrontation since the bloody 1934 general strike on the San Francisco waterfront. Berkeley activists and back-to-the-land types had tried to transform the muddy vacant lot by laying sod, planting flowers, and hammering together swing sets. It came to be called People's Park. The university evicted the kids and erected a high chain-link fence around the perimeter. Thousands marched to retake the park. Police and sheriff's deputies fought them off with riot guns full of buckshot, killing one bystander, blinding another, and wounding some fifty protesters. Governor Ronald Reagan called in the National Guard to occupy the city. A helicopter sprayed clouds of tear gas down onto a student rally. Battles raged on and off for days.

Reagan's extreme crackdown on People's Park earned the episode a legendary status in the counterculture. It also inspired a song that embodied the angst of a nation that seemed to be unraveling. As Mayday approached, the song remained near the top of the Pop, Soul, and R&B charts. It had been the brainchild of the bass singer for the Detroit soul group The Four Tops, which was playing a gig near Berkeley when the violence broke out. The singer, Renaldo Benson, "started wondering what the fuck was going on," as he later told a music journalist. "One question leads to another. Why are they sending kids far away from their families overseas? Why are they attacking their own kids in the street?" Eventually the outline of the song would find its way to perhaps the greatest of the Motown artists, Marvin Gaye, who would render it immortal. Its title was really the question on everyone's lips, no matter their politics: "What's Going On"?

THOSE WATCHING THE SCREEN carefully during the People's Park film might have noticed, among the young people digging flowerbeds, a broad-shouldered man with blond curls, wearing his trademark paisley shirt. Stew Albert had been instrumental at People's Park. In his capacity as a reporter for an underground newspaper, the *Berkeley Barb*, he attended the original community meeting where the idea emerged to beautify the ugly space. Stew wrote it up, triggering the chain of events that led to the violent suppression. Now Stew was camping with the Mayday Tribe at West Potomac Park, feeling some of the same vibe as in Berkeley. His closest ally, Jerry Rubin, also was on the scene. They swallowed some psychedelics, and Stew wandered among the tents in a state of "elevated, romantic innocence."

Stew thought he saw his estranged Yippie comrade Abbie Hoffman walking toward him. He wondered at first if he might be hallucinating. Stew and Hoffman hadn't been on good terms since the Chicago conspiracy trial, mainly due to the bitter feud between Hoffman and Rubin over control and publicity of the Yippies. Yet Hoffman had always admired Stew, considering him a "big golden bear who lumbered through the movement with the determination of an NFL lineman." This really *was* Hoffman in front of Stew. He also was tripping. They stopped, stared at each other in silence, and then embraced. The Spring Offensive was bringing together all the far-flung pieces of the antiwar movement. It had to be a good omen.

At the edges of the crowd, experts in nonviolent resistance were teaching small groups of protesters techniques to keep the peace during the traffic blockade, now only four days away. To one minister visiting the park, this called to mind a line from an old gospel song: "I'm going to lay down my sword and shield, down by the riverside."

One man from the Quaker Action Group instructed his trainees what to do if they came upon a dangerously tense situation Monday: "If you see people are nervous — a little singing, a little hugging, a little contact will help."

• • •

LET THE PRECIOUS, gentle hippies hug and sing and get stoned on the riverfront. Nixon and his men didn't believe for a minute that next week would be some kind of Woodstock, nor did they desire that it unfold that way. They grasped at rumors of violent intent — one aide jotted down some theories of what the protesters might do: "1. Oil burning. 2. T.N.T. 3. Cut tire. 4. Helium balloons." The president privately derided the "soft-headed liberals" in the press and even within his administration who saw the activists as "a lot of nice little peace-loving kids." He told his chief of staff, "You know that's not true, not the bunch that are here now." If only they would prove him right by starting to break things. "I want them to do something God damn it!" he said.

Nixon was trying to thread a very small needle. For his purposes, the protest needed to be just troublesome and violent enough to obliterate any favorable opinion the average American might hold about the April demonstrations. "The next group comes in, just does a little destruction, that's about what we need now," he had told his closest advisers when he was most despondent about the vets' protest. But at the same time, Mayday couldn't be robust enough to cripple the government's operations, because that could make Nixon look weak and incompetent; worse, it might reenergize the protesters. He had to seem outwardly indifferent, while not letting the government's preparations and response prove that the movement was in fact a threat. His chief of staff laid out the danger of saying the wrong thing and publicly predicting violence: "If there isn't violence, then we look foolish, and if there is, we're charged with fomenting it. Thing to do is wait, and if there is violence, then we can play the hell out of it."

So the president had to undermine the protesters and be ready to hammer them down, while keeping both tactics from the public. His desires trickled down through the ranks of his administration. His top aides had begun the week by devoting almost one entire day to strategizing.

On Thursday, the five phone lines listed to the Mayday organizers at their Vermont Avenue building were summarily cut off. The Chesapeake and Potomac Telephone Company claimed a billing problem. It would have been hard to find someone in Washington who believed this was a coincidence.

Then the question had to be answered — should the army be called in?

Walking point on this matter was Richard Kleindienst. As deputy attorney general, he was the second-ranking official in the Justice Department. Kleindienst had met with military officials on Wednesday evening to make sure they would be ready to intervene. The administration wasn't saying troops would definitely be called into the streets. The decision would hinge on the likelihood that the avowed traffic-blockers would become a violent mob that police couldn't handle, the kind of "insurrection" or "domestic violence" that the Constitution recognized as legitimate reasons for the United States to deploy its armed forces against its own people.

Long before the antiwar movement, presidents had summoned troops to quell internal disorders and rebellions fomented by groups ranging from Pennsylvania whiskey distillers to Southern white supremacists during Reconstruction. Such deployments took place in a legal gray area. This fuzziness had roots in the ambivalence of the framers of the Constitution. While the founders were determined not to leave room for executives to act like the monarchs and dictators who used soldiers to suppress their populations, they also recognized that a crisis might call for "no remedy but force," as Alexander Hamilton put it. Still, Hamilton added, "the means to be employed must be proportioned to the extent of the mischief."

Lawmakers tried to set rules to deal with such situations. Over the nation's first century, though, the practice grew progressively looser, reaching the point where low-level federal officials, such as U.S. marshals pursuing fugitive slaves, were summoning the military on their own. So Congress in 1878 had tightened things up again, passing the Posse Comitatus Act, which said federal troops could be used only on presidential authority, and then only after the president issued a proclamation in advance, explaining the reasoning, followed by an executive order. The idea was to ensure the situation was dangerous enough for extraordinary measures. LBJ had issued just such a proclamation and order before calling in the military to restore order in D.C. after the King assassination.

In the spring of 1971, the risks of mixing armed troops and demonstrators were fresh in everyone's mind. It had been only a year since National Guardsmen had fatally shot four students on an Ohio campus. Since then, a new governor had taken over in that state. Speaking to a radio reporter — coincidentally on the same day Kleindienst was developing his military response for Mayday—the governor cited the lesson of an "almost total breakdown" of discipline by the guardsmen at Kent State. "I hope everyone in public office has learned," the governor said, "when using troops among our own civilian population that they must be used with the greatest restraint and the greatest discipline."

Perhaps this caveat was on the minds of the military leaders meeting with Kleindienst, because they pushed back on the deputy attorney general. Since Nixon had made no proclamation about Mayday, they asked, how could he bring in troops without violating the Posse Comitatus Act? Don't worry about it, Kleindienst said. He would check with his legal authority on the matter.

Kleindienst was certain that this legal authority, a lawyer in the Justice Department's Office of Legal Counsel, would present no obstacle. The young man was Kleindienst's Arizona protégé, William Rehnquist. Rehnquist was serving Nixon well. He had found a legal basis for the president to send U.S. troops into Cambodia, the incursion that, among other things, had led to the deaths at Kent State. And Rehnquist already had angered civil liberties advocates on the question of domestic deployment. Back in 1969 he had written a memo saying that the Secret Service had authority to call in the military to protect the president and that Posse Comitatus "does not apply."

On Thursday, Rehnquist reiterated what Kleindienst had implied to the army officials—the law didn't apply in this situation either. "The president has inherent constitutional authority to use federal troops to ensure that Mayday Movement demonstrations do not prevent federal employees from getting to their posts and carrying out their assigned government functions," Rehnquist wrote.

The army had its marching orders, except for one thing: the Justice Department's reasoning didn't persuade the deputy secretary of defense, David Packard. The next day, he told Kleindienst he was dubious. If the president wanted to get the military involved, Packard insisted, he should do things by the book—issue a proclamation declaring the Mayday folks a threat to national security, then sign an executive order federalizing the National Guard and calling in the troops.

By now, Nixon and his entourage had left Washington and landed in California. Kleindienst got on the phone to Nixon's chief of staff at the Western White House to tell him about the speed bump in the plan. Haldeman was furious. No way would they follow the procedures the Defense Department demanded. That's "just what we don't want to do," he said. It would make the president look like he was directly involved in foiling the protesters. He promised Kleindienst that the White House would set Packard straight, make sure he understood that "the president was ordering that the troops be provided without proclamation." As would become much clearer in the future, the usual rules didn't apply to this administration.

EVEN WITH THEIR PHONES cut off, the protesters kept to their schedule of hitting one government agency each day. Thursday it was the Department of Health, Education, and Welfare. Mayday militants joined black protesters led by Hosea Williams, a leader of the Southern Christian Leadership Conference, the civil rights group that had been co-founded by Martin Luther King Jr. The forty-five-year-old Williams, an ordained minister from Georgia who had been in Memphis when King was assassinated in 1968, was now carrying forward King's exhortation that the black movement should oppose the war as well as fight for freedom at home. (Not only was the war cruel and immoral, King had said in the spring of 1967, but it was disproportionately "taking the black young men who had been crippled by our society and sending them eight thousand miles away to guarantee liberties in Southeast Asia which they had not found in southwest Georgia and East Harlem." King's decision to publicly condemn the war immediately cost him support in parts of the black mainstream and the white. The NAACP branded it a "tactical mistake." The *Washington Post* editorialized that King's criticisms were full of "sheer inventions" and declared that he "has done a grave injury to those who are his natural allies . . . He has diminished his usefulness to his cause, to his country and to his people.")

THE FEDERAL HEALTH DEPARTMENT'S officials agreed to speak with the activists in the building's auditorium but erected a wooden wall to keep them out of the main hallway and offices. "The wall must go!" shouted the activists, scuffling with security guards as they tore down the barricade with a crowbar. They carried some of the pieces down to the street and started out for the White House to "dump the wall on

Nixon's lawn!" More than two hundred people were arrested, including Williams.

On Friday a large portion of the West Potomac Park campers, about two thousand of them, marched to the Justice Department at midday. They formed a ring around the building, blocking the entrances and chanting, "Stop the war!" and "Fuck the FBI." Employees returning from lunch had to climb over rows of demonstrators, both seated and prone, or get the guards to drag them through the mass. More arrests ensued: 370 people were taken to jail.

Inside the Justice Department, the deputy attorney general was assuring reporters the government would be ready to meet Mayday with a total of seventy-three hundred police and National Guardsmen. He scoffed at the predictions of Rennie Davis and others that there might be enough protesters on Monday to close down the government. That was "just a lot of hot air," Kleindienst said. "At worst this is going to be nothing more than a minor irritant." Kleindienst didn't mention his behind-the-scenes work to get the regular military involved, in addition to the guardsmen—because if this was going to be minor, why call out the troops?

Kleindienst's boss, Attorney General John Mitchell, was out of town, giving a speech at Southern Methodist University in Dallas, where he took the occasion to blast the news media. He said the nation was "inviting great danger" because of a "sharp erosion in professionalism among many who have the public's ear." Some reporters, the attorney general said, have a "shocking contempt for truth, and cheap surrender for instinct."

The White House at least got some decent press Friday night. The network news shows covered Nixon's visit to Camp Pendleton. The president rode out on the back of a jeep to review the returning division while fighter jets screamed overhead. To date, thirteen thousand marines had been killed in Indochina. But, Nixon told the lineup of fifteen hundred of their brethren, "You left a South Vietnam with the South Vietnamese now assuming the major burden of their own defense." He denounced "those who would have us leave Vietnam even if it means turning the country over to the Communists."

On CBS, the reporter Dan Rather (later to become Nixon's on-air nemesis during the Watergate scandal) had an even more glowing report on how the returning warriors greeted their leader. "Some of those who made it back hoisted their commander in chief to their shoulders and carried him off the parade ground," Rather told the viewers. "No one in his official entourage could remember the last time that Mr. Nixon was carried away joyously on anybody's shoulders."

But it turned out he was rather wrong about that. It was a problem of perspective. From the spot where reporters were contained, they couldn't see that the president was above the marines' heads not because he was borne on their shoulders. He had been perched on the platform of his slow-moving jeep.

BY FRIDAY EVENING, the campsite at West Potomac Park held about six thousand people. They were a diverse mix of college students, old radicals, gay activists, Hare Krishnas, and some of the Vietnam veterans who'd stuck around Washington for more than a week. While the crowd was mostly male, women formed a substantial minority. One thing the multitude was not: racially diverse. Anyone standing on the platform could view a sea of white faces.

"Do people realize that Washington, D.C. is seventy-three percent black?" asked one African American man who strode up to the microphone. "Black people certainly aren't being represented here in this camp."

While black activists had long helped stoke opposition to the war on campuses and off, they generally hadn't participated in large numbers in the big antiwar rallies in the nation's capital. Groups such as the National Black Anti-War Anti-Draft Union, which was founded in 1968 and emphasized the disproportionate conscription of young African American men in the war's early years, tended to focus their work on their own communities.

Some black organizers in Washington, though, had made connections with the Mayday Tribe. They aired pleas for donated food on three black-oriented radio stations. They collected fifty pounds of beans and fatback, then taught the white kids how to cook them. Mary Treadwell, a prominent local organizer, helped pass out the food and then toured the park. "We were the wave of the Sixties and these kids seem to us to be the wave of the Seventies," she said. "We don't want them to think that the wave of the Sixties had turned its back on them."

It almost felt like a pep rally. Only a few observers noted the inherent contradiction at the Mayday camp. The government was both the target of the protest and the enabler of the gathering. Unlike their original plan to place scattered settlements in Rock Creek Park, the Mayday leaders had concentrated their troops in one small area, hemmed in on three sides by a river, a highway, and the Lincoln Memorial. If anyone wanted to round them up, it would be a simple task. For one newspaper columnist, it called to mind the last French military outpost in Vietnam, surrounded and overrun by the enemy: "It kind of looks like Dien Bien Phu."

Yet the euphoria in the impromptu speeches drowned out those worries, as arrivals continued to stream in. "You better be prepared for more people. We're going to have a city!" exulted one man.

And another climbed the stage to assure the crowd "there is NOT going to be a bust. People have talked to the cops and they say no. Would people please not go spreading rumors?"

MAY
1971

Participants in the traffic blockade of May 3, 1971, aim to bring the nation's capital to a standstill to underscore their opposition to the Vietnam War.

15

War Council

Saturday, May 1

RICHARD KLEINDIENST, THE DEPUTY ATTORNEY GENERAL OF the United States, looked around at the dozen men he had summoned to the headquarters of the Department of Justice and gave them dire news. They had vastly underestimated how many Mayday protesters would show up in Washington.

The police had sent up helicopters borrowed from the army that Saturday morning to take pictures of the gathering at West Potomac Park. They confirmed that as many as forty thousand people were already camping there. That was ten times the number the men at the table had expected, and lots more young people would likely arrive over the weekend. If most of them joined the blockade on Monday, police could be facing mobs two thousand strong at each of the twenty-three traffic circles and bridges to be targeted by the radicals.

Kleindienst had told the press earlier in the week that the claims of Mayday organizers were a lot of hot air. A day ago he had promised a group of Republican senators that no military presence would be necessary. But now he admitted to the room that he'd been wrong, that the government now faced a "different kind of situation requiring different planning." It was high time to mobilize the soldiers in force.

For Kleindienst, the looming challenge presented a chance for a kind of vindication. The blustery and profane Arizona lawyer, who carried himself in an imposing stance that looked "like he was about ready to tee off," had been one of the inventors of law and order as a national Republican campaign issue. He had warned for years that the New Left would grow increasingly dangerous if the government didn't come down hard. Even peaceful dissent troubled him, as just one step on the inevitable road to violence. He alerted his son, a Harvard student, that Kleindienst would stop writing tuition checks if he participated in any antiwar protests.

Not long after joining the Nixon administration, Kleindienst told a reporter that protesters who interfered with the business of regular folks "should be rounded up and put in a detention camp." (The Justice Department later said he was misquoted and had only meant that all available tools should be used to preserve order.)

Kleindienst nurtured a particular disdain for one of the Mayday leaders. He could never forget the jitters he felt on a fall day in 1969 when he stood on a balcony at Justice and watched "ten thousand revolutionaries" marching right toward him from the National Mall. They were led by David Dellinger, who was protesting his indictment for the clashes at the Democratic National Convention in Chicago; Kleindienst thought Dellinger "delivered one of the most fiery revolutionary speeches ever given" to a big Washington crowd.

A violent Mayday, a mass frontal assault on the machinery of government, would prove he'd been right all along about the threat.

Kleindienst was used to meddling in the business of keeping order in the city. He once proposed that the National Guard in the District of Columbia get special badges identifying them as "the president's militia." And he had been the one trying to prod Police Chief Jerry Wilson into hiring two thousand new cops to chase crime off the streets.

Now here was Jerry again, one of the dozen members of Kleindienst's war council, trying to figure out how to cool things down without overtly opposing the plan to turn his city into an armed camp.

This was not the first meeting Kleindienst had convened on Mayday. He had called many of the same members of the group together a few times already, starting early in the year, when he first heard that Rennie Davis was talking up the idea on campuses around the country.

Jerry found these meetings tedious. Everyone felt the need to speak up and drone on even if they had nothing to offer. Jerry didn't dislike Kleindienst, exactly. He was a man's man, a bawdy guy you could joke around with. Still, the chief could see why not everyone appreciated his style. Once, after resolving a small dispute over a demonstration permit with Philip Hirschkop, who often handled such details for antiwar groups, Kleindienst offered the lawyer a celebratory whiskey in his office. Turning down the drink, Hirschkop, a former paratrooper and no stranger to offensive language, was disgusted when the deputy attorney general snapped, "What are you, a fucking fag?" A police department lawyer considered Kleindienst smart but not thoughtful: "You never wanted to ask him a question because he gave you an answer right away. He wasn't reflective." John Dean, who had worked for Kleindienst, found him to be someone who "shoots from the hip . . . whether he had enough facts or not."

Still, Kleindienst was more complicated than he appeared. Born and raised on what he called a "bleak plateau" at the edge of the Navajo Nation reservation in Arizona, he had been a teenager when his mother died, and he learned to speak some Navajo from a Native American housekeeper. He worked as a fry cook to help support the family. He was elected president of his multiethnic high school as an outsider, backed by Hispanic, black, and Native American students. His mother's deathbed wish had been that her precocious son would aim for Harvard, which he did successfully.

After law school he became a mover in Arizona politics. Kleindienst helped drive the significant backlash against the social changes of the Sixties. Like other Republicans in the American West, even the many who grew up in comfortable circumstances, he shared some of Nixon's core beliefs. They considered themselves self-made men, closer to the land, less reliant on the government or charity to get by, favoring a personal grace in public while celebrating intolerance in private. It was a political brand that would wrest control of the party from its Eastern moderates.

Kleindienst hooked up with Barry Goldwater's presidential campaign in 1964 and joined Nixon's in the next cycle. Nixon admired him as a "nut-cutter." The president sometimes wondered aloud if Kleindienst wouldn't have been a better attorney general than his taciturn boss, John Mitchell.

In the matter of Mayday, Mitchell had delegated his authority to Kleindienst, who effectively outranked everyone around the table. That put him in charge of keeping order during what Kleindienst later would call a time of "more active demonstrations than any other period in our nation's history." In his view, a government underreaction would lead to the "rule of the mob."

JERRY WILSON THOUGHT Kleindienst was exaggerating the threat. This had happened before. Kleindienst enjoyed friendly gambling. He liked to challenge his underlings to golf-putting contests in the conference room or to rounds of gin rummy. He kept running accounts of who was ahead. Once he had bet the chief a half gallon of Teacher's Scotch on who had better advance intelligence on a particular demonstration — the police or the Justice Department. Jerry won. He wasn't much of a drinker. The bottle sat in an office drawer, lasting for years.

The chief just didn't believe you could really make the argument that the Mayday protesters were fundamentally different than the people who'd been keeping police busy for the past couple of weeks. True, there had been hundreds of arrests for sit-ins and the minor destruction of property. But the overwhelming majority of the demonstrations had been peaceful.

In that belief, Jerry was in an overwhelming minority. Those in the room had all kinds of reasons for wanting the protesters out of the park. Among them was a ramrod-tall lawyer who also worked for Kleindienst at Justice. Harlington Wood Jr. had been born in Springfield, Illinois, like his hero, Abraham Lincoln, and resembled Honest Abe well enough to play him on stage one time, to decent national reviews. He was a straight arrow revolted by the "nudity, immorality and promiscuous behavior" by the Potomac. Wood was a lifelong polo player, so even worse for him was seeing the Mayday Tribe messing up his beloved fields by the river.

Ehrlichman also believed the camp was "an unwholesome situation." It could only mean trouble that the Tribe was consuming "a great amount of apple wine."

Yet the reports about West Potomac Park didn't worry Jerry very much. The leadership was decentralized. The laid-back crowd wasn't indulging much in the usual anti-police shouts of "Pigs!" And face it, the objective of Mayday was not to overthrow the government but to paralyze Washington for a day or so. Jerry could remember the huge blizzard that blew into the city a few years earlier, closing roads for days, crippling public transport, and triggering food shortages that led to some rationing. It was hard to imagine Mayday's impact could be as bad, no matter how many protesters it pulled in.

Before the Spring Offensive, Jerry had asked his officers to research occasions when the military was summoned to Washington. Their memo reported that six people had died in 1857 when marines fired on a mob of thugs who had been hired by the Know Nothing Party to block naturalized citizens from the city's polling places. In 1919, some two thousand soldiers were called in after four deadly days of armed clashes between blacks and whites, during which thirty-nine people died. Then there was the looting and arson that followed the King assassination. Mayday couldn't compare to those crises. A military occupation now might only make things worse.

Even armed with history, Jerry would have no luck changing minds in a room full of Nixon loyalists. They had all heard the president, directly or indirectly, order the protest crushed. Nixon swatted away a proposal by his aides to get Congress to pass an emergency law making it a felony to stop traffic in Washington. It would be better to let the Mayday Tribe launch their protest in full, let them infuriate the city's commuters and the press before snuffing them out. "I'm not too sure we give a damn" if they create a big mess in the city, said the president. "Let them stop the government. Let them screw the things."

Nixon had even mused about how gratifying it would be — "a good fight" — if his men could get some pro-war military veterans or union members to "move in" on any protesters who brandished a Vietcong flag. "If you have a fight about that," Nixon said, "that is on the plus side . . . one way to dramatize our story."

At the Justice meeting, one of the loyalists at the table was Rehnquist, the Justice Department lawyer who had authored the opinion that the president could call in the troops without following standard procedure.

Rehnquist, forty-six, with long bushy sideburns balancing a receding hairline, had done a stint in Washington in the 1950s, when he clerked at the Supreme Court after graduating from Stanford Law School. Since returning to town in the Nixon administration, he had made no effort to hide his contempt for antiwar activists who employed civil disobedience. He labeled them the "new barbarians." In a letter to the *Washington Post* he lambasted the newspaper for encouraging judges to expand the constitutional rights of classes of people who, in Rehnquist's view, were equally undeserving: criminal defendants, pornographers, and demonstrators.

For Rehnquist, this meeting and the hours before Mayday would leave a profound impression. Years later, when he became Chief Justice of the United States, he would dream of a side gig as a writer of Washington thrillers, trying to reproduce the tension of the Mayday preparations in the opening chapter of his first novel.

But for now, his focus was to thwart the protest. The government needed a strong response, a plan on the "high side," said Rehnquist. He backed Kleindienst's proposal to double the number of troops prepositioned in Washington to ten thousand in all.

The army men at the meeting continued to be skeptical. One pointed out that since Kleindienst had already gone on the record saying Mayday was a lot of hot air, putting thousands of troops on the streets might leave the administration open to charges of overreaction and repression. Perhaps better to wait, and see how bad it really gets.

The third hard-liner in the room was John Ehrlichman, who was Bud Krogh's boss in the White House and the president's top domestic policy adviser. He had listened in growing frustration to the reticence of the military men. He suddenly exploded. The president wanted the city kept open at all costs, he snapped. If there aren't enough troops in hand, "it will mean some asses."

As things stand now, he said, the government was "aiding and abetting" the protesters in their illegal plan. President Nixon, he said firmly, was ready to go further than anything that had been proposed so far.

THE MEETING AT JUSTICE broke up late in the morning, with Kleindienst promising to call the dozen men back later in the day to nail down their counterattack. At noon, church bells began tolling all over the country. They rang for an hour. It was an act endorsed by almost every major religious domination in the country — twenty-seven of them, basically everybody but the historically conservative Southern Baptists — in a "call to repentance and renewal" over the war in Vietnam.

"Our nation is sorely troubled," their statement read. "We believe this to be a sickness of the spirit. A major cause is the continuing war in Southeast Asia. Although substantial numbers of combat forces have been withdrawn, the war has been widened geographically and additional thousands of combatants and non-combatants are being killed . . . We are all sick at heart." The bells rang in "mourning for those who have already died in Southeast Asia and our sorrow that the killing continues."

IF PEALS OF CHURCH BELLS reached the river, they were drowned out by jets overhead and the recorded music blaring from the speakers at West Potomac Park, where everyone anticipated the start of an all-day, all-night rock concert. It was the event Rennie Davis had always believed would draw the biggest possible numbers for Monday's activities. It would epitomize the fusion of the radicals and the counterculture, the singularity dreamed into existence by the Yippies.

With his partner David Dellinger still lying in a hospital bed in Georgetown, Rennie was feeling more of the burden of Mayday leadership, and he was showing the strain. His parents, visiting from their retirement home in Florida, worried that their son's voice sounded thin and raspy. He was so busy he skipped meals, munching on nuts and raisins to keep up his energy. They bought him a new sleeping bag so he wouldn't get chilled in the park. Invited to a working lunch at the *Washington Post*, Rennie, with his poise and knowledge, won over the skeptical editors and reporters who came armed with questions about Vietnamese history to trip him up. He turned on the charm for the paper's publisher, Katharine Graham, and "I could see she was impressed by me," he recalled. Graham told her colleagues to back off and "let Rennie eat." She thought he looked particularly skinny.

The Mayday organizers had set their sights on some of the biggest stars of rock and soul who were sympathetic to the antiwar movement. They bandied the names around as come-ons during interviews and campus appearances. "There are over thirty rock groups, Arlo Guthrie, Peter Paul and Mary, Mother Earth, Aretha Franklin and loads of people. James Brown just announced two days ago that he's going to go there," Abbie Hoffman promised a crowd at the University of Oklahoma. But many of the groups were put off by the government's predictions of violence, and it probably didn't help that Mayday's main booker of music talent, Leslie Bacon, had been pursued by the feds and ultimately arrested. Instead of making deals with the musicians, Bacon was at this very moment being questioned in Seattle by the grand jury about the explosion at the Capitol. "They seem to think she knows some people that may have been involved in the bombing," her lawyer told reporters.

A slew of local acts had signed on for the concert in the park, but many of the national ones melted away. The most widely recognized band to show was the Beach Boys. Their surf-music roots had won them wild success in the early Sixties, but as rock grew less sentimental and more visceral, the Beach Boys had been elbowed toward the sidelines, toward irrelevance. (It would be years before their innovative 1966 album, *Pet Sounds,* would be recognized as one of the signature musical achievements of the era.) So now they were on a survival tour, trying to build a countercultural audience. Mike Love, the band's co-founder, agreed to play as long as they were the opening act, so they could finish "before any riots broke out." The band had appeared unannounced the previous week at the Fillmore East in New York, to jam half the night on stage with the San Francisco psychedelic group the Grateful Dead. The night before Washington, they had played to a sparse crowd in Baltimore. Their manager made the dubious claim that this was only because many of that city's young people had decamped to D.C. for Mayday.

The Beach Boys were hardly political, but a huge outdoor audience was not to be passed up.

When they took the stage Saturday afternoon, they found, instead of a riot, fifty thousand people lolling around in the field, singing, chanting, and ingesting tabs of Orange Sunshine LSD sold by itinerant vendors. As the band lit into its vintage hit, "Good Vibrations," the music seemed to break free of its sunny California origins and charge up the euphoria of the gathering. Even a hardened group of self-described anarchists sitting aboard a Hertz rental truck banged the poles of their black flags to the beat.

After the Beach Boys, the parade of bands continued all afternoon and into the night, interrupted only by the occasional announcement or freelance protest. Late in the afternoon, Stew's ex, Judy Gumbo, led some one hundred women on a run through the park. They held hands and shouted, "Hey, ho! Male chauvinism has to go!" They rushed the stage and Judy grabbed the mike. She proclaimed that for all its success, there was much not to like about the gathering. Women were being mistreated, and some reported they had been sexually assaulted. Bands and their lyrics were sexist. Others lined up to speak in favor of alternative lifestyles. "My name is Chamomile, and I'm a male transvestite," said one. Chamomile addressed the men in the crowd, telling them that by growing their hair long "you've gone halfway, and now you should put on a dress and see what that's like, because until you put on that dress, none of us are gonna be free."

The more traditional radicals, who never warmed to the Yippie notion of cultural fusion, felt the gathering was losing focus. One looked on in disgust as Jerry Rubin, certainly on hallucinogens, kissed the ground, threw a handful of dirt up in the air, and proclaimed, "This is better than Woodstock." One hippie argued to an impromptu meeting that Mayday should be a celebration rather than a demonstration. "If we want to send out a vibration of peace, harmony, and love," he said, "the only way we're going to do that is by living it."

Meantime, as the park continued to fill up, Rennie and other Mayday organizers debated their plans for Monday. To make the best use of the swarms of protesters, they decided to reduce the number of rush-hour targets from twenty-three to nine. The nine sites included the four bridges over the Potomac.

Mayday's success or failure would rest largely on an innovation in tactics. The organizers were merging two ideas. Unlike the classic sit-in, in which protesters would take over forbidden property and go limp when the police showed up to haul them away, people of the Mayday Tribe would block a street or bridge, then flee when the police came, so they could hit another spot, preserving their momentum. These so-called mobile tactics had been employed with some success before, most notably during the 1967 protests against the draft in Oakland, California. The second idea was that demonstrators would divide themselves into "affinity groups" or "life action teams," small knots of eight to twelve activists who could move swiftly and collectively without orders from above. The strategy stemmed from "a major shift in activist temper," the journalist and activist L. A. Kauffman later observed. Protesters, she wrote, had "growing disdain for national organizers, movement celebrities, and structured leadership, all of which were felt to stifle creativity and action."*

As a Mayday training manual put it, "a small number of people who get to know each other can give a great deal of moral support to each other in a potentially frightening action." Another leaflet encouraged "variety and inventiveness in tactics" as long as they were nonviolent in character. As insurance, training in nonviolence was to continue at the park right after the rock show.

WHILE THE MUSIC wafted over the Potomac, Richard Nixon held a news conference at his Western White House. He had rehearsed with his aides what to say about the protests. At first Nixon wanted something tough, like "the party's over and it's time to draw the line," but they talked him out of it. He agreed to a more statesmanlike sound bite: "The right to demonstrate for peace abroad does not carry with it the right to break the peace at home." He used it twice with reporters.

The aides were trying to obscure the fact that Nixon, from three time zones away, had been keeping a very close eye. He was doing his best to stay on Washington time so he wouldn't miss anything important, going to bed by 7:45 p.m. About ninety minutes into the Saturday morning war-council meeting, John Ehrlichman had stepped out to give him a briefing by phone.

The president asked to speak with John Mitchell. According to Nixon's private account of the conversation a couple of weeks later, he told the attorney general to bust them. His advice went beyond the encampment to the coming weekday protests: if they don't clear the streets, arrest the whole damn lot.

Nixon also asked to speak with Jerry. When the police chief got on the line, Nixon told him directly what he so far had said only to his inner circle: he wanted the city kept open on Monday. Yes, sir, Mr. President. What else could he say?

Ehrlichman informed Nixon that the military option was now in

---

* L. A. Kauffman, *Direct Action* (London: Verso, 2017), 12. In her comprehensive deconstruction of the tactics of Mayday, Kauffman posits that its American roots lie in an attempt by civil rights activists to block traffic outside the 1964 New York World's Fair.

place. David Packard, the deputy secretary of defense, had dropped his request for a presidential proclamation. On Saturday Packard's office sent the generals a memo: "The president has ordered me and I accordingly direct you to deploy and use such numbers of the armed forces of the United States and of the D.C. national guard as may be required to protect against unlawful interference with the property, personnel and functions of the federal and District of Columbia governments."

The Pentagon soon announced that it had put troops in "raised readiness" at seven bases up and down the East Coast to prepare for possible "illegal conduct" during Mayday. The generals ordered 850 marines from Quantico and one thousand army troops moved to Fort Myer right across the Potomac from the capital. Seven military helicopters would be positioned just south of downtown.

All this was just the beginning, but it worried even the conservative writers for the *Washington Star*'s editorial page. They had been blasting the Mayday Tribe for days. Yet the militarization of the city was more than they'd bargained for. "It is our earnest hope that it will be possible for the police to handle the situation this week without the assistance of the Guard or federal troops," the editorial read. "We do not want a Kent State here."

NIXON'S MEN RECONVENED at the Justice Department at about five o'clock. A few new faces were in the room, including John Dean from the White House. By now, Kleindienst had put the latest plan in place. The military and police forces would be intimidating, and large enough to deal with almost any level of trouble. All told, they'd have seventeen thousand cops and troops available on Monday.

That was good. But what about this weekend? Kleindienst had fallen in love with another idea that had been proposed at the end of the morning meeting.

The impulse had come originally from his Phoenix protégé — Rehnquist, the future chief justice. These people are trying to disrupt the government, Rehnquist had argued, and they shouldn't be indulged. Something should be done, some kind of diversion to prevent them from using the camp as a staging area, to stop the traffic blockade before it got started. The group immediately began discussing whether police could "arrest them on the spot on a trumped-up charge."

It had been Ehrlichman, the president's chief domestic policy aide, who ran with Rehnquist's notion. He'd been in regular touch with Nixon and suggested that the government simply revoke the permit it had granted to Rennie Davis and his crew. Then send in the police for a surprise raid. They would throw the radicals right out of West Potomac Park and force them to scatter through the city, looking for a place to bed down. "Many will go home Sunday if they see we mean business," Ehrlichman believed, and that would be the end of that.

And, he said, there would be a bonus: A raid would prevent the Mayday group from holding its nonviolence training on Sunday, further undermining their discipline and organization in the coming days.

Above all, Ehrlichman would note, "surprise was the most important element."

The chief of police had listened with discomfort to the plan when it arose at the morning meeting. He had pointed out that the camping permit had been properly granted and that so far, at least, the protesters were exercising their right to nonviolent dissent and peaceable assembly. In addition, he told the room, dispersing protesters through the city, carrying all their righteous anger about the raid, would sow its own seeds of trouble, possibly followed by a police response that would raise allegations of repression.

His arguments had fallen on deaf ears.

Perhaps Jerry wasn't pushing back as hard as he could have. But his job depended on the White House, which occasionally had snapped the leash to remind him. Bud Krogh had once called Jerry to say Nixon was unhappy that the police chief had given a public talk about declining crime rates and had failed to mention the president. From then on Jerry made sure he included at least five Nixons in every speech. He also made sure to get Nixon an official police ring after the president visited headquarters.

There was one other thing Jerry couldn't be expected to forget — the people in the room would have a big say in whether he might get a much bigger job, as director of the FBI. The talk that he could take over from J. Edgar Hoover had been teed up again just the night before. The ABC-TV commentator Howard K. Smith said on national television that Jerry Wilson was "possibly the best policeman in the nation" and "would be a fine replacement" for the FBI chief.

So Jerry went along with the majority. But, he said, they needed some pretext to revoke a legitimate camping permit. Perhaps they could cite illegal drug use. Kleindienst agreed. He would have the Drug Enforcement Agency rush dozens of undercover agents to the area to infiltrate the gathering, buy drugs, document their use, and produce reports that later could be used to justify the raid. (The agents would be summoned later that day to the auditorium of the State Department for a briefing before they were dispatched to West Potomac Park. They weren't to bring badges or guns. Instead, each was handed a bent Lincoln penny to show to the cops so they could avoid getting swept up in the arrests. All they'd have to say to the riot squad was "Bent penny!" and they'd be let go.)

One last thing, Jerry asked. Who would take responsibility publicly for the raid if things went south?

As if he didn't know.

Kleindienst replied that it would be presented as a joint decision by the police, the Justice Department, and the Department of the Interior. But it would be Jerry's men who would carry out the raid, and he knew full well he'd be the one taking any hits.

The best he could do was to persuade them to change the timing. Rather than clear the gathering right away, on Saturday afternoon, said the chief, they should wait until dawn on Sunday, after the all-night concert, when everyone would be spent and tired and less likely to resist.

After the war council, Nixon's aides went to work on a cover story for the raid. By seven-thirty in the evening, the press office produced a confidential memo for Ehrlichman and Dean. First, they wrote, the White House must be kept out of it. The public should be told that it was the police who decided to raid the park (never mind any promises to Jerry). "It should be emphasized . . . that the move to clear the park was made with extreme reluctance." The story would be that people were using drugs, that "police had tried to be lenient" but that "the violations became so flagrant and numerous that finally there was no alternative but to act." The press officers suggested that they come up with a fixed number of violations "so as to give newsmen logical peg for leads to their stories."

The press officers further suggested that the police delay any arrests of the Mayday leaders until later in the day, so as not to confuse the matter and give the protesters "an excuse for disruptive tactics . . . such as

Free Rennie Davis." On Monday, if troops had to be used, the decision should be pinned on city officials. All the announcements "should be made by city spokesmen, keeping Federal spokesman in background," advised the memo.

Jerry headed back to police headquarters, where he shut his office door and briefed his top people. He ordered them to mobilize virtually all the city's five thousand cops. He would have to get them out of bed by four in the morning and deploy them in the dark, then make the move at sunup.

At least the park was well suited to a raid. The police would block off the bridge to the south and push the Mayday Tribe in only one direction, out through the streets of Washington. They had cornered themselves in their own Dien Bien Phu after all.

AT THE PARK, the undercover agent John O'Connor ate a dinner of rice and beans along with the hippies and radicals. The music went on. Smoke rose from hundreds of campfires, thick enough to sting everyone's eyes. John made an excuse for leaving, saying he had to get some more supplies.

Instead, he found a phone booth and called the police intelligence office. The atmosphere, he told his handler, really was a bit like Woodstock, with plenty of music and plenty of drugs, but otherwise no trouble.

His boss surprised him. "Don't go back there tonight, 36," he said. Why not? "I can't say," said the detective on the phone. "Don't go back there without checking with us." So John returned to the house he shared with the Vietnam veterans. They still didn't know who he really was, of course. He drank beer and ate pizza with his friends and went to bed wondering the whole time what was up.

16

Revoked

Sunday, May 2

THE BANDS ROCKED ALL NIGHT AND INTO THE EARLY MORNING at West Potomac Park. There were so many musicians and such happy chaos that most of the time no one bothered announcing the group on-stage, and if they didn't identify themselves many in the audience weren't sure who was up there.

One of the invited was the local band Claude Jones (named in honor of their sound technician, who actually didn't play a note), perhaps the best rock group in the Washington region, with a core of enthusiastic fans. They had become regulars at antiwar rallies. The musicians lived in a Civil War–era farmhouse in rural Virginia that was like a big commune, filled with friends and hangers-on. Whenever they got wind that the state troopers might be coming for a drug bust, they buried their stash of pot out back.

Claude Jones had been told they'd go on late Saturday night. It was soon clear that the schedule existed only as an aspiration. No one knew when they'd be called to the stage. The band members didn't mind. They spent the hours wandering the camp, choosing their highs from the smorgasbord of recreational narcotics and flirting with the nurses in the medical tent. Around five in the morning on Sunday it was their turn. The sun wasn't up. On a black moonless night they stared out on a constellation of glowing campfires.

Even without sleep, the band attacked its mix of covers and origi-nals with energy. Around six, the dawn began to glow behind the Washington Monument, and the musicians watched in awe as the faint light slowly revealed how many thousands of people had spread out on the field before them, many just waking up and sliding out of their sleeping bags. One of the Claude Jones singers promised the crowd "just a little music to keep them bones vibrating for a new day," and then, after some soulful strains of his harmonica, launched into one of their favorite Bob Dylan tunes, the waltzy dirge "I Dreamed I Saw St. Augustine." *Come out, ye gifted kings and queens, and hear my sad complaint.* Focused fully on the music, they didn't see a police car parked five hundred yards away on the Memorial Bridge, nor the tall man in a chief's cap who leaned on the wall and watched.

OFFICIAL WASHINGTON HAD been stirring before dawn. Scenes unfolded like a stealth invasion. On the other side of the city from West Potomac Park, military planes ferrying troops from the Eighty-Second Airborne Division in North Carolina roared onto the landing strips at Andrews Air Force Base. They were coming in about every three minutes. About the time Claude Jones took the stage by the river, some two hundred soldiers slipped quietly into the Old Executive Office Building next to the White House.

The army was getting positioned for the Monday traffic blockade. For Chief of Police Jerry Wilson, the action would begin this morning.

Jerry might have been ambivalent about raiding the Mayday encampment, but if they were going to do it, his cops needed to move quickly and cleanly, minimizing the chance for injuries on either side. He had been only half joking when he told the war council that his objective was to get the protesters to leave with smiles on their faces. As a precaution he ordered police boats to patrol the shoreline, so that if the whole thing deteriorated into a stampede, no one would drown in the river. The chief put little stock in the rumors from federal informants that the campers had gotten their hands on dynamite or weapons. But no matter what, his forces had to come in without warning.

Nixon's men held the plan close, keeping it secret not only from the demonstrators, but also from the movement lawyers and city officials whom they had promised to keep fully informed. They didn't alert the local judges either. Even the riot squad wouldn't be told its destination until roll call just before the raid.

Jerry had tried to catch a few hours of sleep at the downtown hotel where he'd been renting a room during the Spring Offensive. He was staying there to be close to the action, leaving his wife, Leona, and their two sons, ages five and ten, back at the house in northwest Washington. At this rate, there was no way he'd be home for their wedding anniversary later in the week.

He had ordered the cops to assemble at four in the morning, outside the multipurpose stadium shared by the Washington Redskins and the Washington Senators, which had recently been named in memory of Robert F. Kennedy. From there, they were being bused to their assignments. The 750 members of the riot squad were stationed near West Potomac Park. Jerry was back in his cruiser before five, as his forces moved quietly through the city. Soon he stood on the bridge and surveyed the encampment. The mist rose from the river and mixed with thick campfire smoke, turning pinkish in the early morning light.

As always the police chief projected calm and probity. This inspired confidence from his men, but it also served to hide the depth of his self-regard and ambition. His portrait on the cover of *Time* the previous year had lifted him to national renown. Now *Life* magazine had been asking to shadow him during the Spring Offensive, to document the almost magical way he seemed to control civil disorder. So Jerry broke his vow of secrecy about the raid. The night before, he had alerted one of *Life*'s Washington reporters, John Neary, who knew Jerry from way back when he covered the police beat at the *Star*. Neary and a photographer would stick with the chief for the rest of the day and beyond.

A little after six, Jerry gave the order. The platoons of white-helmeted riot police, their face visors flipped up, each carrying a baton, moved as quietly as possible to their positions just south of the park. "Tora, tora, tora," the chief said, perhaps a little sadly, echoing the World War II Japanese pilots who carried out the sneak attack on Pearl Harbor. Then he led his deputies into the campground. At Jerry's side, Neary was worried. He had frankly bought into the Nixon line that police faced a mob of hardened and violent radicals. Chicago in 1968 was on his mind. He thought this had a good chance of turning into a bloodbath too.

CLAUDE JONES HAD barely run through "St. Augustine" when the stage manager for the rock concert grabbed the microphone. "People, we have bad news. We have just been told that our permit is revoked!" he said. "Everyone just stay together and stay cool."

Two police helicopters flew in and hovered overhead. As the drowsy campers emerged from their tents and bedrolls, one of Jerry's aides blasted out the official announcement through a loudspeaker mounted to a truck:

> Attention: This is the Metropolitan Police Department. Please be advised that the permit for this demonstration and assembly has been revoked. Further demonstrations and assemblies on these grounds are now unlawful. Everyone on these grounds must leave as soon as possible.

Jerry told the organizers they had until noon. For the next couple of hours, thousands of members of the Mayday Tribe broke into regional groupings to debate, often furiously, what do to next. Should they stand their ground, challenge the revocation and the police? Or leave quietly to fight another day?

On stage, the rattled members of Claude Jones rushed to dismantle their gear and load up their truck. Their manager couldn't believe all the cops. He had been to lots of D.C. protests, but this was the largest mass of riot police he'd ever seen. With their helmets and sticks and tear-gas mortars, they looked like an army of storm troopers.

When the band finally got all the instruments, amps, and sound gear loaded, the keyboardist Mike Henley maneuvered the fourteen-foot box truck out of the park. He was briefly positioned on the road between the encampment and the lines of cops with all their paraphernalia. It suddenly occurred to him — he could twist the wheel, turn the thing sideways across the pavement, run off with the keys, and thus block any police vehicles from getting through. He considered it. He thought about jail.

Then Henley sighed, made the left turn, and headed back to Virginia.

EVEN THOUGH HE had a new sleeping bag, Rennie Davis hadn't spent the night at West Potomac Park. He had gone back to his Lanier Place apartment to bank some rest before the tumultuous week ahead. Shaken awake by the news that the police were moving in, he hurried down to the river in time to plunge into the debate.

The decentralized nature of the Mayday Tribe had many benefits, but Rennie knew the raid exposed one of its weaknesses. Each affinity group was empowered to make its own decision about whether to stay or go. Among them were plenty of hotheads. They'd been stoked by the films about the Algerian revolution and People's Park in Berkeley. Some had already been busted during the past few weeks for other demonstrations, and they had little appetite for meek obedience to the government. Yet Rennie knew that if a sizable number of people stuck around and allowed the police to arrest them, or fought back, the Mayday traffic blockade would be in serious danger of petering out. After all the months of organizing, the last thing Rennie wanted was half the Tribe in jail. There's no way they'd be out on bail in time for Monday morning rush hour. He had to turn the tide of opinion.

Rennie summed it up: "We certainly did not come to Washington, D.C. to fight for a piece of park. We came to shut down the government."

He urged the crowd not to react "in a military way" but rather to think it through strategically. "These fools around us, these police chief Wilsons, these Kleindiensts, these men who command the thousands of troops who are around this city, in anticipation that the government may have to be protected with bayonets from unarmed citizens—they're thinking the military way."

In the end, Rennie's power of persuasion won the day. All but a few hundred decided to clear out and prepare for Monday. "We'll get busted for what we want to get busted for, not 'cause they want to bust us," one young woman declared.

The campers and their vans and VW Beetles began to stream out of the park. The tribe members snuffed out their campfires, dismantled their tents, and stuffed their knapsacks. Trash went into plastic bags. "There's hundreds and hundreds of police at the other end of the park and they all have clubs and they all have guns and they have tear gas," a young man from Poughkeepsie told a reporter from Pacifica Radio. "So we're just going to burn our house to the ground and leave." His affinity group then set their wooden lean-to ablaze.

By the noon deadline, everyone had left but about a hundred people, who sat in one big clump on the grass, surrounded by reporters and police. The cops pulled them one by one, under the armpits and without much resistance, to the waiting buses. They gamely chanted, "The whole world is watching," though it wasn't.

RENNIE HAD HELPED avert disaster. Now he was angry. He charged that the raid was carried out under "virtual martial law." The permit was revoked not because demonstrators violated its conditions but for only one reason — because "too many people are here," he told the press. "Too many people came to shut the government."

The Mayday leader was right, of course, and Jerry knew it. The police chief had been left exactly where he knew he would be — alone to answer the hard questions, no one from the federal government in sight. Reporters asked him point blank if the raid was triggered by the size of the crowd. What could he do? He had to lie. "No," he said. "It was based on repeated violations of the terms of the permit" including "illegal use of narcotics." Then why was it that the Park Police on the scene for the entire week had never warned anyone or arrested a single person for using drugs? Jerry demurred. The reporters pressed. What if there had been only two thousand people, would they still have raided? Jerry stumbled a bit, hesitated, and in the end took some refuge behind the language of bureaucracy: "I was not the sole revoking authority."

A LIGHT RAIN fell as the demonstrators fanned out through the city. Some scuffled with the rest of Jerry's police force, which had been ordered to keep the Mayday Tribe from regrouping at national monuments, traffic circles, or city parks. The cops made scattered arrests throughout the afternoon and evening. Many of the evicted were so frustrated, they headed out of D.C., just as Kleindienst's war council had hoped they would, driving or hitchhiking back to their hometowns.

But thousands stayed, and they set out for the basements of sympathetic churches or to one of the college campuses in town, where a Mayday announcer at the park had claimed they would be welcome.

Great, except they weren't. George Washington University turned most people back from its property. American University did the same, going so far as to erect roadblocks.

An invitation had indeed been issued from the closest campus, Georgetown University. It had come from the student government, however, and not the president's office. The protesters didn't know that. Dozens of their vehicles pulled into the school's main parking lot. They began pitching tents and lean-tos on the football field and the hill near the university's observatory, and crammed into student lounges, until they numbered as many as three thousand.

Georgetown's president was away. His top aides debated whether to call in the police. They were paid a visit by a Jesuit priest who taught at the school, Richard McSorley, a well-known antiwar figure with ties to the Washington elite (he had counseled JFK's widow after the assassination). McSorley had been camping with the Mayday Tribe. Now, still in clerical garb, he steered his bicycle around campus to survey the situation. He rode over to the administrators' offices and implored them not to summon the cops. He convinced them a riot wouldn't look good for the college on television.

So the protesters were able to spend the night. The Raintree Tribe parked its bus on the grounds and cooked everyone rice dinners again.

With most people settled in, the focus returned to Monday's traffic blockade. Weeks into the Spring Offensive, the city's liberal establishment remained skeptical of the protest but had grown more tolerant of its motives. The *Post's* Sunday editorial page wrote, "It seems almost unnecessary to say that the army of anti-war demonstrators who hope to paralyze Washington tomorrow cannot be permitted to succeed." But it added, "There are few of us, we believe, who do not have some sympathy for the way in which these mostly young people have been driven to an act of despair in relation to the savagery and cost of this war . . ."

Dick Gregory, the comedian and activist, showed up at Georgetown and told the park refugees, "You are the soldiers . . . you're gonna meet that monster tomorrow . . . you've got a big job . . . you are the good guys." Rennie and the other Mayday organizers wrote up a new leaflet and rushed to print it. They handed it out all over town and posted it on telephone poles: "Mayday Lives."

David Dellinger, still laid up in the hospital, had previously penned what was both a call to action and a plea for nonviolence. It was published in the newest edition of the Mayday newspaper. "This is one of the most exciting days in history, as Americans begin to express their determination not to be 'good Germans' in the midst of genocide," Dave wrote. He continued:

> The government would like to bait or provoke the protestors into violence. There is evidence that it has infiltrated agents in long hair and freaky clothes, to try to make it appear that the protestors are turning to violence. They may scream "PIG" at the police and guardsmen, or throw things at them, in our name, just as Nixon launches B-52 bombers and anti-personnel weapons in our name. If so we should try to isolate them by maintaining our own good vibes and sticking to our agreed on tactics of non-violent civil disobedience.

LATER THAT NIGHT came the first yellow flag that there might be something untoward about the way the government and the police were handling things.

After clearing West Potomac Park, police had lodged charges of unlawful entry against 166 people. Judges and defense lawyers arrived at Superior Court by two o'clock Sunday afternoon to handle the cases. Hours went by, and not a single defendant was brought in. One judge, suspecting that officials were deliberately dragging their feet to keep the troublemakers locked up, finally issued an order compelling prosecutors to produce the detainees.

Their arraignments started at nine that night and didn't end until five in the morning. Lawyers for the Public Defender Service were on the job. They argued that the police had swept people up haphazardly, failing to distinguish among those snatched as they left the site, those who might just have been bystanders, and those who deliberately stayed put as an act of protest. So challenged, the prosecutor's office quickly dropped charges in all but about twenty of the cases and set everyone else free.

The courthouse was rife with the tension and paranoia of the week, and the anticipation of trouble on Mayday. Some judges dreaded dealing with hundreds of possibly unruly defendants. Separate from the West Potomac Park action, about fifty Quakers had been arrested Sunday afternoon for refusing to leave Lafayette Square, across from the White House, where they were holding a silent prayer meeting. They hadn't filed notice of the demonstration fifteen days in advance, as the

Taking a cue from Hollywood westerns in which settlers circle their wagons against Indian warriors, Nixon's aide Egil "Bud" Krogh Jr. deployed a ring of buses to protect the White House from antiwar protesters. The cordon first appeared at the November 1969 Moratorium march. *Bettmann Archive/Getty Images*

Richard Nixon practiced ruthless politics but also yearned for respect. A year before Mayday, the sleepless and troubled president made a surprise predawn visit, minus his usual security detail, to the Lincoln Memorial on the National Mall, where a hundred thousand people prepared to rally against his expansion of the Vietnam War into Cambodia and protest the killings of four Ohio college students by the National Guard. He struggled to explain his philosophy to young activists. *Bettmann Archive/Getty Images*

David Dellinger helped develop a uniquely American strain of radical pacifism. Above, he stands with Jerry Rubin, in August 1968, as the Yippies nominate a pig for president at Grant Park in Chicago, where theatrics mixed with bloody confrontation during the Democratic National Convention. Almost three years later (below) Dellinger (left) and Rennie Davis (right) would labor to maintain a coalition of dozens of antiwar groups in creating the biggest, most varied protest against the Vietnam War. *Above: Bettmann Archive/Getty Images. Below: Associated Press Photo/Bob Daugherty.*

Just months out of law school, the White House aide Egil Krogh (left, with Attorney General John Mitchell) dealt with an overflowing plate of responsibilities, including antiwar protests, D.C. crime, and drug trafficking. When Elvis Presley appeared without warning at the White House gates just before Christmas 1970 and offered his services as a narcotics agent, it fell to Krogh to escort him to the Oval Office. *Left: White House photograph, courtesy Krogh family. Right: Photo from the Richard Nixon Presidential Library and Museum / Oliver Atkins.*

After the Weather Underground Organization bombed the U.S. Capitol in March 1971, the FBI sought others who might have been involved. Jerry Rubin, Judy Gumbo, and Stew Albert, founders of the Yippies, soon summoned reporters to a news conference. Gumbo said, "We didn't do it, but we dug it." *Washington Star photo by Paul M. Schmick / Reprinted with permission of the DC Public Library, Star Collection © Washington Post*

The Yippie Judy Gumbo was featured on the cover of an underground newspaper that published a guide for participants in the Mayday blockade of Washington. Another member of the Mayday Tribe, Leslie Bacon (right), was seized by the FBI as a material witness to the bomb said to have been set by Bernardine Dohrn (below) and Kathy Boudin, then members of the Weather Underground. *Above, left: Courtesy DC Public Library, Washingtoniana Division. Above, right: Bettmann Archive/Getty Images. Below: Bettmann Archive/Getty Images.*

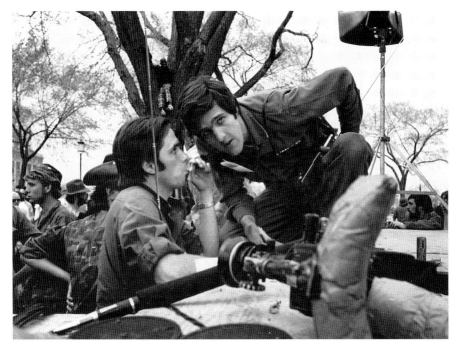

To blunt the success of the antiwar movement's Spring Offensive, the Nixon administration attempted to force members of the Vietnam Veterans Against the War (below, left) out of their temporary camp on the National Mall. One of the group's leaders (above) was a navy war hero named John Kerry. The air force veteran John O'Connor (below, right) kept a secret from his comrades in the group. *Above: © George Butler/Contact Press Images. Below, left: Reprinted with permission of the DC Public Library, Star Collection © Washington Post. Below, right: Courtesy of John J. O'Connor.*

During the week leading up to their traffic blockade of May 3, 1971, antiwar groups targeted federal agencies including the Selective Service System, which ran the military draft. Workers trying to return to their offices after lunch had to be pulled over the crowd by police. *Associated Press Photo/Charles Harrity*

The defense analyst Daniel Ellsberg (kneeling, top right) came to Washington to join the Mayday protest with fellow left-wing academics from the Boston area, including Howard Zinn, to Ellsberg's right, and Noam Chomsky, to his left. Ellsberg had a secret: he'd just given a copy of the Pentagon Papers to the *New York Times*. *Courtesy of the Daniel Ellsberg Collection, Kahle/Austin Foundation*

President Nixon and his inner circle (from left, domestic policy chief John Ehrlichman, national security chief Henry Kissinger, and chief of staff H. R. Haldeman, seated) sought to quell antiwar sentiment long enough to execute their ambitious international objectives. The gathering of the Mayday Tribe in West Potomac Park (below) was one threat to their plans. *Above: Private Collection / Photo © by the Estate of Fred J. Maroon / Bridgeman Images.*
Below: Washington Star photo by Joseph Silverman / Reprinted with permission of the DC Public Library, Star Collection © Washington Post.

Police mounted a surprise dawn raid of West Potomac Park on Sunday, May 2, after Nixon administration officials secretly revoked the Mayday Tribe's camping permit. Some angry protesters burned their makeshift lean-tos. Rennie Davis (below) persuaded most of the thousands of campers to leave peacefully rather than risk jail before the Monday traffic blockade could begin. *Above: Photo © 1971 by Matthew Lewis / Washington Post. Below: Associated Press Photo.*

The D.C. police chief Jerry Wilson was relieved that the West Potomac Park camp was cleared without violence. Nixon's men might be pulling the strings, but the chief knew that if things went bad, he'd be the scapegoat. *Photo by John Shearer / The LIFE Picture Collection / Getty Images*

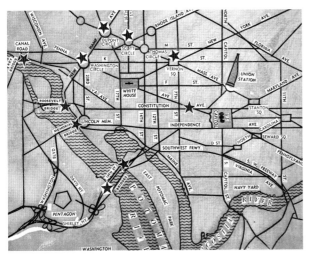

The Mayday Tribe's final map of targets. *Courtesy DC Public Library, Washingtoniana Division*

The cover of its tactical manual. *Author's collection*

On Monday, May 3, Washington came under siege as police and troops moved to stop twelve thousand protesters from blocking traffic. Clockwise from top: Although Nixon's aides called the Mayday Tribe a "vicious and wanton mob," most demonstrators were nonviolent, like the ones lined up here, at the Southeast Freeway. Soldiers protect the Key Bridge. Troops from the Eighty-Second Airborne Division land on the National Mall. Riot squads sweep aggressively though the city's neighborhoods. Military police motor through Georgetown. *Top: Washington Star photo by Joseph Silverman / Reprinted with permission of the DC Public Library, Star Collection © Washington Post. Middle, left: Washington Star photo by Pete Schmick / Reprinted with permission of the DC Public Library, Star Collection © Washington Post. Middle, right: © Ken Light. Bottom, left: Photo © 1971 by Douglas Chevalier / Washington Post. Bottom, right: Washington Star photo by Pete Copeland / Reprinted with permission of the DC Public Library, Star Collection © Washington Post.*

After rounding up thousands of protesters, along with many bystanders who happened to look the part, the police filled all the city's jail cells and looked for places to stash the overflow. Many detainees were trucked to a dusty football practice field next to RFK Stadium (above) and later bused to the Washington Coliseum (below). *Above: Associated Press Photo. Below: Reprinted with permission of the DC Public Library, Star Collection © Washington Post.*

Stew Albert (second from left), one of the original Yippies, was detained with members of his affinity group during the traffic blockade on May 3. He helped another founding Yippie, Abbie Hoffman, to crawl under the fence and escape. *Washington Star photo by Pete Copeland / Reprinted with permission of the DC Public Library, Star Collection © Washington Post*

Those not confined inside the Washington Coliseum remained in cellblocks throughout town, separated by gender. Many were crammed into overcrowded lockups for days without access to legal counsel or anyone else on the outside. *Reprinted with permission of the DC Public Library, Star Collection © Washington Post*

The police and the White House believed that Monday's mass arrests had broken the will of the Mayday demonstrators. But many more showed up on Tuesday, May 4, to protest outside the Justice Department. Minutes after being warned to disperse, another two thousand people were cordoned off and taken into custody. *Washington Star photo by Joseph Silverman / Reprinted with permission of the DC Public Library, Star Collection © Washington Post*

At the age of thirty-three, the criminal defense lawyer Barbara Bowman led the D.C. Public Defender Service. One of the largest such organizations in the United States, it took on the crushing task of freeing the more than twelve thousand people improperly arrested during the three days of Mayday protests. *Photo © 1968 by Bob Burchette / Washington Post*

Attorney General John Mitchell (far right) stands on his office balcony next to his deputy, Richard Kleindienst, watching with approval as antiwar demonstrators are arrested outside the Justice Department. The Mayday protests continued (below) at the U.S. Capitol on Wednesday, May 5, where some twelve hundred more people were rounded up and jailed, despite having been invited to the rally by members of Congress. *Left: Washington Star photo by Joseph Silverman / Reprinted with permission of the DC Public Library, Star Collection © Washington Post. Below: Washington Star photo by Pete Copeland / Reprinted with permission of the DC Public Library, Star Collection © Washington Post.*

As criticism of the mass arrests mounted, President Nixon told Police Chief Jerry Wilson (left) and D.C.'s Mayor Walter Washington to "ignore second-guessers and Monday morning quarterbacks." *Associated Press Photo / Charles Tasnadi*

The Spring Offensive turned out to be the last hurrah of the American antiwar movement. After the protests were over, the leaders, including Rennie Davis (left), Stew Albert, and Jerry Rubin, went their separate ways. *© Leni Sinclair*

The Mayday Tribe slogan. *Author's collection*

Police snared more than twelve thousand antiwar protesters during the three days of the Mayday protest in Washington, loading their prisoners onto buses bound for lockups around the city. The mass arrest remains the largest in U.S. history. President Nixon's reactions to the protests of 1971 helped sow the seeds of his administration's demise. *Washington Star photo by Bernie Boston / Reprinted with permission of the DC Public Library, Star Collection © Washington Post*

rules for that spot required, and the police told them it was an unlawful assembly.

When they got to court, the Quakers were represented by Michael Wald, one of the public defenders. A "very uptight judge" got the case, and she called him up to the bench. She was worried about potential violence in the courtroom. "Mr. Wald, can you control your clients?" she asked him earnestly. An astonished Wald replied, "They're Quakers, your honor!"

The proceedings continued well past midnight, but they came off without trouble. At the end, the judge told the public defender, "I can't thank you enough for having kept this so peaceful."

EVEN THOUGH a few thousand people had found refuge at Georgetown, Nixon's men were satisfied they had broken the back of the Mayday Tribe. "Police very successful in clearing the park," John Ehrlichman noted with satisfaction in his diary. He spoke with Nixon by phone and told him "they'd really broken it up pretty well."

But now that the raid had actually taken place, the president was having some second thoughts. He wondered if his aides had been taking him too literally when he went off on the demonstrators. Maybe we moved too hard, he mused. Maybe it would have been better to let them go ahead and disrupt the city before we disrupted them. Public opinion was still troubling. The latest Harris poll came out Sunday, showing that 58 percent of Americans now believed it was "morally wrong" for the United States to continue fighting in Vietnam. Worse, many no longer found it worth shedding American blood to contain communism: a plurality of 42 percent favored allowing the communists to participate in a coalition government in South Vietnam if that was the only way to end the killing.

While the atmosphere inside the executive mansion was "like war" as Monday approached, First Lady Pat Nixon decided to go ahead with a planned Sunday lunch in the family dining room with her daughters, Tricia and Julie, and Julie's mother-in-law, Mamie Eisenhower, widow of the former president. While they were eating, a guard outside the window accidentally dropped a canister of tear gas, "sending all of us fleeing in tears," Julie said later. The whole town was on edge. Stores and banks boarded up their windows. The usual flood of spring tourists melted away. Workers strategized on how to get to work in the morning. Ehrlichman brought his suitcase so he could stay overnight in the shelter in the White House basement.

The Mayday group had been urging government workers to stay home. They distributed a leaflet explaining their motives. "Your help is needed by the warmakers if they are to continue to keep a façade of legitimacy and power," the leaflet read. "We recognize that most of you who work for the government are not directly involved in making the war, and that most of you in fact wish that the war would be over. But the fact is that this government could not continue to carry on its war without your passive support, by your willingness to do business as usual while the murder continues."

THERE WAS ONE THING the White House didn't yet grasp. Many of the people planning to come out on Monday morning hadn't been sleeping at West Potomac Park at all. Thousands more had filtered into the city and bunked in church basements, dorm rooms, and private homes.

Among these was Daniel Ellsberg, the forty-year-old military analyst now living in Cambridge, Massachusetts. He had come down with his own small affinity group of left-leaning writers and academics. They had debated for weeks whether to join Mayday. While they believed it was time for a more intense protest, they were no longer youngsters and had no desire to get caught up in a second Chicago. Ellsberg, for one, also thought Rennie's group appeared disorganized. He hadn't been sure what mobile tactics really meant, or how that would play out on the ground. He couldn't decide if he should go.

Then, a few days beforehand, Ellsberg was invited as one of the speakers to an antiwar rally in the amphitheater at Brandeis University, outside Boston. He had just watched the film *Little Big Man*, a revisionist western with a sympathetic portrait of Native Americans, starring Dustin Hoffman as a white boy raised by the Cheyenne. An old chief tells Hoffman's character at one point, "It is a good day to die." Ellsberg, at the end of his Brandeis speech, asked spontaneously who'd seen the movie; nearly everyone had. He reminded them of the old chief's quote and added: "Really, it's really never a good day to die. But Mayday is going to be a good day to get arrested in Washington, D.C." The crowd exploded in uproarious applause, people leaping to their feet, and Ellsberg went home and told his wife that he guessed he'd now have to go to the protest after all.

Few Americans could claim as deep a knowledge of the Vietnam War as Ellsberg. A former marine and, at the beginning, a strong supporter of the U.S. intervention, he first visited Indochina during the Kennedy administration as part of a Defense Department research team, and sensed that the Vietnamese independence movement, which had driven out the French, could be strong enough to survive the Americans too. In 1964 he read the original military cables about the clash in the Gulf of Tonkin between U.S. and North Vietnamese ships, and realized that LBJ had mischaracterized the situation to justify an invasion. He spent two years working for the Pentagon in Vietnam, evaluating U.S. efforts to "pacify" the countryside, sometimes walking point with troops to see the war up close.

Returning to the States, Ellsberg joined a team at the RAND Corporation that was producing a secret history of U.S. involvement in Vietnam. Ellsberg had been only the second person to read all seven thousand pages.

On Mayday, Ellsberg had his own secret, shared with only a few confidants. After months of internal agonizing, he had decided to copy key parts of the history and make them public. He knew such a move would mean the end of his career and quite possibly a prison sentence. But he had been absorbing the writings of Gandhi and Martin Luther King Jr., and had been inspired by examples of resistance, particularly by those who refused the draft and went to jail. At first Ellsberg sought help from antiwar Democrats in the Senate. But they were too frightened to abet such a leak. So in March Ellsberg had turned the documents over to the *New York Times*. People at the newspaper were already plowing through the file.

Soon enough the world would learn the shocking contents of the Pentagon Papers. But this night Ellsberg and his group bedded down on the floor of a basement recreation room in someone's Washington home, and prepared to join the Mayday Tribe in the morning.

17

Mayday

Monday morning, May 3

JERRY WILSON WAS BACK IN HIS CRUISER WELL BEFORE DAWN. In the darkness, he picked up his police radio and broadcast to all hands the pre-game message he'd received directly from Nixon's lips on Saturday. "The desire of the president," Jerry told them, "is that this city be open for business this week."

The chief knew he would be under scrutiny like never before, from the demonstrators, the press, city officials — and of course Nixon's men. They were breathing down his neck. Richard Kleindienst, from Justice, arranged for one of his trusted aides to stick close to Jerry for the next three days. This would keep Kleindienst informed and, just as important, make the administration's wishes known to the police chief in real time.

Still, Jerry permitted himself a bit of overconfidence. After Sunday's successful raid, he and his command believed the vast majority of the West Potomac Park crowd wouldn't be back. The youngsters looked to be undisciplined, and there was no reason to think they had the capacity to act decisively as a group. Surprises were unlikely, since the cops had informants inside the Mayday planning meetings. It shouldn't be a big problem to keep things moving this morning. So the police relaxed a little, and the bulk of the department didn't get going until after five in the morning. The paddy wagons, prisoner buses, and patrol cars aimed to get into position by a quarter to six. That would be plenty early, they figured, a good fifteen minutes before the Washington traffic got heavy.

But the police were about to reckon with the consequences of their

Sunday action. While the Mayday Tribe had appeared meek, the early show of force by the authorities had actually toughened the determination of the exiled campers. As for the thousands of other demonstrators in town — the ones who, instead of sleeping by the river, had found lodging in homes, churches, and dorm rooms — they now had absorbed both the news of the park raid and the early reports of troops pouring into town. It erased any doubt that the government would go to extremes. Perhaps the police and the army would try to bottle them up on the campuses, or seal off their targets before they even got started.

As a result many affinity groups decided to hit the streets early, before five. Within an hour, it became obvious to Jerry. This was going to be a tough day after all.

POLICE AND GOVERNMENT agents had been warning for months about the Mayday promise of "mobile tactics," essentially a kind of hit-and-run civil disobedience. Officials largely dismissed it as just another bit of overheated radical rhetoric. So did many of those who joined the demonstration, like Daniel Ellsberg's group. But it didn't take long for everyone to discover its potential.

It never had been a big problem to manage a static act of civil disobedience, one in which demonstrators would simply sit or lie down where they weren't supposed to, refuse to move, and wait to be arrested as a symbolic act. In D.C., the white-helmeted riot police typically would contain them with a formation they called a close squad column, planting themselves on the street like a row of intimidating fence posts. Paddy wagons would pull up to the edge of the crowd, and officers would remove people one by one in an orderly fashion.

If crowds became unruly, the police would aim for dispersal rather than detention. Their columns would sweep in formation through the area, firing tear-gas bombs to panic the crowd into a stampede. Suspects could more easily be picked off after a chase.

Now there were a couple of new wrinkles. During the 1968 King riots, hundreds had been swept up for violating a citywide curfew and were held for many hours without specific charges. A blue-ribbon commission was set up to suggest methods that would both protect civil liberties and smooth the courtroom process in the midst of disorder. As part of the revised rules of engagement, police had agreed that during future mass detentions, they would fill out official records on the spot. These field arrest forms, as they were called, were shorter than the paperwork used at the stationhouses, so they could be completed quickly. In addition, police would have to take a photograph of each suspect with the arresting officer. To that end, the department had purchased a slew of Polaroid Swingers, the first cheap instant cameras, which had created a new mass market for pictures that developed as you held them with your fingers. ("Meet the Swinger," went the ad jingle, sung by a young Barry Manilow.) Jerry ordered officers assigned to patrol wagons to bring lots of extra film and flashbulbs for Mayday.

All this was supposed to discourage indiscriminate arrests, and to make certain there would be no doubt in court who had busted the suspect and why. The 1968 commission had written, "If we are to be concerned with the quality of the justice, as well as the efficiency of the system, it is obvious that the police must be forced to exercise maximum responsibility in completing the record of the offense."

Mayday would stretch this system to the breaking point. These new rules would prove "grossly inadequate" to cope with mobile tactics, as one of Jerry's lieutenants would write in an after-action report.

AT FIRST the action unfolded slowly.

Listed as Site One in the Mayday Tribe's tactical manual was a busy intersection of several highways on the Virginia side of the Potomac, just over the Francis Scott Key Bridge. There, the river valley provided "excellent, low, flat, open areas" for a hit-and-run protest. Many of the drivers passing through every day, the manual noted, were bound for the Pentagon to help manage the reviled war.

Police had copies of the tactical manual, of course, and thus advance warning about every objective. But demonstrators beat them to this target. A little before 5:30 a.m., dozens of people moved into the main feeder road, the George Washington Parkway, and erected barricades across the lanes, using whatever they could find, including small boulders they rolled down from the adjoining woods.

Across the Key Bridge sat Georgetown, the tony neighborhood that housed many of the city's political and media elite, including plenty who had long championed the American presence in Indochina. Near Georgetown University, one affinity group drove their car onto a freeway and managed to overturn it. Others sat down in the middle of George-town's main commercial intersection. Still another cluster of protesters began stringing a cable across one of the busiest roads. Traffic was becoming hopelessly snarled.

Cops with cruisers, motorcycles, or scooters scrambled to the scene. The demonstrators dashed into the adjacent woods or across the highway. The police fired tear gas and grabbed the few they could catch. To try to keep the bridge open, Jerry asked the army to quickly dispatch two hundred soldiers from the Ninety-First Engineer Battalion at Fort Belvoir in Virginia. Before long he would request a caravan of National Guard jeeps to roll down M Street. All day, the military presence would magnify the image of a city under siege, feeding anxiety on all sides.

There seemed to be more Mayday people on the streets than Jerry expected. Still the chief thought the chaos seemed controllable. His conviction didn't last long.

As the minutes ticked by, the police radio began crackling nonstop with reports from all over town. Several police cars broadcast emergency calls at the same time, talking over each other in rising anxiety. "Let one unit go at a time," pleaded a desperate dispatcher. The transmissions became more garbled and distorted. "Lots of groups in the city," reported one cruiser. "Large group at Seventh and D and Ninth and Mount Vernon — can't tell where they are going," said another.

Then faster and faster: "Large groups in Rock Creek stopping traffic on overpasses" . . . "All units — gas is being used on Prospect Street" . . . "Get your men out and lock them up" . . . "Expedite transport" . . . "Need a bus" . . . "Too big a crowd for the men there to handle" . . . "North Capitol Street, group heading south" . . . "Two cars overturned Connecticut and Calvert" . . . "Fourteenth and Jefferson, large crowd" . . . "Mount Vernon Park, large group about one thousand" . . . "a thousand at Nineteenth and New York" . . . "They have southbound Fourteenth Street Bridge blocked" . . . "Seventeenth and Q now being blocked."

And finally, from all over town, with increasing urgency: "Send help" . . . "need more help" . . . "need people" . . . "need more police" . . . "need assistance right away!" . . . "Hurry up!"

By 6:30 a.m., "the entire police operation was in a condition-red status," as one officer would later report, and it would not be long before both procedures and decorum broke down.

DANIEL ELLSBERG AWOKE before dawn in his sleeping bag in the basement. He and his affinity group, which included the left-leaning professors Noam Chomsky, Marilyn Young, and Howard Zinn, had found lodging with one of the hundreds of Washington residents who'd opened their homes that weekend. Still groggy, Ellsberg gazed at the people half his age packed into the house. They looked serious and determined. Their mien took him back to when he was a young marine on a troop ship before an amphibious landing. The kids filled water bottles, inked the Mayday legal aid phone number — 833-9480 — onto their forearms. They all told him they'd never been arrested before, but were ready to go to jail if it would help end the war.

Ellsberg hadn't been arrested before either. He wasn't sure — would the jailers let you bring something to read into your cell? Just in case, he packed a book of essays by the feminist Barbara Deming, a noted apostle of civil disobedience. "A liberation movement that is nonviolent sets the oppressor free as well as the oppressed," she believed.

Under the Mayday plan, each affinity group chose a target. Out on the sidewalk before six, Ellsberg and his friends headed for their designated spot, the Fourteenth Street Bridge. A taxi braked to a stop. "Hop in, this is my second load," said the driver, an African American woman. She was one of many D.C. cabbies who took it upon themselves to ferry protesters for free that morning.

The weather was overcast and cool for May, with temperatures in the mid-forties. As Ellsberg arrived at the approach to the span, the first person he recognized was Benjamin Spock. The sixty-eight-year-old pediatrician had become a standout participant in the peace movement, leveraging his fame as author of the most successful book of child-rearing advice ever published. That made him a popular target of conservatives, who argued, as Vice President Agnew put it in one of his inflammatory speeches, that Spock was partly to blame for the rebellious generation of the Sixties. They'd been raised without proper discipline by parents "enchanted with the advocates of permissive psychology."

Spock had just tried to lead two hundred people onto the ramp, heading for the Pentagon across the river. Some in his group saw their march as a parallel but separate Mayday action, since they didn't intend to block traffic.

The people who had gathered around Spock included both young-sters and more mature protesters like William and Charlotte Kuenning, Quakers in their fifties. They were close to David Dellinger and had lived with him in the small cooperative community of anarchists and pacifists that Dave had helped establish in rural New Jersey in the 1940s. The couple had traveled to Washington a week earlier to see their daughter after she was arrested in the Selective Service sit-in. They had been planning to leave town after that, but, realizing "this might be the most historic demonstration of our time," they decided to stay and put their bodies on the line.

Police didn't differentiate between the clusters of kids and the elders. The riot cops drove Spock and his followers back the way they came, throwing canisters of tear gas into their ranks. On the run, the bespec-tacled baby doctor pressed a handkerchief to his face against the fumes.

Ellsberg now saw Spock conversing with a middle-aged woman. He realized with surprise that she was Barbara Deming. In the lull, Ellsberg pulled her book from his pocket and asked her to autograph it. Behind them, they could see marines with bayonets joining the police on the bridge, now shrouded in clouds of gas.

Rather than make another futile charge, the protesters shifted their attention to the freeway leading up to the span. They sat in the middle of the roadway to halt traffic. Ellsberg's group joined. "Dan manipulated our little affinity group like a platoon in Vietnam," Chomsky said later. They waited for the police to come.

Minutes before six-thirty, a frantic call went out over the police radio: "Help needed at the Fourteenth Street Bridge!"

ALL OVER TOWN it was a similar story. Skirmishes left a heavy fog of stinging gas floating over neighborhoods in Georgetown and along the National Mall, where government workers negotiated their way to the office with handkerchiefs over their faces. Many federal agencies had made arrangements to avoid the blockade. Employees considered essen-tial had been told to sleep overnight in their offices or book hotel rooms nearby. Some were ordered to their desks as early as 3 a.m. At a brand-new arm of the government created by Nixon after the first national

Earth Day — it was called the Environmental Protection Agency — "we were told to be in our offices at a quarter to five this morning so that no one could say that they had stopped the executive process," said William D. Ruckelshaus, the newly appointed administrator. Three of the more robust members of Congress — two Republicans and a Democrat — decided to skirt the bridges by paddling an aluminum canoe across the Potomac from Virginia, fighting the stiff wind. It took them a little more than two hours.

Meantime, the police clashed with protesters on the Theodore Roosevelt Bridge and at Dupont Circle. A contingent of several hundred demonstrators from Illinois blocked traffic at Mount Vernon Square. At the sound of the sirens they ran off through streets and alleys. An elderly woman hid a group of them in her basement. She served them milk and cookies.

On scores of side roads, clusters of youngsters cried, "Motorists off the streets!" They linked arms to stop traffic or turned trashcans and construction equipment into barricades. "We are sorry for your inconvenience," read a leaflet they handed to drivers. "While you are sitting in your car you could take a few minutes to think about things . . . You may not agree with the tactics being used — you may not agree with the points of view of the participants — but we ask you to consider with us the horror, the death, the destruction and devastation continuing daily in Indo-China . . . our actions now need to go beyond what we have done in the past."

Many drivers were furious; many were resigned. Some flashed peace signs. Others gunned their engines and drove straight for the protesters. Among the latter was one of Nixon's speechwriters, an arch-conservative named Patrick Buchanan, who generally put together the president's daily news summary. He had just been over to the Watergate apartments to pick up his fiancée — one of Nixon's receptionists — and they were headed to the White House in his Cadillac convertible when they ran into a Mayday blockade on E Street. Buchanan, who was thirty-two, with a "beefy, beer-drinker's face," thought he might get around on the far right-hand side, where fewer protesters were standing. He hit the gas, and one kid jumped out of the way at the last second. Buchanan bragged about it when he got to work.

Some groups tied ropes across the road or pushed cars out of parking spaces into the middle of the pavement, letting air out of tires or re-moving distributor caps. One of these cars belonged to Nicholas von Hoffman, whose *Washington Post* column had scolded the critics of civil disobedience: "Let's hope that those who think this way are rigid about the legal niceties when the government breaks the law." Having his car stalled didn't appear to weaken Hoffman's sympathy.

Any car small enough to be pushed or lifted was at risk, regardless of its owner's politics. A senior at George Washington University who had joined the D.C. National Guard so he wouldn't be drafted upon gradu-ation was shocked to see his beloved Austin-Healey sports car on the news. It was turned perpendicular in the street, with all four tires flat. "I'm on your side!" he moaned at the TV.

The police scrambled to respond. They radioed for National Guard jeeps to push disabled vehicles out of the way. They sent squads of cops on scooters and motorcycles after protesters, like cowboys chasing a stampede. At one point, several police cruisers, their sirens screaming, gunned right over the curbs and onto the grassy fields around the Wash-ington Monument, firing tear gas out the windows at sprinting demon-strators. But still they felt outnumbered and outflanked.

The tactical advantage underpinning the Mayday plan was now ap-parent, the asymmetrical warfare of a guerrilla force against a stand-ing army. It was nearly impossible to defend against small decentralized bands who could shift on a dime, tie up police or troops at one spot, and then get to another place before the authorities could adjust, choosing spots that weren't even on the original list in the Mayday tactical manual.

Jerry realized that the police department's procedures were being turned neatly against the cops, either on purpose or by lucky accident. Dispersing crowds with tear gas so they could just move on somewhere else wasn't going to work. And the new field forms and Polaroid cameras were slowing arrests to a crawl.

From another police cruiser—apparently the one that held the rep-resentative from the Justice Department who was shadowing Jerry—came what may have been an order masquerading as a question: "Chief, do you think we should disregard field arrest forms and pictures this morning?"

One of Jerry's underlings later summed up the dilemma: "We could either keep the streets of Washington open and the government functioning or we could carefully collect written documentation of arrest information for court. At this stage, we could not do both."

A year before, Jerry had publicly upbraided his riot squad for failing to use field arrest forms in one big bust. And the chief had once promised Judge Greene that no prisoners would be accepted at a booking or holding facility without a field arrest form. He realized that if he broke this promise, it would be difficult, if not impossible, to defend the arrests in court.

Nevertheless, minutes before six-thirty, he made a fateful call: "Cruiser One to Command Center: We will disregard field arrest forms." He had taken the shackles off his cops.

REPORTERS FROM MAGAZINES, newspapers, and television stations scrambled through the city, trying to keep track of Monday's events, a task much more complicated than covering more centralized protests. The day also marked the debut of an innovative American news program.

National Public Radio, an entity spawned by an LBJ-era law aimed at fostering non-commercial broadcasting, had been installed for less than a year at a building on I Street, near the White House. The director of programming, a soft-spoken thirty-six-year-old radio hand from upstate New York, had been working with his team to create a completely new way to report national news, something more experiential and explanatory than the hard, rat-a-tat headlines that were the province of mainstream radio.

The program director was Bill Siemering, who had covered the turmoil of the Sixties at a public station in Buffalo and believed deeply in radio as a potential force for social good. His Washington team had only five reporters, and they'd been together for little more than a month. Their broadcast equipment had been in hand for a couple of weeks. They'd done mockups of a new program, but here was a chance to demonstrate how different it would be from anything anyone had heard before on the radio.

Back when they picked May 3 for the date of the program's maiden broadcast, they had no idea it would mark a day of turmoil in Washington. But that was fine. The new compact cassette recorders Siemering acquired for his reporters — Sony TC-100s — were portable and could be easily carried through the streets. As the trouble erupted, Siemering dispatched his reporters. Later they would edit and splice their hours of tape into an instant radio documentary, which would run on Monday evening for an unheard-of twenty-five minutes. It would paint the "very first brush strokes" of what he hoped the national non-commercial radio network would become.

In a memo to member stations, Siemering had written, "The listener will have a sense of reality, of authentic people sharing the human experience with emotional openness." He wanted to prepare the stations for what it would be like to hear the brand-new show, which they had named *All Things Considered.*

AFTER WEEKS in a city under siege by dissenters, the cops no longer felt restrained. Their chief had freed them from the rules, and they vented their mounting frustration. Instead of arresting protesters one by one and recording which law each was breaking, the tactical squads began chasing down and grabbing big groups. Police were sweeping areas "clean of the Mayday mobs . . . We were hauling demonstrators off the streets in wholesale lots."

Within minutes of Jerry's order, for example, one hundred people were busted in a sweep at Tenth and K Streets. A *Life* photographer captured the unbridled joy on the face of a deputy police chief, Theodore Zanders, as he sprayed Mace into the eyes and noses of one group. Even though the protesters weren't breaking any laws at the moment, he felt justified because "the act of one is the act of all," Zanders later explained.

On the freeway near the Fourteenth Street Bridge, the police went after Daniel Ellsberg's group as they sat in a circle. Two officers approached from opposite angles. One of them pulled down his plastic visor and raised his can of Mace. The protesters jumped away just as the cop let it loose, and it sprayed right in the face of the other cop, whose helmet fell off as he staggered back.

It looked like a Keystone Kops routine, but eventually, after some more mobile tactics, Ellsberg caught a dose so strong, he couldn't see anything or even think for a few minutes. He was rattled. Some in his group stayed and wound up in custody. Ellsberg decided to slip away and avoid arrest.

Vans and buses that had been loading those arrested soon were "jammed to the gunwales." The cops called in the backup transports;

those vehicles filled up just as fast. Then the police started shipping their prisoners in the D.C. transit buses that had been used earlier to carry cops to the scene. They hastily procured more buses from the navy and vans from automobile rental companies.

On the buses the atmosphere was often festive. *We shall overcome,* the protesters sang, and *Give peace a chance.* They banged loudly on the inside of the buses and shouted encouragement out the windows to young people still free on the streets. On some transports the cops warned everyone to be quiet or to risk being "bus gassed."

RENNIE DAVIS HAD risen early. Truth be told, he couldn't really sleep the night before, anticipating the big day. In the morning Rennie didn't join the blockade himself, but rather moved quickly around the city, checking the sites, trying to get a handle on the melee.

About halfway through rush hour, at a quarter to eight, there were already more than one thousand people in custody. The police had planned to bring most of those arrested to the holding area at the federal courthouse, which had about fifty small cells, the largest capacity in the city. The small drop-off zone outside, though, allowed for only one load of prisoners to be taken in at a time. The buses got stuck in a monster traffic jam. The cops couldn't discharge their suspects and return quickly to the trouble spots. So police began stashing hundreds of detainees in the middle of parks and median strips — at Mount Vernon Square and Dupont Circle — where they were penned in by National Guard troops and later by busloads of marines.

Inside the U.S. courthouse, the cells filled up to capacity. Where to put everybody now? The exercise yard at the D.C. city jail was cleared to contain them. But even that wouldn't be enough. What law enforcement needed was a makeshift detention camp, a big enclosed outdoor space of some kind.

IN CALIFORNIA, Richard Nixon tried to appear above the fray. His press secretary put out a statement saying the president expected a normal day.

But in fact Nixon was obsessed. He woke early to follow the news. He demanded an updated report from the White House at least once an hour. Bud Krogh had ceded that job to John Dean. Dean had ordered direct phone lines installed from his White House office to police headquarters, as well as to the FBI, the Secret Service, and the Justice Department. Whenever he or his staff picked up one of the phones, a special White House light went off at the corresponding agency's command center. The pace was frantic. They'd quickly garner the details — which bridges are open, how many arrests? — and they would throw together a summary. Using a Xerox technology called LDX, which predated the fax machine, they'd transmit the typed report to the Western White House, then get working on the next one.

The first reports Monday morning spoke of such unexpected mayhem throughout town that Dean and John Ehrlichman — who had spent the night in the White House — decided they needed a bird's-eye view. A little after seven, they boarded a military helicopter on the Ellipse, the big grassy circle between the White House and the National Mall. As they banked over the city, Ehrlichman stuck his Super 8 movie camera out the window to film what Dean called "a general scene of chaos." They saw "knots of people on the ground . . . burning cars in Georgetown, a confused maze of little figures running through the streets . . . flashing police lights . . . pitched rock battles."

Ehrlichman noted that "sporadic bands clog some streets but, on balance, things are moving pretty well." Yet when they turned for home, they could see clashes and tear gas all around the Ellipse. No way they could land there. They told the pilot to set down instead on the south lawn of the White House, the spot reserved for the president's helicopter. Nixon was out of town, but the First Lady raised hell about the landing anyway.

Just after eight-thirty in the morning came another set of aerial flights. The Justice Department had called the army for more support. At Andrews Air Force Base, troops boarded six huge Chinook helicopters. They took off for the National Mall. A couple of smaller helicopters escorted the Chinooks and set down first, laying pink-and-white smoke flares for the landing zone near the Washington Monument. Then the Chinooks came in, their gigantic dual rotors slicing loudly through the air. Their exit ramps dropped, and out of each craft hustled thirty-three helmeted troops. Off they ran in single file toward the U.S. Capitol.

Another helicopter happened to be hovering above the Mall at that moment, carrying members of the news media. The pilot had flown missions in Vietnam. Looking down, he couldn't escape the surreal feeling he was watching an armed assault on the Washington Monument. The scene made the Mall look something like the site of a military coup, not the bucolic spot intended by its designers.

AT THE MAYDAY headquarters on Vermont Avenue, John O'Connor had already been up all night answering phones. He hadn't been especially eager to hit the streets, but his handlers in the police intelligence division insisted he get out there and report back. If anybody stopped him, John was told, just say the code words "bent penny," and the cops would know you're a good guy.

Famished, John hit his favorite deli on Pennsylvania Avenue for a half-smoke sausage and a cup of coffee. On the way out he ran into a group of hepped-up police on the prowl for demonstrators. "Bent penny! Bent penny!" John cried. The cop growled back, "Bent penny, my ass!" and sprayed Mace in John's face. He dropped the coffee and hot dog and sprinted for safety like a jackrabbit, barely out of range of flying nightsticks. The authorities had apparently forgotten to clue in the police about the plan. When another undercover agent tried using the magic words, a cop knocked out some of his teeth, apparently taking the phrase as a kind of insult.

When John called in to complain to his bosses at headquarters, he also imparted another piece of intelligence. An affinity group made up mostly of John's buddies from the Vietnam Veterans Against the War had got their hands on bags of chicken excrement and planned to dump them on the steps of the Pentagon that morning. Don't worry, John's handler told him, the bridges and approaches are protected by the military. There's no way they can get over there. John asked, Wanna bet? A six-pack? He didn't mention that his friends, the former jungle warriors, had studied the terrain and figured out they could crouch down and creep across the river along an unguarded railroad trestle. When his handler asked if he had any idea what route his friends planned to take, John answered, Hell, no.

Soon, police at the Pentagon took twenty-eight people into custody, but not before they had crossed the Potomac and dumped their odiferous load onto the steps. John would get his six-pack.

THE MORNING TIDE had turned in favor of the cops after Jerry suspended the field arrest rules. Especially euphoric were the hundreds of members of the riot squad, freed to go full-tilt with all their gear and tactics. They were grabbing anyone they could see blocking roads or fleeing the scene.

But that could get them only so far. Many Mayday protesters who used mobile tactics had melted into the city. In addition, there were likely thousands of others in town who hadn't done anything illegal yet. But during the evening rush hour, or later in the week, they might.

The police's idea: As long as we're sweeping the streets clean of these folks, why not get them all?

JERRY HAD PRESSED nearly every cop he had into Mayday service, but most of them weren't on riot duty. Many were stationed as guards around town. One of these was Joseph Green, the rookie officer and Yale graduate whose police academy speech had recently got his bosses in hot water with J. Edgar Hoover.

On Sunday, Green had been told he'd be positioned outside one of the federal office buildings as a precautionary measure. It so happened that his former Yale roommate was in town to join the Mayday protest. He stayed at Green's apartment. Early Monday they rode downtown together. Green parked his car and went off to work. His roommate headed into Mayday action. All morning, standing guard with other cops for an assault that never came, Green followed the reports of chaos on his police radio.

Sometime after nine-thirty, the chatter reflected something new. The cops were now rounding up scads of people who hadn't been observed doing anything wrong.

"Lock up the people on the street," crackled one order. Another said, "Arrest all people on street in groups." And then, an order to arrest "anyone . . . that is not moving" in the ten-block area around two universities, George Washington and Georgetown.

Green found himself wondering, Is that legal?

OFF THEIR LEASH, the cops cruised the streets for likely suspects. The only way to pick them out was by their appearance. An officer near the Mall at Fourteenth Street gave his underlings the order to "arrest anyone that looks like a demonstrator," not realizing, or not caring, that he was within earshot of a reporter for the *Christian Science Monitor*. Another journalist, for the *Los Angeles Times,* observed people being rounded up as police took note of their clothes, the length of their hair, and the political buttons they wore.

Across from the Bureau of Engraving and Printing on C Street, Bruce Soloway, a reporter for the nonprofit Pacifica Radio network, asked one of the riot cops why they were suddenly doing mass arrests. In response, the officer grabbed Soloway, lifted him up by the back of his pants, and forced him to kneel against a concrete fence with a dozen other prisoners, who said they had just been walking down the sidewalk.

David Appelbaum, a George Washington University freshman from Rochester, was taken near the Capitol. He had been on his way to attend a congressional hearing as part of his classwork. "I'm under orders to stop all protesters and in my opinion you're a protester," he was told. (His parents later wrote a letter to Nixon to complain.)

It was payback time at the universities. At the George Washington campus, club-wielding police chased protesters who were seeking refuge there. The cops pursued them right through the entrance to the law school building and then through the hallways. They arrested a law professor, Roger R. Kuhn, who was wearing an armband identifying him as a legal observer. A cop explained that Kuhn, who was teaching a course called Current Problems in Civil Rights that semester, had deliberately bumped him. At the university's hospital, two dozen people who'd been treated at the emergency room for tear-gas inhalation and minor injuries, some of whom had nothing to do with Mayday, were waiting outside for rides home. The police busted all of them, ignoring the protests of doctors and nurses. One of the college's physical education instructors was dragged off the steps of his office building.

In Georgetown, police swept through the streets, arresting kids for any offense they could gin up, such as jaywalking. Young people ran onto the Georgetown campus from the Canal Road entrance with scooter police at their heels. The cops hurled tear-gas bombs against the walls of the Copley Hall dormitory. Michael McCarthy, the son of the U.S. senator from Minnesota who had helped topple LBJ, had come down to Washington for Mayday, but he and his friends never reached their target, the Fourteenth Street Bridge. They were walking back to where they were staying in Georgetown when they were caught in the dragnet.

Other parts of town also became roundup sites. A teacher's aide for deaf students was busted on her way to work in Dupont Circle. A lawyer studying at an institute nearby stopped to help a victim of clubbing; police grabbed him by the neck and loaded him on the bus.

Caught in the arrests were tourists and all kinds of people who happened to appear young, or just dressed as if they were. They included future Washington personalities such as Sidney Blumenthal, a budding journalist who would write for the *New Yorker* and become a White House adviser to President Bill Clinton. Pedestrians weren't the only target. Cops went after drivers and passengers in cars who just looked wrong to them. A young police cadet who had driven from Florida to visit a friend in Georgetown, caught in a traffic jam, got out of his car to take a picture of the protest. After he returned to the driver's seat, a plainclothes officer reached in and beat him with his club, then dragged him out and arrested him.

During the citywide fracas, the civilian lawyer for the police department, Gerald Caplan, ventured from his office onto the National Mall to check things out. The tear gas burned his eyes, but he saw enough to be "shocked." Police chasing kids all over the place, "arresting everyone in sight." The riot cops had been told not to remove their badges, but he saw that many of them had done exactly that, so their prisoners couldn't identify them later. "They had just disobeyed orders," Caplan later recalled.

BY TEN-THIRTY IN the morning, more than five thousand people were in custody. The sweeps wouldn't end until Jerry Wilson's police department had more than seven thousand prisoners on their hands. Never in U.S. history had so many people been rounded up in one day.*

Many, perhaps most, of the prisoners had been part of the traffic blockade. But thousands had not. Loaded onto the buses, they asked

---

* Other notable mass arrests occurred during the riots after the assassination of Martin Luther King Jr. in April 1968, when thousands were rounded up in dozens of U.S. cities, including more than seven thousand in D.C. over four days; after Japan's surprise attack on Pearl Harbor in December 1941, when thousands of Japanese Americans were detained (and ultimately more than 110,000 were imprisoned in World War II internment camps); and in the Palmer Raids of 1919 and 1920, when the Justice Department swept up thousands of suspected radical leftists around the country.

what crime they had committed. Police sardonically answered things like "walking on the sidewalk" or never answered at all. In at least one detention bus, the driver hit the brakes whenever he spotted a young man with long hair and sent the cops out to force him aboard.

Robert L. Ackerly, a lawyer and former federal prosecutor who was out walking near his Dupont Circle office, stopped when he saw police busting people who looked to be doing nothing wrong. He was chatting with a long-haired young man when a cop seized the guy by the arm. Ackerly, who was forty-nine, asked why the longhair was arrested but not Ackerly himself. "Personal judgment, sir," the cop replied. Then Ackerly saw a police lieutenant point to a group of about twelve people, instructing the other cops to "take the one in the Navy pea jacket, take the one in the fatigues," and so on. Personal judgment, Ackerly was told again.

Ackerly, a former fighter pilot who had been shot down and captured during World War II and made a daring escape, was outraged. He marched right back to his office and pounded out a letter to Harold Greene, the chief judge. Ackerly strode over to Superior Court to hand it to Greene in person. "While I recognize the desire of the Chief of Police to remove these youngsters from the scene temporarily," Ackerly wrote the judge, "I still cannot accept indiscriminate, unjustified arrest, and I hope you will not tolerate this either."

A FEW BLOCKS from the courthouse where Ackerly delivered his letter, the lawyers of the Public Defender Service were trying to solve a mystery.

Barbara Bowman, the director of the service, lived on Capitol Hill, about a twenty-minute walk from her office. That morning, on her way in, the tear gas stung her nostrils. News of the mass arrests were all over the radio. Barbara figured her crew was in for an intense day in the courtrooms. She expected the prisoners to show up for arraignment any time now.

But the morning wore on, and no one was appearing at the courthouse. It was eerily quiet. Where was everybody?

She knew that some of her hotshot young lawyers rode motorcycles to work. It was just a couple of years since one of the quintessential films of the Sixties, *Easy Rider,* had romanticized bikes like Harley-Davidsons, and sales were booming. Barbara figured that if anyone could move nimbly around Washington today, scoot past any blocked roads or barriers, it would be these guys.

She sent them off with a mission. Search the city. Locate the prisoners. Go find out what's going on.

18

The Interest of Justice

Later the same day: Monday, May 3

BARBARA BOWMAN'S MOTORCYCLE GANG OF YOUNG LAWYERS located one huge congregation of detainees by mid-morning.

They were out on the east side of the city, near the Robert F. Kennedy Memorial Stadium. Across from the arena, on a dusty football practice field, more than a thousand mostly young people were penned behind an eight-foot-tall cyclone fence. They had been trucked in from all over town. The crowd grew through the morning as more buses rolled up and police marched their loads of prisoners through the gate. Around the perimeter a nervous-looking contingent of cops, air force reservists, and National Guardsmen stood watch.

Nothing but a stretch of grass and dirt, the makeshift detention camp had no provisions, no shelter. The campers found some buckets and trashcans to use as toilets. The temperature remained chilly for May, only in the forties this morning and forecast to rise barely into the fifties later on. A stiff and steady wind didn't help. A few clumps of kids crouched for warmth under part of the big rain tarp stashed at one end of the field. They used the football goalposts to prop it up. Others started little campfires, burning whatever they could scrounge, including scrap wood hurled over the fence by sympathetic guardsmen, who were busy building their own bonfires.

As the hours wore on, the prisoners called out to passerby, "We need food!" From time to time the detainees rushed the fence, a human wave trying to break through. The guards fired tear gas to force them back.

Many of the protesters lettered "POW" in lipstick on their foreheads. At one point they sat and arrayed themselves in a giant human peace symbol for the helicopters hovering overhead to see.

Not everyone in the camp was college age. Older activists including the ex-Yippie Stew Albert were there. So was Benjamin Spock, and the baby doctor was fuming. "This is concentration camp stuff," Spock declared to one of the Mayday Tribe's video cameras.

Among those arrested with Spock by the Fourteenth Street Bridge and bused to the camp were members of Daniel Ellsberg's affinity group. One was Howard Zinn, the forty-eight-year-old Boston University professor who would go on to write a leftist bible, *A People's History of the United States.* An officer had grabbed Zinn when he asked the cop why he was beating another demonstrator. Also present was the author Barbara Deming, who'd signed her book for Ellsberg. At the football field Deming met up with another activist writer, Grace Paley. Deming was fifty-three and Paley forty-eight. Arm in arm, the two women walked briskly around the field, trying to stay warm, and looked for people to huddle with in small circles, making "a kind of slow dance" together.

Despite the conditions, Spock proclaimed he'd rather be inside the fence than free. "These are the people who care about America and have got the courage to do something about it," he said. "So it's really a pleasure to be with them."

Using the field had been a spur-of-the-moment decision, Jerry's assistant chief told reporters: "We had them, and we had to do something right away. Someone can judge the rightness of it later."

BUT IT WAS not exactly spur of the moment. Long before Mayday, Jerry had realized that one way or another, given the course of events in Washington in the late Sixties, there might come a time when he had to find a place to house hundreds or thousands of people after a mass arrest.

Police had calculated that all together, their available detention space could hold about twenty-seven hundred people. That included the cells at the fourteen local precinct houses, the central cellblock at police headquarters, and the lockups in the basement of the U.S. District Court building downtown.

Preparing for Mayday, Jerry had guessed that a maximum of three thousand arrests might be made on any given day. But just in case the police needed more space, he had sent an assistant chief around the region to figure out where they might put any overflow. Perhaps they could go to Virginia, to the former women's prison at Occoquan, or the army base at Fort Belvoir. Also possible was the big hall inside the D.C. Armory, next to RFK Stadium. If not, the assistant chief had noted, the armory owned the nearby field used by the Redskins for football practice.

After the cops had mopped up the city all morning, seizing young people with the wrong appearance as well as citizens who questioned their actions, Jerry had not three thousand, but more than seven thousand prisoners to deal with. They quickly filled all the indoor lockups.

What to do with these thousands? Jerry's deputies reviewed the possible overflow sites. Carting everyone out to Virginia presented a host of logistical problems. The undersecretary of the army, moreover, refused to take detainees at Fort Belvoir. He thought the military would be accused of erecting a concentration camp. The D.C. Armory was no longer an option; it was now full of the National Guard units that Nixon's men had mobilized.

So the football practice field was the next choice. By mid-morning more than seventeen hundred people were confined there. The number would grow to more than twenty-five hundred before the day was out.

And still that wasn't enough. So the police started dumping demonstrators into the exercise yard at the city jail. Soon they numbered sixteen hundred.

Jerry had previously told his cops to honor all press passes, saying such cooperation was "extremely important in promoting good public relations." But it hadn't worked out that way. Among those in the exercise yard were several reporters from the local press and from college newspapers; police had rounded them up for having long hair, beards, and casual clothes, regardless of their credentials. One was Robert S. Anson, a twenty-six-year-old correspondent for *Time* who had been held by Cambodian guerrillas for three weeks in 1970. Another was Henry Allen, an assistant editor at the *Washington Post* and a former marine who had served in Vietnam. Allen hadn't even been trying to cover the event. He was crossing the street near a traffic circle with friends he'd met for breakfast. The cops grabbed them and loaded them into a rented Hertz van, where the other occupants told the same story about the sweeps. When they got to the jail yard, the crowd there cheered and raised their fists in welcome. Asked for his right to call his office, Allen and the others were told the phone was out of order. Allen observed "the tough, almost amused cynicism of people who are no longer surprised that other Americans will sweep them off the streets on charges so ridiculous that no one even bothered to laugh at them."

Another large group languished beneath the federal courthouse, in a cellblock that authorities had previously decided could hold, in an emergency, a maximum of four hundred people. While that many "would be far from ideal, it would permit the humane treatment of persons confined for a relatively short period of time," according to a Justice Department report after the 1968 riots. But now police had crammed in eight hundred detainees.

One of those packed inside a five-by-seven foot cell meant for two people was William Kuenning, the Illinois Quaker activist who had joined the Fourteenth Street Bridge protest with his wife after his daughter's arrest earlier in the week. Police kept pushing more and more people in, ignoring protests of "No more room!" until there were sixteen men in all. He could peer into other cells across the corridor; they held Georgetown students still carrying their books, as well as some ex-GIs. They passed the time singing "Swing Low, Sweet Chariot" and debating political philosophy and tactics. "What's a Quaker?" one of them asked Kuenning. They argued about whether it was productive to call cops "pigs." Tear gas still clung to their clothes. It seeped into the nearby hallway in the courthouse basement, stinging the eyes and throats of employees standing in the cafeteria line.

More than two thousand more were held at the police precinct houses and in the central police lockup. Each cell also got loaded with fifteen or twenty people, so tight there was no room to sit or lie down. Many of the toilets and sinks didn't work. Prisoners chanted, "We need water! We need air!" There were few blankets, and food didn't arrive until well into the evening, if at all.

The jailers at the central police lockup by all accounts were the roughest, manhandling prisoners and calling them names. One detainee who resisted giving fingerprints later reported to his lawyers that he was punched and choked by four policemen until he opened his left hand to allow the booking. Some police told the prisoners untruthfully that the judges were handing out six-month jail sentences. In fact, those few prisoners who got their day in court received wildly disparate treatment, depending on the judge. Bail was all over the map, from ten dollars up to one thousand dollars for the same offense. Some judges were openly hostile. One told a Vietnam veteran, "In the old days we used to shoot veterans who rebelled." Yet other judges expressed sympathy. One called the arrests a "charade," and another handed a defendant bail money from his own pocket.

Almost no one outside the jails had an inkling of the conditions inside. The prisoners weren't permitted to talk to lawyers or make phone calls. Out in the city, the dragnet looked like a big success, having cleared the streets of troublemakers once and for all. But some early warning signs emerged for Jerry, the police, the city, and the Nixon administration. One arrived from an unlikely source: Margaret Kleindienst, the wife of the deputy attorney general, who was growing worried about the welfare of her husband's prisoners. She left at least two phone messages urging Kleindienst to marshal public defenders to help. He apparently didn't return her calls.

BARBARA'S PUBLIC DEFENDERS, of course, were already on the case. One was a twenty-nine-year-old professor on leave from teaching at Stanford Law School. Michael Wald had spent all Sunday night in court, working until three in the morning, dealing with the Quaker case in front of the nervous judge. After grabbing a bit of sleep at his Georgetown apartment, he drove back to work.

The street disorders were mostly over by then, but on the car radio he heard about the mass arrests, and some hints of trouble about the police tactics. After stopping at the office and learning about the detainees, Wald headed to the football field. He met up with his colleagues who'd ridden out earlier. The police and soldiers wouldn't allow any of the attorneys inside the compound. So Wald took his legal pad and pencil and walked over to an empty stretch of fence. He motioned to the prisoners to come over, and he began collecting interviews. No one tried to stop him or the other four defense lawyers from doing the same thing.

One after another, the youngsters pressed their faces to the chain links and told Wald they had been seized while standing or walking on a sidewalk and had never been read their rights, nor told what law they'd broken. As he grasped the scope of the indiscriminate arrests,

Wald grew more determined to help. When the detainees asked Wald what would happen next, he told them the police would book them on a charge and take down their names and addresses for the arrest record. Wald thought hard about his next piece of advice. You should cooperate, he said. But, he added, speaking carefully, I should also tell you that if you were to give them a false name, nothing bad will happen to you.

Those on the other side of the fence smiled. When the police began booking and fingerprinting the suspects that night, there would be dozens of Richard Nixons, dozens of John and Martha Mitchells.

These people clearly would be clients of Wald and his colleagues once they were brought to court for arraignment. But it also seemed obvious that the American Civil Liberties Union or a similar organization now had to intervene in such an egregious matter. Wald drove back to the public defenders' office, reported what he'd seen, and asked Barbara, "So who's filing the habeas?"

A writ of habeas corpus — a judge's order to determine if a jailer can rightfully "have the body" — is a cherished cornerstone of personal freedom in the Anglo-Saxon legal tradition. Fundamentally, it forbids a monarch or state or police official from locking up an individual without a legitimate reason. They must explain in court why the prisoner was taken. The Great Writ of Liberty, as it is known, is rooted in English medieval common law. In the seventeenth century, Parliament decided to write it formally into the code because, despite the tradition, many "sheriffs, gaolers and other officers" were ignoring writs and leaving many of the king's subjects "long detained in prison, in such cases where by law they are bailable, to their great charges and vexation."

The American colonists brought "this darling privilege," as one leader called it, from the mother country. They enshrined it in Article 1 of the Constitution, saying it could be suspended only "in cases of rebellion or invasion." Just two presidents had invoked this suspension clause: Abraham Lincoln, who ordered the seizure of Confederate sympathizers in Maryland during the Civil War, and Ulysses S. Grant, to stop Ku Klux Klan attacks against black people in South Carolina.

During World War II, habeas corpus was simply ignored when President Roosevelt issued an executive order that put tens of thousands of Japanese Americans on the Pacific Coast into internment camps. At the time, first as attorney general and later as governor of California, Earl

Warren backed the roundup, a decision he later "deeply regretted." Many would speculate that, when Warren became chief justice in the 1950s, his guilt about the mass internment helped explain why his Supreme Court did more to extend civil liberties than any other. A few years before Mayday, Warren had affirmed the habeas privilege in his majority opinion for *Terry v. Ohio:* "No right is held more sacred or is more carefully guarded by the common law, than the right of every individual to the possession and control of his own person, free from all restraint and interference of others, unless by clear and unquestionable authority of law."

In May 1971, no suspension had been declared in Washington. Nor had the president invoked martial law. So the seven thousand people held incommunicado still had their constitutional rights. Seeking a habeas order seemed an urgent piece of business. Barbara and her colleagues made some calls to see who was working to get the detainees released by nightfall.

The answer quickly became apparent: nobody. If anyone was to get free, it would be up to the Public Defender Service. Any reservations the lawyers might have had when Judge Greene assigned them to represent the protesters — those evaporated as their native sense of outrage began to simmer and then boil.

Barbara's right-hand man was Norman Lefstein, a thirty-three-year-old lawyer and former national collegiate debate champion, known for his ability to dissect all sides of an issue. Lefstein fled a research job in the Justice Department after Nixon's election, having had no interest in helping design what he feared would be repressive criminal justice legislation. The new attorney general, John Mitchell, and his deputy, Richard Kleindienst, "had pretty radical ideas of things they wanted to do," he said. Barbara's new public defender agency was exciting. So Lefstein had gladly taken a pay cut to become her deputy director.

As the scope of the dragnet dawned on them, Lefstein thought it sounded like "the most lawless thing I've ever heard of." He told Barbara and Wald, "I'm going to go into an office and I'm going to close the door and write some kind of a challenge to what the hell is going on here."

But how to write such a thing? It wasn't just one lawyer filing on behalf of a known client. It was a bunch of lawyers acting for thousands of nameless people. There was hardly time to do any research. Lefstein drafted something that he wasn't sure had been done before.

They called it "Complaint for Habeas Corpus, Temporary Restraining Order, or Any Appropriate Relief." The named petitioners surely were among the more notable in American jurisprudence: "JOHN DOE and approximately 1,700 Detainees Confined Adjacent to Robert F. Kennedy Memorial Stadium vs. Jerry Wilson et al." It asked for the immediate release of everyone on the football field.

Barbara read it and made her edits. She called Judge Greene's office to say her deputy was on his way with an important motion. Lefstein hurried the few blocks to the Superior Court. He swept past the clerk's office, where you were supposed to file your motions, and strode into the judge's chambers. He laid the filing on Greene's desk. This is an emergency and we want a hearing, Lefstein explained to the judge, and we want it as soon as possible.

For Judge Greene, here was another test case as to how the justice system should deal with mass arrests. He agreed to hear the motion, and the government's arguments against it, that very evening.

AT ABOUT THE SAME TIME, John Ehrlichman was making his own inspection of the football field. After his morning helicopter ride he still felt restless, eager to see the action instead of sitting around in the White House command center. He persuaded the Secret Service to chauffeur him through the George Washington and Georgetown campuses so he could shoot more movies of the clashes with his Super 8. And when he heard about the detention camp, he decided to drive over to check things out.

Ehrlichman, of course, had been a prime water carrier for Nixon's hard line on Mayday. He could have been the anonymous "high White House aide" quoted by reporters as crowing about the successful breakup of the gathering at West Potomac Park: "The cleverness of Rennie Davis' plan was to get a lot of bystanders into the demonstration by throwing a rock concert. We probably couldn't have controlled it this morning if we hadn't gotten rid of the innocents."

When Ehrlichman arrived at the detention site across from the stadium, second thoughts began creeping in.

While he found the camp to be calm, "like a crowd at a football game," he saw a potential public relations disaster. The whole arrest operation was "badly run," he observed. Knowing this was Richard Kleindienst's show, he blamed the Justice Department, not the police. The attorney general's office had "failed to provide for heavy arrest rate. Most are illegal. No field note of offense." He headed back to the White House to await Nixon's imminent return from California and to figure out how to get these people inside for the night.

He noted in his diary, "Concern re: 'concentration camp' at RFK Stadium."

AS GRACE PALEY and Barbara Deming had found, the detention camp was also a big reunion for people who'd been part of the movement but isolated in their own small groups during the planning. Stew Albert didn't find his Yippie ex-girlfriend Judy Gumbo, though. She hadn't been among those arrested. As it turned out, after all the preparation, she hadn't even participated in Mayday. She would explain later that she and her affinity group, which had gotten royally stoned Sunday night, decided they were too strung out to get up before dawn like everyone else. They slept in. They would join the protest, as a second wave, a little later in the morning. But by the time they hit the streets, looking for action, it was all over. For years Judy would cite it as an embarrassing leadership lesson she learned — you can't let self-indulgence get in the way of your commitments.

The police chief had ordered hamburgers for the first arrivals at the field. ("You've got a real sense of power, Mr. President," Jerry later told Nixon, with some exaggeration, "when you call up McDonald's and say I want five thousand Big Macs.") That food was gone by the time the bulk of the arrestees arrived. Other than some apples and bananas tossed over the fence by sympathetic visitors, most of those penned in the field had to wait six hours for food, until the police brought bologna sandwiches and sodas. Later, activists from the black community, the same ones who had helped feed the kids at West Potomac Park, talked their way through the police lines to throw sandwiches and fried chicken over the fence. The army summoned a water truck and ran a hose into the compound.

The protesters within the crowd tried to keep their spirits high. To the tune of the Beatles' "Yellow Submarine," they sang, "*We all live in a concentration camp, concentration camp, concentration camp.*" Other times they chanted a plea for their beverage of choice: "Boone's Farm! Boone's Farm!" Someone lettered a crude sign naming their detention camp and nailed it up. They would shout out this camp nickname whenever the buses brought a new wave of detainees: "Welcome to Insurrection City!"

One young couple from New York State — he from Staten Island, she from Newburgh — were engaged. They said they had nothing to do with Mayday and got swept up after walking out of a restaurant. In the compound they found a Baptist minister from Georgia among the throng to marry them on the spot.

Another couple recognized Abbie Hoffman, who had showed up with a broken nose he secured while fighting with cops in Georgetown. "My god," Stew told him. "You're a bloody mess." The young lovers wanted a mock wedding and asked the Yippie star if he would officiate. Hoffman agreed, on the condition that they help him escape. After the ceremony, the wedding party, which included Stew, found an unguarded part of the fence and managed to dig under it just deep enough for Hoffman to squeeze through to freedom. (That was Stew's version, anyway. Hoffman later variously claimed he'd been smuggled out in a medical orderly's jacket or inside a garbage can.) The FBI would track down Hoffman in New York and arrest him Wednesday night, on charges of incitement to riot.

Word of the detention camp filtered through Washington. Four Democratic members of Congress decided to inspect the scene. A little after four in the afternoon, they pushed their way inside. One of them was Bella Abzug, a New York civil rights lawyer who had been among a crop of antiwar Democrats swept into office in the midterm elections the previous November. Marching through the crowd in her trademark cape and big hat, to cheers of "Bella, baby!" the congresswoman recognized the writer Grace Paley from their common Manhattan literary and progressive circles. For years the two women had been debating the value of straight politics (Abzug) versus direct action (Paley). Well, Abzug told Paley, "I guess you're where you want to be. And I'm where I want to be." They had a good laugh over it.

After leaving the detention area, though, Abzug flashed with anger as she denounced the roundup. "Under the American system of justice, you are arrested and charged," she said. "They are penned in there like animals."

• • •

IN MID-AFTERNOON, Jerry Wilson reversed his order concerning the field arrest forms. All units were instructed to use them. But by then the action had ended.

Like Ehrlichman, Jerry had toured the campus of George Washington University. As he walked, angry students taunted him, calling him a "pig." Around noon, the police chief rode over to the Justice Department to meet with Kleindienst and others. No one took the minutes, but Sanford J. Ungar, a *Washington Post* reporter whose beat entailed staying in close contact with Kleindienst, was told by sources that Justice officials had decided it would be good policy to "keep those arrested out of circulation" for at least twelve hours.

Whatever went on behind closed doors, it was clear the authorities were dragging their feet in getting prisoners processed or moved. Kleindienst and other hard-liners had previously broken with American legal tradition in their new D.C. crime law, which allowed for preventive detention for certain people suspected of violent crimes. Now they were taking the opportunity to apply it to nonviolent suspects on a massive scale.

AT THE SUGGESTION, or order, of the Justice Department, Jerry's chief counsel, Gerald Caplan, put in a call to Philip Hirschkop, the lawyer who negotiated the permits for the Mayday Tribe. If the protest groups promised to leave the city quietly and end all the demonstrations, Caplan told him, the ten-dollar collateral system would be resumed and the prisoners could bail themselves out. But even if Rennie Davis and his fellow organizers wanted to make such a promise — which they didn't — they couldn't speak on behalf of all the affinity groups. That just wasn't how it worked, which was something that the authorities still didn't understand.

As the dust settled, the Mayday Tribe summoned reporters to the Executive House hotel at Scott Circle. Rennie, still rattled by Sunday's police raid in the park, had been up most of the night regrouping and looked "hollow cheeked and blank-eyed with exhaustion." (But he still managed to dress well, "elegant in a suede jacket," noted one writer.) On Monday morning he had moved around the city, observing first the fruits of his months of organizing and then the enormous police dragnet.

In less than peak condition, Rennie badly bungled his public statement. While he called Mayday "almost the most major nonviolent demonstration" in U.S. history, he also said, "We want to make clear that we failed this morning to stop the U.S. government. Our biggest problem was not appreciating the extent to which the government would go to put people on the skids."

Many years on, Rennie would explain that he was obsessed that afternoon with what he had believed was a fatal tactical mistake. The mass of protesters had been so worried about the police and military that they'd hit the streets too early, in his view — more than an hour before the peak of the morning rush hour. Thus they didn't tie up the traffic as definitively as he'd hoped. "We dropped a ball, that's all," he would say later. "I was just acknowledging that."

But at the time, Rennie's cohorts watched with astonishment as he seemed to admit total defeat. Sidney Peck, a Cleveland professor who along with Dave Dellinger had been one of the longtime stalwarts of the movement, found it "ridiculous." What exactly did it mean to fail? Had anyone on either side really expected the American government to come to a dead stop — the White House to go dark, the Pentagon to stop issuing orders, the Treasury to stop writing checks, the Selective Service to stop sending draft notices — because of traffic tie-ups, even big ones?

To Peck and others, Mayday had been "a major political statement, a victory." By any measure, they had achieved their goal of disrupting Washington, of forcing the government and its citizens to pay attention. They had turned out some twelve thousand people willing to put themselves in harm's way to stop a war, many of them first-time demonstrators. Thousands of motorists had been inconvenienced, and while lots of them were irritated, plenty of people stuck a fist out the window in support — even some National Guardsmen. The White House had turned the city into an armed camp on questionable authority, police went on a rampage, and the jails were full to bursting.

And despite thousands of frustrated radicals running through the streets, there had been few casualties. There was scattered property damage — some broken windows, slashed and punctured tires, trashcans in the roads. The small number of injuries came almost exclusively at the hands of aggressive riot cops wildly swinging their sticks. The pledge of nonviolence from Dave, Rennie, and other organizers had been kept.

If that was failure, then what would success have looked like?

But no matter. Even before noon, Attorney General John Mitchell had declared victory over Mayday. "The city is open, the traffic is flowing, the government is functioning," he proudly told reporters. The newspaper headlines and network news would contrast Mitchell's statement with Rennie's words — "We failed." The first summation of the protest conveyed to the public would be, at best, incomplete. Contributing to that impression was a new kind of radio report, which contained its own glitches.

WHEN THE CLOCK struck five that evening, the reporters and editors of National Public Radio weren't ready. Their audio news magazine, *All Things Considered,* was supposed to sign on for the first time, live on about ninety stations across the country. They had been rushing to mix down the hours of recordings they'd made all over the city. At least one of the five reporters had been tear-gassed and another briefly detained by the cops. Their documentary was not quite done. So the program manager, Bill Siemering, told the host of the show, Robert Conley, a former reporter for the *New York Times,* to ad-lib until producers could cue up the finished tape.

"The day started out almost before dawn," began Conley, sounding a tad nervous and unprepared. He filled the dead space with bits of scenes that he recalled from the editing process or wire service reports. The protesters "spread nails and puddles of oil" on the roads, he said, and "a truck filled with paper was set afire." He said some demonstrators "cut fuel lines on buses" while others ran up to stalled cars, "pulled open the hood of the car and yanked out the distributor caps so the engine couldn't run anymore."

The documentary was ready within a couple of minutes. Siemering, in the control room, tried to alert Conley. Something was wrong, though, and Conley couldn't hear him through his headphones. So the host rambled on for six minutes in all. He quoted the attorney general's pronouncement that the blockade had failed and the government's claim that attendance had been normal at federal offices. While acknowledging the seven thousand arrests, the only consequence he cited was "a sizeable crush in the courts," which of course wasn't true, since no one was being brought to court. The sizable crush in cells and detention camps went unmentioned.

When he finally realized the tape was ready, Conley explained, with palpable relief, "Rather than pulling in reports from all over town, we thought we might try to take you to the events to get the feel, the texture of the sort of day it's been."

What followed was twenty-five minutes of powerful, if chaotic, vérité reporting. Anyone who listened carefully after Conley's introduction received an impression far more sympathetic to the protest. "Thousands of young people came to Washington willing to risk being arrested in order to end the war," a reporter began. "It was their Freedom Ride, their Selma march, their Mayday." The piece went on to paint the scenes of tear gas, sirens, shouts, helicopters. "Sir, it's another Saigon," offered one Vietnam veteran, not a protester but a minister volunteering at an emergency room jammed with kids who needed stitches in their heads from encounters with billy clubs. There were interviews with several federal workers who said that despite the inconvenience of the blockade, they recognized that the antiwar movement needed to try new tactics.

For its brilliant originality in programming, *All Things Considered* would win NPR a Peabody Award the following year. But the maiden broadcast, at least, demonstrated the weakness of an approach eschewing narration, context, and analysis. It touched on the police roundup only obliquely: "Today in the nation's capital it is a crime to be young and have long hair," one of the reporters said. There was nothing about the effective suspension of civil liberties. It would be a while yet before NPR figured out how to combine creative use of audio with thorough reporting, a marriage that eventually would build the program into one of the nation's major and most respected news sources.

AFTER HIS PRESS CONFERENCE, Rennie, tired and frustrated, headed back to the Mayday offices with Sidney Peck and other fellow organizers and lawyers. They argued about what to do. Before they even reached the next intersection, two unmarked cars carrying FBI agents slammed on the brakes next to them on Massachusetts Avenue. The agents took Rennie, drove him to federal court, and booked him on charges that he conspired "to injure, oppress, threaten, and intimidate United States citizens in the free exercise and enjoyment of rights and privileges secured to them by the Constitution and the laws of the United States." Told of the arrest, Nixon's chief of staff approved, saying, "Rennie Davis symbolizes it."

Prosecutors requested bail to be set at $100,000. Rennie's lawyer, Philip Hirschkop, told the judge that was excessive, given that the civil disobedience in Washington was analogous to the civil rights movement. "Just like sitting in a drug store," the lawyer said. "It's the same principle." The judge reduced Rennie's bond to $25,000. He would be in jail for two days until his supporters could raise the cash.

The Justice Department had decided to charge, in addition to Rennie, two other members of the Chicago Seven, John Froines and Abbie Hoffman. So far, the officers had been unable to find either. David Dellinger, the spiritual godfather of Mayday, still in the hospital with eye trouble, wasn't mentioned.

THE WEATHER in the late afternoon remained cool, cloudy, and windy. It would drop into the thirties after nightfall. The police and the White House could face a backlash if they kept thousands of people outside overnight at the football field and in the jail yard.

The authorities put in a call to a printing and publishing executive named Charles Lockyer. A couple of years earlier, Lockyer's company had acquired a D.C. landmark known as the Coliseum. Originally built in the 1940s by a man who thought a skating arena would be a natural extension of his booming ice business, the Coliseum still hosted the Ice Capades, and it had over the years also become the home of hockey and basketball teams, boxing and wrestling matches, and the circus. In February 1964, it was the site of the Beatles' first public performance in America, accompanied by the deafening screams of eight thousand hysterical fans. The group had opened with "Roll Over Beethoven."

Now the police were on the phone, asking Lockyer if they could put a few thousand prisoners inside his facility. They could pay him five hundred dollars a day. Lockyer didn't much like the idea. Saying no would, however, pit him against all the powers in the city, right in the middle of an emergency.

The buses were called back into service, to ferry the detainees to the

Coliseum. They were herded inside and onto the main floor. The temperature was more comfortable than it had been outdoors, but still only about fifty degrees.

AS THE BUSES ROLLED, Barbara and her associates climbed the steps of the Superior Court, just before sunset. They carried hastily prepared briefs as well as affidavits the lawyers had taken from about a hundred prisoners through the fence outside RFK Stadium.

In his courtroom, Judge Greene called the case of *JOHN DOE v. Jerry Wilson* at about seven-thirty. In the hours since the public defenders had written their habeas motion, they'd heard reports of the other sites in town filled with detainees. They now were asking for the immediate release of everyone held and arrested on Mayday.

Barbara deferred to Lefstein, her deputy, who stood and held up for the judge the front page of the afternoon newspaper, the *Washington Evening Star*, with the headline "City Shutdown Foiled, 6,000 Protesters Held."

"Your honor," Lefstein began, "we have witnessed in the District of Columbia probably the largest number of arrests that this city has ever seen in a given day."

The judge impatiently waved this off. He already knew it. "You don't have to read from the paper," he said.

"Seven thousand persons have been arrested in the District of Columbia to date, approximately," Lefstein went on, "and the allegation made in our complaint is that in large numbers of cases these persons were arrested in a dragnet fashion." There were no field arrest forms and thus no records of who arrested them, or why. Therefore, Lefstein argued, there was simply no possibility of prosecuting these people.

The judge asked Lefstein, "How do we know that they don't have some other method of identifying them or connecting them up with an offense?"

The lawyers for D.C. and the Justice Department asked for more time to do just that, saying the habeas action had been filed too soon. A more "reasonable time" to seek release, said the city's lawyer, might be "a week or so." What's more, he attempted to have the public defenders removed from the case, on the theory that they had no authorization to handle misdemeanors like disorderly conduct. Perhaps the government lawyer didn't know that Judge Greene himself had invited them.

THE ARGUMENTS CONTINUED in the courtroom. At Andrews Air Force Base, where the big B-52s that had carried in the troops still lined the tarmac, Air Force One came home with the president on board.

Early news reports were running against the protest. On the flight back from California, Nixon had grown excited, anticipating a public relations victory and a reversal of the favorable image the Spring Offensive had earned so far. En route, the president had even wondered out loud to Haldeman if it wouldn't be smarter for them to release the prisoners tonight, so they could engage in more "trashing" and get more bad press tomorrow. "Pic on evening news is critical," Haldeman wrote in his notes.

The president's helicopter landed at the White House around eight in the evening, and he immediately summoned his two top aides to the Lincoln Sitting Room for another update and a discussion of what was to come.

Nixon said he wanted his aides to get to work on tagging his most liberal Democratic opponent, George McGovern of South Dakota, with any negative publicity from the demonstrations, just the way the Democrats had, he said as a reminder, tried to link him to the extreme-right-wing John Birch Society. "Be sure McGovern can't avoid these demonstrators," he told them.

The three of them agreed that Mayday "has gone extremely well for us. At least so far," Haldeman recorded in his diary.

Nixon was hoping for more good news on Tuesday, perhaps some injuries that could be blamed on the protesters. "Be sure police are hurt tomorrow," the president instructed his aides.

AFTER THE HABEAS HEARING, Judge Greene retired to his chambers to consider what to do.

The proceedings had made it quite clear — an overwhelming number of the arrests were indefensible in court. The lawyers for the city government and the administration hadn't shown otherwise. To boot, they had also displayed zero interest in speedy justice. No protester had been presented for arraignment until almost twelve hours after the arrests began, and by nightfall only a few hundred had appeared in court. "You can't say that the greatest haste was made in bringing these cases before the court," the annoyed judge had admonished D.C.'s attorney. The same thing had happened Sunday night, when another judge had to threaten prosecutors to get the city to produce the people arrested after the raid on West Potomac Park.

But the case wasn't cut and dried. If Greene ordered the immediate release of thousands of people, there would be no way to hold responsible that small number whose guilt might be provable. On the other hand, if he didn't release them, the court would be implicitly endorsing an arguably unconstitutional mass detention.

A little before midnight, he issued his order. The police and the city would have to show they had cause for holding the prisoners, or release them. "It is extremely unlikely," Greene wrote, "that a successful prosecution can be brought under the circumstances without a field arrest form or the equivalent and a photograph." Greene added a concise and elegant summation of the Great Writ: "The interest of justice requires that persons against whom charges cannot be sustained shall not be held in confinement."

But though it sounded like a win for Barbara and her public defenders, that wasn't quite the case. The judge made a concession to the city and the Justice Department, giving them until eight the following evening to prove they had usable evidence against the prisoners. Which meant that people who already had been locked up for more than half a day could be confined for at least another twenty hours.

Then even that slim victory evaporated. The lawyers for the city went to the next-highest authority, the D.C. Court of Appeals, the equivalent of a state supreme court. The public defenders loathed the conservative panel for its propensity to side with the prosecution no matter what. Three of its judges held a telephone conference shortly after midnight. They issued a stay on Greene's order and agreed to hear arguments about it first thing in the morning.

It would be another night without sleep. The public defenders now felt like they were at war.

19

A Heavy Cloud

Tuesday, May 4

BY EARLY TUESDAY, TWO THOUSAND PRISONERS WERE stretched out uncomfortably on the oval concrete floor of the Washington Coliseum, a sea of exhausted refugees lying hip to hip, right up to the wooden barriers at the edges. Many more sat in the bleachers. Red, white, and blue banners hung from the ceiling, where the overhead lights glared all night. Thousands more detainees were scattered in various lockups around the city, but this was the largest group.

Inside the arena, the cool air was sour with tear-gas fumes, which lingered in the clothes of the crowd; it blended with the body odor of people locked up together all day. Late in the night the National Guard provided blankets (according to credible reports, Justice officials had deliberately delayed this action), but there weren't quite enough to go around. Lots of people were lying on a jacket. Or right on the bare floor.

Hundreds were standing in line to get released. That was because late on Monday, Police Chief Jerry Wilson had revived the bail system he'd suspended the previous week. Jerry had done this while the public defenders were in the courthouse across town, making the case that the arrests and detentions were illegal. Whatever the judge decided, it was becoming clear that authorities no longer could drag their feet in processing their prisoners just to "keep them out of circulation."

A police official took the microphone for the Coliseum's public-address system, the same one that usually announced a hockey play or gravity-defying trick by a circus acrobat. His voice echoed through the arena, informing the detainees that they could now pay ten dollars in collateral and earn their freedom.

There was a catch, though. Each would have to give a name and address, submit to fingerprinting, and have a mug shot taken, thus creating an official arrest record. Like all such documents, it would be sent to the FBI. For the majority, that would be their first entry into the criminal justice system. (A secret FBI review would find that only 1,415 of the 9,000 Mayday fingerprint cards it received came from people with prior records.) This wasn't normal police policy for minor offenses like disorderly conduct or trespassing, usually handled without creating such a record. The Justice Department was, however, eager to identify any known troublemakers among the crowd. "I want to see what we turn up here," Assistant Attorney General Will R. Wilson, whom Kleindienst had put in charge of the scene, told an underling.

Jerry had also sent his most trusted deputy to keep an eye on things at the Coliseum, the same man he'd dispatched to the National Mall to make sure the Vietnam veterans weren't arrested. Maurice Cullinane couldn't remember ever having seen anything so bizarre. Cully had grown up in Washington and spent his life on the force. One day he would be chief of police himself.

National Guardsmen would appear with sandwiches or cigarettes, throw them over the barrier into the crowd on the floor. Someone sent boxes of oranges, and these too were lobbed into the air, one by one. It looked like feeding time at the zoo. The group would break out into song and chants. Once, a small cluster of male and female protesters caught Cully's eye. They turned around, bent over, and pulled down their pants. They had used a black marker to draw a letter on each cheek. The message they bared spelled out "F-U-C-K N-I-X-O-N."

Cully just shook his head. It didn't exactly improve his impression of the protesters. But neither did he feel very proud of how his colleagues were handling things. When he'd arrived late Monday, he was pained to see wagonloads of young people hauled into the arena without any paperwork. He wondered how the police could now fill out an arrest record if they had no idea who did the bust. "You can't tell me one policeman's name?" he said. "Who am I going to book 'em to?"

He had identified the key problem. And the Justice Department had stepped in with a solution.

Richard Kleindienst had shipped a group of young Justice lawyers to the arena, to sit behind the tables and process the prisoners. As they filled out the forms, they were instructed to fuzz up the time and place of arrest. In those boxes they were to write simply "3rd of May, 1971" and "Public Street." Their bosses handed them a list with names and badge numbers of seven policemen. They were to randomly enter one of them in the space for arresting officer.

In other words, the Justice lawyers were told to falsify the record to establish grounds for an arrest that otherwise would be indefensible in court. When some of the lawyers questioned whether this was ethical or legal, they were told it was being done on the authority of the attorney general's office, and those who didn't like it could leave.

No one did. One Justice lawyer assigned to the arena, James P. Turner, a deputy assistant attorney general in the civil rights division, called Kleindienst in the early morning hours, urging that everyone be released instead. Kleindienst refused.

Meanwhile, lawyers for the other side, from the public defender service, the ACLU, and other groups, had been trying for hours to get into the arena. They were bunched on the other side of the Coliseum doors, standing with dozens of friends and relatives who were waiting for news of the kids who'd been busted.

It wasn't until nine on Monday night that police permitted five of the defense lawyers through the door, including Ralph Temple, the legal director of the Washington ACLU. A *Washington Post* reporter, James Mann, managed to slip in quietly with them, and for hours he would be the only working journalist documenting the situation.

Up until then, the prisoners had no access to anyone on the outside. The demonstrators asked Temple why they hadn't been permitted so far to use the Coliseum's pay telephones or talk to a lawyer. "Yes, you have those rights," Temple answered, "and they're being violated because the court system has broken down." Okay, one demonstrator told Temple, this is a lesson in why the liberal establishment is wrong on how to bring about change: "You tell us to work within the system, and when we try to, they ignore the system . . . they smash us with naked power."

In the early morning hours the defense lawyers got word of Judge Greene's habeas order. They were elated. They told the prisoners that if they waited until the hearing scheduled for Tuesday night, there was a good chance they would never have to submit to processing or create an arrest record.

But by dawn the lines of ragged protesters at the tables were just as long. Most of the prisoners told the lawyers they would rather pay ten dollars, get out, and take the consequences than wait any longer for the justice system to protect them. Henry Allen, the assistant editor at the *Washington Post* who had been held first in the D.C. jail yard and then bused to the arena, paid his collateral. At eight in the morning on Tuesday, Allen stepped out on the street. He had been detained for twenty-one hours. He and the hundreds of others knew they were giving up their rights. But they couldn't imagine tolerating another day in that place.

WHEN HE WOKE Tuesday morning to the news coverage of Mayday, President Nixon was delighted.

For the most part the newspaper stories remained unsympathetic to the demonstrators and appreciative of Jerry's police. They focused on the fact that the protesters hadn't stopped the government and emphasized instances in which demonstrators had destroyed property. With most prisoners still held incognito, only a very few reporters and other observers were raising questions about the nature of the arrests and the detention centers. The president passed around to his aides "good comments" from the broadcast journalist Eric Sevareid, who had branded the protest as ghastly and declared that not even the most extreme civil libertarians could object to the police tactics.

The *Washington Post*, which Nixon considered the mouthpiece of the capital's liberal elite, editorialized that the protesters had "obliterated" their message, and their legitimate criticism of the war, by resorting to a "rampage" of blocking streets with trashcans and their own bodies, by their "invitation to violence, the battling with police." Law enforcement agencies acted with "skill and discipline," the editorial said.

Unmentioned by the *Post* editorial was the almost complete lack of reports of acts of violence attributed to any of the twelve thousand protesters. (There had been scattered incidents of vandalism, such as slashed tires and broken mailboxes or lampposts. A handful of kids had thrown rocks or bottles at police who gassed them, but only a few cops got hit. By contrast, many more protesters were treated for cuts and bruises caused by police officers' nightsticks and for respiratory distress.) Nor did it devote a single word to the dragnet, the swinging billy clubs, the tear gas.

The *Post* editorial conceded one thing — a pretty big thing, really, though it was mentioned offhandedly — to the people who organized Mayday. They had been "among the first to sense a wrongness in the war," and the majority of the American people probably wouldn't be supporting a pullout "had they not been in the streets several years ago, shouting for attention, shattering the indifference." But the editorial argued that the Mayday protest had set back the antiwar movement — something you could read "in the words and faces of frightened, outraged citizens, surveying the damage."

Who were these frightened, outraged citizens? One, anyway, was the deputy editor of the *Post*'s editorial page. At the age of forty, Meg Greenfield was already an influential Washington journalist as well as one of the highest-ranking women in the business. So moved against Mayday was Greenfield that, besides writing or helping to write that day's stinging editorial, she penned a personal column published on the same page. It went a long way toward explaining her antipathy. Greenfield lived in an elegant brick townhouse in Georgetown. Early Monday morning, she wrote, she had watched the demonstration from her window, becoming enraged by the "scruffy" and "tattered" demonstrators who had the temerity to turn "our small street" into a staging area for the protest. They parked their "bedroll-laden U-Haul truck" and pulled obstacles into the intersections to block traffic. Greenfield put down her coffee and, still barefoot and in her bathrobe, ran down to retrieve her trashcans from the middle of the street.

At their mid-morning meeting in the Oval Office, Nixon and Haldeman, his chief of staff, crowed over the coverage. They chuckled merrily about Greenfield's garbage run. Nixon had been worried that the press might hit him for hiding out in California most of Monday, or that the protest might "hurt us" as did the "emotional" medal-throwing ceremony by the Vietnam veterans. Instead, "the *Washington Post* editorial this morning just smashed 'em," Haldeman told the president. A pleased Nixon said of the demonstrators: "I think that they were bad people." Haldeman agreed. "It's not even like Chicago, where the bad guys were the police for a while," he said. "In this one, the media aren't making the police the bad guys."

It was Nixon's first full day back at the White House. He held meetings all morning and afternoon with his aides, administration officials, and Republican lawmakers. They discussed not only Vietnam but dozens of topics, including a proposed supersonic passenger plane, the upcoming presidential "Salute to Agriculture," and the economic troubles of West Germany. Yet time and again Nixon steered the conversation back to the Mayday protests. He sought reassurance that they would help his public image. "The country this time," Nixon marveled, "is on our side." He checked in with his personal secretary and longtime friend, Rose Mary Woods, asking, "What do you think of these people that have been raising hell?" and she answered, "They're awful-looking people . . . long hair and dirty and just crummy-looking people. Just the lowest of the low." And Nixon agreed: "What a lousy bunch of bastards they were." At another meeting he told Ehrlichman, "These are really animals, aren't they?"

Haldeman had only one concern about the government's response. He saw potential danger in the military assault on the National Mall. The startling images caught by the press could be used against them. "Maybe it wasn't a very good idea, this helicopter landing on the Monument grounds," he said. "What was the point? The streets were open, they could have driven in. Why did they come in helicopters and stage a big thing, you know?"

Nixon retorted he had no problem seeing the choppers on the Mall. And, he said, it was fun for the troops. The happy day was putting him into one of his expansive moods. He imitated the sounds for his aides: "Coming in there with a helicopter, you know: dih-dih-dih. You know, the kids get out their toy pistol: Bih-bih-bih-bih-bih-bih-bih. Hell, they love it. If we're right on the basic issue, it adds to the drama."

In fact, the president thought the squelching of Mayday could be held up as a national model, a law-and-order success story. Soon he would instruct Bud Krogh to assemble a packet to be mailed to every mayor, police chief, and governor in the country, containing a cover letter from the D.C. mayor Walter Washington, a police handbook on managing public disorders from Police Chief Wilson, and a copy of an opinion poll showing the public's disapproval of the protesters. (Later, Bud would report back that there was no such police manual because Jerry "operates pretty much out of his hip pocket," and the idea for the mailing would wither away.)

More important, Nixon said, the bad impression of Mayday was a political opportunity. They could hang it around the necks of his Democratic challengers in the next year's presidential election. "Goddam it, smear 'em!" said the president. "They deserve it!" At another point he advised: "Kick 'em in the balls." And forget any nuances, he instructed his aides, perhaps recalling his work as a communist-hunter during his Congress days. "Just charge that they endorsed the demonstration," Nixon said. "Then let them deny." At another point he said, "Only way to do it is to keep making the charge."

Yet few mainstream Democrats were defending the protest. They took their cues from the early news coverage. Those who had voiced support for the rest of the Spring Offensive, including leading senators and John Kerry of the veterans' protest, distanced themselves from Mayday. A Democratic congresswoman from Oregon rose on the House floor to proclaim that though she opposed the war, she could not back "the crazies who have been in Washington this week."

Even Senator Sam Ervin, the North Carolina Democrat who was at that moment presiding over hearings on illegal government surveillance of domestic dissenters, praised the police for "a rather fine job." His comments ran against his usual position. He had, for example, just published an article in the *Denver Law Review* accusing the administration of playing "a dangerous game" as it "nurtured, encouraged and fostered" a national mood "toward the acceptance of harsher laws and the cutting of Constitutional corners" in the name of security. "Tyranny," Ervin had written, "can come just as surely if the people are willing to deliver over their freedom in search for safety."

Nixon's men were surprised and pleased that their nemesis — "the great defender of constitutional liberties and all," as Haldeman described Ervin — was supporting their response to Mayday. Still, Haldeman recognized that this was only the first round of coverage. "Civil rights types," the chief of staff warned, would soon "start squealing about they shouldn't have been arrested."

Neither were the streets yet quiet, Haldeman told Nixon. A few hundred more young people milling around town had been arrested early Tuesday in sweep tactics similar to Monday's, mostly on charges unrelated to demonstrations, such as jaywalking. Worse, he informed the president, the militants who weren't in jail, or who had been released, planned another big action today "to prove they've got some balls." They were to gather at a park near Pennsylvania Avenue and then march to the Justice Department. As soon as they start, Haldeman said, "we arrest them." Then tomorrow, he told Nixon, the Federal Employees for Peace in Vietnam planned to rally in Lafayette Square across from the White House, where the cast of *Hair*—that damn group again!—was set to provide entertainment. The Park Service had granted the organization a permit, but at the Justice Department, John Mitchell and Richard Kleindienst were trying to figure out if they could obtain an injunction to revoke it.

The Federal Employees for Peace were probably a "bunch of goddam State Department bastards," Nixon mused. At one point in the day he acknowledged that most government workers in D.C. were probably Democrats, and against the war. "Christ's sake," Nixon said, "they can't be anything else in this town."

If Mayday was looking like a win for the administration, it didn't lack for other signs of growing opposition to its Vietnam strategy, even in the heartland. It had been exactly one year since National Guardsmen had shot four students to death during the demonstration at Kent State University. As the Mayday protesters sat in confinement, some seven thousand people attended a memorial service at the Ohio school. The day before, the *Akron Beacon Journal* was awarded a Pulitzer Prize for its reporting on the Kent State killings. (Coverage of the nation's tumult dominated the Pulitzers, as prizes went to John Paul Filo, the local news photographer who captured the moment of death that would forever exemplify Kent State; and to United Press International, for diving into the life of a young woman in the Weather Underground who died in the explosion of the group's bomb factory in New York.)

The same day, the twin cities of Fargo, North Dakota, and Moorhead, Minnesota, held a referendum on whether the United States should pull out of Vietnam by the end of the year. It passed with 71 percent of the vote.

AND, JUST AS Haldeman feared, voices with a different opinion than Meg Greenfield's began to be heard. The *New York Times* editorial page criticized the "mass preventive detention" of seven thousand people. While it also gave the police credit for not resorting to the thuggery of the Chicago cops in 1968, the editorial went on to make a quite different point:

This victory for public order, however, is morally empty. It was achieved only by turning the center of the nation's capital into an armed camp with thousands of troops lining the bridges and principal streets, helicopters whirring overhead and helmeted police charging crowds of civilians with nightsticks and tear gas. To evict thousands of peaceful campers from West Potomac Park at dawn on Sunday may have been shrewd police tactics, but it is never a reassuring spectacle to see a Government trying to outmaneuver its own citizens . . . a nation so fevered with unrest, so troubled in its conscience, so much at war with so many of its young people, is a nation under a heavy cloud.

Jerry Wilson had started his day after Mayday with a message of praise to his troops. "Your performance yesterday was magnificent. Be ready to do an encore if needed." But by the time he appeared at a press conference Tuesday afternoon, reporters were asking him whether he didn't now believe the arrests might have gone too far. "I'll leave that up to the American people," said the chief. "I feel I have discharged my duties." In response to another question he parsed his words as carefully as any Washington politician or lawyer: "There was no blanket policy of arrests."

Not all local officials toed the line. At another press conference at city hall, the Rev. David H. Eaton, chairman of the city's human relations commission, whose day job as a Unitarian minister didn't depend on the White House, bristled when asked if Mayor Walter Washington had made or concurred in the decision to run a dragnet: "Every source I've been able to check shows it was made by the President of the United States, passed on to Attorney General Mitchell to Kleindienst to Chief Wilson. The mayor was not consulted in any way whatsoever."

WITH THE MAYDAY TRIBE locked up, life in official Washington carried on. The annual luncheon of the Ladies of the Senate proceeded on schedule. Its members were the wives and widows of present and former lawmakers. The group had met at the Capitol most every Tuesday since World War I to don Red Cross uniforms, roll bandages, and provide other items for the charity. At the lunch the women wore large black-and-white tags, lettered not with their names but those of their husbands. The guest of honor was the First Lady. Pat Nixon occasionally opined in public about the left. In March she had told reporters that the Capitol bombing "must have been the work of a madman because no one would bomb his own property." ("Excellent quote!" the president observed.) Now asked about Mayday, she said, "It sort of failed, I understand." She said she was glad of that, adding she had "no sympathy with people who break the law or try to deny freedom to others." "I agree," rejoined Judy Agnew, who as the vice president's wife was by tradition the club's president. The First Lady reported back to the White House that the guests told her the president had "saved our country."

As the lunch progressed, though, a second big Mayday protest was gearing up. At noon, John Dean, who was continuing to issue blow-by-blow memos from his West Wing office to Nixon's inner circle, reported that demonstrators were gathering at Franklin Square, with plans to march about ten blocks to the Justice Department in protest of the mass arrests. With so many kids locked up, and with Monday's aggressive tactics surely providing a deterrent, police and Justice officials had figured on a small crowd.

But instead, Dean wrote, they already numbered two thousand and were growing. "Mass arrests expected," Dean added. As Haldeman had promised the president, Dean had little doubt the police would sweep up this latest manifestation of Mayday.

At first, Justice officials thought they might be able to prevent the march from reaching them by busting everyone for violating the city law against parading down the street without a permit. They were surprised when the protest leaders at Franklin Park acceded to Jerry Wilson's suggestion to walk down the sidewalks, no more than four abreast. The police chief strolled along the route with them, but in the middle of the road, between the rows of demonstrators on each side. As was his custom, he wore his soft chief's hat instead of a helmet, and an earphone for his radio.

The protesters spread out over almost the entire three-quarter-mile route from the park to Justice. By early afternoon, about four thousand people were sitting down, first on the sidewalks and then the pavement of Tenth Street, on the west side of the building. Riot police wearing helmets and carrying gas masks sealed off both sides of the block. For more than an hour the protesters sat peacefully, chanting slogans and singing songs.

Attorney General Mitchell, sometimes accompanied by Kleindienst and other aides, stepped through the French doors in his office onto a small fifth-floor balcony, puffing on his pipe while taking in the scene. Mitchell realized he wasn't going to make it to the White House for a three-thirty appointment with the president. He called Haldeman to ask if they could reschedule.

From the White House you could hear the military helicopters heading to Justice headquarters for aerial surveillance. Mitchell is "under assault over there," Haldeman reported to Nixon.

The president agreed. "It may look as if, if he's here, as though we're planning a war," Nixon said.

A little later, the president wondered out loud if police could clear out the demonstrators any faster with the techniques that cops in the South had used to break up civil rights marches. He asked, "Any reason that we don't use fire hoses on these people rather than that darned tear gas?" His aides told him that they had indeed raised the idea with Jerry Wilson on Monday, but the chief had nixed it. (Secretly horrified, Jerry had told the White House that it would be counterproductive because it would only make the streets slippery and tie up traffic even further.)

Nixon's press secretary, Ron Ziegler, added gently, "Fire hoses turned on the crowds; that makes a worse picture than tear gas."

"Does it?" Nixon asked. He added, "It's awfully effective."

At Justice, FBI agents surveyed the crowd. They cared little for the rank and file. They were looking for the two men, in addition to Rennie Davis, whom the government wanted to charge with conspiracy for organizing Mayday: Abbie Hoffman and John Froines. Like Rennie, both were members of the Chicago Seven. They spotted Froines outside Justice and tracked him. "The package is now moving east toward the flagpole," one agent reported by radio. Then, "He's standing south of the flagpole talking to a man with a bald head." Then, "We have him! We have him! We have him!"

Minutes after Froines was grabbed, Jerry went off to consult with Justice officials on his next move. He came back shortly before three and soon announced through a bullhorn that the gathering was "an unlawful assembly."

Within minutes, before any more than a small portion of the crowd could find their way out through the police lines, the riot squad moved in to make arrests. Two thousand people were taken. Again, no violence.

"Offenders are dancing and singing and offering no resistance," Dean reported to Nixon. This time, Jerry ordered that the cops use the field arrest forms. It took hours to stick to the rules. But that would not keep this latest roundup from being questioned in court too.

UNTIL MAYDAY, Ralph Temple of the ACLU had thought of Jerry Wilson as a friend, a tough cop but "not a brute." He considered the chief one of the "restraining forces on this administration's desire for repression." Now he saw things differently. For three days in a row, Jerry had carried out actions that reflected the wishes of the president and his men to neutralize a political threat.

If Jerry's goal was to win approval at the White House, it was working. He had become a source of delight and speculation. Most of Nixon's men knew nothing of Jerry's ambivalence, nor did they know that he enjoyed reading books about human behavior, or that he had been pressing to diversify the force with black and female officers. What they loved about the police chief was that he executed the plan and that he made for good photographs when he mounted a motorcycle sidecar to scoot more nimbly around town.

"You know, he's a sort of George Patton–type guy, in a way," Haldeman told the president and Charles Colson, the White House lawyer who Nixon had put in charge of figuring out how to hurt the Democrats.

Haldeman continued, "He was zooming all over the city . . ."

". . . in his motorcycle." Colson finished the sentence.

"Great guy," Nixon agreed. "Aren't we lucky to have him?"

"And he programs beautifully," added Colson. "We talked to him Saturday night about things he should say and he just, just took it word for word, and he did the same thing Sunday."

"What's his background?" Nixon asked.

"Gotta find out," said Haldeman. "Nobody knows. He has a Southern drawl."

"The guy's got to be a hell of a fella," said Nixon. "He's gotta be. And he's got great talent. I don't care whether he went to school or not. He's got talent such as you don't have among most of our bureaucrats, you know, judgment, talent, poise, style. He's got that stature."

The trio also discussed what they considered the challenge of managing Jerry's department.

Haldeman said, "With this kind of police force you've got to have a guy like Patton 'cause you got a —"

"Half of 'em are Negroes," Nixon interjected.

And Haldeman agreed. "You got a potentially shaky police force in here, because they keep pouring these blacks in."

MOST OF THE PEOPLE arrested at Justice were carted to the precincts or the cellblock in the federal court building, replacing those who had been released on collateral over the previous twenty-four hours. This time, there was paperwork for the arrests. Other protocols remained the same: the detained were denied phone calls or legal advice.

Among those grabbed in the sweep, despite his press pass, was a young *Washington Evening Star* reporter named John Mathews. His colleagues lost track of him for more than eighteen hours. He spent much of that time jammed in a cell so crowded, people had to sleep in shifts, the ones on the floor lying head to toe, like sardines in a tin. Real sardines might have been welcomed in the cell. After many hours Mathews and the other prisoners were fed the sandwiches supplied each day by the local restaurant on contract with the city jail — one slice of bologna with "a dab of rancid mayonnaise," served between slices of fluffy white bread.

Mathews and his cellmates passed the hours calmly, sharing cigarettes and debating politics. Spending time with his more radical peers, Mathews came away thinking that "the young people most concerned and analytical about their generation really think they are developing a new culture with new systems of values, or at least old values resurrected and reconsidered." He even let one of his cellmates sleep at his house after they were released.

Once the cells around the city were full up, the last three hundred of those arrested at Justice were brought to the Coliseum. They arrived to cheers from the stalwarts who'd now been there for thirty-six hours because they had refused to be booked and fingerprinted. The new arrivals were herded into the arena's seats, separated from Monday's crowd by a line of police. The new ones soon began a call-and-response chant. "Fuck!" they yelled, as the ones below answered, "Nixon!" Down on the floor, a small group began a nude dance as others circled around them, clapping and chanting, "Body power!"

After subsisting on the bologna sandwiches, the Coliseum prisoners were ecstatic when the guards admitted a group of Washington's black activists, who had arrived at the arena in twelve cars full of donated food and blankets. "I think they collected every blanket in Washington," recalled a civil liberties activist who handed one over herself. They were led by Walter Fauntroy, the city's nonvoting delegate to Congress, and Mary Treadwell, head of Youth Pride, Inc., a community action group that had been started by a former civil rights activist (and future mayor) named Marion Barry. When it came to antiwar protests, African Americans "are not going to put their bodies on the line, we're not going to get our heads beat, but we can at least support these people," Treadwell declared.

The prisoners were convinced Judge Greene would free them all after the hearing he'd scheduled for eight o'clock that night, where the government was supposed to explain why people were still locked up. They began counting down how much longer before the deadline. "Three hours and thirty-five minutes to go!" one yelled out, setting off loud cheering.

NIXON REMAINED A little disappointed there hadn't been more violence and destruction to blame on the protesters. At one point, told that the bomb squad had defused a possible explosive device under one of the Potomac bridges, Nixon exclaimed, "Why the hell didn't they let it blow up?" (The bomb turned out to be fake, only a prank.)

The president knew the man pulling the strings was the deputy attorney general. "Ol' Kleindienst has just been sitting at his desk since Saturday over there and doing a hell of a job," one aide told Nixon, who responded, "He's done very well." Late in the afternoon, the president phoned Kleindienst to check on the protest outside Justice. "What kind of animals you got out there today?" Nixon asked. Kleindienst admitted the protesters had "really fooled us" into thinking the Justice march would only bring in a few hundred people because "we had them all in the clink" Monday night. "And good God Almighty, they showed up with four or five thousand of them . . . they just came like ants from everywhere."

Still, Kleindienst said, in the end it fit their detention plans. The outcome was "pretty good . . . it permitted the chief to just round 'em all up instead of chasing them all over town." There was a tiny pause while

Nixon must have weighed some of the criticism of Monday's sweep, then a touch of wariness in his voice as he asked about the justification for the latest roundup: "On the grounds they were told to disperse and did not, huh?"

In any case, Nixon pronounced, "They're really a crummy lot, aren't they?" He promised to "do something special" to thank Jerry Wilson.

Nixon's aides also alerted him to the situation in the Coliseum. So far the Justice Department had fended off the legal challenges from the public defenders — the lawyers for the administration had "outmaneuvered these guys," said John Ehrlichman, the domestic policy adviser. Yet they still had the problem of fifteen hundred people who were refusing to be fingerprinted and were sticking it out until Greene's hearing that night.

"What can you do to get them out?" the president asked Ehrlichman.

"Oh hell," Ehrlichman said, "starve 'em if necessary. Just turn off the water and food, you know."

"That's easy," said Haldeman.

Nixon acknowledged that no one could force them to be fingerprinted. So he agreed that maybe the best thing was to "turn off their food."

BY THE TIME Barbara Bowman and her public defenders walked into Judge Greene's courtroom at eight Tuesday night, all but about eleven hundred of the seven thousand people arrested in Monday's dragnet were out of detention. Most of those who got out of the Coliseum had paid their ten-dollar collateral and reluctantly accepted a falsified arrest record. In most cases, it turned out, those who had paid collateral, whether in the Coliseum or the cellblocks elsewhere in town, were told incorrectly by police or Justice lawyers that they could be released only if they checked the box agreeing to forfeit the money, rather than the box insisting on a trial date. That amounted to a guilty plea.

Barbara and the other public defenders — now joined by lawyers from the ACLU and other civil liberties groups in town — were infuriated by this process. So when they appeared before the judge, they not only asked for the immediate release of the remaining prisoners but insisted that he order police to tear up the arrest records. Otherwise they would be sent to the FBI, which would thus have the fingerprints and mug shots of thousands of people who were either innocent or had never been properly caught in the act of committing any violation. "We would submit, your honor," said Lefstein, Barbara's deputy, "that law violation by the authorities should be no less subject to the law than violations by demonstrators."

The city's attorneys insisted they had one way to possibly tag the detainees with their infractions. On Monday, police photographers had shot hundreds of feet of movie film and hundreds of still photographs of the protest. The authorities were hustling to develop the film, and when it was ready, they could try to blow up the images and match up the faces in the pictures with those taken to jail.

The hearing didn't end for four hours. It was nearly midnight. This time, Judge Greene took very little time to come back with his decision. He ruled that the government had not shown it had any cause to arrest or hold these people. All remaining detainees were to be released now. They were not required to post any collateral or bail nor sign any arrest form.

Greene did craft a compromise on one point. Those released would have to agree to be photographed and fingerprinted. But their records would be held back from the FBI. If police couldn't come up with evidence strong enough to convict them within ninety days, the records would be destroyed.

Even with that condition, it was another victory for the public defenders. The cops had no realistic hope they could match the filmed faces of running protesters with real people in the lockups, not in a way that would ever hold up in court. The lawyers rushed over to the Coliseum with the good news. Many of the jubilant holdouts began lining up to give fingerprints and photographs, relying on the judge's protective order. Over the next few hours more than six hundred more people were released.

That is, until four o'clock in the morning. Another piece of news was passed around. It turned out that after Judge Greene's ruling, the government's lawyers had called the judges for the D.C. Court of Appeals in the middle of the night and secured from them an emergency stay.

Once again, all the activity at the Coliseum froze. The public defenders would have to be back in court in a few hours to fight it out again.

20

The Holdouts

Wednesday, May 5

FIRST THING WEDNESDAY MORNING, THREE JUDGES OF THE D.C. Court of Appeals considered Judge Greene's order to release the holdouts at the Coliseum. Standing before them, Barbara Bowman, running on little more than righteous fury after two wild days without proper sleep, was resorting to exaggeration in service of her arguments, something she'd always been careful to avoid in criminal cases. "This is not a small deprivation of liberty," the public defender lectured the judges. "People are being kept in conditions that animals in slaughterhouses aren't kept in."

When the arguments ended, Barbara's deputy, Norman Lefstein, too worked up to go back to the office, waited around the court clerk's desk for the decision. Like Barbara, he felt a rising anger. He regarded the basic principles of American law as sacred, and here he was seeing them violated in a most cavalier way by the people who were supposed to preserve, protect, and defend them.

Finally the court clerk handed him the ruling from the judges. They had upheld Greene's order to release the prisoners from the Coliseum. But Lefstein was shocked to see that the appeals panel had killed Greene's instruction about holding back the arrest forms. The paperwork could indeed be sent to the FBI, they said. Those grabbed in Monday's dragnet would now have an official arrest record, even though there was every reason to believe virtually every man and woman among them was either innocent or improperly busted.

Lefstein crumpled the order in his fist and stormed out. He headed back to the public defender office. "How did it go?" one of the other lawyers asked. It didn't go well, Lefstein admitted. Yeah, the lawyer said, I figured. I heard on the radio a few minutes ago that you took the order and crushed it.

Great, thought Lefstein. He didn't realize reporters had been watching. He guessed he'd just given the appellate judges another reason to despise the public defenders.

Barbara was also thunderstruck. As she saw it, the appellate panel stubbornly refused to consider the facts and the law, so eager were they to buy the law enforcement version. "It was terrible to stand up there in court," she would say, "knowing that you were absolutely right in appealing to the judges to understand that not far away thousands of people's basic rights were being abused and to suddenly realize that nothing was going to be done, because no one cared."

BY LATER THAT WEDNESDAY, though, more people did care, as details spread about the roundup and incarceration. Senator Ted Kennedy, who had courted the Vietnam veterans on the Mall a couple of weeks earlier, but then blew hot and cold on the rest of the Spring Offensive (undoubtedly mulling how to position himself for a possible 1972 presidential bid) now came out strongly against the police tactics. He vowed to call hearings on how the government had handled Mayday. Speaking to the graduating class at Iona College in New York, Kennedy charged that the administration had "undermined the Constitution" and that the dragnet wasn't a police action but a "high-level political decision." He added, "In the name of law and order, they have violated the laws and ignored the orders which make us secure in our liberty and free from fear of arbitrary government interference in our lives."

Such sentiments began to leach into the pages of the *Washington Evening Star*, thus far a reliable bulwark of support for the authorities. It carried a news analysis headlined "Mass Arrests Tarnish Public Image of Police." The piece began, "For the first time in recent years, the arrest tactics of the Metropolitan Police Department during a massive protest have brought serious criticism."

All this was watched closely at the White House. Tuesday's euphoria was giving way to a nagging worry about a backlash. A member of John

Dean's staff—a former New York City cop named Jack Caulfield, who had been hired to spy on the Democrats—dashed off a memo to Dean, suggesting they mobilize quickly to blunt the "liberal media thrust at our 'repressive' tactics."

Also alarmed was Pat Buchanan, the White House speechwriter who was a few days from marrying the president's receptionist. "There is an undertow beginning to move now *against* our actions in the Washington disorders," he wrote to Haldeman. Rather than fight back, Buchanan's idea was to invent a counter-narrative: Authorities were badly outnumbered and had swept everyone up for their own good, to protect the protesters from harm. If the cops had taken the time to properly process each bust, he wrote, "the demonstrators would have successfully shut down the city, some might have been injured or killed in battles with citizens whose own right of movement had been violated." Buchanan didn't mention that he himself could have been one of those battling citizens, since he had nearly run down some kids.

NIXON ADOPTED NEITHER Caulfield's suggestion nor Buchanan's disinformation plan. Instead, he decided that the White House shouldn't respond directly to the growing criticism; doing so might only confirm his role behind the scenes of Mayday. He directed his press secretary to dodge any questions related to the Constitution and simply say the president was pleased with the performance of the police.

As a result, the first government official to publicly and specifically defend the legality of the response to Mayday was another of its architects, William Rehnquist.

Rehnquist, who headed the Office of Legal Counsel at Justice, had attended the department's Mayday war-council meetings. A few months after Mayday, Nixon would nominate Rehnquist to the Supreme Court, where eventually he would be named chief justice and would seek to dismantle the decisions of the Warren Court that expanded civil liberties. During his initial confirmation hearings, in the fall of 1971, Rehnquist would acknowledge his presence at "two or three" of the Mayday sessions, but during his testimony he would assert, "I do not really think I had any significant input or contribution to make at those meetings." In fact, he had been a major contributor. Rehnquist had written the legal opinion that the president could avoid constitutional restrictions when calling in troops for Mayday. At the meetings he urged the sharpest possible crackdown on the protesters, and his exhortations had instigated the police raid on the West Potomac Park encampment. So he had every reason to defend the outcome.

Like Senator Kennedy, Rehnquist had been invited to deliver a commencement speech on Wednesday. He was down in North Carolina's Blue Ridge. Rehnquist told students at Appalachian State University that the "extraordinary" conditions on Monday justified suspending normal rules of arrest and detention. He raised the doctrine of "qualified martial law," under which, he claimed, actual or threatened violence "is held to outweigh the normal right of any individual detained" to exercise his or her constitutional rights.

Civil liberties lawyers greeted his statements with astonishment. A state of martial law could have existed only if formally declared by the president. He hadn't done so, nor, in fact, would such a proclamation have been justified. "Martial law is an extreme remedy reserved for armed insurrection or cataclysmic disasters," the American Civil Liberties Union would write. "It is not an appropriate reaction to a traffic blockade."

Later, during the same Supreme Court nomination hearings where he would misrepresent his role in the planned response to Mayday, Rehnquist would again skirt the truth, insisting that the press had taken his statements about martial law out of context. He said he had been discussing the doctrine merely as an academic question, not something that he thought applied to Mayday. The disbelieving senators would point out that his speech had been widely reported for six months and that he never tried to correct the record. The Ripon Society, a centrist Republican organization, would pile on, stating that "even if one believes the capital was in dire jeopardy on Mayday, the Rehnquist rationale is legally slovenly."

ONE REASON THE PRESS was growing more critical by Wednesday was that editors at newsrooms, including *Time*, the *Washington Evening Star*, and the *Washington Post*, were getting firsthand stories from their own writers who had been caught in the net.

In the lingo of the Sixties, middle-of-the-roaders and liberals could get "radicalized" by firsthand experience. Many bright-eyed civil rights volunteers from the North in the mid-1960s had tacked sharply left after witnessing the brutality of the South's police and the deadly terrorism of white supremacists. In the antiwar movement, getting clonked on the head by riot cops for no good reason, or seeing it happen to your peers in person or on television, had a similar effect.

In Washington, two reporters, one each from the *Post* and the *Star*, wrote that they had been radicalized by Mayday. Ensnared by police, thrown into crowded confinement, they found not the "animals" or "bums" described by Nixon but rather hordes of young people who worked together to share food and blankets, soothe troubled detainees, and hammer out collective strategies. The demonstrators appeared thoroughly sincere in the belief that they had to lay their bodies down. By the end of a twenty-one-hour stint in his small cell, John Mathews of the *Washington Star*, who initially had been skeptical about the protesters, wrote that he wasn't sure whether to flash his new mates a peace sign or a raised fist. He gave them both.

There were plenty of other examples of radicalization all over town. A twenty-three-year old student at George Washington University, Janis McDonald, was a liberal Democrat, a former volunteer in the Kennedy campaign, and a resident adviser at the main girls' dormitory. Her brother was a marine wounded by a land mine in Vietnam. She had occasionally attended marches but always stayed away from anything intense. She couldn't bring herself to curse in public, which made it hard to join in the popular chant "One two three four, we don't want your fucking war."

On Monday, though, McDonald watched in anger as helmeted riot police rolled through the campus, sweeping up anyone who looked like a member of the counterculture. By Wednesday, she decided it was her moment to join the third and final mass action of the week. This time the Mayday Tribe was going to the U.S. Capitol.

RENNIE DAVIS WAS now free on bail, along with John Froines. (Some of their followers didn't take kindly to seeing them sprung while thousands remained behind. "There was a feeling that we were, I guess, elitists," Froines admitted.) The third man charged by federal prosecutors in the so-called Mayday conspiracy, the Yippie leader Abbie Hoffman, whose organizational work for Mayday didn't extend much beyond showing up, had made his way to New York City after escaping the prison compound outside RFK Stadium. FBI agents grabbed him Wednesday in the lobby of his Manhattan apartment building.

Nixon, told by his chief of staff that "another of the Chicago Seven guys" was busted, expressed satisfaction. It led to one of the president's periodic outbursts against what he sometimes called the "fucking Jews" who were "disloyal" and unworthy of his trust. Even the growing antiwar sentiment in the District of Columbia, he said, could be attributed to the fact that many residents were Jewish and "the gentiles have moved out."

"Aren't the Chicago Seven all Jews?" asked the president. "[Rennie] Davis is a Jew, you know."

"I don't think Davis is," Haldeman said.

Nixon tried again. "Hoffman. Hoffman's a Jew."

"Abbie Hoffman is and that's so," the chief of staff said.

They discussed the rest of the day. Haldeman told Nixon that the Justice Department couldn't find legal grounds to stop a lunchtime demonstration planned by Federal Employees for Peace in Lafayette Square, across from the White House. "Forget it," Nixon said. It wasn't worth the trouble. So the rally went off as planned, drawing about a thousand government workers in office attire. No one was arrested.

But the protest at the Capitol would be a different matter. Rennie and other Mayday leaders had decided to go ahead with their plans to bring to the steps of Congress their People's Peace Treaty — the one negotiated between American and North Vietnamese students, which called for a cease-fire and a withdrawal of U.S. troops in exchange for the release of prisoners of war. They would demand that the lawmakers consider it seriously.

Early in the afternoon, a couple of thousand people gathered on the National Mall to prepare for the rally. They included some who'd recently been released from the Coliseum and new recruits like Janis MacDonald. Marching on the sidewalks to stay legal, they made their way toward the Capitol grounds, where they explained to police that they were invited guests. The invitation had come from four liberal Democrats. These were freshmen swept into office in November on the issues of civil rights and Vietnam: Bella Abzug (who had visited the RFK Stadium detention camp) and Charles Rangel of New York, Ron Dellums of California, and Parren Mitchell of Maryland. They were outsid-

ers in the club of congressional white men — a woman and three Afri-·
can Americans.

Abzug and her colleagues confirmed to the police that the protesters
were invited. They were then allowed to file onto the east steps of the
Capitol at about three o'clock. They set a microphone up top, outside the
building entrance now sealed off by police. Someone unfurled a banner
printed with the People's Peace Treaty. The four lawmakers prepared to
address the gathering.

NIXON'S MEN had been well aware of the planned action. Jerry Wilson
and Richard Kleindienst had met that morning at seven by the Capitol
to scope things out.

Later in the day, from the Oval Office, the president followed the
demonstration as closely as he had watched the others. Haldeman told
him with a laugh that the protesters promised to stay on the steps until
Congress approves "this peace treaty they signed with North Vietnam."

"Trouble very likely," added Haldeman.

"Good!" Nixon replied.

Nixon's political instinct told him not to give an inch on what he called
"the whole business about repression and so forth." He asked whether
their friends in Congress could work up a resolution "supporting the
president on the handling of the demonstrations" or at least make some
speeches in that vein.

Criticism of the Mayday arrests — Nixon called it "the overreaction
thing" — was to be expected. The correct response was not to back off
but to "play it hard," the president went on, to "stay firm and get credit
for it" and not look like "we're sorta sitting here embattled and doing the
best we can." Instead they should push the decisive response as a model
for other cities or universities: "These people try something, bust 'em."

Nixon insisted, "We may have more going for us than we think here,
Bob."

When he was done, he asked Haldeman, "Convinced?"

"Yeah," said Haldeman. "We stay with that all the way."

As for the protest on the Capitol steps, Haldeman indicated that the
president might see some results from Charles Colson, the White House
lawyer in charge of undermining Nixon's opponents. "I think there'll
be some folks out there to tear down the Vietcong flags today," he said.

"There'll be some confrontation on that in the Hill thing. We're trying for that."

Colson had been busy. The crates of oranges the National Guard tossed to the kids in the Coliseum as a supposed gift from Edmund Muskie, one of the Democrats' presidential contenders, had actually come from Colson, just like the oranges delivered in Muskie's name to the Vietnam vets on the Mall a couple weeks earlier. The idea was to tie Muskie to the Mayday protest even though he had never endorsed it.

Haldeman laughed heartily about the prank. Nixon loved it too, and would later try to spread the fake news around Washington.

They marveled at Colson's ability to "get stuff done here." While Colson had occasionally been caught with his fingerprints on dirty political tricks, he "has got a lot done that he hasn't been caught at," Haldeman said.

It felt to Haldeman like a good dry run for their plans for the coming year. Colson's brand of mischief would come in handy during Nixon's re-election campaign. The chief of staff told Nixon about a plan to create a crew that could "tear things up" while remaining "completely removed" from the campaign.

But that was for later. For now, Haldeman said, he had advised Colson to get "hardhats and legionnaires" — meaning conservative construction workers and Teamsters, and pro-war military veterans — to "dig up . . . thugs" and send them after the radicals, especially the ones carrying Vietcong flags.

"They've got guys who'll go in and knock their heads off," Nixon said approvingly.

"Sure," Haldeman agreed. "Murderers. Guys that really, you know, that's what they really do . . . they're gonna beat the shit out of some of these people. And hope they really hurt them. You know, I mean go in with some real — and smash some noses."

AT THE CAPITOL, tensions built quickly, just as Colson had predicted, or in fact had instigated. Two conservative congressmen separately rushed groups of demonstrators, ripping from their hands a Vietcong flag and a copy of the peace treaty printed on a bed sheet. "It shouldn't be on the Capitol steps," declared G. V. "Sonny" Montgomery, the Mississippi Democrat who grabbed the treaty. The lawmaker bragged that he'd landed a punch during the fracas, during which one demonstrator was knocked to the ground.

The head of the Capitol police force, James Powell, was unnerved. He'd known in advance he'd have to deal with a crowd on Wednesday. He had expected a few hundred people, though, not two thousand. All the recent flaps about permits in Washington confused him. Protests had been illegal near the Capitol for a century, but then the big march last week had been allowed to rally there. The Vietnam vets came to throw their medals on the steps. So Powell wasn't sure he had authority to kick out this latest group.

First, he tried to get permission from the Speaker of the House, Carl Albert. Through an aide, Albert initially refused, saying that members of Congress were addressing the protesters. But later on, after Powell sent him a message claiming the crowd was "loud and boisterous," Albert indicated that he would be okay with dispersing them.

Soon the phone rang at police headquarters, in the office of Jerry Wilson's counsel, Gerald Caplan. Powell wanted to check on what the law allowed: "Should we lock 'em up?"

Caplan was twenty-seven, fairly new on the job, and already shell-shocked from the chaos of Mayday. He'd seen firsthand how the riot police lost control. He had been fighting court battles and dealing with constant questions from reporters. When Monday's prisoners languished in the jails, Caplan had to give the press the company line that the delay in bringing them to court was the fault of the public defenders, not the police. When he said it, he inwardly cringed.

Truthfully, Caplan had no idea what to do about the Capitol. Above all, he didn't want to be the one to approve another mass arrest. He decided to pass the buck. He called an assistant U.S. attorney, who had been on the job two years longer than Caplan. No one picked up the phone, so Caplan left a message, saying he wouldn't reply to Powell's legal question. "I'm not gonna answer," Caplan said. "I want you to answer it."

After getting Caplan's message, the assistant U.S. attorney, Gil Zimmerman, hustled down to the scene to look things over and consult with Chief Powell. Zimmerman had already been involved in other legal fights during the Spring Offensive, including trying to keep the Vietnam vets from sleeping on the Mall. He told Powell that as far as he was concerned, the demonstration looked to him like a clear violation of the nineteenth-century law. Powell decided to go ahead with the arrests.

But Caplan had a feeling they weren't clear on the rules either.

By now, Bella Abzug was speaking at the top of the steps. Chief Powell, still nervous, stood at the bottom. He held a bullhorn. His hand was shaking. The gathering was an "unlawful assembly," he announced. Anyone refusing to leave would be arrested in ten minutes. Few heard Powell above Abzug's amplified speech and the chatter of the crowd. Police soon sealed off the bottom of the stairs and began the arrests. No one at the top had any idea what was happening.

Powell later claimed he made a second announcement. He was standing next to Jerry Wilson. A *Washington Star* reporter overheard him ask Jerry if he should try yet again, because he still didn't think a lot of people on the steps had heard. No, Jerry said, according to the reporter, "Let them tell their story in court."

After her speech, with the Capitol doors behind her still sealed, Abzug walked down the steps to leave the rally. That was when she noticed the police grabbing protesters. She found Powell and told him no one had heard his order. An aide to Ron Dellums also noticed. "Congressman, they're making arrests down there," he told Dellums, who then set off through the middle of the crowd to confront police. The aide tried to follow but was grabbed by the cops and shoved down the steps. Dellums rushed over to help. A cop swung a billy club into his ribs when he tried to push through the police line. "They didn't give a damn about the fact that I was a congressman. I'm a nigger, and that's exactly the way many of those people up there in that front line treated us," Dellums told reporters. (Nixon would explode when told the story: "Balls! He's lying! He's lying, he's lying!")

As they had done at the Justice Department protest the day before, police filled out the field arrest forms for each prisoner. But as Caplan had feared, confusion reigned as to what law had been violated. At first the protesters were charged with unlawful entry. Later on, police began marking the arrests based on charges of unlawful assembly, in violation of a law banning speech "with intent to impede, disrupt or disturb orderly conduct" of the Congress. It was hard to see what was being disrupted. Before the march had even reached the steps, security guards had cleared the Capitol of visitors and sealed the entrances. Both the Senate and House had adjourned by the time the lawmakers addressed the crowd. Later on, aides working inside would testify in court that they hadn't even heard the rally.

Nevertheless, in the end, twelve hundred more people were arrested. That brought the Mayday grand total of arrests to twelve thousand.

"DO YOU THINK we're repressing?" Nixon asked the group gathered in his office. One of them was the man in charge of the Justice Department, Attorney General John Mitchell. Another was the top Republican in the House, Gerald Ford of Michigan.

"No, not enough," someone said. That set off a burst of laughter.

"What the hell more do you want?" the president joked, to more mirth.

Serious again, Nixon said the protests were going to be bad for "those clowns" — those Democratic lawmakers he said were sympathizing with the prisoners.

Nixon told Ford one story to illustrate the point: "Muskie, sending oranges to these people — twice!"

That surprised Ford. "I didn't know that," he said.

Ford then outlined his own theory about Mayday, centered on the tactical manual the Tribe had published, listing all their methods and targets. "Why did the demonstrations around here fail? Because they told the enemy in advance what their plans were."

"Um-hmm, they sure did," Nixon replied.

"And if they'd kept their mouths shut," Ford said, "and come down here and then spontaneously done what they planned to do, you wouldn't have been prepared to the degree that you were."

"I think that possibly could be so," the attorney general said, to more general laughter.

"Sure, tell the enemy what you're gonna do, and you run into a little more trouble," said the minority leader.

In line with the president's wishes, his men would stick with the hard line. But they decided to buy some insurance. They told Jerry Wilson to step up and get ready to take the blame. And Jerry did what he was told. He put out a statement. The Justice Department, he said, "has purposely declined to tell me how to operate the police force in this city." He added:

"I wish to emphasize the fact that I made all tactical decisions relating to the recent disorders. The decision to temporarily suspend the use of field arrest forms and to immediately arrest all violators of the law was mine and mine alone. I took these steps because I felt they were necessary to protect the safety of law-abiding citizens and to maintain order in the city."

Perhaps the statement had the ring of a confession tortured out of a prisoner of war, but it went with the territory, Jerry knew. There never had been any doubt in his mind about that. Also, as he certainly realized, his willingness to fall on his sword earned him even more appreciation at the White House.

"Wilson went to the mat today," John Ehrlichman informed Nixon.

"Good for him!" said the president.

Ehrlichman added, "We programmed him to do this this morning, and he did better than you could possibly have programmed . . . he has never let us down yet."

And then Nixon added words that, if Jerry had heard, would have made any abasement well worth it: "We might have a guy who can be the next head of the FBI."

Haldeman told the president that the chief was working so hard, he missed his own wedding anniversary. He said Jerry's wife, Leona, had told reporters, "I guess I'll have to take him a sandwich with two candles."

The president grabbed the phone on his desk: "Get me Mrs. Wilson, the wife of the Chief of Police, Washington."

AT A PRESS briefing that afternoon, Nixon's press secretary, Ron Ziegler, had been bombarded with questions about whether the president regretted anything about the way the protesters had been treated, the apparent violation of their constitutional rights. Ziegler pointed to Jerry's statement and said the president wasn't second-guessing the decisions Jerry had made on his own.

When Ziegler told Nixon about this later, the president exclaimed, "I wish they'd have hit me with that. I'd have kicked them right in the balls."

"They were looking for a quote which said that the president regrets that the constitutional rights of some of those who were arrested were violated."

"Oh, shit," said Nixon.

Nixon told his aides not to let anyone in the White House express any public doubt about the way it went down. "I see anybody do that, the whole goddam staff is fired," he said. "No leaks, no concerns, [no] 'People around the president are worried, di di di di di.' If anything, I think we should have clubbed a few more of the bastards." After talking to Ziegler he put in a call to Henry Kissinger, always someone to reinforce Nixon's hard line. The national security adviser assured the president from California that there was still a "violent backlash" against Mayday among the public.

Later, the president reached Jerry's wife to extend his anniversary wishes. Nixon expected her to be thrilled to hear directly from the president. But she never put much stock in Jerry's hobnobbing with big shots, and the call didn't impress her. Nixon sounded wooden and insincere, she told her husband, like he was reading from a script.

BY WEDNESDAY EVENING, Judge Harold Greene, by nature polite and well mannered, burned through just about all of his patience with the police, the prosecutors, and the appellate judges who kept undoing his carefully crafted legal compromises. He was shocked and angered that the higher court had rejected his attempt to protect the people detained on Monday by ensuring that no permanent records of their arrests would be filed with the FBI. Thousands of prisoners had been coerced into having their fingerprints and photographs taken if they wanted to get out into the fresh air, and now they would have histories of arrest that Greene considered unjustified.

At the Coliseum, only the hardcore from Monday's arrests remained. There were just under four hundred of them — the ones who steadfastly refused to give their names for booking. Their arrests were illegal, they said, so they wouldn't submit to any process, no matter what the police, attorneys, or prosecutors said.

Judge Greene had ordered that, whatever the circumstances, prosecutors had to produce the anonymous holdouts in court by six that night. In preparation, the lawyers from the city and the Justice Department had cobbled together records on each defendant, calling them John or Jane Doe, and charging them with obstructing sidewalks or streets in the District of Columbia. No location, no arresting officer, no other detail.

When they showed up in court, Greene was in no mood for further delay. He told the lawyers for both sides they had thirty minutes before the courts would convene. He split the prisoners into two groups. He conferred with two of his most liberal judges and assigned them to hear the cases in adjoining courtrooms.

Thirty minutes? The exhausted public defenders realized they hadn't fully researched the issues. After all, their experience was in defending people charged with felonies. They scrambled for the next half hour, tearing frantically through the D.C. code books, trying to find precedents in other cases. Some called around, trying to reach civil rights lawyers for advice.

The clock ran out. Michael Wald, the public defender assigned to one of the two courtrooms, grabbed whatever he had. He rushed in to argue the case. He hadn't any idea what the public defender next door was telling the other judge; there hadn't been time to coordinate their efforts.

Wald watched the two hundred Mayday protesters file into the benches. The bailiffs locked the doors, so no outsiders could get mixed into the crowd and no defendants could mix their way to freedom.

For forty-eight hours straight, Wald and his colleagues had been litigating the Mayday arrests. This was the first time he'd been in a courtroom with actual clients. These exhausted, hungry, unwashed people, he realized, had been in custody in difficult conditions for as many as sixty hours. Some of them had resisted being moved out of the Coliseum to the courthouse at the end, locking arms and holding on, while some police officers removed their badges (so the protesters wouldn't know whom to charge with misconduct later) and smacked them with batons to make them let go.

But the public defender was glad to see them — he had been uneasy doing legal work for people he'd never met.

He cleared his throat and raised his voice: "Hi, I'm Michael Wald. I am here to represent you in these proceedings. You don't know me, have no reason to have confidence in me, but you really have no choice about it if you want to be released today. Anybody who wants another attorney may return to the jail." No one did.

When the judge took the bench, Wald told him that his clients couldn't be properly arraigned. The John and Jane Doe paperwork was faulty. There were no specifics, no time or place of arrest. How could a defense be prepared in such a case? Even if they were acquitted on the vague charges, how could the defendants be protected from double jeopardy, from being charged again with the same crime? The situation was completely untenable.

With dizzying speed, to the surprise of both sides, the judge agreed. He dismissed all the charges.

In a panic, the attorney for the city begged the judge to stay his decision. What if a higher court disagreed with this ruling and later allowed the suspects to be arraigned? If the defendants were freed right now, having given no names, no fingerprints, no one would ever find them again.

But like Greene, the judge seemed to have had quite enough of the Court of Appeals. He refused to consider a stay. Wald didn't know it yet, but the judge next door had made the same call.

It took a few seconds. Then the defendants realized they'd just been handed their freedom.

The room exploded in cheers. Two hundred people leapt from their seats, hugged each other. Many of them rushed over to surround their lawyer. In a moment that Wald would always remember as one of the best in his life, certainly the best in his long and distinguished legal career, they hoisted the public defender up onto their shoulders. Shouting with joy, they burst through the doors, joined the happy kids flowing from the neighboring courtroom, and streamed out into the fading light of day.

21

Aftermath

"I approved this plan."

THE SPRING OFFENSIVE HAD ENDED BY THURSDAY, THE SIXTH of May. Or at least its presence on the streets was over. But in the courts the battle would go on, not for days and weeks, but for months and years.

In the end, the justice system turned out to be far less favorable ground for Richard Nixon and his team. The story of Mayday initially embraced by the press ("the worst reviews of any demonstration in history," as one columnist put it) and Congress, and the public, would be reversed. The administration would lose; the demonstrators would win.

An occasional judge would note an apparent contradiction in the strategy behind Mayday, saying that a group aiming to slow or stop the operations of the government and fill the jails wasn't well positioned to complain later, when that system broke down. But overwhelmingly the courts held that regardless of their motives, the detainees were entitled to the same rights and treatment as anyone else.

Compared with the demonstrations, the legal actions related to them would receive almost no public attention. Yet the cases born in that season would have lasting effects on the country.

They would sweep away limits on how citizens can demonstrate their dissent in Washington, D.C. and chill the chance that future mass arrests could be made anywhere in America. They would create the standard by which judges can delete criminal records that were improperly created. They would set guidelines for detaining material witnesses during grand jury investigations.

One case would even touch on the power of the presidency, restricting the authority of Nixon and future executives to keep their records, including audio recordings, secret.

Then there was the political butterfly effect. Within two years the Mayday perturbations would combine with other forces in a cyclone that would shred the White House and send more than twenty of Nixon's men to prison.

THE PRESIDENT'S AIDES could feel the shift. Outsiders were now raising questions not only about the sweeping arrests, but how people were treated in custody.

Even after the judges freed the four hundred holdouts Wednesday night, more than a thousand prisoners remained. The other eleven thousand people arrested on Monday on the streets, Tuesday at Justice, or Wednesday at the Capitol had been let go after giving their fingerprints and addresses. Many had been arraigned and released on bail, pending a trial; the rest had, knowingly or not, pleaded guilty by paying ten dollars in collateral and checking a forfeit box on a piece of paper.

Most of the thousand people left inside had been busted on the steps of the Capitol the day before. They languished in the cellblock below the federal courthouse. About half had refused to be fingerprinted, insisting their rally had been legal and the arrests not. But police wouldn't allow public defenders down there to talk with their clients. They believed the lawyers would only advise the kids not to cooperate.

No doubt the jailers had a second motive: to keep the crowded and unsanitary conditions under wraps. For days they had stuffed more than twice as many people into the courthouse cellblock as the Justice Department had previously set as the maximum emergency capacity.

At the pleading of the public defenders, Judge Greene told the jailers to admit two lawyers. The police ignored his order and still wouldn't let them in.

On Thursday, Barbara Bowman crucified one of the police lawyers before the judge: "When you received the information that Judge Greene had issued the oral order, your concern was for a reasonable way out of that order, was it not?" The witness answered, "Yes, ma'am." Greene listened in amazement, wondering aloud why some police officials believed their department "is really completely independent of any civilian authority, either judicial or prosecutorial."

Greene made his message clear to the government's lawyers: defy me again, and you'll be held in contempt. So the jailers let Michael Wald and another defense attorney through the steel doors on Thursday night. The lawyers' hearts sank. Cells meant for two people held twenty to forty detainees each. "Some were sick; others were asleep on the floor or so exhausted they were unable to communicate. Isolated from counsel or any outsiders for nearly 40 hours, they had little idea of what was likely to happen to them," Wald reported.

The other public defender, Kirby Howlett — he had been one of Barbara's motorcycle riders — was shocked at how some guards were abusing their charges. Howlett half expected to see angry militants screaming obscenities at the cops through the bars, but instead found most of the kids to be sincere and thoughtful. Yet the police "had a hatred for them unlike anything I'd ever seen before — far worse than their reaction to blacks or even to black cop-killers," Howlett said later. "I had nightmares afterward — here it was, unbridled police power encouraged by the highest authority in the country."

Some public-health doctors got inside as well, including a cardiologist from D.C. General Hospital. They saw some detainees sick with infectious diseases, others suffering emotional trauma and exhaustion. Appalled, they asked the court to remove the prisoners from their dangerous conditions. One of Greene's judges, James Belson, agreed to tour the cellblock. The judge then retired to his chambers. The doctors had to wait until six the next morning for his decision, but they won the point. Belson agreed that "petitioners are experiencing cruel and unusual punishment and irreparable injury." He ordered they be moved from the cells, given blankets, and allowed to speak with attorneys.

At this point Wald was still in the lockup. He'd never left. The public defender had been going from cell to cell, explaining to the detainees they could submit to fingerprinting or eventually face a contempt charge. He decided to accompany the first group of weary prisoners who agreed to be booked. Down they went to the underground garage. The jailers herded Wald and his clients onto a bus, which took them across the street to the basement of the central police station. "The trip, in the middle of the night, surrounded by armed guards, gave me the feeling that I was being taken forever to a faraway place, isolated from the rest of the world," he would write.

Wald spent five hours with the prisoners as they were processed. He was unable to contact anyone, afraid to leave them unrepresented. Like Howlett he was dismayed to observe some officers cursing kids who tried politely to explain their politics. The attitudes of the guards, the capricious decisions of some of the judges, hadn't seemed completely foreign to him. As a public defender he observed every day just how much of a nightmare the justice system could be for poor black people. But when Wald finally was outside again, at nine on Friday morning, "I felt like I had escaped rather than just walked out. For the first time that week I had a sense of what my clients had been experiencing."

NIXON'S MEN SOUGHT to block any drift toward sympathy for the detainees. Attorney General John Mitchell called the protesters a "mob," likening them to Hitler's brown-shirted thugs. If the Nazis had been dealt with as firmly as Washington handled the Mayday crowd, Mitchell said, "the world might have been spared a whole era of violence and misery." Not content to compare antiwar protesters with fascists, Mitchell reiterated his belief that communist influence and money were behind the whole movement.

The president was closely following the controversy over the mass arrests. When a group of lawmakers visited the White House on Thursday, he joked, "Glad you could all make it down here today. At least the streets are clear — though I see all of you got haircuts just to be on the safe side."

Nixon too wanted to keep up the fiction that the protesters had been violent and destructive and that police had no choice but to grab them all. "Do they have any kind of statistics with regard to damage done, or anything, or aren't they good enough to use?" the president asked his chief of staff.

"They have some," Haldeman responded. "They didn't do a hell of a lot of damage."

Nixon was disappointed. "Well, then, use the horrible examples: They slashed tires . . ."

The president schooled his press secretary, Ron Ziegler, on how to frame things for reporters. As the president riffed, and riffed some more, Ziegler scribbled so hard, the sound was picked up by the tape machine secretly running in the Oval Office.

Nixon wanted the press secretary to stress that police had hurt few if any protesters: "They ran over one jerk who was laid down in front of a car, that's too goddam bad." Getting himself worked up, banging on his desk for emphasis, the president ordered Ziegler to declare that not only did the White House fully support the police tactics but would handle future demonstrations the same way. "We're not going to allow peaceful citizens and millions of law-abiding citizens in this country to have their peace [*bam!*] destroyed [*bam!*] by the violent [*bam!*] few."

Haldeman, the chief of staff, tacked even harder to the right, floating new rules and laws to control dissent. He said the city should force demonstrators seeking permits to post a bond to cover any potential damage from their protest, which might dissuade some organizations from coming at all. Furthermore, Haldeman said, "I don't see any reason why we shouldn't now develop a plan, publicize it, for the declaration of martial law, in effect, in this city, which suspends the right of a proper trial and all that."

That rang even Nixon's alarm bell. Well, the president counseled, "we don't want to appear to be Gestapo, living in a police state and all that kind of crap."

It might help to have Congress formally condemn the Mayday protesters and the few lawmakers who had supported them, and to issue praise for Jerry Wilson and his police. Charles Colson, the czar of dirty tricks, drafted a resolution and instructed a colleague to get "one of our tougher guys in the House" to introduce it. "Let's for a change be demagogues," Colson added.

In a meeting with Colson, the president suggested, "Let's give Wilson a medal or some damn thing."

"He's a folk-hero type," Colson agreed. "He's got what the Jewish people called chutzpah."

That was something Nixon hadn't heard before. "What do you call it?"

"It's a little pizazz," Colson explained.

The president invited Jerry, Mayor Walter Washington, and leaders from the National Guard and the army to the Oval Office for a fifteen-minute photo opportunity. Nixon told them to ignore "second-guessers and Monday morning quarterbacks . . . we back you all the way."

On Nixon's schedule for the coming weekend was the annual dinner of the White House Correspondents Association, where the president was supposed to submit with good nature to gentle roasting. The timing wasn't great. Nixon already despised most news people; now they could wield Mayday as another club against him.

Nixon's aides had met for an hour in the West Wing to plot a press strategy. Ziegler worried that, at the daily briefing, reporters would go after him about the legality of the arrests. The domestic policy adviser, John Ehrlichman, scoffed. "Newspapermen are the least competent men to judge constitutionality," he said, adding that reporters swept up in the dragnet "wanted to be arrested." If anyone should ask Ziegler directly if the president thought the Constitution had been violated, "don't take the question," ordered Ehrlichman. Blame the roundup on the police chief. If all else fails, deny the facts with a straight face, and take the line that the busts were all done by the book: "There were no mass arrests."

That Saturday night, after swinging by the wedding of his speechwriter and his receptionist, Nixon headed for the correspondents' gala in the ballroom of the Sheraton Park Hotel. He immediately regretted it. Sitting up front, he tried to hide his mounting dismay. He thought the "clowns" in attendance were "disgusting" and full of "barbed insults." The reporters and their guests were "drunk, crude, and terribly cruel" to any speaker with something good to say about the administration.

The part when they gave out journalism awards especially grated. Nixon later complained to his aides that the winners were "way out left-wingers," each honored for "a vicious attack on the administration," including the top prize for exceptionally meritorious Washington coverage, which went to a reporter who dug into illegal military surveillance of the New Left: "I had to sit there for 20 minutes while the drunken audience laughed in derision as the award citations were read."

Police Chief Jerry Wilson also attended. In another hotel ballroom a few months earlier, he'd been honored by the National Conference of Christians and Jews for his humane treatment of antiwar protesters. That was before Jerry told the world that he had been the sole decision maker on Mayday.

Now, when the chief was introduced, there was a bit of polite applause, but Nixon saw reporters "deliberately turning up their noses." Some news outlets were still supporting the police actions — a *Washington Star* editorial stressed that "constitutional niceties are quite beside the point" — but others had grown critical or damned Jerry with faint praise. "We were good," recalled Jerry's deputy chief, Maurice Cullinane, "and then we were not so good." *Life* magazine, which had embedded a reporter with the chief during Mayday, wrote, "If the round-ups showed more respect for practicality than for constitutional rights, at least they worked." The city's biggest coalition of business leaders prepared a full-page newspaper advertisement that, while generally supportive of the police, also allowed that "perhaps in retrospect some things might have been done a little differently." Jerry felt compelled to send a message to his force: "Stand firm. The calls and telegrams are 91 percent for the police."

SOON A HARDER rain began to fall. The Massachusetts senator Ted Kennedy, a member of Nixon's least favorite political family, who polling showed had now become the Democrats' leading choice for the 1972 nomination, denounced the detention of "masses of innocent pedestrians" and the manufacture of "fraudulent arrest papers." A newspaper columnist wrote, "It was the week when traffic was not stopped but the Constitution was." Another writer blasted the government's overreaction, saying he "refused to be troubled that a protest march for peace caused a few people to be a half-hour late for work or required the D.C. police to be paid a few extra hours of overtime." New York City's police commissioner, who had recently been Jerry's boss in Washington, decried the tactics of his former department as unnecessary and unconstitutional.

One of the Superior Court judges who had heard Mayday cases, Charles W. Halleck, declared publicly that "citizens were arrested under conditions that betrayed a blatant disregard for the civil liberties of protesters and innocent bystanders alike, but more importantly, they were arrested in a fashion that totally abandoned any hope of successfully prosecuting the vast majority of those arrested." He reproved officials who engaged in "public preening and self congratulations on a job well done."

In the increasingly tense atmosphere, Nixon and his people tried to have it both ways. They hoped to reap political credit for enforcing order without risking any liability for perhaps trampling the Bill of Rights. Mitchell, the attorney general, told a gathering of police officials in California that Jerry Wilson had been fully in charge those days — the "courageous" move to sweep the streets of protesters had been "his decision and his alone." He reiterated to reporters that Justice had no role "whatsoever." That led Senator Kennedy to ask, "If the attorney general is so pleased with these activities, I wonder why he is so anxious to disclaim the administration's responsibility for them."

Mitchell continued to falsely deny his involvement in the roundup and detention, both in his public statements and in an affidavit he later would file in court. His deputy at the Justice Department, Richard Kleindienst, would also testify that Justice hadn't been in charge — despite the fact that Mitchell had given him authority to carry out the president's directives about demonstrations in D.C. and that he had run the war-council meetings, where he stated that "the general impetus" was to arrest as many demonstrators as possible. Jerry would later acknowledge in court that he had been in contact with Kleindienst at least thirty-six times during the Mayday protests.

The minutes of the war councils, which would get little attention when they surfaced years later as evidence in lawsuits, clearly document Kleindienst's role, as well as those of William Rehnquist, John Ehrlichman, and, of course, Jerry Wilson. But long before this evidence came to light, the president, within days of Mayday, privately contradicted the story put forward by his aides.

Nixon's own accounts, caught on tape, have remained unreported until now. They leave no doubt that the responsibility for the Mayday dragnet can be laid at the doorstep of the Oval Office.

In the taped conversations, the president acknowledged he had called in from California on the weekend before Mayday and given Mitchell a direct order for Justice to pass on to Jerry Wilson.

"I don't want the impression that this being tough on these people is just the idea of Wilson and the Attorney General," Nixon told his aides. "It's my idea, you know. I gave the signal to everybody. I said, 'Now bust these bastards.'"

Later, speaking to a visitor in the Oval Office, the president recalled,

"I got a hold of Mitchell on that Saturday night. I said, 'Bust them.' And don't hurt anybody. I don't want anything like Chicago, but I says, 'Arrest the whole damn lot, if they don't clear the streets.' And they arrested them and the police chief did a hell of a job."

Nixon would state it even more clearly to a group of conservative congressmen he invited to a meeting in the Cabinet Room at the White House. Referring to the war councils held at Justice, he said the plan for dealing with the demonstrators had been fully worked out in advance by federal and local officials. "Now, you can get into a lot of fine arguments as to whether or not individuals should be arrested under those circumstances," said the president, but he vowed not to "run away from it just because some people in the press don't like it."

He added, "The point is, I had the responsibility . . . I approved this plan."

BY THE TIME Nixon attended the press gala, virtually all the Mayday protesters were out of detention. Barbara Bowman and her public defenders spent the weekend at home, recovering from exhaustion. On Monday, they regrouped for the next stage. While many demonstrators had forfeited a trial, lawyers for the city and the administration still planned to prosecute some five thousand people.

Some of the lawyers felt a bit of competitive pique that the American Civil Liberties Union had now entered the fray. During the intense first day or two of the protests, the ACLU had been caught off-guard. Like the rest of the city's establishment, its leaders were slow to recognize the import of the mass arrests. That left the grinding legal tasks to Barbara's people, who filed the habeas motions and stayed up all night to free the imprisoned. Some of the public defenders resented filling a void that should have been occupied by the civil liberties organization. Once the Mayday legal challenges got moving, ACLU officials had begged the public defenders to list the group on their motions, even though they hadn't really been part of it. "They said, 'It would be really bad if our names weren't on the papers,'" Wald recalled.

But now the ACLU was fully engaged. The group's leaders got to work, preparing a class action on behalf of the detainees. Since so many of them had scattered, the best way to reach them would be through advertising. To collect witness accounts and raise money for a legal war chest, "I got this ad together which was just a killer," recalled the executive director of the group, Florence Isbell. Under the headline "The Vietnamization of America," Isbell's copy compared the sweep arrests to the free-fire zones in Vietnam, where troops were authorized to shoot anyone who looked like an enemy. A donor named Philip Stern, who was heir to the Sears Roebuck & Company fortune and was outraged by the police roundup, came through with more than $30,000 to buy full-page advertisements in the *Washington Post* and the *New York Times*. The notices would bring in hundreds of affidavits and thousands of donations.

When he opened the morning newspaper the following Monday and saw the ad, Charles Colson practically climbed the White House walls. To Colson, who knew a thing or two about ethics violations himself, the ACLU was improperly trying to drum up business for itself. "I don't believe I have ever seen anything as gross as this," he told John Dean. "Would it not be possible immediately to get the D.C. Bar Association to take steps to block this? As a lawyer, I find this terribly offensive and it seems to me that someone, obviously not us, should raise this issue." Dean replied that while he too found it offensive, challenging the move would raise "a cry of attempted repression and a lot of free publicity for the ACLU. It would be a much happier situation to have their efforts fail for lack of support, or fail in the courtroom."

But the efforts would not fail. Warning signs already flashed. His bosses had asked Dean to determine how many innocent people really were caught in the dragnet, so they would have some numbers to use, to undercut Kennedy. Dean delegated the research to another administration lawyer. The memo he got back laid out the genuine legal jeopardy faced by the police and the government. In his review, the lawyer noted legitimate arguments that the arrests and the delays were improper. Furthermore, even if some individual arrests could be justified, "the question may be raised as to whether the application of such laws on a massive scale for the purpose of breaking up a political demonstration does not constitute an abridgment of freedom of speech."

The memo accurately divined the mood of the judicial branch. The first decision came from Halleck, the Superior Court judge who had criticized the government in his speech. He dismissed a slew of arrests that happened a few days before the main thrust of Mayday, outside the headquarters of the Department of Health, Education, and Welfare.

Some two hundred people had been charged with violating a D.C. statute that outlawed any "processions and parades" without a permit. The judge struck down the 1934 law as unconstitutionally vague and arbitrary.

Soon, the ACLU, armed with affidavits netted by the newspaper ads, filed its class action, asking a federal judge to halt all prosecutions of the people detained on May 3, the day of the traffic blockade, unless the police had filled out field arrest forms or taken Polaroids of them. Although the judge initially rejected the ACLU's request, an appeals court quickly reversed him and granted the injunction. The decision forced the government to drop charges against twenty-five hundred people, admitting it had no evidence against them.

As for the other thousands, prosecutors notified the court it would pursue convictions, beginning with a batch of twenty-four cases. First up was Michael B. McCarthy, a Harvard sophomore, the son of the U.S. senator who had helped force LBJ from office over Vietnam. But when McCarthy traveled back to Washington and arrived at the courthouse on the appointed day, he was met by a clerk from the city's legal office who told him never mind, the charge had been dropped for no evidence. The rest of the cases were put on hold.

In the end, charges against virtually all of the seven thousand people arrested on May 3 were dropped.

There was rapid vindication too for the two thousand people arrested at the Justice Department sit-in on May 4, the day after the traffic blockade. Prosecutors tried to bring a few cases to trial. Despite the fact that police had filled out field arrest forms for some defendants, almost every one was acquitted when the government failed to prove that police had given people enough time to disperse before the busts began. By mid-June virtually all the arrests from that day had been dismissed.

Authorities fared no better with those arrested on the steps of the Capitol on May 5. In a test case, a group of eight defendants were tried together — including Janis McDonald, the George Washington University student who had been radicalized by the police dragnet outside her dormitory. In July a Superior Court jury acquitted them all, accepting the defense claim that the rally didn't disrupt any official business. (Jerry would later admit that "it was a reasonably orderly crowd.")

Some individuals took the government to court on their own. Two young Department of Labor employees who'd been scooped up on their way to the office on May 3 won damages of $4,500 each for false arrest.

What of the arrests by police who raided West Potomac Park the day before the traffic blockade? Judge Greene dismissed them all. He ruled that the government's revocation of the Mayday Tribe's permit — the scheme hatched at the war-council meetings at the Justice Department — was illegal.

So it went for the rest of the year. By December, only twenty-one cases related to Mayday remained unresolved. The final tally looked very bad for the police and the government. Most of the more than twelve thousand people arrested during the three days of Mayday, plus more than two thousand busted in different actions over the weeks of the Spring Offensive, had been released without prosecution.

Of the rest, most had been so desperate to get out of detention, they had forfeited their collateral or had pleaded guilty or no contest to charges that would turn out to be improper. Only 128 people had been convicted at trial. Only a single one of those convictions stemmed from the three main days of Mayday; the other 127 all had been arrested on April 28 for blocking the doors of the Selective Service — the administrator of the military draft. (Convicted of disorderly conduct, they had to pay a ten-dollar fine or spend one day in jail, with credit for time served.)

It was a rout. The battered lawyers for the city and the administration were ready to put Mayday behind them. The civil liberties lawyers on the opposite side were not. Next, the ACLU would seek compensation for the protesters and the destruction of their arrest records.

FOR ALL THE ADMINISTRATION'S warnings of potential violence during the Spring Offensive, there had been only one truly destructive act. That was the explosion at the Capitol on March 1. The attack had helped Nixon's men justify their aggressive preparations for Mayday. Now they knew that if the bomb could be linked to the Mayday Tribe, it would support the argument that the protesters deserved arrest and detention.

It had been two months since the Weather Underground had placed the bomb, which the group considered "one of our most visible and satisfying actions" — and still the FBI hadn't caught those responsible. Nor had they been able to charge anyone with rendering assistance.

Still in custody, though, was the woman whom authorities claimed was a material witness, the nineteen-year-old Mayday organizer Leslie Bacon. Agents had flown Bacon to Seattle, where a grand jury had been impaneled to investigate the radical left.

The Weather Underground, which claimed responsibility for the bomb, had also done something it never did before and wouldn't do again. The guerrillas tried to exonerate Bacon. They made public a note they had sent to Bacon's mother in California the day of the traffic blockade. "Your confidence in Leslie is justified because she is completely innocent of any involvement in the bombing of the U.S. Capitol," Weather wrote. "We know this for a fact because, as the FBI and Justice Department well know, our organization did the bombing." At the "appropriate time," they promised, they would prove it by revealing details known only to the bombers and the FBI. Perhaps not doing the young woman any favors, the letter went on to say, "Mrs. Bacon, we cannot turn ourselves in to save Leslie. She is a committed revolutionary and understands this."

In Seattle, Bacon's lawyers initially told her she had no reason to defy the grand jury and risk a contempt charge by refusing to answer questions about the Capitol: "Since I knew nothing about it, it was absurd that I should go to jail." As she later explained, she agreed to discuss other matters, acknowledging, for example, that she had previously helped members of Weather survey a New York bank, which they later attempted to firebomb. According to Bacon, she had dropped out of that plot long before it got underway. She figured that once she'd explained all that, "everything would be cool, and we'd all go home. That wasn't exactly what happened." When the prosecutor's questions got more pointed, she clammed up, and on May 19, two weeks after the Mayday protests ended, she was jailed for contempt. "The government is trying to frame us and other innocent people to make their own paranoid fantasies legitimate," she told reporters.

A few days later, the Justice Department decided to seek answers directly from Bacon's associates — including Stew Albert and Judy Gumbo. They were summoned to a grand jury as well. "It's a total frame-up," said Judy. Stew ripped up his subpoena in front of reporters and scattered the scraps on the grass. "An FBI agent has told me I was a suspect in the Capitol bombing," he said. "I had nothing to do with it. Neither did Miss Bacon nor Miss Gumbo."

In addition to Seattle, the government convened grand juries in Detroit and New York City and called at least eight people from the Mayday crowd. Having learned a lesson from Bacon's initial appearance, all of them refused to answer a single question. The two other men who'd been in Judy's car in Pennsylvania, Michael Tola and Colin Neiburger, burned their subpoenas at a press conference.

OVERDUE FOR a press conference himself, Nixon agreed to schedule one for June 1, despite his lingering fury with the correspondents' gala. He hadn't been meeting with reporters as often as his predecessors. One reason was his history of strained relations ("You won't have Nixon to kick around anymore," he spat at correspondents in 1962 after failing in his bid to be governor of California). To veteran Washington reporters, there was another reason for his elusiveness: he just seemed personally uncomfortable up there. "I think he is a rather solitary man," one observed. Nixon liked to gird himself beforehand by jogging in place for four hundred paces to "get the wind up."

The televised session started out fairly easy. Softball questions gave the president a chance to display his facility with issues like NATO and the recently announced framework for SALT, the talks on nuclear arms reduction with the Soviets. As usual, a reporter would ask a question, get an answer, and the next reporter would move on to another one-shot topic.

At the halfway point, the mood changed. Herbert Kaplow of NBC asked if Nixon, with a month's perspective, had changed his mind about the propriety of the police response to Mayday, now that the courts had thrown out thousands of the arrests.

The president doubled down. He reiterated support for the crackdown without, of course, revealing his own role. Unlike peaceful dissenters, he said, "when people come in and slice tires, when they make a trash bin out of Georgetown and other areas of the city, and when they terrorize innocent bystanders, they are not demonstrators, they are vandals and hoodlums and lawbreakers, and they should be treated as lawbreakers."

The next question to Nixon dealt with a different topic. But then the reporters returned to Mayday. One asked if it was really so important to keep traffic flowing "that some method of suspending constitutional rights was justified." Nixon began to lose his cool. It was "really an exaggeration" to say that rights were violated, he said. Two more questions came at him. Why, if the arrests were justified, were the courts releasing thousands of people? Why were they being ruled improper? Agitated, Nixon gripped the sides of the lectern as he struggled to answer. His voice grew shakier. Richard Lee Strout, a reporter for the *Christian Science Monitor* who had covered presidential press conferences for fifty years, through nine presidents, thought it was the sharpest exchange he'd ever seen.

Afterward, Nixon headed upstairs to the residence and, as was his style, picked up the phone to seek reassurance. He called Haldeman first and got right to the point.

"Well, they all ganged up apparently on that damn Mayday thing," Nixon complained. "You know, Bob, of all the big questions, they should be veering in on SALT, China, the USSR. They covered it tangentially, but Jesus Christ, they screwed around on Mayday?" His voice dripped with disdain. "Goddam it, these people are thugs, vandals, terrorists. That's what they are. You know they really are. Don't you agree?"

"Sure," Haldeman said.

The president called the FBI director, J. Edgar Hoover.

"What do you think of that press corps? Aren't they a bunch of bastards?"

"Yes, a bunch of SOBs," the director said. "Sometimes I'd like to punch them in the jaw."

Nixon laughed. "That's what I felt!"

The president knew one person who would always praise his public performance, Rose Mary Woods, his personal secretary. When he got Woods on the line, his voice lost its stiffness and took on an almost tender quality. "That was *marvelous*," Woods told Nixon. "They were really rough questions and they just stayed with it. You answered just beautifully." Of the reporters, she said, "When they ask questions they just look so evil. Oh! Just straight-out evil!"

Nixon also checked in with his national security adviser, Henry Kissinger. "The way they badgered along on that Mayday thing was disgusting," said the president. "Isn't it interesting though that out of that thing six questions were on that stupid issue? Good god, the goddam thing's over! We did the right thing. We kept the government going. These people were a bunch of dope addicts and the rest."

After Kissinger reassured him he was right, Nixon hung up and called Haldeman back. He wasn't sure that he had gotten across his position on the legality of the arrests.

"Bob, let me tell you what happened," Nixon said. "We arrested a hell of a lot of people. In a strictly legal sense, it was not legal."

"That's right," Haldeman said.

"But we had to do it. Now that's all there is to it. And we'll do it again. Because keeping this government going is more important than screwing around. Because nobody was thrown in the can, nobody was kept in the can, they were all released. So what are they squealing about?"

Then Nixon concluded, "And don't worry about this little, technical legal question."

PERHAPS, AS THE PROTESTERS racked up victories in the courtroom, the little technical legal question might have ballooned into a political scandal, with reporters uncovering the role of the White House, the official falsehoods, and the cavalier attitude toward the Constitution shown by the nation's top law-enforcement officials. As a top Republican lawyer in the Justice Department later warned his colleagues privately, Nixon's conversations about Mayday that were captured on tape "may themselves conceivably be criminal acts," persuasive evidence that the president was part of a "conspiracy" against demonstrators to "deprive them of their civil rights." But less than two weeks after Nixon's press conference, an explosive new story shoved everything else aside.

It happened on Sunday, June 13, a day when the Nixon family could finally relax after a roller coaster of a spring. The day before, Tricia Nixon's wedding at the White House had been a triumph. Four hundred guests gathered in the Rose Garden. The president positively glowed as he danced with his daughters and his wife at the reception in the East Room.

The main headline on the front page of the Sunday *New York Times* ended the reverie: "Vietnam Archive: Pentagon Study Traces 3 Decades of Growing U.S. Involvement." Inside, the paper published six full pages about the study and promised this was just the first installment in a series. The secret papers leaked by the former Defense Department analyst Daniel Ellsberg had become public.

Ellsberg had given copies of the Pentagon Papers to the *New York Times* reporter Neil Sheehan in March. On Mayday, after being Maced along with his Cambridge, Massachusetts, affinity group, he returned home. He knew that staff at the *New York Times* had been reading and analyzing the documents, but didn't know until the day before that the newspaper was about to publish.

The White House realized that only a few people had access to the confidential study. Ellsberg was immediately suspected.

At first, Nixon wasn't especially concerned, though he told his chief of staff that the leaker and the newspaper were being "criminally traitorous." The study dealt with the blunders and deceit of the previous two administrations, both Democratic, and ended before Nixon had even taken office.

Kissinger, who knew Ellsberg from his work for Defense and the RAND Corporation, wasn't as sanguine. Ellsberg was brilliant, but he'd moved far to the left, Kissinger said. He goaded Nixon, telling him the revelations in the Pentagon Papers would get in the way of peace talks with North Vietnam. As Nixon later recalled, Kissinger also told the president "we were in a 'revolutionary' situation,'" as Ellsberg used the papers to "promote the concept of unlawful dissent."

Aides soon held several "panic sessions" to craft a strategy. After the *New York Times* published for a third day, the Justice Department, on the grounds of national security, obtained a temporary court order barring the newspaper from printing any more installments. Ellsberg quickly passed a copy of the papers to the *Washington Post*. The publisher, Katharine Graham, went against the advice of some of her lawyers, who warned of dire legal and financial consequences (the *New York Times* had grappled with the same questions before publishing). She decided to go ahead with the *Post*'s own stories. William Rehnquist, the Justice Department lawyer who had pushed to cripple the Mayday Tribe, telephoned the newspaper's editor, Ben Bradlee. The *Post* was violating laws against espionage, warned Rehnquist. He demanded they halt publication and hand over the documents. Bradlee refused.

Within two weeks, the battle pitting the First Amendment against national security wound up in the Supreme Court, which, in a historic victory for journalism, ruled on June 30 that the government could not prevent the newspapers from publishing.

The Pentagon Papers would reveal much about the war: how deliberately the United States became involved, how officials ignored the realities of Vietnam and justified the intervention with misleading information, how early in the game many generals and politicians realized the bombing wasn't effective and victory was unlikely. The story hewed more closely to the claims of the antiwar movement than any government account had. It was playing out as Ellsberg had hoped.

While the newspapers were no longer in legal danger, Ellsberg certainly was. Just before the Supreme Court ruling, he turned himself in, saying he was ready to accept the consequences. He would be indicted for theft and espionage by a grand jury in Los Angeles.

HAD COOLER HEADS prevailed at this point, Nixon and his men might have saved themselves.

They could have let the Ellsberg prosecution take its course and blamed the revelations in the Pentagon Papers on the previous Democratic administrations. Although trouble was brewing about the mass arrests, they could have banked on the short attention span of the American press and public. While they'd been battered by the Spring Offensive, they had survived what would turn out to be the antiwar movement's last hurrah. Nixon and Kissinger could have continued to point to troop withdrawals as evidence that the Vietnam War was coming to an end. The president could have trained the full focus of the administration on his creative diplomatic initiatives with China and the Soviet Union, and his bid for reelection in 1972, as a global peacemaker.

This was not to be. Nixon was a man who nursed grievances, particularly in a "time of high national passion," as one aide put it, with the White House facing an unrelenting siege. Even before the Pentagon Papers, said the aide, "we were surrounded by critics and demonstrators. We had been shaken by antiwar demonstrations, the wave of bombings, the massive May Day attempt to shut down Washington." Mayday and Ellsberg "intensified the pressures to find out what our 'enemies' were up to," the aide wrote. It could all be one big conspiracy, from the Vietnam Veterans' protest all the way to Ellsberg's. "They don't all happen at once by accident," argued Kissinger, who would famously brand Ellsberg as "the most dangerous man in America today."

At the same time, the success of their tactics emboldened the president and his inner circle — the bending of constitutional rules, the pranks and schemes against their opponents, without any serious consequences so far. There was every expectation that such methods could work on a larger scale. "Once we get the war over," Nixon said in the midst of Mayday, "we'll beat the living bejesus out of those people out there cause they're on the wrong side." The prediction of one of the Chicago Seven defendants had been borne out: the sleeping dogs of the right had wakened.

Less than a year before, the president had accepted Tom Huston's plan for break-ins and other illegal actions to counter the New Left, before he was forced by an angry J. Edgar Hoover to rescind the document (even though the FBI was secretly carrying out the same acts). Now Nixon wanted to revisit those methods and use them against Ellsberg, who, the president and his men believed, could be working with foreign agents. He gave impatient orders to Haldeman: "Bob, you remember Huston's plan? Implement it."

Nixon had been told that a liberal Washington think tank, the Brookings Institution, might have another secret government report on Vietnam locked in a safe. He wanted someone to break in and crack it. "Get it done! I want it done!" he told Haldeman. Haldeman turned the order over to Charles Colson, the White House lawyer in charge of dirty tricks, who, according to John Dean, drew up a plan to case the building and then set off a firebomb, so his operatives could slip inside and complete the job. Dean would later claim he talked his bosses out of the "crazy scheme."

However it fizzled, it left Nixon frustrated. He decided to establish a special unit to execute his off-the-books instructions.

Who could run this new unit? Dean had disqualified himself by opposing the Brookings caper. Charles Colson was too busy playing Nixon's dirty tricks on the Democrats. The president suggested bringing Tom Huston back to the White House, but Nixon's aides disliked Huston too much for that. "I really need a son of a bitch, like Huston," Nixon insisted. Not "a high-minded lawyer" but someone who wouldn't worry about legal niceties. "We're up against an enemy, a conspiracy," said the president. "They're using any means. We are going to use any means."

EARLY IN HIS ADMINISTRATION, Nixon harbored some doubts about Bud Krogh. The president had considered replacing him with Huston as overseer of the government's counterattack on the antiwar movement. But by the spring of 1971, Bud had won over the president by representing himself as a hard-liner who could be trusted, who could see how to turn the Capitol bombing into a political plus, who was taking an increasingly fierce line on his other big responsibility, illegal narcotics. Bud's boss, Ehrlichman, sent the president in mid-May a "hard hitting memorandum on the drug problem" written by Bud.

"I couldn't feel better about drugs because I know Krogh is a tough son of a bitch," Nixon told his chief of staff on the phone one evening, a couple of weeks before the Pentagon Papers became public. "He believes as I believe. He's going to do what I want. Right?"

"Sure," said Haldeman. "And he will. He won't give up."

"And he won't give up, and he'll needle everybody, and we're going to do something," Nixon said.

Having ceded direct White House oversight of the Mayday demonstrations to Dean, Bud had turned his focus back to international drug smuggling. In early July, he left on a two-week foreign trip. He stopped last in Vietnam, to further explore the patterns of heroin abuse among GIs.

Just before Bud arrived back in the United States, where he was to brief the president at the Western White House, Nixon surprised the world. He announced he'd become the first American president to visit China since the communist revolution. Bud was thrilled by this political and diplomatic triumph. When it came to domestic issues, though, Bud already was sensing Nixon's waning interest in his portfolio of drugs and crime, particularly after the Spring Offensive. The president was shifting "his wrath" to the antiwar movement, an obstacle to his foreign policy and a threat to his reelection.

Arriving at San Clemente in mid-July, Bud and two colleagues presented their findings about heroin to Nixon and to Bud's boss, John Ehrlichman. Afterwards, Ehrlichman invited Bud into his office. He shut the door.

Bud had been right that Nixon was losing interest in the drug war. "The president," Ehrlichman said, "has a project for you." He handed Bud a file labeled "Pentagon Papers."

Nixon and his men were convinced that Daniel Ellsberg hadn't been working alone. In their view he was "very likely" at the center of a conspiracy to undermine U.S. influence in Southeast Asia, with help from the Russians. To Nixon, it resembled the historic case he had taken on as a young congressman, when he helped prove a State Department official named Alger Hiss — another Ivy League elitist — had been part of a Soviet spy ring. The president gave a copy of his book, *Six Crises,* to Ehrlichman and told him to have Bud read the chapter on Hiss, for guidance.

With little experience in national security, Bud was impressionable, and he didn't question the conspiracy theory. He thought Ellsberg really might be a traitor. Before long, he moved out of his West Wing digs. He and a member of Kissinger's staff, David Young, set up shop in Room 16, a "hideaway office," a former mailroom in the basement of the Old Executive Office Building. They assembled operatives to carry out the president's wishes, to undermine Ellsberg and plug other leaks. They were officially known as the Special Investigations Unit, but playfully called themselves the White House Plumbers.

The following year, after five men were arrested while breaking into the Democratic National Committee headquarters in a building called the Watergate, the cover-up of the plumbers' activities would lead to the demise of the Nixon administration.

Epilogue

BUD KROGH HAD LEFT THE WHITE HOUSE BEFORE THE BREAK-IN at Democratic headquarters. Nevertheless he became, of all people, the first member of the administration sentenced to prison — for lying about what had happened in Room 16 in the months following the Mayday demonstrations.

His fate underscored, as John Dean put it later, how "the whole anti-war, Ellsberg stuff, it just merges right into Watergate."

Bud's downfall began when he approved a plan cooked up by his operatives to steal Daniel Ellsberg's file from his former Beverly Hills psychiatrist on Labor Day weekend in 1971. The idea was to discredit Ellsberg, perhaps find evidence of foreign contacts, and thus diminish the impact of the Pentagon Papers. The bizarre caper featured a red wig, fake thick glasses, $2,000 in secret cash, and a miniature camera on loan from the CIA. Bud's field men were G. Gordon Liddy, a former FBI agent, and E. Howard Hunt, ex-CIA. For the dirty work, Hunt recruited three Cuban Americans from Miami who'd been involved in clandestine CIA efforts against the Cuban leader Fidel Castro. The Cubans busted a window, climbed into an office building, and jimmied the psychiatrist's door.

They trashed the place but found nothing usable. Hunt and Liddy, who sold themselves to Nixon's men as tough and seasoned spies, proved to be astonishingly clumsy and amateurish. For example, during reconnaissance, Hunt snapped a picture of Liddy, wearing sunglasses and standing "proud as punch" right next to the parking space marked as reserved for Ellsberg's doctor. When Hunt returned the camera, he left that film inside. The CIA had it developed and kept it on hand.

A few months later, Bud moved to the Department of Transportation as an undersecretary. Then in June 1972, Liddy and Hunt, now working for Nixon's reelection campaign, launched the operation to plant bugs at the Watergate, sending in two of the same Miami Cubans they'd used in the Ellsberg job. After their lack of good tradecraft got them all caught, the CIA gave Liddy's file, including the Beverly Hills photo, to federal agents, who began interviewing White House officials to try to puzzle out what it meant.

When Bud learned he was next on the list to be questioned, he sought advice from Dean, the counsel he had originally recruited to the White House staff. Bud didn't realize it, but Dean might have nurtured a bit of resentment toward him because he thought that the job of running the plumbers "should logically have been mine."

To protect the president and his aides, the Watergate break-in had to be painted as a one-off "third-rate burglary" by rogue characters — when it was actually part of a wide-ranging clandestine campaign to cripple the president's critics and opponents. Room 16 was its wellspring. As Bud later recalled, "John Dean said, 'Well, you're going to have to lie like you've never lied before in your life.'" So that's what Bud did. He told investigators he knew nothing about trips made by Hunt and Liddy to California. ("Never told Bud to lie," Dean recently told me. "Bud somehow jumbled the facts." Dean said his only advice would have been that if Bud believed the Ellsberg operation to be a classified national security matter, "You can't reveal it.")

In September, Hunt, Liddy, and the five Watergate burglars were indicted. Though FBI agents and the *Washington Post* were on the trail, finding information that would lead to a greater scandal, the issue was still obscure to voters and gained no traction in the 1972 presidential campaign. Pete McCloskey, the California Republican whom Bud Krogh had met in Saigon, dropped a feeble challenge to Nixon in the primaries. The president's plunging popularity in opinion polls had reversed direction in February, after he pulled off his triumphant visit to China. He easily won renomination. In November he buried Democrat George McGovern in a landslide. The following month he sent a fleet of B-52 bombers over North Vietnam to pound Hanoi back to the bargaining table — the so-called Christmas bombing.

At his second inaugural, just after his sixtieth birthday, Nixon was ebullient. He knew he was about to announce, finally, an agreement with the North Vietnamese to end the war. "Let us pledge," he said in his address, "to make these *next* four years the *best* four years in American history."

Days later, on January 23, 1973, Henry Kissinger and the chief negotiator for Hanoi, Le Duc Tho, initialed the peace deal in Paris. Strangely, it happened only hours after the man who made the conflict a full-scale war, the former President Lyndon B. Johnson, died of a heart attack at his Texas ranch, at the age of sixty-four. The terms of American withdrawal, which included a promise (never fulfilled) that the United States would pay war reparations, were arguably closer to a surrender than those contained in the People's Peace Treaty proposed by the Mayday Tribe. In the twenty months since the crowd had unfurled a copy on the Capitol steps, to the ridicule of Nixon's men, another thirteen thousand U.S. soldiers and tens of thousands more Vietnamese had died, not to mention the destruction caused by U.S. ordnance and chemical agents.

Nixon's political power appeared to be at its height. But the Watergate investigators in the FBI, in Congress, and especially at the *Washington Post*, persisted. Within a couple of months they confirmed the role of the White House. The cover-up intensified — Hunt was paid $75,000 to keep quiet about the fiasco of the Ellsberg burglary, after warning he would otherwise disclose the "seamy things" he'd done for Ehrlichman and Krogh. The dam burst in April 1973. Dean, who had been instrumental in the cover-up, flipped on the president. The puzzling CIA photos from the Ellsberg burglary? They were evidence that the White House was obstructing justice, Dean told investigators. He would agree to plead guilty and testify against his colleagues, and would spend four months in jail. Dean said his personal ethics had left him no choice but to break rank. Nixon's men never forgave him. "He was a traitor and a liar and out for himself from the beginning," Nixon later insisted privately.

John Ehrlichman, Bud's boss and the president's chief domestic policy adviser, had approved the covert Ellsberg job, "if done under your assurance that it is not traceable," as he wrote on Bud's memo. He now tried to hide that evidence and told the FBI that he hadn't known about the plan in advance, leaving Bud as the fall guy.

So much for Bud's father figure.

Until then, Bud's life had appeared to be on the mend. He had the new job, and had reconciled with his wife, Suzanne. He was back living with her and the two boys. He kept up his running; he was first to cross the finish line in a city-sponsored race around the Mall. Bud could not, however, outpace his recent past. As the scandal spread, he resigned his transportation post, and in the autumn of 1973, he was indicted in Los Angeles for directing the Ellsberg break-in and in D.C. for lying to Watergate investigators.

Strikingly, the Washington sport of anonymous character assassination did not extend to Bud. Instead, his former colleagues told reporters they didn't believe he would ever lie under oath. He was just too much of a straight arrow.

Yet Bud compounded the lies by pleading not guilty in both cases, all the time struggling with the knowledge that, as he put it later, the Ellsberg caper was "the most extreme and unconstitutional covert action taken to that date." His initial public silence impressed Nixon. "Someday when you call him," the president told an aide, "just tell him that I think he's a hell of a guy, would you?"

Bud couldn't bear the falsehood for long. He was haunted by it. Over the Thanksgiving holiday, a friend lent him his house in Williamsburg, Virginia, for the weekend. Bud drove the family down in their Volvo, with bicycles in the back. As he toured the city's living museum of colonial times, he felt the presence of the founders who built a nation dedicated to the individual's rights. How could he continue to defend what he'd done?

He talked it over with his wife. They packed up and headed home, where Bud changed his plea to guilty. In February 1974 he began serving four months at the Allenwood minimum-security prison camp in central Pennsylvania. He was assigned to the farm, where he cleaned cow dung out of the pens and learned to drive a tractor. He kept up his daily run. He found himself almost enjoying the sense of peace and calm that had been missing from his life in Washington. After four years in the Nixon White House, he had a new appreciation of the need for "mercy and gentleness" in the public sphere.

"I think what we've got here," a member of the Watergate prosecution team said of Bud, "is a long dead light of the soul, and a conversion."

MOST OF BUD'S COLLEAGUES fought the charges brought against them. Eventually they ended up behind bars too. Ehrlichman served eighteen months for the Ellsberg break-in and his role in the Water-gate cover-up. H. R. Haldeman, Nixon's chief of staff, also served eigh-teen months for conspiracy and obstruction of justice. Gordon Liddy was inside for almost four and half years, Howard Hunt for nearly three. Charles Colson, who had tried to undermine the Vietnam vets, who had promised to instigate fights over Vietcong flags, and who had sent or-anges to protesters in the name of the Democrats, spent seven months in prison after pleading guilty to disseminating false and derogatory in-formation about Ellsberg. "My motive was to neutralize Dr. Ellsberg as an antiwar spokesman in order to further the president's aims for ending the Vietnam war," Colson told the court.

Besides Ehrlichman and Dean, three other participants in the govern-ment's Mayday war councils were among the dozens of Nixon officials ensnared in Watergate.

Attorney General John Mitchell went to prison for nineteen months. He had left Justice to run the Nixon reelection campaign, where among other things he controlled a clandestine fund used for illegal activities, including paying off the Watergate burglars. Richard Kleindienst, who had presided over the Mayday meetings, succeeded Mitchell as attorney general but resigned when the scandal broke. Though he wasn't charged in Watergate, Kleindienst pleaded guilty to lying to the Senate about a different matter. Robert Mardian, who ran the Justice division investi-gating the New Left and filed conspiracy charges against Rennie Davis and the other Mayday organizers, was convicted in Watergate, though he later won his freedom on appeal.

A more felicitous outcome awaited William Rehnquist, the Justice lawyer who had pushed for a way to bust up the Mayday encampment. Nixon named him to the Supreme Court months after the Spring Of-fensive. Fifteen years later, President Ronald Reagan would elevate him to chief justice. In recent years scholars have cast even more doubt on the testimony Rehnquist gave at his confirmation hearings about a 1952 memo he wrote as a young Supreme Court clerk. (The memo praised the high court's notorious 1896 *Plessy v. Ferguson* decision, upholding racial segregation; Rehnquist claimed he was stating the views of his boss, not his own.) Rehnquist was never held accountable for that, nor for misleading, if not lying outright to, the Senate about his role in the pre-Mayday meetings.

The spring of 1971 nevertheless left a deep impression on Rehnquist. As chief justice, he pitched his literary agent on a Washington potboiler built on the fictional murder of an assistant attorney general during Mayday. His thirteen-page outline was rejected as "thin" and "illogical."

RICHARD NIXON'S ROLE in the Watergate cover-up would lead the House of Representatives to begin impeachment proceedings. Before the full House could vote, he resigned, on August 9, 1974.

Ten months earlier, he had replaced Vice President Spiro Agnew with the House Minority Leader, Gerald Ford. Agnew, who had attacked the antiwar movement and New Left for corrupting American values, had resigned because a grand jury in Maryland, where he'd been governor, was preparing to indict him for taking kickbacks and bribes from developers, including accepting cash in the vice president's office.

A month after ascending to the presidency, Ford granted Nixon a full pardon.

IN CONTRAST, almost all of the people targeted by Nixon's men would wind up with no criminal history. Daniel Ellsberg spent no time in jail. A federal judge dismissed all charges against him and his co-defendant, Anthony Russo, for leaking the Pentagon Papers, citing the illegal and "bizarre" conduct of the White House.

The arrest records of Ellsberg's friends, along with the thousands of others jailed during Mayday, were wiped away. Instead of being fined tens of thousands of dollars, as many Watergate figures were, the detainees got paid for their trouble, and then some.

Over the years, thanks to class actions filed by the ACLU as well as individual lawsuits, juries and judges awarded millions of dollars to thousands of detainees, for violations of their right to free speech, assembly, and due process. Some got back what they spent on bail and collateral. Others received compensation for false arrest and imprisonment. Congress acknowledged, in a backhanded way, that the fault lay as much with the federal government as the police; it appropriated more than $3 million to the city to help defray the costs of settlements and damages.

Because the money came through so many years after the events, the ACLU had difficulty finding everyone entitled to compensation. Many had given their jailers false names or addresses. Most had moved multiple times since 1971. So the civil liberties group hired skip tracers — the people whose usual job it is to track down suspects who've skipped out on bail. Still, dozens were never found.

The biggest checks went to those dragged away from the rally on the Capitol steps. The lead lawyer for the ACLU in that case was Warren Kaplan, a Washington attorney originally drawn into Mayday when he was asked to spring a friend's daughter from jail. In the stirring final argument he prepared for the jury, Kaplan acknowledged that, technically, the matter at hand dealt only with the Capitol rally. He added:

> But in a very real sense it is more than a story about 1,200 people who got arrested on May 5th, 1971. It is the story of a period in American history when certain high-ranking law enforcement officials concluded that they were above the law. It is about a period in American history when the largest mass arrests known to the history of our country took place, a period in which in the space of three short days some 15,000 people* were arrested while attempting to express their First Amendment rights. It is about a period in our history which must not be repeated.

The jury agreed, deliberating for only a few hours before awarding the plaintiffs $12 million in damages, at the time said to be the largest judgment in a civil lawsuit not involving a big corporation.

The government appealed the $12 million award as excessive, and years later an appellate court agreed, ordering the original trial judge to come up with a more reasonable amount. In the end the award was cut by 90 percent. Still, more than a thousand people arrested on the steps received as much as $3,200 each. One of them was Janis McDonald, the George Washington University student who had been one of the eight defendants in the original criminal case against the protesters. By the

---

* For effect, Kaplan was citing the biggest estimate of mass arrests being made at the time, but the number fifteen thousand was misleading. Over the three days of the Mayday protests, more than twelve thousand people were rounded up. More than two thousand other arrests took place over the ten weeks of the Spring Offensive, so the overall total was between fourteen and fifteen thousand, by most accounts.

time it was settled she had graduated, gone to law school, passed the bar, and joined Kaplan's legal team.

THE SUPREME COURT declined to hear the government's appeal of the Capitol steps judgment. Yet even without a high-court ruling, the case would, like other Mayday actions, echo for years through the justice system. For the first time, a federal court had acknowledged that individuals had an implied cause of action against federal officials for violations of their First Amendment rights of free speech and assembly. And the case reinforced the right of demonstrators to receive fair warning before being arrested. It would be cited and referenced in hundreds of lawsuits about false imprisonment and improper police procedures.

The case had consequences as well for secret government records. When the Watergate scandal revealed the existence of Nixon's White House tapes, Kaplan sought recordings made during Mayday, looking for evidence the president and his men had directed the counterattack. Nixon's lawyers fought the matter long past the resolution of the Capitol steps trial, arguing that even though the tapes had to be turned over in the Watergate criminal case, executive privilege protected them from disclosure in civil actions. In the end, a court determined Nixon had to surrender the tapes,* using a standard that would be cited in future key decisions on government records, including the Whitewater investigation of President Clinton; the prosecution of Clinton's secretary of agriculture, Mike Espy; and the dispute over Vice President Dick Cheney's secret task force on energy policy.

The Capitol arrests also got a cameo when the government finally came to grips with compensating the more than a hundred thousand Japanese Americans herded into West Coast internment camps during World War II. Representative Ron Dellums, the California Democrat who had been billy-clubbed on the steps during Mayday, called on

---

* Nixon's conversations relevant to Mayday were transcribed by the National Archives at the trial court's request. By the time they were complete, the legal case was long over. For more than forty years the transcripts sat in file cabinets in College Park, Maryland, along with other Nixon records. Warren Kaplan, who had requested them in 1971, didn't know they existed until they surfaced during research for this book.

his colleagues to take heed of the 1971 case and consider it precedent. In 1988, Congress approved payments of $20,000 to each surviving Japanese American detainee.

Besides the Capitol steps litigation, the other major Mayday case was the ACLU lawsuit that sought to delete the arrest records of the seven thousand people arrested during the traffic blockade. That set precedents too. It was said to be the first class-action suit certified by a court where plaintiffs sought damages for violations of their Fourth Amendment due-process rights. After the arrests were declared unconstitutional, a judge told the FBI to return any fingerprints and paperwork they'd received from the D.C. police. Sixteen years of legal skirmishes later, the court ordered the records destroyed, not only for all of those detained on May 3 but during the entire week. It remains a leading case in determining when courts can require expungement of arrests, cited today in legal-procedure manuals in states from Alabama to Washington.

Taken together, the aftershocks of 1971 discouraged police from making indiscriminate busts. A few years after Mayday, one D.C. cop told a reporter the cases had made them "overly cautious" during demonstrations, leading them to ignore minor infractions and seek to disperse troublemakers rather than make mass arrests.

Besides these effects on the police, the protests had a direct impact on the rules future dissenters encountered in Washington.

One judge erased the 1882 law that effectively prevented demonstrations on the Capitol grounds. It was found unconstitutional on its face. Without the change, dozens of protests might have been kept far away from Congress, including very large ones, like the Million Man March in 1995.

In the aftermath of the Spring Offensive, the courts also put a stop to attempts to shrink the size of allowable demonstrations near the White House; both LBJ and Nixon had sought to do this. The idea was to limit crowds to no more than one hundred people on the sidewalk in front of the executive mansion, and no more than five hundred in Lafayette Square, across the street, to protect the president from possible harm. Judges suggested it was a thinly veiled attempt to suppress dissent in the name of an unlikely security threat. "The White House sidewalk, Lafayette Park, and the Ellipse constitute a unique situs for the exercise of

First Amendment rights," they wrote. After Mayday, Nixon's aides also explored Haldeman's idea of forcing protest organizers coming to Washington to post a bond to cover any potential property damage. That was scotched by administration lawyers, who noted the judiciary was in no mood to approve prior restraints that were probably unconstitutional. (Almost fifty years later, these ideas would be revived by the Donald Trump administration, which sought to impose fees on demonstrations and ban protests from 80 percent of the White House sidewalk.)

Years after the Spring Offensive, an appellate judge reflected that the authorities had learned from "what was done in the past and what the courts have said about those incidents," and had since managed an "avoidance of ugly confrontation." The lessons of Mayday restored the right of dissent to the streets of Washington.

THERE WERE AFTERSHOCKS too from the Capitol bombing, though some of these reduced rather than expanded civil liberties.

Among them was the question of whether government agents could arrest and detain a material witness who they feared might flee, without first giving the person a chance to answer a subpoena. That's what had happened to Leslie Bacon, the nineteen-year-old Mayday organizer accused of having knowledge about the bombers. Her lawyers challenged her arrest. Judges in the Ninth Circuit ultimately ordered her released pending trial, saying prosecutors failed to prove she wouldn't have come in under her own power.

Fatefully, though, the court didn't address the larger constitutional question of whether material witnesses could be arrested in grand jury proceedings at all. Which was why, thirty years later, after Al Qaeda's 2001 attacks on the World Trade Towers and the Pentagon, Bacon's case had "a singularly far-reaching influence" in allowing government agents, without showing probable cause, to seize and hold dozens of people of Middle Eastern descent.

The 1971 explosion also closed out an age of innocence in Washington. For the first time, guards at the Capitol began examining briefcases, purses, and packages. Authorities installed X-ray machines at ten entrances and video cameras at other spots. It would be the biggest single step-up in security in Washington for thirty years.

• • •

IN THE MATTER of the Capitol bombing itself, for which the Weather Underground had claimed responsibility, no one would ever be charged. With no suspects to bring to trial, nor any injured victims, the spectacular assault on the arena of U.S. democracy simply disappeared from public memory. As it faded, it left some important questions unresolved. The acts of a relatively small band of radical guerrillas helped provoke the authorities to deploy wide surveillance of the left and the suppression of dissent. If those guerrillas counted on significant aboveground assistance, that still wouldn't excuse the government's desperate and illegal activities, but it might make them easier to explain or understand.

The FBI director, J. Edgar Hoover, admitted to Congress that the bureau had been highly optimistic that it would break the bombing case but then was stymied. It wasn't the only investigation of the Weather Underground that frustrated the FBI. Agents found it nearly impossible to crack the discipline of the fugitives. Their "commune-type" organization, members living in close quarters with no secrets from one another, "very often prevents law enforcement officer penetration," one White House aide complained.

So the bureau would have to try to solve the case by working from the outside in. But the government's own zealotry shut that door. In June 1972, in a case unrelated to Mayday, the Supreme Court ruled unconstitutional the Justice Department's practice of wiretapping the New Left and others without a warrant from a judge. That meant prosecutors no longer could claim a threat to national security in order to avoid disclosing such illegal surveillance in court. Rather than spill the secrets, the Justice Department dropped the one charge it had laid against Leslie Bacon: allegedly lying to the grand jury by claiming she hadn't visited the Capitol the day before the bombing. (Nixon himself gave the order to shelve the Bacon case. With the FBI and the press beginning to dig into Watergate, the last thing the administration needed was another wiretapping scandal.)

Bacon walked free. Her friends, colleagues, and acquaintances no longer faced the danger of charges of contempt for refusing to testify.

At first, the outcome seemed likely to cut Stew Albert and Judy Gumbo loose from FBI scrutiny. Even better, the hubbub eventually helped bring the couple back together romantically. They moved to a cabin in the Catskills, north of New York City.

Yet the FBI didn't leave them alone. Given the wiretaps and eyewitness reports, the agents never believed Stew and Judy when they consistently denied knowledge about the Capitol bombing or Weather.

Some details of the government's suspicions had surfaced in questions that prosecutors put to Leslie Bacon before the grand jury. They asked her about conversations at the house on M Street, where she had stayed with Stew and Judy in the days before the bombing. She was asked why, on the morning of the explosion, Stew had suggested to someone in the house that the device contained twenty sticks of dynamite — a comment allegedly overheard by an informant or a hidden microphone. They asked about the contents of the green knapsack Stew brought with him to D.C. from New York a few days earlier. And they wanted to know why Stew, Judy, and two others from the house had rushed out of town instead of remaining in D.C. to work on Mayday.

In the version given by Stew and Judy, the knapsack was full of high-quality weed, which Judy and her roommates asked Stew to bring down from New York because they'd run out. If Stew commented on dynamite, they said, it was only because he was quoting something he'd read or heard in the news. Judy, Stew, and the others in Judy's car — Michael Tola of Chapel Hill, North Carolina, and Colin Neiburger from Boston — fled D.C. not because they transported explosives or were otherwise involved in the bombing but because they knew the harassment they already were enduring would crank up to an unbearable level. FBI and police officers stopped and searched their car because they couldn't find anyone from Weather and needed to round up "the usual suspects," as Judy contended. "This is the honest-to-God truth," Neiburger would say later. "I'm terrified of firecrackers. Never held a stick of dynamite in my hand."

Stew and Judy stuck by their story. But its weak points were numerous enough to keep any investigator interested. For example, with hundreds of hippies, ex-Yippies, and radicals living and visiting in D.C. in late February 1971, and marijuana readily available, why did the M Street folks need to summon Stew on a five-hour bus ride from New York to replenish their stash? (Asked about this recently, Judy elaborated, saying that she had wanted not only free pot but another quick fling with Stew.) Mystery too surrounded the activities at the M Street house. One resident mentioned during a phone call that "people are here from all over the country" working on a "secret" project, a comment that got him thrown out of the house by the others, according to a private memo prepared for Stew and Judy's defense.

It's unclear what news report Stew might have seen about dynamite, since authorities didn't speculate on the explosive material used by the bombers until a Senate hearing held the following day. Finally, most of the Mayday people in town knew they were under surveillance, so it's also unclear why that particular foursome would be the ones to decide, as Judy put it, to "get the hell out of Dodge."

While Stew and Judy continued to tell authorities they didn't know who put the device in the Capitol, the word was out in some radical circles that the bombers were Bernardine Dohrn and Kathy Boudin. It would be surprising if none of the Yippies heard this, since they and Weather had been expressing mutual admiration for years. If Stew didn't know, why did he show up for his grand jury appearance that summer in a sequined shirt embroidered with a bomb and the phrase "Bernardine Lives"? In a little-noticed radio interview in the fall of 1971, Judy told listeners that Stew's shirt was "referring to Bernardine Dohrn, who was one of the people who was underground, who in fact according to the own admission of the Weather Underground was in fact responsible for the Capitol bombing, not us."*

In 1976, true to the promise they made in their Mayday letter to Leslie Bacon's mother, Dohrn, Boudin, and other Weather leaders appeared with obscured faces in a documentary film and proudly laid out how they pulled off the caper. It was the only one of its many attacks the group ever discussed in public. In the film they didn't reveal which of them did it, but in subsequent years, members of Weather, their associates, and their relatives told several researchers anonymously that it was Dohrn and Boudin. Two teams carried out the action, people close

---

* Judy recently asserted to this author that in the 1971 interview, she had meant to say that the Weather Underground Organization was responsible, but not specifically Dohrn, because she didn't know the identity of the bombers then, and still does not today. She acknowledged that she and Stew did come to know some Weather fugitives, but not until sometime after Mayday. She said that at the time of the bombing, "I didn't know any of those people."

to Weather would tell the author Ron Jacobs. One group "scouted the target area and provided detailed information to the other team," which then planted the devices.

Knowing at least some of this, the FBI set up a long-term stakeout of the Catskills cabin where Stew and Judy lived, in case anyone from the Weather Underground showed up. "We may consider use of all types of investigative techniques," Hoover instructed the local FBI office. On several occasions agents searched the home while the couple were away. They never found evidence, but in fact, some Weather people did visit. Stew later obtained his FBI files and, based on the memos, would calculate that the agents and fugitives had come close to overlapping "on several occasions."

The FBI surveillance was particularly helpless when Judy got behind the wheel; she drove so fast on the rural highways, they couldn't keep up without tipping their hand. So in the winter of 1975, agents attached a tracking device to her car. Unfortunately for the FBI, Stew and Judy spotted it. They drove to their lawyer's office, and he immediately went to the press. Stew and Judy sued the FBI for harassment. The bureau settled for $20,000. Stew and Judy used the money to buy a new Audi. To rub the agents' noses in it, they ordered a vanity plate with the FBI code name for the case: CAPBOM.

Eventually, Stew and Judy married and ended up in Portland, Oregon. Stew focused on his writing and support for progressive Jewish causes. Judy became a prolific fundraiser for Planned Parenthood. They had a daughter. Stew never abandoned his political beliefs or his conviction that his work in the movement had been valuable. "I was a shaper of history," he wrote to the author Norman Mailer, his erstwhile marching companion, "not a barker in a sideshow."

Many of Stew's friends and associates moved on, however. His alter ego Jerry Rubin became a consultant and entrepreneur. Rubin went on the road to debate Abbie Hoffman in a series of talks dubbed "Yippie v. Yuppie." As for Hoffman, he fled underground for several years to escape a drug charge and eventually killed himself with an overdose of barbiturates in 1989. Rubin died in 1994 after being hit by a car while crossing a Los Angeles street. Eldridge Cleaver, the black revolutionary, condemned psychedelic culture as "silly," singling out Stew. He returned home from

Algeria to serve eight months in prison; he briefly rejoined the Panthers before becoming a born-again Christian who backed Ronald Reagan for president. He died at sixty-two. Timothy Leary, the LSD guru freed from prison by the Weather Underground, whom Stew helped find temporary exile with Cleaver in Algeria, was captured abroad by U.S. agents and served three more years behind bars. He died of cancer at seventy-five.

With age, Stew mellowed a bit. He never forgot that the Sixties "were a wonderful time to be 25 years old with nothing on your mind but a good time and a desire to change the world." Yet, writing after Leary's death, he admitted some second thoughts about the acid-fueled Yippie life: "It became increasingly apparent that if reality was ever going to yield to the transformative images of our compassionate ideals, it would take place slowly and only after much hard thinking and practical political work."

The Weather fugitives continued to stage nonlethal bombings in the 1970s, notably a blast inside a Pentagon bathroom and at the State Department, but by 1980 the group had effectively disbanded. Dohrn, along with her husband and fellow member, Bill Ayers, came out of hiding and surrendered. A year later, Boudin, who had remained underground, helped a group called the Black Liberation Army rob an armored truck outside New York City. Two police officers and a guard were killed, the radicals were captured, and Boudin went to prison for twenty-two years. She left her fourteen-month-old son to be raised by Dohrn and Ayers.

When Dohrn was back aboveground in the early 1980s, Stew and Judy kept in touch with her, inviting her to their daughter's birthday party. Dohrn wrote back that she couldn't wait to talk over the old days.

In Portland, Stew's health deteriorated. He developed hepatitis C and then liver cancer. He died in 2006 at the age of sixty-six. The night before, he posted to his blog. "Still me," he wrote. "Still me."

In a eulogy, Dohrn lauded Stew as a facilitator of the marriage between surrealism and radical politics. "The yippies and Weather Underground were kissing cousins," she wrote. Three years before his death, Stew published a memoir of his life and times. He had originally planned to frame the book as a letter to his daughter. "Explain why the end of the 60's were justifiably violent," reads one of his research notes. His note hinted he might divulge untold secrets. "You need to decide here what you want to tell her about Weatherman, if anything. You could talk about early Weatherman, or about CAPBOM, or not at all." For his book, he ultimately chose not at all.

THE GOVERNMENT NEVER prosecuted Rennie Davis, Abbie Hoffman, or John Froines on the trumped-up charges of a conspiracy to foment riots on Mayday, because a federal judge ruled that the FBI would have had to reveal the identities of its informants and the nature of its wiretaps. Neither did Rennie, Hoffman, Froines, Jerry Rubin, David Dellinger, or any other members of the Chicago Seven go to prison in that case. In 1972 an appeals court voided their Chicago convictions, ruling that the trial judge had conducted himself with prejudice. The government would decide not to try them again, especially given the new rules for disclosing illegal surveillance.

David Dellinger had been discharged from Georgetown University Hospital for his eye problems by the end of May 1971. He and the other organizers regrouped. They tried to mount a new spate of civil disobedience near the White House that October. Rennie and Dave were among the nearly three hundred people arrested. They spent a night in jail, but the thousands of protesters they expected didn't show up, and the action fizzled. "When Mayday was over," observed Froines, "that was in a sense the end of the antiwar movement."

The following summer, protesters made an appearance at the Republican National Convention in Miami but, outside of the McGovern campaign, the most visible organized action against the war in 1972 was the brainchild of Tom Hayden, another member of the Chicago Seven and Stew's one-time Berkeley roommate. Hayden had met and fallen for Jane Fonda. The two of them organized a traveling show they called the Indochina Peace Campaign, which played in dozens of cities that fall, aiming to pressure Congress to not only end the war but cut off aid to the South Vietnamese regime. (Fonda would become known to the American right as "Hanoi Jane" after making a trip to North Vietnam and posing behind an anti-aircraft gun, a moment she'd later call naive and would forever regret. She would return to acting, and Hayden would become a California state legislator.)

When the peace agreement was signed in Paris in 1973, Rennie left the cause. His quest for revolutionary change shifted with dizzying speed from the political to the spiritual. To the great dismay of his former ac tivist colleagues, he became ensnared in a religious movement that heralded a fifteen-year-old guru from India as the earth's "one perfect master." Rennie soon told reporters he would "cross the planet on my hands and knees to touch his toe."

The Spring Offensive did permanent damage to David Dellinger's health, but he didn't stray from his path. After the Pentagon Papers emerged, he bolstered his stump speech with an I-told-you-so about the war. "Now the facts appear in headlines with the official stamp of the perpetrators," he said. In 1971 he made a prediction: "At some point — some fifty to a hundred thousand senseless casualties later — the government will do a little fancy footwork and withdraw all or most of its overt combat troops from Vietnam while continuing its imperialist policies throughout the world. Similarly, in the normal course of events, the country will elect more and more black mayors and fund more and more black capitalists while continuing to deny the masses of people, black and white, the joys and dignity of political and economic equality."

South Vietnam fell to the North Vietnamese army in April 1975, unifying the country under communist rule. Dave was among fifty thousand people who gathered in Sheep's Meadow in Central Park in New York to celebrate the true end of the war. Eventually he moved to Vermont with his wife and lived out the rest of his eighty-eight years in a modest house on a dirt road near Burlington. He didn't stop writing and speaking about pacifism and social change until he developed Alzheimer's and died in a nursing home in 2004.

AFTER THE INTENSITY OF 1971, John O'Connor decided he'd had enough of undercover work. He told his D.C. police bosses he was coming in from the cold. He'd claim his long-delayed spot at the police academy. He lied once again to his pals in the Vietnam Veterans Against the War, telling them he was moving to California. He cut off his long hair and tossed away his ragged clothes so no one would recognize him.

Yet he couldn't bear to shed his beloved red Mustang. One day, as he waited at a stoplight in Washington, one of his former housemates happened to come up alongside. "John," the vet asked incredulously, "is that you?"

So John came clean, though it took some serious convincing before his old crowd even believed he was a police officer — he had to bring his

gun to their apartment for show and tell. John wasn't sure how they'd react. There was shock and anger at first—"kicked in the balls" was how
Jack Mallory felt—but pretty soon they all were able to laugh about it.
John's police bosses didn't like it that he stayed friends with the vets, and
they threatened to fire him if he didn't dump them. In turn, John warned
his bosses he'd go straight to TV or the newspapers with his story. They
left him alone after that. John stayed on the D.C. force for more than
twenty years before he retired and started a second career as a nurse; he
remains in touch with his old buddies today.

As for the Vietnam Veterans Against the War, a few weeks after Mayday, on Memorial Day, they reprised their Spring Offensive protest by
camping on the Lexington Green in Massachusetts. This time, police
moved in, arresting more than four hundred veterans and supporters.
John Kerry was part of it. But soon after, he left the group, finding that
it was too dominated by the militant faction. Kerry reentered Massachusetts politics, eventually becoming a U.S. senator. When he finally
made his run for president, against the incumbent, George W. Bush,
in 2004, his antiwar activities during the Spring Offensive surfaced as
a campaign issue. Right-wing conspiracy theorists falsely claimed not
only that he hadn't deserved his Vietnam service commendations, but
also that he hadn't really thrown any of his own medals or ribbons onto
the Capitol steps.

The election was close; had Kerry switched just sixty thousand votes
in Ohio, he would have gotten to the White House. In 2012 President
Barack Obama appointed him secretary of state. In that capacity, Kerry
returned for the first time in more than forty years to Vietnam's Mekong
Delta, where he'd won his Silver Star, this time to talk about the dangers
of climate change.

THE LAWYERS AND JURISTS who saved the government from aban-
doning the principles of law on Mayday prospered.

Harold Greene, the chief judge of the Superior Court, the first line of
defense against improper arrests and detentions, was named to a federal
judgeship a few years later. There he presided with distinction over one
of the weightiest antitrust cases in U.S. history, facilitating the breakup
of the AT&T telephone monopoly, kick-starting the telecommunica-
tions revolution that would lead to an internet-connected world.

Michael Wald, the public defender who had been carried away on the shoulders of jubilant Mayday protesters, returned to teaching at Stanford. He became a national expert on youth and children's issues and served for a time in Washington during the Clinton administration.

Norman Lefstein, Barbara Bowman's deputy director at the Public Defender Service, also left for academia, teaching at the University of North Carolina before being named dean of Indiana University's law school. His research and practice remained focused on how to get proper legal representation for the indigent.

Not long after Mayday, Barbara divorced her husband; reclaimed her family name, Barbara Babcock; and became the first woman appointed to the regular law faculty at Stanford. After the Democrats retook the White House in the wake of Watergate, she interrupted her academic career to serve as assistant attorney general in charge of the civil division of the Justice Department in the Carter administration.

At her swearing-in, Barbara made clear to the hundreds of people in her division that she no longer felt ambivalent about the women's movement. "I gave a little speech and I told them I was a feminist and scared the shit out of them," she would recall with a laugh. While at Justice, Barbara successfully argued a landmark case before the Supreme Court that helped enshrine the federal Freedom of Information Act. She also worked to get talented women and minorities on the list for potential federal judgeships, including one named Ruth Bader Ginsburg, who would later credit Barbara with her appointment to the D.C. Circuit. "I do not believe I would have gained that good job," Ginsburg said, "without her constant endeavors to place and move up my name on the candidates list."

J. EDGAR HOOVER died exactly a year after Mayday. For the first time since the FBI was founded, a president had a chance to fill the top job.

Police Chief Jerry Wilson never got the call.

Instead, Nixon elevated L. Patrick Gray, the Justice Department lawyer who had tried to kick John Kerry and the Vietnam veterans off the National Mall.

Soon Jerry left the force. He was only forty-six. He wrote a book about urban law enforcement. After Nixon resigned, President Gerald Ford considered naming Jerry head of the Drug Enforcement Administration. But Ford dropped the idea; the controversy over the Mayday arrests, as well as continuing revelations about the police department's surveillance of the New Left, would have made it impossible to get his name through the Senate. Instead, Jerry went back to school. He grew a mustache and earned a college degree. Among other things he taught at the University of Maryland and worked for a time as director of security for a big drug-store chain.

NOT LONG AGO I visited Jerry Wilson several times at his home, in a sleek retirement complex on the western edge of Virginia's Washington suburbs. Pushing ninety and in good health, the tall ex-chief was only slightly stooped and a little unsteady as he meandered through his apartment, showing me the pictures of him with Richard Nixon, which still hung on the walls.

After nearly fifty years, Jerry remembered that he had suspended the rules about field paperwork on the chaotic morning of May 3, 1971. But he couldn't — or wouldn't — close the question of what happened after that: who then authorized his cops to sweep through the city, arresting thousands of young people without evidence they'd broken any laws?

He told me that until he heard it from me, he hadn't known about President Nixon's message to the attorney general just before Mayday, which Nixon recalled as an order to "arrest the whole damn lot." I pointed out that the police logs, and multiple witnesses, suggest that some version of the order was passed to the riot squad. It was also the case that Mitchell's Justice Department had sent one of its men to shadow the police chief that day and facilitate communication with Jerry. Nevertheless, Jerry said he still didn't know how the idea might have made its way from Mitchell to the cops on the streets.

"They should not have been arresting anybody who was not at least blocking traffic," Jerry told me. "I certainly didn't suggest people do it . . . I know it happened. I mean, because we got sued, I know it happened. I could not tell you why."

His version tracks with what he said decades ago in court depositions. If he were to tell me anything different now, of course, it would mean he'd been less than truthful under oath.

Two men who'd been Jerry's colleagues on the force in 1971, the department's lawyer, Gerald Caplan, and deputy chief Maurice Cullinane, theorize that police had acted on their own, out of anger and frustration after weeks of protests and then the mobile civil disobedience of the Mayday Tribe. "I think it was contagious, I think that's how it got started, and then it got the mob mentality, they just start sweeping up," said Cullinane.

Cullinane, who later became chief himself, added, "If Jerry Wilson told you he didn't order it, you should believe him." But however it got started, he allowed, Jerry "didn't do anything to stop it."

At the time, and for years after, Jerry implicitly rejected the idea that his conduct on Mayday was calibrated to convince Nixon to appoint him as director of the FBI. He wasn't after the job, he would say. While his name was raised by the press, the White House never formally mentioned him as a candidate, he would point out.

After the president backed off the idea, there was speculation that Jerry's lack of a college degree was a factor, or that Nixon bowed to pressure from his party leaders to appoint a loyal Republican like L. Patrick Gray. But it seems equally likely, if also ironic, that Jerry doomed his candidacy at the Mayday war councils, with his initial resistance to the administration's hard line and his ambivalence about turning D.C. into an armed camp. By several accounts, Richard Kleindienst, who presided over those councils, turned out to be the main opponent to promoting Jerry.

It seems just as possible that Jerry desired the director's job much more than he let on. Minutes after we first met, I explained that I had spent many hours listening to the White House tapes for my research. His eyes lit up.

"Do you know," he asked me, "why I was never made head of the FBI?"

IN HIS EXILE, Richard Nixon never forgave those who mounted mass protests against the Vietnam War and laid siege to his administration during his first term. "It is difficult, if not impossible, to convey a sense of the pressures that were influencing my actions and reactions during this period," he wrote later. The best he could come up with for reconciliation was to call the movement "a brotherhood of the misguided, the mistaken, the well-meaning and the malevolent."

One government lawyer who attended the Mayday war councils reckoned that the 1971 protests — which he called "the most massive, sustained and varied period of public demonstrations" in Washington's history — "may have helped to bring down a president." Yet Nixon showed no desire to relive the weeks he'd obsessed over that spring; in his memoir he gave Mayday a single sentence.

The interplay between Nixon's paranoia, his goading of the intelligence community to move against the New Left, and the stiffening resolve of the antiwar movement had another long-lasting result — congressional investigations into how the FBI and CIA carried out illegal surveillance and disruption of domestic groups they deemed subversive. The probes, the first of their kind, took place after the revelations of Watergate, but the fuse had been lit in March 1971 by the band of eight Philadelphia-area activists who stole files on the FBI's counterintelligence program a week after the Capitol bombing. (Unlike the bumbling Watergate and Ellsberg burglars, they never were caught.) By the mid-1970s, lawmakers had installed a constellation of new restraints on the agencies' activities, which largely remained in place until the antiterrorism laws enacted after the 2001 attacks.

The 1970 Huston Plan to undermine the New Left surfaced during the Watergate investigation, to the dismay of Nixon, who realized it made him look like a "repressive fascist." Huston, who had moved back to Indiana to launch a successful career as a real estate lawyer, later told congressional investigators he regretted his role in encouraging the administration to adopt extralegal tactics in fighting its critics. He said he had come to believe there was danger in opening a door that could lead people in charge of the tools "to move from the kid with a bomb to the kid with a picket sign, and from the kid with the picket sign to the kid with the bumper sticker of the opposing candidate. And you just keep going down the line."

Bud Krogh, who crossed that line, finished serving his prison term in the summer of 1974. He visited Seattle to see if he could regain his Washington state law license. (He ultimately succeeded.) While there, he decided to fulfill a longtime dream of climbing Mount Rainier, whose snow-capped 14,000-foot peak, on a clear day, seems to float over the city's skyline like an offering. With a family group Bud ascended to the summit in early August. On their way down, they got the news: Nixon had just resigned.

Later that month, Bud arranged to visit the ex-president in San Clemente. He felt compassion for the tired and frail-looking man he found sitting at his desk. Nixon wondered out loud if he should follow Bud's example and plead guilty to the cover-up. Bud asked, Do you feel guilty, sir? "No I do not," Nixon replied.

Afterward, Bud began working on a memo to Nixon, suggesting that the former president would find resolution and serenity if he took full responsibility for his actions. But before he could send it, Ford's pardon rendered Bud's advice moot.

Asked much later by a documentary film producer how he would describe Nixon to someone landing from Mars, Bud said:

> I would tell him that he is probably a man that is almost impossible to completely understand . . . I was never quite sure what he was feeling about something. Many things were said for effect that maybe masked what he was really feeling. A man of enormous intellect at least as I observed it and read in his books. A person who could on one hand be extremely kind and courteous to some people and extremely ruthless and cruel on the other hand. A man of tremendous contradictions and who I don't have a clue as to where the real core was.

ON THE FORTY-FIFTH anniversary of Mayday, a few dozen of the organizers and participants came back to Washington to reminisce. They held their reunion downtown, at the venerable Hotel Harrington, in a windowless ballroom on the second floor, with discolored and loose ceiling tiles, well-worn tables and chairs. A few radical posters hung on the walls for inspiration. The scene wouldn't have been unfamiliar to anyone suddenly teleported from a 1971 movement meeting, except for the preponderance of gray hair and walking canes.

Outside, the capital was rainy and cool, and a different place than they remembered. Million-dollar condominiums rose along the avenues once lined with burned-out row houses. Wild prosperity had pushed the poor farther to the city's fringes. Washington was no longer a majority-black city, but an African American president occupied the White House. The arena across town, which had confined thousands of Mayday detainees, including some now attending the reunion, was about to reopen as a gleaming showcase store for the outdoorsy retailer REI. On the National Mall, a few minutes' walk from the encampment broken up in 1971 by Jerry Wilson's cops, the Vietnam Veterans Memorial, built in 1982, had become a major draw for tourists and mourners, ex-soldiers and ex-protesters, all staring reverently at the polished black marble wall covered with the names of the 58,276 Americans who died or went missing in the nation's most divisive modern war, the monument to a disastrous chapter that still looms like a specter behind conflicts abroad and at home.

Rennie Davis, his graying hair falling in a ponytail down his neck, came to D.C. from his home deep in the Colorado foothills to give the opening remarks at the Mayday Tribe reunion. His 1970s detour into the guru cult seemed forgiven, if not forgotten. Rennie's rhetoric remained more New Age than New Left, but still intact was his wide, welcoming grin and his strong speaking voice. He noted that the medical establishment now takes much more seriously what he used to rail about in his campus speeches — that exposure to Agent Orange caused serious health problems not only for soldiers and civilians exposed to the chemical in Vietnam, but also their children.

Switching on the old charisma, Rennie told the group that although "we weren't the most brilliant tacticians," they had mounted one of the most significant protests America had ever seen. He said he shared their frustration that Mayday had been "all but forgotten in the footnotes of history."

Also in the room was Judy Gumbo, now white-haired but as passionate and energetic as ever. After Stew's death she had moved back to Berkeley. She had helped organize the reunion. Atop a long table at the side of the ballroom sat two models of federal buildings, molded out of chocolate. One was the shape of the U.S. Capitol and the other the Pentagon. Both had been the targets of dozens of antiwar protests as well as bombs from the Weather Underground. At the right moment, Judy invited the aging militants to smash the state once again. They raised their fists and brought them down hard, spraying flakes of chocolate around the room.

IN THE HARSH and hopeful times of the Sixties and early Seventies, when the flaws of American democracy threatened to overcome its promise, when national institutions shook to the breaking point, many people felt tempted to try to smash the state or pervert the Constitution. In the end, none succeeded. The republic survived, thanks in large part to a system of laws and the people sworn and determined to conserve it.

It took sixteen years before the law put the legacy of Mayday to rest.

No one in Washington on July 30, 1987, would have paid attention to a truck motoring through the streets and stopping outside the big municipal trash incinerator on Benning Road. It was ninety-three degrees and humid, no day to be anywhere in the proximity of a giant oven, even one that sat on the banks of the Anacostia River a few miles upstream from where it emptied into the Potomac.

The whole summer had been miserable, not only with more days over ninety than ever before, but with the heat of the latest scandal. The administration of Ronald Reagan stood accused of funneling military aid, against the explicit will of Congress, to anti-communist guerrillas in Nicaragua, and secretly paying for the scheme with arm sales to Iran, which were banned. The revelation had already ignited one of the biggest mass protests at the Capitol since Vietnam. The authorities had learned the lessons of 1971; no one was arrested.

At the riverfront, the truck brought a load of boxes, along with a representative from the ACLU, who was supposed to witness a final act of legal contrition. Inside were the fading records of Nixon's season of suppressed dissent: police computer printouts, bail receipts, collateral slips, photographs, and thousands of white index cards scrawled with names and addresses. A judge had ordered the documents destroyed so that the Mayday detainees would have no criminal histories. That order had been given in 1974. Government lawyers kept trying to head off what they termed an unnecessary and "ritualistic" act, but now the years of legal wrangling had come to an end.

Up went the boxes, lifted into the flames by a mechanical bucket. Somewhere inside was a collateral slip noting that I had paid ten dollars to secure my own release early in the morning of May 4, 1971, after twelve hours in a crowded jail cell in the station house of the Third District. The records burned, and flecks of black ash sailed up through the smokestacks as tall as twenty-story buildings, floating into the sky on the prevailing winds and out toward the spot where the rivers meet.

Acknowledgments

Many people gave patiently of their time and memories to reconstruct these events of the 1960s and 1970s, especially Jerry V. Wilson, Barbara (Bowman) Babcock, Judy Gumbo Albert, Rennie Davis, John Froines, Paul Krassner, John Dean, Gerald Caplan, Norman Lefstein, Michael Wald, Jack Mallory, Tim Butz, and John Scagliotti. John O'Connor shared not only his recollections but also his as-yet-unpublished memoir. I owe special thanks to Jerry Wilson, as well as to Philip Hirschkop and his associate Beth Richelieu, for digging out dusty fifty-year-old file boxes and entrusting them to me. Appreciation too to Matt Krogh, who worked with his dad, Bud Krogh, to enrich this story.

Before he died, Warren Kaplan, a lifelong champion of civil liberties who was one of the Mayday lawyers, agreed to be interviewed and then enthusiastically helped me track down the relevant Nixon tapes. He is sorely missed.

A first-time author quickly learns to lean on some of the nation's most extraordinary public servants at university libraries and at institutions like the National Archives, the Library of Congress, and the Richard Nixon Library and Museum. Their labors to protect priceless historical records and disseminate the truth deserve the gratitude of every citizen. Among archivists who helped point the way: Cary McStay at the National Archives; Dorissa Martinez and Ryan Pettigrew at the Nixon Library; Krista Gray and Angela Waarala at the University of Illinois; Julie Herrada at the University of Michigan; Kendall Newton at the University of Texas; Christian Lopez at the University of Georgia; Laura Schnitker at the University of Maryland; and Susan Stawicki-Vrobel at Marquette

University. Thanks too to government officials like the FBI's Rebecca Bronson, who hold fast to the letter and spirit of public records laws.

The photographic record of dissent in the nation's capital has been diligently tended by Craig Simpson and his colleagues at Washington Area Spark, as well as by the dedicated archivists of the Washingtoniana Collection in the city's Martin Luther King Jr. Memorial Library. Thanks also to Eddy Palanzo at the *Washington Post*, who ventured deep into storage to track down some key images.

Others shared invaluable expertise to make this book possible. Arthur Spitzer, presently legal director of the American Civil Liberties Union of the District of Columbia, provided crucial early guidance about the Mayday court battles and remained an important touchstone throughout. My gratitude to Laura Darkins for inestimable advice about legal research, and to Fred Reiner and Susan Schiffman for their help in tracking the journey of the Mayday arrest records. I'm indebted to a number of august journalists and historians of the 1960s and 1970s, especially Susan Braudy, Todd Gitlin, Ron Jacobs, James Mann, Sanford J. Ungar, and Tom Wells. They offered up wisdom and encouragement.

Those who read early versions of the manuscript include authors who have been my longtime mentors, colleagues, and friends: Jeff Leen, leader of the *Washington Post's* magnificent investigative unit, who is my former boss and journalism partner; Laurel Leff at Northeastern University; and Rob Rosenthal at Wesleyan. Their suggestions mightily improved the book, as did the keen eyes of Ellen Berlinsky, Tim Cuerdon, Deborah Duffy, Tom Green, Stephanie Nichols, Jim Savarin, Gary Schine, and John Whitesides. Any lapses, of course, are mine alone.

I had the good fortune to learn much of my trade at the *Washington Post* when it flourished under the brilliant stewardship of Steve Coll, Robert Kaiser, Leonard Downie, Bo Jones, and Donald Graham. There, and in other great newsrooms, I cribbed best practices from world-class reporters, while benefiting from the friendship and support of outstanding editors, including Pam Luecke, Jill Dutt, Barbara Vobejda, Christine Spolar, Daniel Hertzberg, Martin Heerwald, Bjorn Edlund, Alec Fisken, Dick Clever, and Susan Chadwick.

Big thanks as well to my more recent colleagues at ProPublica, especially Stephen Engelberg, Robin Fields, Richard Tofel, and Paul Steiger, for their generous forbearance as I worked on this project. With dizzying speed they have built a beautiful machine of investigative reporting that is serving the public interest all over this nation.

If you are lucky in life, you get to navigate the years with your own affinity group. When I was swept up in the 1971 Mayday roundup, as a nineteen-year-old college student protesting the Vietnam War, the police separated me from my ragtag little band of poets, pranksters, and potheads. To my lasting benefit, we've never lost touch. Gary, Jim, Alan, Tim, and the other Alan — you guys will always be my brothers.

My literary agent, Gail Ross, instantly recognized the need to revive this history. The idea ripened with her backing and advice, and the refinements from her team at Ross Yoon. Gail had the foresight to match me with Deanne Urmy, my editor at Houghton Mifflin Harcourt. No one writing his first book could be luckier than to fall into partnership with Deanne, to tap into her broad editorial vision and love of narrative. Gentle and resolute, she guided me to the finish line. Thanks to the rest of Bruce Nichols's fine team at Houghton: copyeditor Susanna Brougham, who brought precision to the text, and David Eber, Mark Robinson, Megan Wilson, Michael Dudding, Chloe Foster, Lisa Glover, Beth Burleigh Fuller, Leah Petrakis, Emily Snyder, Jenny Xu, Mary Cait Milliff, and Jessica Vestuto.

Years spent on an endeavor like this book would be lonely without a patient, loving, and talented family. My son Jacob, a writer of history in his own right, provided close readings along the way, as well as contributing important elements of the research. In addition to her considerable gifts as a hunter-seeker of historical photographs and a keen editor of images, Nancy Walz has been my sounding board and my therapist, my constructive critic and my tireless promoter, and my partner for life, to whom I owe all things. To borrow a line, her questions are like directions to the truth.

Notes

The secret voice-activated White House taping system installed by President Richard M. Nixon in February 1971 recorded more than 22,000 meeting and telephone conversations — about 3,700 hours of tape in all — before it was disconnected in July 1973, in the midst of the Watergate investigation. Conversations quoted in this book are taken from recordings preserved on cassettes at the National Archives at College Park, Maryland, which I listened to directly; transcripts prepared over the decades by federal archivists and other scholars, including at the Miller Center at the University of Virginia; the well-chosen excerpts in *The Nixon Tapes, 1971–1972* (Boston: Houghton Mifflin Harcourt, 2014) by Douglas Brinkley and Luke A. Nichter; and nixontapes.org, the most complete digital repository, an extraordinary public service created and maintained by Nichter, a professor of history at Texas A&M University.

Quotes from the diaries of H. R. Haldeman, Nixon's chief of staff, come mostly from his written and taped entries, stored at the Richard Nixon Presidential Library and Museum in Yorba Linda, California; several are drawn from edited transcripts he published in *The Haldeman Diaries* (New York: Putnam 1994).

The following abbreviations are used for frequently cited sources:

- **AGP:** Stew Albert and Judy Gumbo Albert Papers, Joseph A. Labadie Collection, Special Collections Research Center, Hatcher Graduate Library, University of Michigan, Ann Arbor
- **DDP:** David T. Dellinger papers, Tamiment Library/Robert F. Wag-

ner Labor Archives, Elmer Holmes Bobst Library, New York University

- **EJEP:** Edward Jay Epstein collection, Howard Gotlieb Archival Research Center, Boston University
- **EKP:** Egil Krogh Jr. papers, White House Special Files, Richard Nixon Presidential Library and Museum, Yorba Linda, California
- **FOIA:** FBI files obtained through author's Freedom of Information Act requests
- **HI:** Hoover Institution Archives, Stanford University
- **HVF:** J. Edgar Hoover Official and Confidential Files, FBI Series 16, Box 12 Special Collections, Raynor Memorial Libraries, Marquette University, Milwaukee
- **JDP:** John Dean papers, White House Special Files, Richard Nixon Presidential Library and Museum, Yorba Linda, California
- **JEP:** John Ehrlichman papers, Hoover Institution Archives, Stanford University
- **JWF:** Jerry V. Wilson personal files
- **NL:** Richard Nixon Presidential Library and Museum, Yorba Linda, California
- **NT:** President Richard Nixon's White House tapes
- **NYT:** *New York Times*
- **PHF:** Philip J. Hirschkop personal files
- **PU:** Manuscripts Division, Rare Books and Special Collections, Princeton University Library
- **SPC:** Swarthmore College Peace Collection, Swarthmore, Pennsylvania
- **WES:** *Washington Evening Star*
- **WP:** *Washington Post*

Prologue: Nixon's Insurrection City

page

xvii *"spectre of social chaos"*: May Day Tactical Manual, 1971, Mayday Collective, author's collection

xviii *"I don't see what"*: LBJ to McGeorge Bundy, 5/27/64 phone conversation, cited in H. R. McMaster, *Dereliction of Duty* (New York: Harper Perennial, 1998), 325

two million Americans: By the end of the war, the number of U.S. troops who served would total 2.7 million. James C. Bradford, ed., *Atlas of American Military History* (London: Oxford, 2003) 194; *Newsweek,* 3/29/71, 27

275,000 U.S. troops: President's radio address, 2/25/71, transcript, Miller Center of Public Affairs, University of Virginia, Charlottesville

just ticked past 45,000: Associated Press, "U.S. Combat Death Toll over 45,000 in Vietnam," *WP,* 4/30/71, A20

more tons of explosives: Eight million tons in all, according to Mark Clodfelter, "The Limits of Airpower or the Limits of Strategy," *Joint Force Quarterly,* 3rd quarter 2015, 111

xix *nineteen million gallons:* "Research on Vietnam Veterans," U.S. Department of Veterans Affairs, Office of Research & Development, https://www.research.va.gov/topics/vietnam.cfm

xx *all over the country:* D.C. Police acting director, operations, Herbert Miller to Chief of Police, May 14, 1971, JWF. The police found that those ultimately arrested came from all fifty states, as well as D.C., the Virgin Islands, Argentina, Canada, and Denmark.

design a federal city: For in-depth discussions of the plans by Washington and L'Enfant, see Joel Achenbach, *The Grand Idea* (New York: Simon & Schuster, 2004) and Scott W. Berg, *Grand Avenues* (New York: Pantheon, 2007).

xxi *"It is this cause":* Report, "Reclamation of the Marshes of the cities of Washington and Georgetown," 1/26/1882, Committee on the District of Columbia, chairman, Rep. Henry Safford Neal, R-Ohio

"the unexpectedly grand": L'Enfant-McMillan Plan of Washington, D.C., Historic American Buildings Survey, National Park Service, 1993

"the most beautiful place:" "Original Plan of Washington," *House & Garden,* July 1940, 63

"The whole will acquire": Elizabeth S. Kite, *L'Enfant and Washington* (Baltimore: Johns Hopkins Press, 1929), 58. Lucy G. Barber writes that the Mall was transformed into the first "national public space," in *Marching on Washington* (Berkeley: University of California, 2002).

xxiii *Of those in the room:* Accounts of the May 1971 planning meetings at the Department of Justice are taken primarily from the meeting minutes archived in the American Civil Liberties Union Records, Subgroup 2, Series 4, legal case files, *Dellums v. Powell,* Box 1336 PU, Princeton University.

xxvi *instant induction:* Amid complaints that local draft boards disproportionately produced low-income and minority conscripts, Nixon in 1969 adopted the idea of a draft lottery based on birth dates, a system that had been first proposed under the LBJ administration.

    "patient, discreet and solicitous": Special Order No. 12, Wilson to MPD, April 28, 1971, JWF

xxvii *On short notice:* Associated Press, "Nixon Considers San Clemente Trip," *WP,* 4/21/1971, A2

    on Friday morning: President's Daily Calendar, April 30, 1971, NL

    radicals had bombed: Bart Barnes, "Dynamite Charge Suspected in Blast," *WP,* 3/3/1971, A1

xxviii *"the lowest point":* Richard Nixon, *RN* (New York: Simon & Schuster, 1990), 497

    "little bastards," "animals": Various Nixon tapes, 1971

xxix *getting "thugs":* NT 491-14, 5/5/71, 9:53 a.m., NL

xxx *"all those asses":* Harlington Wood Jr., *An Unmarked Trail* (Petersburg, IL: self-published, 2008), 120

1. This Is Real

3 *a stained-glass window:* Bart Barnes, "Dynamite Charge Suspected in Blast," *WP,* 3/2/1971, A10

4 *assassination attempt:* "J. P. Morgan Shot at His Home; Capitol Damaged by Time Bomb," *Washington Times,* 7/3/1915, A1

    the phone rang: Author interviews with Judy Gumbo, 5/4/2016 and 9/5/2017; also see Agis Salpukas, "2 Youths Tell of Their Discussions with Girl in Bombing Inquiry," *NYT,* 6/2/1971, 21

    red-brick townhouse: Described in Phyllis Richman, "Turning Tables," *WP,* 9/11/1983

    place to place: Various MPD police intelligence memos, including a 2/24/1971 report identifying the M Street house as home of the "Rennie Davis collective," JWF

    ironic bow: "Capitol Bombing Affidavit Draft," Box 9, AGP, Michigan

5 *Civil disobedience:* Author interview with Colin Neiburger, 4/22/19

    "we didn't do it": Paul W. Valentine, "Some Found 'Joy' in Capitol Bombing," *WP,* 5/26/1971, B1

    set out for Boston: Gumbo interviews

    high boots: Judy Gumbo, "Brave New Life," undated essay published on Yippie Girl website, https://www.yippiegirl.com/articles-brave.html

    block the doors: "Oakland Seven Indicted," *The Movement,* San Francisco, February 1968

    wild curly brown hair: Stew Albert, *Who the Hell Is Stew Albert?* (Los Angeles: Red Hen, 2003), 71

6 *she'd never forget:* Gumbo interviews

    burst through the front door: Capitol Bombing Affidavit Draft, AGP, Michigan

7   *its main architect:* Author interview with Paul Krassner, 12/10/2016; also see Paul Krassner, "Hippies, Radicals, Pranksters," *Los Angeles Times,* 8/31/2017

8   *"who observed these events":* Stew Albert, "My Generation" Drafts, Box 2, AGP, Michigan

9   *"wise old rabbi":* Krassner interview

10 *They learned that:* Film, *Vietnam Day, Berkeley,* Berkeley Art Museum & Pacific Film Archive, University of California
    "I sometimes wonder at": Dean Rusk, Address, American Society of International Law, 4/23/1965

11 *"Typical":* Stew Albert, Manuscripts and Writings, Box 1, AGP, Michigan
    "We're going to raise": Norman Mailer, *Armies of the Night* (New York: New American Library, 1968), 234
    tea into Boston Harbor: Tom Wells, *The War Within* (Berkeley: University of California Press, 1994), 180
    "Maybe a little might": Stew Albert, Manuscripts and Writings, Box 2, AGP, Michigan

12 *suits, ties, and dresses:* Wells, *War Within,* 181
    West Potomac Park: Newsletter, National Mobilization Committee to End the War in Vietnam, Subject Vertical Files, Labadie Collection, University of Michigan Library, Ann Arbor
    "like the legions of Sgt. Pepper's": Mailer, *Armies,* 108–9
    seven hundred were arrested: Wells, *War Within,* 203
    Kennedy wasn't impressed: Stew Albert, speech transcript, Manuscripts and Writings, Box 1, AGP, Michigan

13 *"soulful socialism":* Jonah Raskin, *For the Hell of It: The Life and Times of Abbie Hoffman* (Berkeley: University of California Press, 1997), 195
    wandered alone: Krassner interview
    kind of baptism: Krassner, "Hippies, Radicals, Pranksters"
    a gathering spot: Gumbo interviews
    "That was his job": Ibid.

14 *against white terrorists:* For an excellent history of armed self-defense among U.S. blacks, see Charles E. Cobb Jr., *This Nonviolent Stuff'll Get You Killed: How Guns Made the Civil Rights Movement Possible* (New York: Basic Books, 2014).
    Little Red Book: Michael Kazin, *America Divided: The Civil War of the 1960s* (New York: Oxford, 2015), 187; also see *Berkeley in the Sixties,* documentary film, directed by Mark Kitchell, 1990
    yellow Pontiac: Stew Albert, Manuscripts and Writings, Box 1, AGP, Michigan
    it stuck: Jonah Raskin, "Judy Gumbo Albert, Yippie Girl," *The Rag Blog,* 4/17/2012; Gumbo interviews

15 *Wise Men:* Todd Gitlin, *The Sixties: Years of Hope, Days of Rage* (New York: Bantam, 1987), 303
    people over fifty: Hazel Erskine, *The Public Opinion Quarterly,* vol. 34, Spring 1970, 134–50

16   *McCarthy appealed:* Fred Halstead, *Out Now!* (New York: Anchor Foundation, 1978), 409
      A Night at the Opera: Stew Albert report, FBI San Francisco field office file 100-56066, 4/28/1969, Box 10, AGP, Michigan
      "Boys, I have bad news": Albert, *Who the Hell,* 89
17   *"These Yipps with their":* Frank Kusch, *Battleground Chicago* (Chicago: University of Chicago Press, 2008), 50
      first blood shed: David R. Farber, *Chicago '68* (Chicago: University of Chicago Press, 1988), 177–78
      crying and swearing: Jack Hoffman and Daniel Simon, *Run, Run, Run* (New York: Putnam, 1996), 100
18   *target in Washington:* Author interview with Rennie Davis, 8/14/2018; also see Peter Collier and David Horowitz, *Destructive Generation* (New York: Summit, 1989), 105
      valedictorian in high school: Rennie Davis, *The New Humanity* (Las Vegas: BlissLife Press, 2017), 32
19   *"practiced organizational talent":* Halstead, *Out Now!,* 407
      "that most romantic": Bill Ayers, *Fugitive Days* (Boston: Beacon Press, 2009), 246
20   *"such a network":* David Gilbert, *Love and Struggle* (Oakland, CA: PM, 2012), 159. Gilbert, serving a sentence of seventy-five years to life for his role in a deadly 1981 armored car robbery, was the partner of Kathy Boudin and the father of their son.
      "we were very careful": Ayers, in *The Weather Underground,* documentary film, 2002
      the GI coffeehouses: Donald Janson, "Antiwar Coffeehouses Delight G.I.'s but Not Army," *NYT,* 8/12/1968, A1
      working with the Weather: Davis interview; B. D. Colen, "Rennie Davis: From 4-H to SDS," *WP,* 10/25/1971, C1
21   *"Dynamite became":* Ayers, *Fugitive Days,* 223
      "That was a nightmare": Davis interview
      two women: Neither Boudin nor Dohrn has publicly admitted or denied she did the bombing. According to Weather sources cited by Horowitz and Collier (*Destructive Generation,* 105), Dohrn called Rennie Davis the morning of March 1, 1971, to alert him that she and Boudin had done it. Davis confirmed in a recent interview with the author that he was alerted about the bomb in advance, but said he wasn't given details. He said that he doesn't recall who called him before or after the explosion, but doesn't think it was Dohrn. He also said he doesn't remember, if he ever knew, who actually set the device. Associates of Boudin gave details of how the two women prepared for and set the bomb to the author Susan Braudy for *Family Circle: The Boudins and the Aristocracy of the Left* (New York: Anchor, 2004), 240–45. Dohrn and Boudin didn't respond to questions from this author.

"second team": Ron Jacobs, *The Way the Wind Blew: A History of the Weather Underground* (London, New York: Verso, 1997), 61

visitors weren't frisked: "Suggested Security Measures, United States Capitol Buildings," 3/4/1971, in FBI Series 16, Box 12, HVF, Marquette

22 *strapped the dynamite*: Braudy, *Family Circle*, 240–43

new mechanism: Weather members gave these details, speaking with obscured faces, in their authorized documentary *Underground*, 1976.

"You may have other calls": Box 12, HVF, Marquette

looked into the bathroom: Ibid.

23 *"Okay boys, you stay"*: Author interview with Colin Neiburger, 4/22/2019

contained a knapsack: "State of New York Deposition," Stew Albert affidavit, June 1971, Box 14, AGP, Michigan

army bomb-disposal unit: FBI teletype from Philadelphia field office, 3/2/1971, Box 11, AGP, Michigan

"They thought we blew up": Bill Kovach, "2 Yippies Charge Harassment in Investigation of Capitol Bombing," *NYT*, 3/4/1971, 17

San Francisco apartment: "WUO Pine Street Bomb Factory," in FBI Weather Underground Summary, 8/20/1976, Part 6 of 6, page 384, FBI Online Vault, https://vault.fbi.gov/

24 *Mitchell had authorized*: NT 752-13, 7/25/72, 2:29 p.m.

trying to interrogate them: Leonard Weinglass to J. Edgar Hoover, 3/15/1971, PHF

searched a car: Author interview with Tim Butz, 6/12/2018

selected Stew's picture: Witness affidavit, FBI files, Box 10, AGP, Michigan

declined to take the bag: FBI memo 174–318 from Washington Field Office, 3/2/71, Box 10, AGP, Michigan

"set-up, a liar": Judy Gumbo, "CAPBOM revisited," undated essay published on Yippie Girl website, https://yippiegirl.com/articles-capbom.html

25 *"rather portly"*: Author interview with retired FBI agent Thomas Strentz, 6/15/2018; Strentz transcript for FBI Oral History Project, Society of Former Special Agents of the FBI

2. We Need Time

26 *down to the river*: Krogh family interviews, 8/7/2018, 12/11/2018, 12/22/2018

an outstanding miler: "Athletics," University of Chicago magazine, February 1923

less of a burden: Craig Waters, "The Agony of Egil Krogh," *Washingtonian*, May 1974

27 *rarely made it home*: Donald P. Baker, "215 Run for Their Health on Ellipse," *WP*, 10/8/72, B1

often felt lonely: Waters, "The Agony"

oversized head: Krogh family interviews

show tunes: Egil Krogh with Matthew Krogh, *Integrity: Good People, Bad Choices, and Life Lessons from the White House* (Washington: Public Affairs, 2007), 7

"The problems are closing in": Krogh to Richard Kummert, 6/25/69, Box 1, EKP, NL

"The work gets heavier": Krogh to William Fite, 11/19/69, Box 1, EKP, NL

"bruised heads, drained": Krogh to Richard O. Kommert, 6/5/1969, Box 1, EKP, NL

speed-reading system: Krogh to Jay Wilkinson, 3/13/1969, Box 1, EKP, NL

detail and paperwork: Richard Kleindienst, *Justice* (Ottawa, IL: Jameson Books, 1985), 49–51

28   *a promise he and his father*: Dan Baum, *Smoke and Mirrors* (Boston: Little, Brown, 1996), 13

been up all night: Jeb Stuart Magruder, *An American Life* (New York: Atheneum, 1974), 68

"boundless gratitude": Albert Losche to Krogh, 7/25/1969, Box 64, EKP, NL

29   *nuclear submarines*: Krogh oral history, 9/5/2007, NL; also see "Disturbances Greet Atom Ship in Japan," *NYT*, 11/12/1964, A1

"the best-looking man": Aldo Beckman, "Tough Tasks Routine for Chicagoan," *Chicago Tribune*, 5/24/1970; Krogh family files; Waters, "The Agony" 60

piled into a red Buick: Krogh, *Integrity*, 86

30   *behind the easy chair*: Krogh family interviews

"Nothing stirs animals more": Krogh to Daniel Patrick Moynihan, 10/20/1969, Box 1, EKP, NL

"rather hard core": Krogh interview transcript, Box 9, EJEP, Boston University

more of an opportunity: Krogh to John Ehrlichman, "President's Reaction to Capital Bombing," Undated, Box 19, EKP, NL

31   *points behind*: "Poll Finds Muskie Leads President by 43% to 40%," *NYT*, 2/2/1971, 12

"Impeach Nixon": Haldeman diary, 3/1/1971, NL; Don Oberdorfer, "President, Visiting Iowa, Gets Cool Reception," *WP*, 3/2/1971, A3

"All of it could very": Haldeman diary, 3/1/1971, NL

32   *"a virtual blueprint"*: Robert Dallek, *Kissinger and Nixon: Partners in Power* (New York: Harper, 2007), 21

"You ever hear that music": NT 249-6, 8:59 a.m., 4/15/1971

"an underlying unease": Dallek, *Kissinger and Nixon*, 7

33   *"a brighter, more handsome"*: "Jessamyn West's Frank New Best Seller Upsets Some of Her Friendly Persuasion Fans," *People*, 8/11/1975

"certain resentments": Stephen B. Bull Oral History, NL

hire no more of them: Memo, 3/16/1970, Box 1, JEP, HI, Stanford

"And we've got to remember": NT 001-150, 4/18/1971, 1:28 p.m.

"the cacophony of seditious": Jules Witcover, *Very Strange Bedfellows: The Short Unhappy Marriage of Richard Nixon and Spiro Agnew* (New York: PublicAffairs 2007), 91

"That whole thing": John Ehrlichman interview, "Cold War," CNN series, 1999, Episode 16, transcript at National Security Archive

34   *"what may be the severest":* Nixon address, 6/3/1969, transcript at American Presidency Project, University of California at Santa Barbara
"We have a Constitution": Ibid.
"They would like to keep": Public Papers of President Richard Nixon, 1971, *Federal Register,* 81

35   *as the limo accelerated:* Krogh, "Responsibility for Demonstrators," 1/23/1969, Box 1, EKP, NL
"Nixon, go home!": Dallek, *Kissinger and Nixon,* 25
granted the right to gather: Krogh, *Integrity,* 107
"seem to aggravate": Bruce Oudes, *From the President: Richard Nixon's Secret Files* (New York: Harper & Row, 1989), 8–11
previous occupants: Lady Bird Johnson, cited in Wells, *War Within,* 584
"Hey, hey, LBJ": Luci Baines Johnson, interview with LBJ Presidential Library, 11/12/2013
the president's safety: Secret Service to Ehrlichman, 2/18/1969, Box 21, EKP, NL
"in a sense he was": Daniel P. Moynihan to Nixon, 1/3/1969, cited in "Text of a Pre-Inaugural Memo," *NYT,* 3/11/1970, 30
"greatest comeback": Haldeman meeting notes, 11/7/68, Box 41, Haldeman papers, NL
figure of destiny: Haldeman memo, 9/5/1968, Box 35, Haldeman papers, NL

36   *dropped the idea:* Wells, *War Within,* 378
"decent interval": Daniel Ellsberg, *Secrets* (New York: Viking, 2002), 229–30
stage a great retreat: Richard Reeves, *President Nixon: Alone in the White House* (New York: Simon & Schuster, 2001), 203
"the nutty opposition": Haldeman meeting notes, 9/26/69, Box 32, Haldeman papers, NL

37   *"As you know, we need":* Krogh to Clark Mollenhoff, "Game Plan for Moratorium/Mobilization Protest," 9/25/1969, Box 1, EKP, NL
out of his league: Waters, "The Agony," 60
"subservient and pliant": Clark Mollenhoff, *Game Plan for Disaster* (New York: Norton, 1976), 38
"get the word out": Charles Stuart, *Never Trust a Local* (New York: Algora, 2005), 49
an iceberg: Nixon to Alexander Haig, per Haldeman diary, 4/30/1971, NL
"good, recent literature": Ehrlichman to Moynihan and McCracken, 6/2/1969, Box 69, EKP, NL
"liberal and radical thinking": Sally Quinn, "White House Interns Take a Cruise on the Stormy Potomac," *WP,* 8/2/1969, E2
Wellesley College: James Stack, "Sen. Brooke Upstaged at Wellesley Commencement," *Boston Globe,* 6/1/1969; Box 66, EKP, NL

38   *urns of hot coffee:* Unsigned, "1,400 College Students Converge on Washington to Picket for Peace," *NYT,* 2/17/1962, A1

3. The Hot Buttons

39 *"go to the heart"*: "Transcript of President's Address," *NYT*, 5/1/1970, 2

40 *"Is this because of me"*: Reeves, *President Nixon*, 213

41 *"We implore you to"*: "City, U.S. Officials Meet on Protest," *WES*, 5/5/1970, A1
"The two hundred year old": "Notes and Comment," *New Yorker*, 5/16/1970
"The blood is on the hand": Unsigned, "Plans Mapped for Saturday," 5/5/1970, *WES*, A1
on the curb in tears: William Greider, "Fires Hit Campuses," *WP*, 5/10/1971, A1
"a very strange feeling": H. R. Haldeman, *The Haldeman Diaries* (New York: Putnam, 1994), 163
millions of cicadas: Peter Haldeman, "Growing Up a Haldeman," 4/3/1994, *NYT*, 30

42 *found himself wondering*: Beckman, "Tough Tasks," Krogh family files
"the very fabric of government": Henry Kissinger, *White House Years* (Boston: Little, Brown, 1979), 513
tennis court: Haldeman, *Diaries*, 161
"is to panic us": Ibid., 161
"hit them hard": Ibid., 163
out of bed: Nixon to Haldeman, taped memo, 5/13/1970, Dictabelt Collection, NL

43 *"We all felt threatened"*: Magruder, *American Life*, 73
"turned out to be huge": Haldeman, *Diaries*, 108
"Custerism": Beckman, "Tough Tasks," Krogh family files

44 *"Searchlight is on"*: This account of the early morning's events is drawn from multiple published and unpublished sources, as well as Krogh, *Integrity*, and author interviews with the Krogh family and others.

45 *rambled from subject*: Krogh to president's file, 5/9/1970, Box 77, President's Meeting Files 1969–1974, NL
"I couldn't muster": Jon Shure email to author, 11/25/2018

46 *"trying very hard"*: Krogh to president's file, 5/9/1970, Box 77, President's Meeting Files 1969–1974, NL
into the Mercury: Krogh family email to author, 12/18/2018
"Whose idea": Krogh, *Integrity*, 117

47 *through six takes*: George Schlatter, in "The Interviews: An Oral History of Television," 3/6/2002, Television Academy Foundation
the Laugh-In *producer*: President's Daily Diary, NL
"It's too bad": Reeves, *President Nixon*, 223
"The tidal wave": Kissinger, *White House Years*, 512
"You do have an obligation": Meeting notes, 6/19/1970, JEP Box 1, HI, Stanford

48 *the two hit it off*: Christopher Lydon, "Conservative Architect of Security Plan," *NYT*, 5/24/1973, 34

portrait of John C. Calhoun: William Safire, *Before the Fall* (New Brunswick: Transaction, 2005), 296

"These fellows are careful": Huston to Haldeman, 5/20/1969, Box 1, EKP, NL

"are unwilling to admit": "A Report on the Huston Plan," Staff, Senate Select Committee on Intelligence Activities, 4/23/1976

"the most logical target": Reeves, *President Nixon*, 175

"Everything he wrote": NT 919-32, 5/16/73, 3:02 p.m., cited in Stanley Kutler, *Abuse of Power* (New York: Simon & Schuster, 1998), 507

49   *"credit-card revolutionaries"*: "A Report on the Huston Plan," 4/23/1976, Staff, Senate Select Committee on Intelligence Activities

twenty-five dollars a week: Krogh to Ehrlichman, "Financing of Campus Disorders," 6/5/1969, Box 1, EKP, NL

"does not have specific information": Ehrlichman to Nixon, "Communist Financial Support of Campus Disorders," 6/5/1969, Box 1, EKP, NL

"Give Huston the job": Alexander Butterfield to Ehrlichman, 6/10/1969, Box 1, EKP, NL; see also Senate Select Committee report; see also Carla DeLoach, Oral History, Society of Former Special Agents of the FBI

Nixon's "dark side": Tom Huston, Oral History, 4/30/2008, NL

"Other weapons in": Huston to Nixon, "Foreign Communist Support of the Revolutionary Protest Movement in the United States," June 1969, Internet Archive

50   *"assume it goes no further"*: Krogh to Haldeman, "Internal Security Organization," 2/23/1970, Box 1, EKP, NL

"isolation of the Peace Now": Krogh to Haldeman, "Internal Security," 1/26/1970, Box 214, Haldeman papers, NL

"invited and got": Curt Gentry, *J. Edgar Hoover: The Man and His Secrets* (New York: Norton, 1991), 650

"Certainly hundreds": Senate Select Committee, "A Report on the Huston Plan"

51   *recommended action items*: Ibid.

approved by the president: Ibid.

"that snot-nosed kid": Gentry, *Hoover*, 653

"bullheaded as hell": Senate Select Committee, "A Report on the Huston Plan"

"went through the ceiling": Ibid.

52   *"just to be sure that we can"*: NT 450-10, 2/16/1971, 10:28 a.m.

odds at fifty-fifty: Haldeman diary, 3/30/1971, NL

"For us the objective": NT 451-23, 2/28/1971, 6:16 p.m.

"It can be anticipated": Intelligence Evaluation Committee report, Box 95, JDP, NL

53   *"A relatively small number"*: "Report on Mayday," 2/18/1971, Box 95, JDP, NL

"Well I don't know": NT 457-5, 2/24/1971, 12:34 p.m.

"from middle-of-the-road": Krogh to Ehrlichman, "President's Reaction to Capital Bombing," Box 19, EKP, NL

54   *lay bare two years:* C. D. Brennan to W. C. Sullivan, Exhibit 17, Church Commit-
      tee investigation into intelligence activities, 1976
55   *the report existed:* Thomas Oliphant, "Only 3 Have Read Secret Indochina Re-
      port; All Urge Swift Pullout," *Boston Globe,* 3/7/1971, A1

4. A Mighty Waters

56   *The ninth floor:* PCPJ Permit Application, 3/26/1971, PHF
      One floor up: Andrew E. Hunt, *The Turning* (New York: NYU Press, 2001)
57   *"You could work with":* Author interview with Jack Mallory, 7/31/2017
      the older brother: David Dellinger, television interview, July 1981, Alternative
      Views No. 119, Alternative Information Network
      never cancel a meeting: Roxanne Dunbar-Ortiz, *Outlaw Woman* (San Francisco:
      City Lights, 2002), 174
58   *"It's all so terribly real":* Dellinger to family, 11/2/1966, Box 10, DDP, NYU
      a "key activist": FBI memo, 6/10/1968, cited in Ward Churchill and Jim Vander
      Wall, *The COINTELPRO Papers* (Boston: South End Press, 2001)
      "They insisted upon his": Tom Charles Huston, "Foreign Communist Support of
      the Revolutionary Protest Movement in the United States," 1969, 62, declassified
      copy in Internet Archive, https://archive.org/details/Huston-Foreign-Support-
      Communist
      "colorful and symbolic": Todd Gitlin, *The Whole World Is Watching* (Berkeley:
      University of California, 1981), 174
      "dissolved a few preconceived": Bill Branton to Dellinger, 5/11/1971, Box 8, DDP,
      NYU
59   *"Gandhi-like serenity":* Judy Collins, *Sweet Judy Blue Eyes* (New York: Crown,
      2011), 226
      "I would not be a Moses": David Dellinger, "Communists in the Antiwar Move-
      ment," in *Revolutionary Nonviolence* (New York: Doubleday, 1971), 245
61   *"It was a part of this":* Rennie Davis interview, "Cold War," CNN series, 1999, Ep-
      isode 13, transcript at National Security Archive, https://nsarchive2.gwu.edu/
      coldwar/interviews/episode-13/davis1.html
      "the state of disunity": Bradford Lyttle, *Peace Activist* (Indianapolis: Dog Ear,
      2014), chapter 32
      Calvin Coolidge: Family obituary, Box 2, DDP, NYU
62   *"I dropped to my knees":* David Dellinger, *From Yale to Jail* (New York: Pantheon,
      1993), 40
      "the hardest decision": Ibid., 85
      "If you hang up": Dellinger interview with Terry Gross, NPR, 4/9/1993
      "near the breaking point": Raymond Dellinger to David Dellinger, 10/8/1943, Re-
      cords of the Bureau of Prisons, 1870–2009, Notorious Offenders File 1919–1975,
      National Archives
63   *"nonviolent war":* Dellinger editorial, *Direct Action,* cited in Dellinger, *Yale to
      Jail,* 139–42

"the vision of love": Staughton Lynd, *Nonviolence in America*, (New York: Bobbs-Merrill, 1966), xvii

"We can expect to face": Dellinger, *Yale to Jail*, 142

"Go ahead and hit me": Ibid., 156

"I would warn any would-be": Jesse Lewis, "350 Arrested in Capitol Hill Protest," *WP*, 8/10/1965, A1

64 *"That's what I believe"*: Dellinger, NPR interview, 1993

"There was never a meeting": Dellinger interview with LBJ Library, 12/10/1982, Box 10, DDP, NYU

break the tie: Halstead, *Out Now!*, 140

"What a zoo!": Dellinger interview with Ron Chepesiuk, February 1994, Louise Pettus Archives, Winthrop University, Rock Hill, South Carolina

"We have to leave in": Dellinger interview with LBJ Library

65 *dominated the left*: Ibid.

"enchanted all kinds": Ibid.

"a bit insane": Transcript of government tape recorded Grant Park in Chicago, 8/28/1968, ACLU records, Chicago 7 Case, Box 1752, PU, Princeton

"Think of Dave as": Author interview with Todd Gitlin, 10/10/2018

different approaches: Dellinger interview, Alternative Information Network, 1981

"a mighty waters": Wells, *War Within*, 178

They cast their eyes: Gitlin, *Sixties*, 320

Dave made the case: Ibid., 321

"a massacre": Gitlin interview

"One, is there any": Gitlin, *Sixties*, 323

66 *"arouse the sleeping dogs"*: Ibid., 289

Even Rennie had considered: Davis interview

gotten Daddy in trouble: Stew Albert note, Box 1, AGP, Michigan

67 *"joined at the hip"*: Davis interview

"Dave doesn't need to": Dellinger interview, Alternative Information Network, 1981

"stand on the rubble": J. Anthony Lukas, "Prosecutor Calls Chicago 7 'Evil,'" *NYT*, 2/14/1970, 19

"The winter days blurred": "Remembering David Dellinger," Democracy Now, broadcast 5/27/2004

"You want us to be": Andrew E. Hunt, *David Dellinger: The Life and Times of a Nonviolent Revolutionary* (New York: NYU Press, 2006), 221–22

68 *"somehow shucked two marshals"*: John C. Tucker, *Trial and Error* (New York: Carroll & Graf, 2003), 155

"More marshals joined": Ibid.

a shoving match: Jay Craven, "David Dellinger Remembered," *Judevine Mountain Emailite*, 6/14/2004

top-ten list: "Leading New Left Revolutionaries," Box 99, JDP, NL

changed his name: Dellinger, NPR interview, 1993

69   *"by all odds the correct"*: Arthur Waskow, "What Happened," *WIN* magazine, 6/1/1970

      "Proposal": Halstead, *Out Now!*, 568n.

      blocking bridges: Metropolitan Police Department intelligence report, 2/24/1971, JWF

      four votes short: Randy Furst, "Vietnam War Era Activists Reconvene at Macalester College," *Minneapolis Star-Tribune*, 5/4/2016

      "we would just humiliate": Davis interview

      "I was one of the Chicago": Ibid.

      donated $100,000: FBI memo, Funding of Demonstrations in Washington, 5/28/1971, Box 89, JDP, NL

70   *they saw pews packed*: Sam Hemingway, Bill Leogrande, and Ken Grant, "We Are the Revolution," *Daily Orange*, Syracuse, 10/27/1970; Davis interview

      "If the government won't": Ibid.

      "really brought the house down": Author interview with John Froines, 4/1/2019

      the FBI tracked: Attorney's court notes, 5/5/71, PHF

      a hundred stalled cars: "May 1971 Demonstrations," Justice Department intelligence report, Box 95, JDP, NL

      "We're going to paralyze": University of Texas–El Paso *Prospector*, 11/3/1970, clipping in Protests Against War, Box 1, Swarthmore College Peace Collection, Swarthmore, Pennsylvania

      its own peace treaty: Rennie Davis, "A Hard Look at Vietnam Peace," *NYT*, 10/16/1970, 35

      the godfather of: Jay Craven, essay in *The People Make the Peace* (Charlottesville: Just World, 2015), 127

71   *"Lack of unity"*: FBI intelligence digest, Box 90, JDP, NL

      By acclamation: Press release, Ann Arbor Student and Youth Conference on a People's Treaty, 2/7/1971, PHF. See also manifesto in Collected Document Groups, Mayday Collective, SPC, Swarthmore

      face the shutdown: Halstead, *Out Now!*, 591

      "Davis' actions and statements": "Demonstrations at Washington, D.C. beginning April 24, 1971," Justice Department intelligence report, 3/26/1971, Box 95, JDP, NL

      "What madness has brought": Halstead, *Out Now!*, 589

      at the Hamilton Hotel: Metropolitan Police Department intelligence report, JWF

72   *"absolutely not involved"*: William L. Claiborne and Sanford J. Ungar, "Bomb Figure Taken to Seattle," *WP*, 4/30/1971, A1

      $10,000 reward: Leonard Weinglass to J. Edgar Hoover, 3/15/1971, PHF

73   *Since 1965, more than*: Neil Sheehan, "Should We Have War Crimes Trials?" *NYT Book Review*, 3/28/1971

      "Yes, it is a protracted": Michael T. Kaufman, "Antiwar Teach-In on Again at N.Y.U," *NYT*, 3/31/1971, 7

5. The Pivot Point

74   *lurid details:* Author interviews with Jerry Wilson, 3/22/2014, 7/9/2015, 7/25/2015, 10/9/2015, 11/16/2018

       stand on a box: Author interview with Maurice Cullinane, 10/5/2017

75   *"We used the same general":* William C. Sullivan, *The Bureau: My Thirty Years in Hoover's FBI* (New York: Norton, 1979), 149

76   *their graduation ceremony:* Author interviews with Joseph B. Green, 4/27/2018; Maurice Cullinane, and Jerry Wilson; see also Paul W. Valentine, "Rookie Urges Police Graduates to Join in Dialogue with Critics," *WP,* 2/13/1971, B1

       "wish to see their own": Joseph B. Green, speech transcript, February 1971, author's collection

       "I assure you this": Valentine, "Rookie Urges Police Graduates"

       "There's two FBI agents": Cullinane, Wilson interviews

       deputy felt embarrassed: Cullinane interview

77   *complain once more:* Krogh memo to file, "Hoover-Chief Wilson Conflict," 2/26/1971, Box 4, EKP, NL

       marked "damaged in transit": Green interview

       as a possible successor: "Wilson for Hoover? Justice Dept. Says No," *WP,* 5/8/1971, B2

       hoped to replace him: Haldeman diary, 2/4/1971, NL

       first cop: Alfred Lewis, "Wilson Is First Police Chief Cited by Christians, Jews," *WP,* 2/18/71, B3

       "He died hating me": Wilson interviews

78   *"marauders and criminals":* Ben A. Franklin, "City of Fear and Crime," *NYT,* 1/22/1969, 49

       "I hate those moldering": Daniel Patrick Moynihan to Ehrlichman, 1/28/1970, Box 7, JEP, HI, Stanford

79   *more than a dozen years:* Jerry Wilson, *Police Report* (Boston: Little, Brown, 1975), 45

       now more dangerous: General Accounting Office report cited in U.S. Senate testimony, 3/20/1970

       hiring armed guards: "Cops v. Crime: Ready for a Hot Summer," *Time,* 7/13/1970

       two dozen holdups: Crime blotter, *WP,* 8/5/1970, C6

       more than 70 percent: Matthew B. Gilmore, "District of Columbia Population History," Washington D.C. History Resources, https://matthewbgilmore.word press.com/district-of-columbia-population-history/

       ratios of cops to citizens: GAO report cited in U.S. Senate hearing, 3/20/1970

80   *"frightened liberal cohorts":* Krogh to Ehrlichman, "D.C. Crime — Police," 11/11/1969, Box 1, EKP, NL

       "embarrassed for my profession": Moynihan to Mitchell, Ehrlichman, 10/24/1969, NL online, https://www.nixonlibrary.gov/sites/default/files/virtuallibrary/doc uments/jul10/65.pdf

81   *"not one thousand"*: Ibid.

they grumbled: Green interview

"The department was going nuts": Cullinane interview

such a thinker was needed: Krogh interview transcript, Box 10, EJEP, Boston University

82   *black and growing*: Gilmore, "D.C. Population History"

"Send white officers only": Wilson interviews

83   *"start raining like hell"*: "The City's Turmoil: How It Began," *WP*, 4/14/1968, A1

a hundred separate riots: Senate Permanent Investigations Committee report, 11/1/1967; also see Paul Scheips, "The Role of Federal Military Forces in Domestic Disorders, 1945–1992," Center of Military History, U.S. Army, 192

84   *the destabilizing influence*: Scheips, "The Role," 207

Washington burned: Special Anniversary Section, *WP*, 3/28/2018

"the bearings at the pivot": Wilson, *Police Report*, viii

85   *more than one per day*: D.C. civil defense office memo to deputy mayor, 5/24/1971, JWF

"Two, four, six, eight": "Police Bar March on Mitchell Home," *NYT*, 2/20/1970, 24

was swept up: Wilson to Hirschkop, 4/23/1970, PHF

86   *without any paperwork*: D.C. Circuit Court of Appeals files, *Washington Mobilization Committee v. Maurice Cullinane* et al., 1976

"We've handled a lot": Leonard Downie, "Chief Critical of Police Action," *WP*, 3/17/1970, C1

the chief's back was turned: Ibid.

"I don't stand behind": Unsigned, "Expert at Curbing Demonstrators" *NYT*, 5/5/1971, 26

87   *"somewhat unethical"*: Eric Wentworth, "Wilson Defends Undercover Agents," *WP*, 7/17/1970, A1

go undercover: Wilson interviews

"The thing that surprised": Cullinane interview

police covered the waterfront: Current Activity Report, 2/17/1971, JWF

88   *"The people involved"*: Thomas I. Herlihy, director, police intelligence division, "1971 Spring Anti-war Offensive," 2/24/1971, JWF

cranked up the concern: Ibid.

full command: Deposition, *A Quaker Action v. Morton*, 6/8/1972, PHF

6. This Is 36

89   *"in Vietnam, about nineteen"*: Rod Kane, *Veteran's Day* (New York: Orion, 1990), 90

across the Pacific: Christian G. Appy, *Patriots: The Vietnam War Remembered from All Sides* (New York: Viking, 2003), 28

90   *"Where does this money"*: Dick Howard, "Vietnam Veterans Against the War," 4/1971, Box 77, Haldeman papers, NL, cited in Wells, *War Within*, 490

filed a lawsuit: "Sues," *WP*, 8/28/1966, A26

"This must not be approved": Daily News Summary, 2/25/1971, Annotated News Summaries, Box 30, President's Office Files, NL

91   *her confidential settlement*: Butz and Mallory interviews

"known and suspected": Demonstrations and Domestic Intelligence, Box 85, JDP, NL

"We are asked to lead": Letter, "Fire Base Pace," 7/26/1970, Box 674, Paul McCloskey papers, HI, Stanford

"There's never been a more": Col. Robert D. Heinl Jr., *Armed Forces Journal*, cited in Gitlin, *Sixties*, 418, and Hunt, *Turning*, 122

92   *At a firebase*: Appy, *Patriots*, 438

"83 instances": Krogh and Lehman to Kissinger, 11/11/1970, Box 3, EKP, NL

tiny "tiger cages": Reuters, "Saigon Is Investigating 'Tiger Cage' Cells at a Prison," *NYT*, 7/11/1970, 9

93   *another vote was likely*: The proposed Senate cutoff was sponsored by the South Dakota Democrat George McGovern and the Oregon Republican Mark Hatfield. The amendment was defeated twice, by votes of 52–44 in 1970 and 55–42 in 1971.

"We pointed out that": Krogh to Ehrlichman, "Vietnam trip," 9/15/1970, Box 3, EKP, NL

the big peace demonstration: Hunt, *Turning*, 12

"In a sensible world": Ibid.

gathered a small band: Gerald Nicosia, *Home to War* (New York: Crown, 2001), 17

94   *on a TV talk show*: David Jackson, "John Kerry: Veteran Politician," *Chicago Tribune*, 12/04/2003, A1

set off to recruit: Author interviews with John O'Connor, 8/18/2017, 5/15/2019

95   *"had a feeling it was"*: Mallory interview

"We didn't tell each other": Ibid.

"much as America regards": Transcript, The Sixties Project, Institute for Advanced Technology in the Humanities, University of Virginia

"America was asleep": John Kerry interview with Gerald Nicosia, 1/31/1989, transcript, Box 2008-224/10, Home to War/Vietnam Veterans Archive, Briscoe Center for American History, University of Texas at Austin

96   *contentious meeting*: Jackson, "John Kerry"

Kerry who crystallized: John Kerry interview in *Vietnam: A Television History*, 11/5/1982, WGBH. Some of the militant VVAW leaders later disputed Kerry's assertion that he came up with the idea for Dewey Canyon. One of these was Mike Oliver, as quoted in Nicosia, *Home to War*, 98.

"looked like a Lincoln": John O'Connor interview, 8/18/2017; Mallory interview

eye on the White House: Jackson, "John Kerry"

97   *middle of rush hour*: O'Connor interviews

"No, I don't love them": Butz interview

98   *go undercover:* O'Connor interviews; John O'Connor, unpublished manuscript, "Strictly Undercover," author's collection

99   *twenty paid informants:* Paul W. Valentine and Lee A. Daniels, "Report Says CIA Lent D.C. Police Men, Equipment," *WP,* 3/13/1975, A1

       ten thousand U.S. leftists: "'Confirmation' of CIA List Story," Associated Press via *San Francisco Chronicle,* 1/5/1975

       directed agents: Scheips, "The Role," 381

       "Agent personnel": Testimony prepared for Senate hearing by Assistant Army Secretary Robert Froehlke, 3/2/1971, Box 94, JDP, NL

       leased 450 lines: Ronald Kessler, "FBI Wiretapping: How Widespread?" *WP,* 2/7/1971, A1

100   *"for plenty of reasons":* Betty Medsger and Ken W. Clawson, "Thieves Got over 1,000 FBI Papers," *WP,* 3/25/1971, A1

       the same man who led: "State of New York Deposition," Stew Albert affidavit, June 1971, Box 14, AGP, Michigan

       suspending him without pay: Tim Logue, "Secrets Revealed in 1971 Burglary of FBI Office in Media," *Delaware County Times,* 2/9/2014, A1

       "got carried away during": FBI memo, 9/16/1970, *Media Files,* Liberty Publications, 1971

102   *so crestfallen:* O'Connor interviews; O'Connor, "Strictly Undercover"

       Kerry described it: William Claiborne, "Protest Planned Near Capitol," *WP,* 3/17/1971, 13

7. The Courage Part

105   *more than a million copies:* UPI, "Calley Disc Tops Million," *WP,* 4/20/1971, B7

106   *"our people are more divided":* John W. Finney, "2 Georgians in House Shift to Opposition to the War," *NYT,* 4/2/1971, A1

       "That's the one place": Haldeman, *Diaries,* 265–66

       Allowing the reaction: Ibid.

       "look at their hole card": NT 469-12, 3/18/1971, 6:25 p.m.

       keep arming the South: Memo to file, Alexander Haig, 3/26/1971, Box 81, President's Office Files, NL

       "If our domestic situation": NT 469-12, 3/18/1971, 6:25 p.m.

107   *spate of air-crew deaths:* Robert Sander, preface, *Invasion of Laos* (Norman: University of Oklahoma, 1971)

       hideaway office: Haldeman, *Diaries,* 268

       "American involvement": Nixon, "Address to the Nation on the Situation in Southeast Asia," 4/7/1971, transcript, American Presidency Project, University of California at Santa Barbara

       "Whatever you or I": "5 Top Democrats Ask Nixon to Set Date for Pullout," *NYT,* 4/23/1971, A1

108   *"You know when you really":* NT 476-14, 4/9/1971, 11:40 a.m.

"If we went out and shot": Ibid.

"Mr. President, how does": Buchanan to Nixon, 4/20/1971, Box 81, President's Office Files, NL

"I truly think the day": John Ehrlichman, *Witness to Power* (New York: Simon & Schuster, 1982), 45

109   *"something about Christ died"*: President's Daily Diary, NL; Haldeman, *Diaries*, 270

       "Good job": News Summaries, 4/12/1971, NL

110   *"We're fighting a delaying"*: NT 477-1, 4/12/1971, 9:10 a.m.

       a personal best: President's Daily Diary, NL

       "Let's face it": NT 001-101, 4/15/1971, 7:31 p.m.

       "RN is less affected": Reeves, *President Nixon*, 103

       "We need a little more": Meeting notes, 12/3/1970, Box 2, JEP, HI, Stanford

       "hard work, how he": Meeting notes, 2/2/1970, Box 1, JEP, HI, Stanford

111   *"For Christ's sake can't"*: NT 249-6, 4/15/1971, 8:59 a.m.

       "I do not enjoy fishing": Nixon to Rose Mary Woods, copy to Haldeman, 3/31/1971, Box 1, Lawrence Higby papers, NL. The memo contains the notation "THIS MEMORANDUM IS NOT TO BE HANDED TO ANYONE TO READ—IT IS FOR TALKING PURPOSES OF HRH AND RMW."

       "Primarily," the aide wrote: Dwight Chapin to Haldeman, 1/22/1971, Box 2, President Returned Materials Collection, NL

       "The Nixons Nobody Knows": *McCall's*, May 1971

       gazing alone: Gene T. Boyer and Jackie Boor, *Inside the President's Helicopter* (Brule, WI: Cable Publishers, 2011), 212

       "manner and tone": Krogh to Ehrlichman, "Domestic Policy Issues—1971–1972," 4/16/1971, Box 4, EKP, NL

112   *"The people that lead this"*: NT 249-6, 4/15/1971, 8:49 a.m.

       "trouble will be inevitable": Krogh to Dean, 4/15/1971, Box 89, JDP, NL

       a "tinder box that is": This was Minority Leader Robert Dole, according to Haldeman memo to file 4/14/1971, Box 81, President's Meeting Files, NL.

       "We can't afford to let": Haldeman diary, 4/15/1971, NL

       "Rennie Davis is": NT 477-1, 4/12/1971, 9:10 a.m.

113   *"I think that thinking"*: NT 477-10, 4/12/1971, 2:30 p.m.

       talk some sense: Ehrlichman, "Cold War," CNN

       a Sunday think piece: "Youth Greening May Turn Blue," *WP*, 4/11/1971, C1, copy in Box 12, EKP, NL

       "quell the current excitement": Krogh to Ehrlichman, "Domestic Policy Issues—1971–1972," 4/16/1971, Box 4, EKP, NL

8. Move On Over

114   *they'd slept together*: Gumbo interviews

       thousands of such watches: FBI Washington Field Office to Hoover, "Explosive and Incendiary Devices," 3/3/1971, Box 12, HVF, Marquette *only to disappoint them:* FBI NY Field Office File 174-1340, 3/11/1971, Box 10, AGP, Michigan

115   *"a girl to handle":* Jennifer Frost, *An Interracial Movement of the Poor* (New York: NYU Press, 2005), 43

"could not help but": Karin Aguilar-San Juan and Frank Joyce, eds., *The People Make the Peace* (Charlottesville, VA: Just World Books, 2015), 59

"huge arguments": Robin Morgan, cited in Ruth Rosen, *The World Split Open* (New York: Penguin, 2006), 136

116   *built by a woman:* Samuel Z. Goldhaber, "Police Trail One Woman in Bombing," *Harvard Crimson*, 10/16/1970, 1

the Women's Brigade: Bryan Burrough, *Days of Rage* (New York: Penguin, 2015), 150

FBI's most-wanted list: "New Left Summary," Box 89, JDP, NL

117   *"quite a number of":* Neiburger interview

"Freaks are revolutionaries": Bernardine Dohrn, "A Declaration of a State of War," 5/21/1970, reproduced in Dohrn, Bill Ayers, and Jeff Jones, *Sing a Battle Song* (New York: Seven Stories, 2006), 150

"changed our diets": Gilbert, *Love and Struggle,* 165

"had the closest association": Abbie Hoffman, *The Autobiography of Abbie Hoffman* (New York: Four Walls, 2000), 249

"revolutionary first aid": Albert, "Sixties Memoir," Box 2, AGP, Michigan

118   *"We will have to swim":* Stew Albert, "Panthers, Yippies Shoot Up Oakland Hills," *Berkeley Barb*, 11/29/1968, 11

"fear of violence": Dellinger, *More Power,* 168

"explore the shrouded world": Tom Hayden, *Reunion* (New York: Random House, 1988), 421–22

International Liberation School: Gitlin, *Sixties,* 351

"to educate and train": Judy Gumbo, "Remembering Tom Hayden," *Counterpunch,* 2/14/2017

two boxes of dynamite: "My Generation Drafts," Box 2, AGP Michigan. In an interview with the author, Judy Gumbo said Stew never told her he had possessed dynamite, and she suggested Stew made up the story for dramatic effect. That would be inconsistent with everything else in Stew's unpublished memoir, which conforms with known facts.

119   *the movie* Woodstock: Leary went to the film with Bernardine Dohrn and Jeff Jones, according to unpublished drafts of Stew Albert's memoir, Box 2, AGP, Michigan.

"Total war is upon us": Robert Greenfield, *Timothy Leary* (Orlando: Harcourt, 2006), 385–88

"For a while, there was": Jonah Raskin, "Looking Backward," in *Sing a Battle Song,* 122

Judy was on her way: Unsigned, "Up Against Judy Gumbo's Wall," *Boston After Dark,* 6/8/1971, 1

120   *"Hi, Mom!"*: Witness accounts given at Mayday Tribe Reunion, 5/3/2016

a meeting in Indonesia: Gitlin, *Sixties*, 265; one attendee was his wife, Nanci Hollander.

121   *ordering them to leave*: Ibid., 362; see also *She's Beautiful When She's Angry*, documentary film, 2014, Mary Dore, director-producer

"'Girls say Yes!'": Gitlin, *Sixties*, 292; also see memo from FBI Philadelphia office, 105–170160, "Stop the Draft Week," 10/25/1967, Clergy and Laity Concerned file, Part 1 of 2, page 20, FBI Online Vault, https://vault.fbi.gov

"Free dope, free food": Letter from "Maisie" to Yippie, 2/1/1971, Box 1, AGP, Michigan

"White males are most": Robin Morgan, "Goodbye to All That," *Rat*, 1/1970

"Our minds have been fucked": Judy Gumbo, "Why the Women Are Revolting," *Berkeley Barb*, 5/16/1969, 5

122   *the housework situation*: O'Connor and Mallory interviews

"assist in all aspects": Angus MacKenzie, *Secrets: The CIA's War at Home* (Berkeley: University of California Press, 1999), 34

"some shuddering in": Jeannette Smyth, "Girl Pages," *WP*, 5/7/1971, B1

"physical beauty, per se": Ronald Sarro, "AF Defends Photos of Women Recruits," *WES*, 5/3/1971, A14

the rank and file dragged: Cullinane interview

123   *they could wear slacks*: Green interview

recruit females: Sarah Booth Conroy, "Women Recruiter," *WP*, 4/23/1971, B3

"It's so easy to burn": Tricia Nixon interview, *WES*, 5/6/1971; wedding announcement, *WP*, 4/15/1971

a tool kit instead: "Tricia's Shower Gifts," Box 65, First Lady's Press Office files, NL

124   *Linda Evans*: Jacobs, *The Way the Wind Blew*, 52

"it's up to us, to hide": Nancy & Gumbo, "Linda Evans," *Berkeley Tribe*, April 24–May 1, 1970, 26

9. Fringe Group

127   *last-minute scramble*: John Kerry, *Every Day Is Extra* (New York: Simon & Schuster, 2018), 129

"not mobilizing very well": NT 477-1, 4/12/1971, 9:10 a.m.

"a little harder": Timothy Hutchins and William Holland, "Cemetery–Capitol Hill March Opens Viet Veterans' Protest," *WES*, 4/19/1971, A1

Down it went: Richard Stacewicz, *Winter Soldiers* (New York: Twayne, 1997), 242

bed down for the night: O'Connor interview

They were as diverse: Carl Bernstein, "Viet Veterans Camped on Mall Resemble Basic Training Outfit," *WP*, 4/22/1971, A14

128   *"instinct for the political jugular"*: Nixon, *RN*, 496

Nixon's dark side: Magruder, *American Life*, 64

"Department of Dirty Tricks": Ibid., 66

decorations over the fence: Status Report, Dean to Haldeman, Ehrlichman, 4/15/1971, Box 4, EKP, NL

"downgrading the importance": Colson to Dean 4/19/1971, and Dean to Haldeman, Ehrlichman 4/22/1971, Box 89, JDP, NL

129   *Joe Frazier:* Red Smith, "Champ Raps with Politicos," *WP,* 4/22/1971, D5

    "We're behind you in": NT 001-150, 4/18/1971, 1:28 p.m.

130   *"This, I think, is the":* Hutchens and Holland, "Cemetery–Capitol Hill March"

    Gold Star mothers: O'Connor, "Strictly Undercover," 183

    "Groups will not enter": Richard Kleindienst, cited in minutes of Justice meeting 4/14/1971, Box 23, Harlington Wood Jr. Papers, Illinois History and Lincoln Collections, University of Illinois, Urbana-Champaign

    "There just must be more": Michael Kranish, "With Antiwar Role, High Visibility," *Boston Globe,* 6/17/2003, A1

    "It is absolutely incredible": Paul W. Valentine, "Vets March on Hill, Protest Their War," *WP,* 4/20/1971, A1

    "We have come to Washington": VVAW leaflet, John O'Connor personal files

131   *"we are the troops":* John Kerry et al., *The New Soldier* (New York: Macmillan, 1971), 104

132   *"The Executive will have":* Farrand, *The Records of the Federal Convention of 1787, Vol. 2* (1911)

    "what action has been": President's Daily News Summary, 2/24/1971, Box 30, President's Office Files, NL

    quietly arrange: Haldeman memo, 2/22/1971, reproduced in Oudes, *From the President,* 220

    Douglas MacArthur: MacArthur would go on to distinguish himself in the Pacific during World War II but would be fired by President Harry Truman in 1951 after he agitated publicly for a big U.S. expansion of the Korean War.

133   *The vets could stay:* Sanford J. Ungar, "Vets Can Use Mall," *WP,* 4/20/1971, A12

    "Poor old Hoover": NT 485-4, 4/21/1971, 4:18 p.m.

134   *"The petitioner just doesn't":* Edward B. Fiske, "Ali Is No Pacifist, U.S. Tells Court," *NYT,* 4/20/1971, 24

    their DD214s: Sanford J. Ungar and William L. Claiborne, "Vets' Camp on Mall Banned by Burger," *WP,* 4/21/1971, A1

135   *begging for an end:* Mike Feinsilber, "Senate Told of GIs Killing Own Officers," *WP,* 4/21/1971, A1. The word "fragging" is derived from "fragmentary grenades." Mansfield cited 209 fragging incidents in 1970, up from 96 in 1969, in which thirty-four died.

    a mixer and fundraiser: Nicosia, *Home to War,* 124

    "Those guys on the Mall": Dorothy McCardle, "A Thousand Years in Vietnam," *WP,* 4/21/1971, B3

136   *grabbed a couple of crates:* Mallory interview

invitation to testify: Nicosia, *Home to War,* 124

nearly broke the phone: O'Connor interview

137 *bowling alone:* President's Daily Diary, NL

handle public statements: Status Report, Dean to Haldeman, Ehrlichman, 4/15/1971, Box 4, EKP, NL

"good Negro for HUD": Meeting notes, 10/23/1970, Box 1, JEP, HI, Stanford

dumber than you are: Wilson interviews

"I trust we are not going": Buchanan to Haldeman, 4/21/1971, reproduced in Oudes, *From the President,* 240

138 *The final vote came out:* Nicosia, *Home to War,* 131

"I'm going to stay": Henry Aubin, "Vets Defiant over Ban," *WP,* 4/21/1971, A14

"I'm glad" it's going: NT 485-4, 4/21/1971, 4:18 p.m.

139 *"The policy — which the VVAW":* Dean to Haldeman, Ehrlichman, 4/21/1971, Box 89, JDP, NL

"The president asked me": Wilson interviews

"This capital never looked": Marquis Childs, "Veterans' Camp: What They Seek," *WP,* 4/23/1971, A23

140 *wanted them arrested:* Dean to Haldeman, Ehrlichman, 4/22/1971, Box 77, Charles Colson papers, NL

"If all our guys get arrested": William L. Claiborne, "Police Move Quickly, Gently in Arresting Protesting Vets," *WP,* 4/23/1971, A6

"I deem the present": George L. Hart Jr. to Attorney General, 4/22/1971, Box 23, Harlington Wood Jr. Papers, Illinois History and Lincoln Collections, University of Illinois, Urbana-Champaign

"The judiciary has been degraded": William L. Claiborne and Sanford J. Ungar, "Judge Lifts Ban on Vets, Scolds U.S.," *WP,* 4/23/1971, A1

thought about resigning: Sanford J. Ungar, *FBI* (Boston: Little, Brown, 1976), 504

"a bad guy": NT 486-3, 4/22/1971, 12:30 p.m.

10. The Last Man

141 *"pretty chopped up":* Haldeman, *Diaries,* 278

what people saw on TV: NT 487-7, 4/23/1971, 11:56 a.m.

"the rattiest-looking people": NT 486-3, 4/22/1971, 12:30 p.m.

The only silver lining: Haldeman, *Diaries,* 278

"God knows": NT 486-3, 4/22/1971, 12:30 p.m.

far more positive rating: Opinion Dynamics polls, cited in Mark D. Harmon, *Found, Featured, Then Forgotten: U.S. Network TV News and the Vietnam Veterans Against the War* (Knoxville, TN: Newfound Press, 2011), 65–66

142 *"The only conclusion":* Haldeman, *Diaries,* 278

"I'm sure a significant": NT 487-1, 4/23/1971, 9:15 a.m.

"burning with this anger": John Kerry interview with Gerald Nicosia, 1/31/1989, transcript, Box 2008-224/10, Home to War/Vietnam Veterans Archive, Briscoe Center for American History, University of Texas at Austin

143   *chased the enemy:* Documentary film, *Going Upriver: The Long War of John Kerry,* 2004, George Butler, director

had little affection: John Kerry, WGBH interview, 1982

Kerry told the senators: Quotations from "Text of Speech by John Kerry," *Boston Globe,* 4/25/1971, 49. Kerry's speech and actions in 1971 would become sources of dispute more than thirty years later during his campaign for the presidency, in 2004. A right-wing political group named the Swift Boat Veterans for Truth claimed that in his speech to the Senate committee, Kerry had repeated unproven allegations about U.S. atrocities in Vietnam and thus painted all the troops with a sinister brush.

145   *informants posing as vets:* John Prados, *Vietnam: The History of an Unwinnable War* (Lawrence: University Press of Kansas, 2009), 434

new spontaneous demonstration: Secret Service memo, Box 89, JDP, NL

with his daughter Tricia: President's Daily Diary, NL

blankets or quilts: Fred Barnes, "Veterans," WES, 4/23/1971, A6

"Come in, sister, join us": Mary Anne Dolan, "Women in the March Dedicated," WES, 4/23/1971, C3

146   *given Jerry full authority:* Status Report, Dean to Haldeman, Ehrlichman, 4/16/1971, Box 4, EKP, NL

a born diplomat: Wilson interviews

147   *join the Republican Party:* Murray Chotiner to Mitchell, Haldeman 4/26/1971, NL Virtual Library https://www.nixonlibrary.gov/sites/default/files/virtual library/documents/contested/contested_box_24/Contested-24-04.pdf

"And then for one full week": NT 487-1, 4/23/1971, 9:15 a.m.

eighth clandestine session: Memorandum of Conversation, Paris, 6/26/1971, Nixon Presidential Materials, NSC Files, Box 1039, National Archives, accessed at https://history.state.gov/historicaldocuments/frus1969-76v42/d9

"that uneasily dormant": Kissinger, *White House Years,* 1010

secret negotiating position: For insight on this change, see George McTurnan Kahin, "Nixon and the PRG's 7 Points," in Jayne Werner and David Hunt, eds., *The American War in Vietnam* (Ithaca, NY: Cornell University Press, 1993), 57–70

148   *"use nuclear weapons":* NT 487-7, 4/23/1971, 11:56 a.m.

A firm American withdrawal: Kissinger, *White House Years,* 1019

Sunny's Surplus: O'Connor interview

149   *"part of America that was not":* Kerry, WGBH interview, 1982

150   *threw their symbols:* "Ex-GIs Discard Medals," WES, 4/23/1971, A1

Hundreds of spectators: Art Goldberg, "Vietnam Vets: The Anti-War Army," *Ramparts,* July 1971, 11

sobbing, he embraced others: William L. Claiborne, "Yesterday's Hero Now Feels Clean," WP, 4/24/1971, A9

He lobbed: Going Upriver documentary

151   *ten thousand of "our" vets:* Haldeman diaries, 4/25/1971, NL

"On Saturday anyway": NT 486-3, 4/22/1971, 12:30 p.m.

11. The Saturday March

152 *preserve "quiet and dignity"*: An Act to regulate the use of the Capitol Grounds, July 1, 1882 (22 Stat. 143)

went to jail: Scott Hart, "Army of Coxey Set Pace for D.C. 'Invasions,'" *WP*, 12/6/1937, 5

153 *a distance of at least*: Mary Spargo, "Capitol Police Rules Change Is Promised," *WP*, 4/19/1946, 4

turned away hundreds: John J. Lindsay, "400 Storm Capitol for Home Rule," *WP*, 7/29/1959, A1

"minimizing adverse PR": Status Report, Dean to Haldeman, Ehrlichman, 4/16/1971, Box 4, EKP, NL

Vice President Spiro Agnew: Letter, 4/16/1971, PHF

154 *"The peace movement has"*: Mary McGrory, "They Woke the Country Up," *WES*, 4/26/1971, 7

"under substantial communist": "Fulbright Panel Hears Antiwar Vet," *WP*, 4/23/1971, A4

"some of the people": Jack M. Kneece, "200,000 Join Anti-War March," *WES*, 4/24/1971, A1

"ridicule and disrupt": FBI memorandum, New York to Director, 4/2/1971, Box 12, AGP, Michigan

"all efforts [would be] made": FBI memorandum, Director to New York, 4/9/1971, Box 12, AGP, Michigan

155 *"has conspicuously and"*: Editorial, "Up the Hill and Down Again," *WP*, 4/24/1971, 18

"Even though they are": NT 477-1, 4/12/1971, 9:10 a.m.

TV "has zeroed in": NT 487-7, 4/23/1971, 11:56 a.m.

"want to destroy you": Ibid.

156 *"self-righteousness and brutality"*: Kissinger, *White House Years*, 510

"I gather you don't know": Kissinger telephone recordings, 4/23/1971, 7:50 p.m., transcript, National Security Archive, George Washington University

"take Henry Kissinger out": Secret Service memo 4/22/1971, Box 89, JDP, NL

157 *spend the weekend*: President's Daily Diary, NL

"these demonstrations are": Lance Gay, "Cathedral Eulogy," *WES*, 4/24/1971, A20

159 *A holiday atmosphere*: *Post* and *Star* reporting

161 *"we promised an apolitical"*: Gerald Caplan, book review, in *McGeorge Law Review*, vol. 41, 2010

"What is he trying": Wells, *War Within*, 377

The chief typed it: Wilson to Krogh, undated in May 1970, JWF

162 *"downplayed as much as"*: Haldeman diaries, 4/24/1971, NL

revising the number down: Fred Barnes and William Holland, "Protest Takes on Keystone Kops Air," *WES*, 4/26/1971, A6

"All the jackasses": NT 490-7, 4/29/1971, 12:53 p.m.

163 *admit to himself*: Davis interview

12. What's the Harm?

164 *footing the bill:* Ken Kelley, "Blissed Out with The Perfect Master," *Ramparts,* July 1973, 32–34

a lot of oatmeal: Martin Weil, "Protesters' Camp Becomes Carnival of Counter Culture," *WP,* 4/26/1971, A15

165 *cluster of Quaker families:* Robert F. Levey and Jean R. Hailey, "10-Day Protest to Begin," *WP,* 4/26/1971, A1

"If millions of people": David R. Boldt and Sanford J. Ungar, "For Many, This Was First Time," *WP,* 4/25/1971, A17

"Unless tens of thousands": Nicholas Von Hoffman, "Clenched Knuckles," *WP,* 4/26/1971, B1

166 *"has become the prime fact":* "The Advocates," WGBH-Boston, broadcast 4/20/1971

167 *"it's possible to use force":* Speech transcript, David Dellinger, 4/12/1971, Chapel Hill, North Carolina, copy in FBI files, Charlotte, North Carolina, 5/7/1971, FOIA

"The theme of Non-Violent": Undated pamphlet, Mayday Video Collective, PHF

168 *"Throughout American history":* "The Advocates," WGBH-Boston, broadcast 4/20/1971

branded its members as "terrorists": UPI, 4/24/1971, via *NYT*

"be sure we're alert": Haldeman diaries, 4/24/1971, NL

"We should let the nuts": Ibid., 4/25/1971

169 *"should not be raised":* Haldeman note on William Timmons to Nixon, 4/27/1971, Box 301, Williams Timmons papers, NL

the dog made a break: Associated Press, "Nixon's Dog Runs Off at Camp David," *WP,* 4/26/1971, A2

bribe King Timahoe: Stephen Bull oral history, NL

the lowest level: Orr Kelly, "Draft Calls Cut for Rest of 1971," *WES,* 4/27/1971, A1

roamed the halls: "Draft Office Doors Blocked in Protest," *WES,* 4/27/1971, A10

170 *"crude, foul-mouthed":* William Holland and Lance Gay, "Police Clear Entrance," *WES,* 4/28/1971, A6

"There were approximately": Rolapp to Robert C. Mardian, 4/27/1971, Box 95, JDP, NL

"hundreds of tents": "After Action Report, Anti-War Demonstrations April-May 1971," Prisoner Control Center, Metropolitan Police Dept. 13, JWF

"for the entire peace movement": Unsigned, "Churchmen Ask Nation to Repent War," *WP,* 4/28/1971, A1

campuses around the country: FBI Nitel 176-1410, from Chicago office to Director, 4-19-1971, FOIA

171 *adult education classes:* Natasha Dellinger to David Dellinger, 4/11/1971, Box 10, DDP, NYU

injected morphine: FBI Airtel, Washington office to Director, 4/30/1971; also FBI Washington office memo, 6/28/1971, FOIA

"I saw you on TV": Nancy Moore to Dellinger, 5/4/1971, Box 8, DDP, NYU
to justify violence: Staughton Lynd, ed., *Nonviolence in America: A Documentary History* (Indianapolis and New York: Bobbs-Merrill, 1966), xlii
"Sometimes the people": FBI transcript from recording of Dellinger speech, 4/12/1971, at University of North Carolina, Chapel Hill, FOIA
"The actions this spring": "Massive Antiwar Demonstration Set for April 24," Underground Press Service, in *The Olive Branch*, Vol. 1, No. 3, Jacksonville, FL, in Independent Voices Collection, voices.revealdigital.com

172   *"shyly kissed me"*: Dellinger, *More Power*, 153. According to Dellinger, the Weather Underground member Kathy Boudin also admitted to him two days before the 1970 townhouse explosion that she had been having second thoughts about the group's direction. Nevertheless, the following year Boudin reportedly helped plant the bomb in the Capitol.
"They think they know": NT 482-17 and 482-18, 4/19/1971, 3:03 p.m.
admit to a grand jury: Wallace Turner, "Judge Bids Miss Bacon Reply to Questions on Bank Bombing," *NYT*, 5/7/1971, 17

173   *"act a little goofy"*: Paul W. Valentine and Robert H. Williams, "D.C. Police Acts Cited," *WP*, 3/20/1975, A1
secret transmitters: Report of the U.S. Commission on CIA Activities Within the United States, 1975, Appendix VII
rescinded his predecessors' orders: MPD General Order 12, 3/29/1971, cited in Frank J. Donner, *Protectors of Privilege* (Berkeley: University of California, 1990), 340
placed the lamps: Dougald D. McMillan, secret Justice Department task force report on Rockefeller Commission, 6/30/1976, 10–12, first obtained by James Bamford for *The Shadow Factory* (New York: Doubleday, 2008)
"Leslie, get the fuck": "Goodwin Is Scared to Death of Rainbows," interview with Leslie Bacon, Colin Neiburger, and Michael Tola, *Liberation News Service*, 7/18/1971

174   *at his private island*: Stephen Bull to Haldeman and Chapin, 4/27/1971, Alphabetical Name Files, Rebozo, NL
clandestine visit to China: Dallek, *Kissinger and Nixon*, 288; Haldeman diary, 4/27/1971, NL
"these bearded weirdos": NT 488-24, 4/27/1971, 4:57 p.m.

175   *more relatable*: Author interview with John Dean, 12/18/2018
Bud was unaware: Krogh interview, 2/5/1997, Box 1, *Eye of the Storm*, documentary film collection, Russell Library, University of Georgia; also see "Dean, Nixon's Counsel, Was Dismissed from First Law Job in 1966 in 'Disagreement,'" *NYT*, 4/5/1973, 33
It's just too good for: Dean interview
"He's terrific conceptually": Krogh to Donfeld, attachment to 4/17/1970 memo from John Dean, Box 10, EJEP, Boston University

"very smooth, cool, calculated": Dwight Chapin to Haldeman, 6/30/1970, Box 14, WH Central Files, NL

Dean's transparent effort: Stuart, *Never Trust*, 53

"I was often stunned": Dean interview

their office space: John Dean, *Blind Ambition* (New York: Simon & Schuster, 1976), 48

unlisted phone number: Ibid., 26

176 *flag lapel pin*: Ibid., 134

secretly blackballed: Seymour Hersh, *The Price of Power* (New York: Summit, 1983), 396n.

if things went well: Maureen Dean, *Mo: A Woman's View of Watergate* (New York: Simon & Schuster, 1975), 82

"I could play the admiring": John Dean, *The Nixon Defense* (New York: Viking, 2014), 155

Bud began to worry that Dean: Krogh family email to author

"Tried this. Credibility": Note on 4/27/1971 status report, Box 4, EKP, NL

the secret tunnel: Dean, *Blind*, 28

having the air force fly: Air Force Brig. Gen. W. P. Anderson to D.C. director military support, 4/29/1971, Box 86, JDP, NL

177 *"to combat dissent"*: Army memo to Kleindienst, 4/28/1971, Box 89, JDP, NL

13. Public Defenders

178 *could see the flames*: Harold Greene interview, *D.C. Bar Report*, April/May 1996

179 *"A mass arrest situation"*: Harold Greene, "A Judge's View of the Riots," *D.C. Bar Journal* 35, 1968, cited in William A. Dobrovir, "Justice in Time of Crisis," D.C. committee staff report, 17

stop accepting collateral: Marine Beasley, "Mayday Weakens Court, Police Ties," *WP*, 5/30/1971, A9

"precipitating another Chicago": Carl Bernstein and Donald E. Graham, "200 Arrested," *WP*, 4/29/1971, A1

180 *course at Yale Law School*: Author interview with Barbara Babcock (known in 1971 by her married name, Barbara Bowman), 8/28/2017

181 *shuffled to sedate fields*: Cynthia Grant Bowman, "Women in the Legal Profession from the 1920s to the 1970s," *Maine Law Review* 2009, vol. 61, 1

182 *bested a fellow student*: Eleanor Holmes Norton and Joan S. Lester, *Fire in My Soul* (New York: Simon & Schuster, 2002), 95

scared Barbara to death: Babcock interviews; Babcock oral history, "Women Trailblazers in the Law," American Bar Association, 2006–7; Barbara Babcock, *Fish Raincoats* (New Orleans: Quid Pro, 2016)

"hardly the classic": Louise Lague, "Lady Lawyer to Teach Lib via Law," *Washington Daily News*, 7/7/1970

183 *Christian woman who prayed*: Babcock, *Fish Raincoats*, 9

184   *representing Mafia chieftains:* Evan Thomas, *The Man to See* (New York: Simon & Schuster, 1991), 20

"had the transmission": Babcock oral history

186   *encouraging a backlash:* Stephen E. Ambrose, *Nixon, Vol. 2: The Triumph of a Politician, 1962–1972* (New York: Simon & Schuster, 1989), 154

"We are going to make": Reeves, *President Nixon*, 28; Unsigned, "Thieves Throw D.C. Woman, 81, Down Stairs," *WP,* 1/18/1969, E3

$5,000 worth of jewelry: "Burglary of Nixon Aide Spurs Fight on Crime," *WP,* 3/4/1969, A13

political window dressing: Krogh interview with Epstein, Box 9, EJEP, Boston University; also see Edward Jay Epstein, "The Krogh File — The Politics of 'Law and Order,'" *The Public Interest,* Spring 1975, 104

"literally a garbage pail": Robert F. Levey, "Senators Urged to Fight Crime Bill," *WP,* 5/2/1970, C1

"is intent upon the diminishment": Richard Harris, "The New Justice," *New Yorker,* 3/25/1972, 64

187   *"No Senator can possibly":* William Proxmire, transcript of Senate Hearings regarding 1971 D.C. appropriations, 3/16/1970

graduating law-school class: National Observer, 12/8/1969

"The people who weren't successful": Author interview with Michael Wald, 8/28/17

188   *the wrong use of:* Babcock, *Fish Raincoats,* 88

Addie was on the way: Philip A. McCombs, Addison Bowman profile, *WP* magazine, 1/23/1972

14. Barricades

190   *personal calendar:* NT 491-14, 5/5/1971, 9:35 a.m.

"John, P plans keep": Undated note in "Demonstrations May 1971," Box 89, JDP, NL

191   *Go with makeup:* Haldeman diary, 4/28/1971, NL

"In my case it would": NT 251-27, 4/29/1971, 10:24 a.m.

"I would not want": Nixon news conference transcript, *NYT,* 4/30/1971

"Let me just make one": Carroll Kilpatrick, "President Says Protests Won't Intimidate Him," *WP,* 4/30/1971

the 45,000 mark: "U.S. Combat Death Toll Over 45,000 in Vietnam," *WP,* 4/30/1971, A20

"a precious, gentle people": Jim Mann, "New Potomac Campers Older, More Serious," *WP,* 5/1/1971, 5

192   *squeeze their spiels: Liberation News Service,* 5/1/1971

cassette players: Meridith Lair, *Armed with Abundance: Consumering & Soldiering in the Vietnam War* (Chapel Hill: University of North Carolina Press, 2011), 129

193   *makeshift screen:* Author interview with members of Videofreex collective

"well-dressed Arab women": Jack Caulfield to Krogh, "White House Tour Poses Serious Presidential Safety Hazard," 3/11/1970, Box 9, EKP, NL

inspired a song: Ben Edmonds, *What's Going On?: Marvin Gaye and the Last Days of the Motown Sound* (Edinburgh: MOJO Books, 2001), 149; WOOK-Washington Radio 1340 chart, April 5, 1971, Anacostia Community Museum, Washington, D.C.

194   *"elevated, romantic innocence"*: Albert, *Who the Hell,* 162

"big golden bear": Hoffman, *The Autobiography,* 150

"I'm going to lay down": Barbara Deming, *We Cannot Live Without Our Lives* (New York: Grossman, 1974), 28

"If you see people are": Mann, "New Potomac Campers"

195   *"1. Oil burning"*: Undated notes on "Mayday Demonstrations," Box 77, Charles Colson papers, NL

"You know that's not": NT 490-7, 4/29/1971, 1:06 p.m.

"The next group comes": NT 487-1, 4/23/1971, 9:15 a.m.

"If there isn't violence": NT 251-27, 4/29/1971, 10:24 a.m.

one entire day: NT 489-23, 4/26/1971, 6:40 p.m.

phone lines: "All Phones Cut Off, Protesters Protest," *WP,* 4/30/1971, A8

196   *"no remedy but force"*: *The Federalist* (New York: Modern Library, 1937), 170–71, cited in Robert W. Coakley, *The Role of Federal Military Forces in Domestic Disorders, 1789–1878* (U.S. Army: Army Historical Series, 1988).

LBJ had issued: Scheips, "The Role," 284

197   *"almost total breakdown"*: "Ohio Governor Pleads for May Day Restraint," *WP,* 4/30/1971, A6

Posse Comitatus Act: Confidential memo from Army to Kleindienst, 4/28/1971, Box 89, JDP, NL

"does not apply": Cited in Scheips, "The Role," 351n

"The president has inherent": William H. Rehnquist, "Authority to Use Troops," 4/29/1971, U.S. Department of Justice, Office of Legal Counsel Opinions, 343

198   *"just what we don't"*: Haldeman diaries, 4/30/1971, NL; Kleindienst also refers to this discussion at the May 1 war-council meeting, the minutes show.

"taking the black young men": Martin Luther King Jr., "Beyond Vietnam," speech, 4/4/1967, New York, https://kinginstitute.stanford.edu/king-papers/documents/beyond-vietnam

"sheer inventions": Editorial, "A Tragedy," *WP,* 4/6/1967, A20

199   *"just a lot of hot air"*: Henry Aubin and Paul Valentine, "7,300 Police, Guardsmen Readied to Counter Disruptions," *WP,* 5/1/1971, A1

"At worst this is": "U.S. Acts to Keep Streets Open," *WES,* 4/30/1971, A1

"inviting great danger": "Mitchell Assails Media Coverage," *WP,* 5/1/1971, A2

200   *slow-moving jeep*: Frank Murray, "Did Nixon Get a Ride on Marine Shoulders?" *WES,* 5/2/1971, A3

"Do people realize that": "Getting It Together in West Potomac Park," *Liberation News Service,* 5/1/1971, 7

They aired pleas: The three stations were WOL, WOOK, and WUST.

201 *"It kind of looks like"*: Robert Dechard and Michael S. Feldberg, "D.C. Disruptions Continue Despite Arrests at HEW," *Harvard Crimson*, 4/30/1971
"there is NOT going to be": "Getting It Together in West Potomac Park"

15. War Council

205 *vastly underestimated*: Minutes, 5/1/1971 Justice meeting, ACLU files, Princeton
no military presence: Richard Halloran, "30,000 Protesters Routed in Capital, *NYT*, 5/3/1971, A1
"like he was about ready": Wood, *Unmarked Trail*, 111

206 *stop writing tuition checks*: Kleindienst, *Justice*, 71
"should be rounded up": Elizabeth Drew, "Report: Washington," *Atlantic*, May 1969, 4
"ten thousand revolutionaries": Kleindienst, *Justice*, 73
"the president's militia": Krogh to Ehrlichman, 5/27/1970, Box 3, EKP, NL
these meetings tedious: Jim Mann, "Wilson Gives Policies on Mass Arrests," *WP*, 6/4/1972, A1

207 *"What are you"*: Author interview with Philip J. Hirschkop, 6/11/2019
"You never wanted to": Author interview with Gerald Caplan, 8/31/2017
"shoots from the hip": Dean interview
a "nut-cutter": Memos, 3/26/1970, Box 1, JEP, HI, Stanford
a better attorney general: Memos, 12/3/1970, Box 1, JEP, HI, Stanford

208 *"more active demonstrations"*: Kleindienst, *Justice*, 89
friendly gambling: Dean, Wilson interviews
"nudity, immorality": Wood, *Unmarked Trail*, 126
lifelong polo player: Wilson interviews
"an unwholesome situation": Minutes of Mayday post-mortem, Roosevelt Room, 5/6/1971, Box 89, JDP, NL

209 *asked his officers*: "Disorders in Washington Where Military Assistance Was Requested," undated, JWF
"I'm not too sure we give": NT 489-23, 4/26/1971, 6:40 p.m.
"If you have a fight": NT 251-17, 4/27/1971, 2:25 p.m.
"new barbarians": William H. Rehnquist, excerpts from Law Day speech, 5/1/1969, *Congressional Record*, 11/15/1986
he lambasted: Rehnquist letter to the editor, *WP*, 2/14/1970, A14

210 *the opening chapter*: Rehnquist book proposal, "Death in the Paw Paw Tunnel," Box 7, Rehnquist papers, HI, Stanford
"it will mean": Wood, *Unmarked Trail*, 120
"Our nation is sorely": "Churchmen Ask Nation to Repent War," *WP*, 4/28/1971, A1

211 *a new sleeping bag*: Barry Kalb, "Portrait of a Radical Leader," *WES*, 4/30/1971, A2
"I could see": Davis interview

"*let Rennie eat*": Author interview with attendee Jim Mann, 5/1/2018; Davis interview

"*There are over thirty*": Abbie Hoffman, speech, University of Oklahoma, 4/29/1971, cited in FBI Abbie Hoffman files, Part 15 of 50, FBI Vault online

212 "*They seem to think*": UPI, 5/2/1971, in *WES*

"*before any riots broke*": Mike Love, *Good Vibrations: My Life as a Beach Boy* (New York: Blue Rider, 2016), 234

213 *lyrics were sexist*: FBI undercover report, Box 10, AGP, Michigan; also Robert F. Levey and Bart Barnes, "Visitors Mass to Tie Up City," *WP*, 5/2/1971, A16

"*you've gone halfway*": *Mayday RAW*, video documentary by Videofreex collective

"*This is better than Woodstock*": Michael Lerner, "Mayday," *Ramparts*, July 1971

"*If we want to send*": *Mayday RAW*

214 "*a small number of people*": PCPJ Spring Training Manual, PHF

"*variety and inventiveness*": Leaflet, "Movin' Together," 4/17/1971, PHF

briefing by phone: President's Daily Diary, NL

speak with John Mitchell: Minutes of Mayday post-mortem

arrest the whole: NT 500-17, 5/18/71, 12:16 p.m.

the city kept open: Wilson interviews; NT 490-24, 5/4/1971, 3:07 p.m.

215 "*The president has ordered*": Memo from Pentagon to army, Box 89, JDP, NL

Seven military helicopters: Robert F. Levey and Bart Barnes, "Troops Move In to Area," *WP*, 5/2/1971, A1

"*It is our earnest hope*": Editorial, "Demonstrations, Tribesmen and Rationality," *WES*, 5/2/1071, C1

"*arrest them on*": Minutes of Mayday post-mortem

216 "*Many will go home*": Ehrlichman diary notes, Box 2, JEP, HI, Stanford

"*surprise was the most*": Minutes of Mayday post-mortem

217 "*Bent penny!*": Charles Lutz, "Operation Bent Penny," 8/4/2011, at HistoryNet; Frank Dunne Jr., "Larry McElynn, Undercover Man," *Celebrate Hilton Head*, May 2009; Tom Clifford, *Inside the DEA* (Bloomington, IN: AuthorHouse, 2005), 18–19

"*It should be emphasized*": "Public Information Suggestions from Ziegler/Scali," 5/1/1971, Box 77, Charles Colson papers, NL

16. Revoked

220 *thousands of people*: Author interviews with Mike Henley and Michael Oberman of Claude Jones, and with Wilson; also see Jim Mann and Tom Huth, "Peace City Exodus," *WP*, 5/3/1971, A1; "Mayday 1971: The End of Algonquin Peace City," Pacifica Radio broadcast, 5/2/1971; "The Camp Bust Came Early," *WES*, 5/3/1971, A1; Ralph Graves, "Inside Cruiser One," *Life*, 5/14/1971, 3

two hundred soldiers: Bart Barnes and J. Y. Smith, "Campers Ousted," *WP*, 5/3/1971, A1 *drown in the river:* Minutes of Mayday post-mortem

They didn't alert: Barnes and Smith, *"Campers Ousted"*

221 *"Tora, tora, tora":* John Neary, "The Day Washington Did Not Shut Down," *Life,*
5/14/1971, 30

222 *"Attention: This is":* Transcript, West Potomac Park police warning, JWF

back to Virginia: Henley and Oberman interviews

he hurried down: Davis interview

223 *"We certainly did not come":* Carl Bernstein, "Political Victory Seen by Protesters," *WP,* 5/3/1971, A19

"These fools around us": "Mayday 1971," Pacifica Radio broadcast

224 *"too many people are here":* Ibid.

225 *steered his bicycle:* Richard T. McSorley, "Life Taught Him About Peace, Justice,"
National Catholic Reporter, 8/1/1997, 2

"You are the soldiers": Duncan Spencer, "It Gets 'Scary' as Demonstration
Nears," *WES,* 5/3/71, A3

"Mayday Lives": Nicholas Von Hoffman, "Good Morning Commuters," *WP,*
5/3/1971, D1

226 *"The government would":* *Washington Spring,* Mayday newspaper, 5/3/1971, PHF

Their arraignments: Michael Wald, "Mayday Revisited," *Criminal Law Bulletin,*
vol. 10, no. 1, 1974, 395

everyone else free: "The Camp Bust Came Early," *WES*

227 *"very uptight judge":* Wald interview

a plurality: Louis Harris, "Tide of Public Opinion Turns Decisively Against the
War," *WP,* 5/3/1971, A14

"sending all of us": Julie Nixon Eisenhower, *Pat Nixon: The Untold Story* (New
York: Simon & Schuster, 1986), 317

228 *brought his suitcase:* Ehrlichman, May 1971 diary, 5/2/1971, Box 2, JEP, HI, Stanford

"Your help is needed": "Mayday — What Does It Mean for Federal Employees?,"
movement pamphlet, JWF

He couldn't decide: Ellsberg, *Secrets*; also, Ellsberg video interview with Judy
Gumbo, 2016, author's collection

17. Mayday

230 *"The desire of the president":* Neary, "The Day Washington Did Not"

stick close to Jerry: The emissary was Fred B. Ugast, head of the Justice Department's tax division, described in his oral history in *Washington Lawyer,* Febru-
ary/March 1997

231 *close squad column:* "Riot Formations," MPD manual, undated from 1960s,
JWF

232 *lots of extra film:* MPD special order 12b, 4/29/1971, JWF

"If we are to be": Task Group 5 report, "Paper Flow Process in the Court of General Sessions," 23, Box 23, Harold Greene papers, Library of Congress

"excellent, low, flat": Mayday Tactical Manual, author's collection

233 *crackling nonstop:* "After Action Report, Anti-War Demonstrations, April–May 1971," Prisoner Control Center, MPD, JWF; see also "Progress Report for Special Events or Emergencies," 5/3/1971, JWF; "Transcript of all radio communications pertaining to the May Day Demonstration," 5/1/1972, MPD communications division, JWF; Neary, "The Day Washington Did Not"

234 *his affinity group:* Ellsberg, *Secrets,* 377; Ellsberg video interview

"A liberation movement": Barbara Deming, *Revolution and Equilibrium* (New York: Grossman, 1971), 211

"enchanted with the advocates": Transcript of Agnew speech, Honolulu, 5/2/69, Box 66, EKP, NL

235 *anarchists and pacifists:* Dellinger, *Yale,* 146

"this might be the most": William H. Kuenning, *Free to Go: The Story of a Family's Involvement in the 1971 Mayday Activities in Washington* (Lombard, IL: Unicorn Publications, 1971), 10

"Dan manipulated": J. Anthony Lukas, "A Month in the New Life of Daniel Ellsberg," *NYT Magazine,* 12/12/1971

"Help needed at": MPD radio communications, JWF

236 *"We were told to be":* "City Shutdown Foiled," *WES,* 5/3/1971, A6

an aluminum canoe: Ibid.

milk and cookies: Bill Zimmerman, *Troublemaker* (New York: Doubleday, 2011) 207–11

"While you are sitting": Copy in Mayday Demonstrations, Box 89, JDP, NL

"beefy, beer-drinker's face": Magruder, *American Life,* 70

He hit the gas: Patrick J. Buchanan, *Nixon's White House Wars* (New York: Crown Forum, 2017), 211

237 *"Let's hope that those":* Columbia University *Daily Spectator,* 5/4/1971

Austin-Healey sports car: Lee McGavin, "May Day Demonstration 1971," Story Chip World History Project

"Chief, do you think": MPD radio communications, JWF

"We could either keep": MPD After Action Report, 37, JWF

238 *promised Judge Greene:* Wilson to Harold Greene, 9/2/1969, Box 24, Harold Greene papers, Library of Congress

239 *instant radio documentary:* Author interview with Bill Siemering, 6/7/2019; Cokie Roberts, *This Is NPR: The First Forty Years* (San Francisco: Chronicle, 2010); Michael McCauley, *NPR: The Trials and Triumphs of National Public Radio* (New York: Columbia, 2005); Marc Fisher, *Something in the Air* (New York: Random House, 2007); Steve Oney, "The Philosopher King and the Creation of NPR," Spring 2014, Shorenstein Center, Harvard University

"The listener will have": William H. Siemering to NPR member stations, "Some Things to Consider About ALL THINGS CONSIDERED," 4/8/1971, https://current.org/2016/01/nprs-1971-all-things-considered-launch-memo-to-stations/

"clean of the Mayday mobs": MPD After Action report, 40, JWF

"the act of one is": Testimony in *Washington Mobilization Committee et al. v. Maurice J. Cullinane*, U.S. Court of Appeals, 1976

"jammed to the gunwales": "After Action Report, Anti-War Demonstrations April-May 1971," Prisoner Control Center, Metropolitan Police Dept., 38, JWF

240   *They banged loudly: Mayday RAW*

"bus gassed": Angus Phillips, "But Officer, I Was Only . . . ," WES, 5/4/1971, A1

more than one thousand: MPD After Action Report, JWF

they were penned in: Unsigned, "Shutdown Foiled: 6,000 Protesters Held," WES, 5/3/1971

241   *The pace was frantic*: Dean, *Blind*, 42–43

"a general scene of chaos": Ibid., 43

the First Lady raised hell: Ehrlichman, May 1971 diary, 5/3/1971, Box 2, JEP, HI, Stanford; Dean, *Blind*

Then the Chinooks: "Shutdown Foiled," WES, 5/3/1971; Paul W. Valentine, "7,000 Arrested in Disruptions," WP 5/4/1971

watching an armed assault: Bart Barnes, "The Morning as Viewed from a Copter," WP, 5/4/1971, A14

242   *"bent penny"*: O'Connor interview and unpublished memoir

243   *"arrest anyone that looks"*: Trudy Rubin and Robert Hey, "Mayday Protesters Ask: Did Police Use Legal Procedures?" *Christian Science Monitor*, 5/5/1971, 11

244   *police took note of*: Stuart H. Loory, "Many Arrests Illegal, Public Defender Says," *Los Angeles Times*, 5/5/1971, 14

back of his pants: Bruce Soloway, "Insurrection City," radio documentary, 5/25/1971, Pacifica Radio Archives, BC0582

"I'm under orders to stop": "Mayday 1971: Order Without Law," ACLU study, July 1972, 11

deliberately bumped him: William Basham, "Mass Arrests Tarnish Public Image of Police," WES, 5/5/1971, A9

caught in the dragnet: Bart Barnes, "Mayday Charge Dropped," WP, 6/11/1971, C1

aide for deaf students: "Mayday 1971: Order Without Law," ACLU study, July 1972, 7

245   *Sidney Blumenthal*: Ibid., 12

A young police cadet: Bart Barnes, "Mayday Victims Cite Police Improprieties," WP, 5/30/1971, A1

more than five thousand: MPD After Action report, JWF

246   *"Personal judgment, sir"*: Ackerly to Greene, 5/3/1971, Box 24, Harold Greene papers, Library of Congress

"While I recognize": Ibid.

247   *Go find out*: Babcock interview

18. The Interest of Justice

248   *one huge congregation*: Babcock interview and oral history; Wald interview

249   *human peace symbol*: Deming, *We Cannot Live*, 21

"a kind of slow dance": Conversations with Grace Paley (Jackson: University Press of Mississippi, 1997) 96; Deming, *We Cannot Live,* 21

"We had them, and we": "2000 Confined at Redskins' Practice Field," WES, 5/3/1971, A3

That included the cells: MPD After Action report, 26, JWF

250   *Fort Belvoir:* Meeting notes, Box 23, Harlington Wood Jr. Papers, Illinois History and Lincoln Collections, University of Illinois, Urbana-Champaign

more than twenty-five hundred: Ibid., 45

"extremely important": MPD special order no. 12, 4/28/1971, JWF

251   *"the tough, almost amused":* Henry Allen, "Busted on a 'Disorderly' Rap: 21 Hours in D.C. Jail," *WP,* 5/5/1971, C1

"would be far from ideal": Civil Disobedience and Emergencies, Box 22, Harold Greene papers, Library of Congress

punched and choked: "Mayday 1971," ACLU, 41

252   *expressed sympathy:* Wald, "Mayday Revisited"

Margaret Kleindienst: Unsigned 4 p.m. memo to Richard Kleindienst, 5/3/1971, Box 23, Harlington Wood Jr. Papers, Illinois History and Lincoln Collections, University of Illinois, Urban-Champaign

253   *give them a false name:* Wald interview

"sheriffs, gaolers, and other": Habeas Corpus Act of 1679

"this darling privilege": Cited in Francis Paschal, "The Constitution and Habeas Corpus," *Duke Law Journal* 1970, 605

254   *debate champion:* Babcock, *Fish Raincoats*

"pretty radical ideas:": Author interview with Norman Lefstein, 9/20/2017

"the most lawless thing": Lefstein, Babcock, and Wald interviews

255   *"The cleverness of Rennie Davis' plan":* Valentine, "7,000 Arrested"

256   *"Concern re: 'concentration camp'":* May 1971 diary, 5/3/1971, Box 2, JEP, HI, Stanford

embarrassing leadership: Gumbo interview

"You've got a real sense": NT 494-3, 5/8/1971, 10:15 a.m.

water truck: "1500 Still Await Release," WES, 5/4/1971, A4

257   *"Welcome to Insurrection City!":* Deming, *We Cannot Live,* 22

One young couple: Dash and Edwards, "Portrait of a Prison Compound"

a broken nose: "Mayday: 12,000 Busts Can't Stop People's Peace," *Liberation News Service,* 5/8/1971, 1, PHF; Hoffman, *The Autobiography,* 260; "Suicide Abbie," Box 1, AGP, Michigan; Hoffman interview with *East Village Other,* 5/25/1971

"I guess you're where": Paley, *Conversations,* 97

"Under the American system": Leon Dash and Paul G. Edwards, "Portrait of a Prison Compound," *WP,* 5/4/1971, A14

258   *meet with Kleindienst:* Minutes of Mayday post-mortem

"keep those arrested out": Sanford J. Ungar, "Controversy Mounts Over Arrests Here," *WP,* 5/5/1971, A1

put in a call: "Mayday 1971," ACLU, 53

"hollow cheeked and blank": Mary McGrory, "A Day Filled with Anger," *WP,* 5/4/1971, A3

259 *"almost the most major"*: Carl Bernstein, "Rennie Davis: Make Clear . . . We Failed," *WP,* 5/4/1971, A12

"We dropped a ball": Davis interview

found it "ridiculous": Wells, *War Within,* 505

260 *about ninety stations:* "Debut Broadcast of *All Things Considered,*" 3/29/2017, WNYC

detained by the cops: Oney, "Philosopher King," 3, https://shorensteincenter.org/wp-content/uploads/2014/07/d87-oney.pdf

filled the dead space: All Things Considered, 5/3/1971, recording, NPR archives, University of Maryland

Conley couldn't hear him: Siemering interview

261 *FBI agents slammed:* Davis interview; arrest warrant issued 5/3/1971, PHF

262 *"Rennie Davis symbolizes"*: NT 490-12, 5/4/1971, 10:12 a.m.

acquired a D.C. landmark: S. Oliver Goodman, "Coliseum to Get New Owner," *WP,* 8/13/1969, B7

didn't much like the idea: Morris Siegel, "Siegel at Large," *WES,* 5/7/1971, A3; MPD memos, JWF

263 *"Your honor"*: Partial trial transcript, Box 22, Harold Greene papers, Library of Congress; Public Defender Service, "Legal Services During the 1971 Mayday Demonstrations," 9/1971, 7, Georgetown Law Library

264 *more "trashing"*: Haldeman diary, 5/3/1971, NL

"Pic on evening news": James Rosen, *The Strong Man* (New York: Doubleday, 2008), 111

"Be sure McGovern": Ehrlichman diary, 5/3/1971, Box 2, JEP, HI, Stanford

"Be sure police are hurt": Ibid.

265 *"You can't say that"*: Public Defender Service report, 4

threaten prosecutors: Wald, "Mayday Revisited," 395

"It is extremely unlikely": Show Cause Order, 5/3/1971, Harold Greene papers, Box 22, LOC

issued a stay: Bart Barnes and William L. Claiborne, "2700 More Arrested in Protests," *WES,* 5/5/1971, A1

19. A Heavy Cloud

266 *sea of exhausted refugees:* "Mayday 1971," ACLU; Wald, "Mayday Revisited"; Jim Mann, "Coliseum Diary," *WP,* 5/8/1971, A7; unsigned, "1500 Still Await Release," *WES,* 5/4/1971, A1

267 *only 1,415 of:* L. M. Walters to John Mohr, "9/3/1971, May Day Demonstrations, 1971," Box 10, AGP, Michigan

"I want to see": "Mayday 1971," ACLU, 40; Will R. Wilson, *Fool for a Client* (Austin, TX: Eakin Press, 2000), 135

feeding time: Jim Mann, "Spirits Run High in Coliseum 'Jail,'" *WP,* 5/5/1971, A9
"You can't tell me": Cullinane interview

268 *the lawyers questioned:* Affidavit, DOJ lawyer Eileen M. Stein, cited in "Mayday 1971," ACLU, 39–40
called Kleindienst: Witness testimony, *Dellums v. Powell,* Box 1336, ACLU papers, PU, Princeton
the only working journalist: Mann, "Coliseum Diary"
"Yes, you have those": Harris, *"The New Justice,"* 103

269 *twenty-one hours:* Allen, "Busted"
"good comments": President' news summary, 5/5/1971, Box 30, President's Office Files, NL
protesters had "obliterated": "The Movement, the Medium, and the Message," *WP,* 5/4/1971, A16

270 *a personal column:* Meg Greenfield, "Notes from the Georgetown Front," *WP,* 5/4/1971, A16
might "hurt us": NT 490-12, 5/4/1971, 10:12 a.m.

271 *"The country this time":* NT 490-22, 5/4/1971, 2:14 p.m.
"What do you think": NT 490-16, 5/4/1971, 12:29 p.m.
"Coming in there": NT 490-16, 5/4/1971, 12:09 p.m.
"operates pretty much out": May 1971 Memos, Box 4, EKP, NL

272 *"Goddam it, smear":* NT 490-16, 5/4/1971, 12:09 p.m.
"Only way to do it": NT 490-22, 5/4/1971, 2:14 p.m.
"the crazies who": "President Satisfied on Protest," *WP,* 5/7/1971, A12
"a rather fine job": Ungar, "Mass Arrests Directed by Justice Department," *WP,* 5/5/1971, A1
"a dangerous game": Sam Ervin, "Constitutional Casualties in the War on Crime," *Denver Law Journal,* special edition 1971, cited in Richard Harris, "Reflections: The New Justice," *New Yorker,* 3/25/72, 69–70; also see Karl E. Campbell, *Senator Sam Ervin, Last of the Founding Fathers* (Chapel Hill: University of North Carolina Press, 2014), 337
"the great defender": NT 491-14, 5/5/1971, 9:55 a.m.
"Civil rights types": NT 490-12, 5/4/1971, 10:12 a.m.

273 *"bunch of goddam State Department":* NT 490-16, 5/4/1971, 12:03 p.m.
"Christ's sake": NT 490-24, 5/4/1971, 3:07 p.m.
"mass preventive detention": "Empty Victory," *NYT,* 5/4/1971, 46

274 *"Your performance yesterday":* Written statement, JWF
"I'll leave that up to": Trudy Rubin and Robert Hey, "Mayday Protesters Ask: Did Police Use Legal Procedures?" *Christian Science Monitor,* 5/5/1971, 11
"Every source I've": Ungar, "Mass Arrests"

275 *"must have been the work":* President's news summaries, March 1971, Box 30, President's Office Files, NL
"It sort of failed": Unsigned, "Red, White, Blue, and Satisfied," *WP,* 5/5/1971, C3

"saved our country": NT 491-14, 5/5/1971, 9:55 a.m.

"Mass arrests expected": Status report, Mayday Demonstrations, Box 77, Charles Colson papers, NL

276   *"under assault over there"*: NT 490-22, 5/4/1971, 2:30 p.m.

"It's awfully effective": NT 490-24, 5/4/1971, 3:07 p.m.

"The package is now moving": Unsigned, "The FBI Homes In and Gets Its Man," *NYT*, 5/5/1971, A1

277   *"Offenders are dancing"*: Dean to Nixon, "Demonstration Status Report May 4, 5:00 p.m.," Charles Colson papers, Box 77, NL

"not a brute": Author interview with former ACLU Executive Director Florence Isbell, 3/29/2014

"restraining forces": Fred J. Cook, "Are Mass Arrests the Right Answer?" *NYT*, 6/6/1971, E7

"You know, he's a sort": NT 490-16, 5/4/1971, 12:09 p.m.

278   *"a dab of rancid"*: John Mathews, "New Sense of Community," *WES*, 5/6/1971, A5

sleep at his house: Ken Wachsberger, *The Ballad of Ken and Emily* (Ann Arbor: Azenphony Press, 1997)

279   *"I think they collected"*: Isbell interview

"are not going to put": Bart Barnes and William Claiborne, "2700 More Arrested in Protests," *WP*, 5/5/1971, A9

"Why the hell didn't": NT 490-22, 5/4/1971, 2:30 p.m.

"Ol' Kleindienst has": NT 490-24, 5/4/1971, 3:19 p.m.

"What kind of animals": NT 2-76, 5/4/1971, 4:29 p.m.

280   *"do something special"*: Ibid.

"outmaneuvered these guys": NT 490-24, 5/4/1971, 3:19 p.m.

"Oh hell," Ehrlichman said: Ibid.

281   *"We would submit"*: Babcock, Lefstein interviews; Public Defender Service report 11

20. The Holdouts

282   *"This is not a small"*: Unsigned, "Appeal Panel Upholds Prisoner Release Order," *WES*, 5/5/1971, A1

283   *crumpled the order*: Lefstein interview; Wald, "Mayday Revisited"; Public Defender Service report

"It was terrible": Harris, "The New Justice," 102

"undermined the Constitution": Woody West, "Justice Official Defends Procedure in Arrests," *WES*, 5/6/1971, A1

"For the first time": William Basham, "Mass Arrests Tarnish Public Image of Police," *WES*, 5/5/1971, A9

284   *"liberal media thrust"*: Jack Caulfield to Dean, 5/5/1971, Box 89, JDP, NL

"There is an undertow": Buchanan to Haldeman, 5/5/1971, Box 77, Charles Colson papers, NL

seek to dismantle: Stephen E. Gottlieb, *Morality Imposed: The Rehnquist Court and the State of Liberty in America* (New York: NYU Press, 2000), 3

285 *"Martial law is":* "Mayday 1971," ACLU, 14

never tried to correct: Senate Judiciary Committee Hearings, November 3–10, 1971, Supreme Court nominations of William H. Rehnquist and Lewis F. Powell

"even if one believes": Congressional Record, 92nd Congress, 12/2/1971 to 12/7/1971

286 *a raised fist:* John Mathews, "New Sense of Community," *WES,* 5/6/1971, A5

watched in anger: Author interview with Janis McDonald, 11/15/2018

"There was a feeling": Froines interview

287 *"fucking Jews":* George Lardner Jr. and Michael Dobbs, "New Tapes Reveal Depth of Nixon's Anti-Semitism," *WP,* 10/6/1999, A31

"Aren't the Chicago Seven": NT 491-14, 5/5/1971, 9:35 a.m.

288 *met that morning:* Plaintiff filing, *Dellums v. Powell* case file, Box 1336, ACLU records, PU, Princeton

the president followed: NT 491-14, 5/5/1971, 9:35 a.m.

289 *"They've got guys":* Ibid.

"It shouldn't be on": James M. Naughton, "Protesters Failed to Stop Congress," *NYT,* 5/6/1971, A1

290 *Powell, was unnerved: Dellums v. Powell* case file, Box 1336, ACLU records, PU, Princeton; also see *Dellums v. Powell,* U.S. Court of Appeals for the D.C. Circuit, 1977, 566 F.2nd, 167

"Should we lock 'em up?": Caplan interview

291 *clear on the rules:* Ibid.

an "unlawful assembly": Naughton, "Protesters Fail"

"Let them tell their story": Dellums v. Powell case file, PU, Princeton

Dellums rushed over: Trudy Rubin, "Arrest Tactics Placed in Legal Glare," *Christian Science Monitor,* 5/8/1971, 1

"They didn't give a damn": William L. Claiborne and Bart Barnes, "1,200 Protesters Arrested at Capitol," *WP,* 5/6/1971, A1

"Balls! He's lying!": NT 493-3, 5/6/1971, 9:41 a.m.

"with intent to impede": Naughton, "Protesters Fail"

292 *"Do you think we're":* NT 493-3, 5/5/1971, 3:31 p.m.

"has purposely declined": Richard Prince and Henry Aubin, "Wilson Says He, Not Justice, Made Arrest Decision," *WP,* 5/6/1971, A14

293 *"Wilson went to the mat":* NT 492-7, 5/5/1971, 5:45 p.m.

"I wish they'd have": NT 492-7, 5/5/1971, 6:03 p.m.

294 *"I see anybody do that":* Ibid.

"violent backlash": NT 002-095, 5/5/1971, 6:13 p.m.

shocked and angered: Wald, "Mayday Revisited," 421

histories of arrest: Babcock, Wald, Lefstein interviews; Public Defender Service for the District of Columbia, "Legal Services During the 1971 Mayday Demonstrations," 1971; Wald, "Mayday Revisited"

295 *smacked them*: Findings, *Dellums v. Powell*, U.S. Court of Appeals, D.C. Circuit 1977, 566 F.2nd, 216

"Hi, I'm Michael Wald": Wald interview and Wald, "Mayday Revisited", 422

296 *handed their freedom*: Wald interview; William N. Curry and Maurine Beasley, "Judges Free 382 Confined Since Monday," *WP,* 5/6/1971, A8

21. Aftermath

297 *"the worst reviews"*: Mary McGrory, "Mayday: Act One, Act Two," *WES,* 5/9/1971, B1

298 *Bowman crucified*: Wald, "Mayday Revisited," 519

299 *"had a hatred"*: Harris, "The New Justice"

300 *"the world might have been"*: UPI, "Protesters Like Nazis," *WES,* 5/12/17, D1

"Glad you could all": John Andrews to President's file, 5/6/1971, Box 81, President's Office Files, NL

"Do they have any kind": NT 493-3, 5/6/1971, 9:26 a.m.

301 *"They ran over one"*: NT 493-9, 5/6/1971, 11:09 a.m.

"we don't want to appear": NT 496-12, 5/10/1971, 2:40 p.m.

"one of our tougher": Oudes, *From the President*, 247–48

"Let's give Wilson": NT 493-20, 5/6/1971, 5:05 p.m.

302 *"second-guessers and"*: NT 494-3, 5/8/1971, 10:23 a.m.

"don't take the question": Minutes of Mayday post-mortem

"drunk, crude, and terribly": Oudes, *From the President*, 250–54

"deliberately turning up": Ibid.

303 *"We were good"*: Cullinane interview

"perhaps in retrospect": "Demonstrations in Washington," advertisement, *WES,* 5/10/1971, back page

"Stand firm. The calls": Jerry Wilson, typewritten statement, JWF

Democrats' leading choice: "Kennedy Passes Muskie in Poll as 1972 Choice of Democrats," *NYT,* 5/16/1971, 23

"masses of innocent": William L. Claiborne, "Mitchell Warns on Protests," *WP,* 5/11/1971, A1

decried the tactics: Unsigned, "Protest Arrests Held Not Justified," *WP,* 5/12/1971, B9

"citizens were arrested": Marine Beasley, "Mayday Weakens Court, Police Ties," *WP,* 5/30/1971, A9

304 *"his decision and his"*: William L. Claiborne, "Mitchell Warns on Protests," *WP,* 5/11/1971, A1

"the general impetus": Plaintiff's exhibit, *Dellums v. Powell*, Box 1336, ACLU papers, PU, Princeton

in contact with Kleindienst: Ibid.

"I don't want the impression": NT 493-20, 5/6/1971, 5:05 p.m.

305 *"I got a hold of Mitchell"*: NT 500-17, 5/18/1971, 12:16 p.m.

"Now, you can get": NT 59-2, 6/3/1971, 9:51 a.m.

"They said, 'It would be'": Wald interview

306 *"I got this ad together"*: Isbell interview; *WP* advertisement, 5/17/1971

full-page advertisements: Ibid.

"a cry of attempted": Dean to Colson, 5/17/1971, Box 89, JDP, NL

innocent people: Colson to Dean, 5/11/1971, Box 89, JDP, NL

"the question may be": Dapray Muir to Dean, undated 5/1971, Box 89, JDP, NL

307 *The judge struck down:* B. D. Colen, "Parade Permit Law Again Overturned," *WP,* 1/8/1972, B5

"it was a reasonably": Timothy S. Robinson, "Liability of D.C. Police Chiefs in Protest is Upheld," *WP,* 7/4/1978, C1

308 *Department of Labor employees:* "2 in Capital Win Suits on Arrest," *NYT,* 10/4/1972, 36

the government's revocation: UPI, "Judge Calls U.S. Voiding of Mayday Permit Illegal," *NYT,* 7/10/1971, 7

twenty-one cases: "21 Demonstrators Face Mayday Trial," *WP,* 12/9/1971, B1

"one of our most visible": Gilbert, *Love and Struggle,* 170

309 *"We know this for"*: Copy of Weather Underground letter, PHF

"Since I knew nothing": "Tell Us All About Your Friends: The Grand Jury System," interview broadcast, 10/18/1971, WBAI, Pacifica Radio Archives, BC0364

"The government is": Wallace Turner, "Miss Bacon Is Sent to Jail," *NYT,* 5/20/1971, 20

"It's a total frame-up": Unsigned, "Cambridge Woman Subpoenaed," *Boston Globe,* 5/24/1971, 29

"An FBI agent has told": UPI, "Activist Denies Any Role," *NYT,* 5/21/1971, 20

310 *jogging in place:* Ehrlichman memo, 1/9/1971, Box 2, JEP, HI, Stanford

"when people come in": Transcript, President's News Conference, *NYT,* 6/2/1971, 24

311 *the sharpest exchange:* "All Things Considered," 6/2/1971, NPR archives, University of Maryland

"Well, they all ganged up": NT 4-6, 6/1/1971, 9:20 p.m.

"What do you think": NT 4-17, 6/1/1971, 10:23 p.m.

"That was marvelous": NT 4-14, 6/1/1971, 10:17 p.m.

"The way they badgered": NT 4-8, 6/1/1971, 9:38 p.m.

312 *"Bob, let me tell you"*: NT 4-10, 6/1/1971, 9:51 p.m.

"may themselves conceivably": Memo, "Re: Dellums v. Powell, D.D.C.," U.S. Solicitor General Robert H. Bork to Philip Buchen, 6/3/1976, Box 29, Philip Buchen papers, Gerald R. Ford Presidential Library, Ann Arbor, Michigan. Bork wrote this memo three years after he famously obeyed Nixon's order to fire Watergate prosecutor Archibald Cox following the resignations of two other Justice officials who refused to go along with the president. Bork became a well-known conservative judge and in 1987 was nominated by President Ronald Reagan to

the Supreme Court. His nomination was rejected by the Senate after a tumultuous political battle.

313 *"criminally traitorous"*: Tom Wells, *Wild Man: The Life and Times of Daniel Ellsberg* (New York and London: Palgrave Macmillan, 2001), 459
far to the left: Hersh, *Price of Power*, 384
"we were in a 'revolutionary'": Nixon, *RN*, 513
"panic sessions": J. Anthony Lukas, "State of Siege," *NYT Magazine*, 7/22/1973
demanded they halt: Ben Bradlee, *A Good Life* (New York: Simon & Schuster, 1995), 308

314 *"time of high national"*: Magruder, *American Life*, 197
"intensified the pressures": Ibid., 165
"They don't all happen": NT 521-13, 6/15/1971, 5:13 p.m.

315 *"the most dangerous man"*: Hersh, *Price of Power*, 385
"Once we get the war": NT 490-22, 5/4/1971, 2:30 p.m.
"Bob, you remember": NT 525-1, 6/17/1971, 5:15 p.m.
"crazy scheme": Dean interview
"I really need a": NT 534-5, 7/1/1971, 10:27 a.m.

316 *Ehrlichman, sent*: Ehrlichman to Nixon, 5/20/1971, Box 4, EKP, NL
"I couldn't feel better": NT 4-23, 6/3/1971, 7:43 p.m.
shifting "his wrath": Epstein, *"The Krogh File,"* 123

317 *handed Bud a file*: Krogh, *Integrity*, 17; Krogh Watergate testimony

Epilogue

318 *"the whole antiwar"*: Dean interview
"proud as punch": Ibid.

319 *"should logically have been"*: Dean, *Blind*, 47
"You're going to have to": Transcript, Krogh interview, 2/5/1997, Box 2, "Eye of the Storm" Documentary Film Collection, Russell Library, University of Georgia
"Never told Bud to lie": Dean interview
polls had reversed: Gallup Poll release, "President Nixon's Popularity at Highest Point in 14 Months," 3/9/1972

320 *"seamy things"*: NT 886-8, 3/21/1973, 10:12 a.m.
"He was a traitor": Monica Crowley, *Nixon in Winter* (New York: Random House, 1998), 297
tried to hide: Seymour Hersh, "Young Says Ehrlichman Took 'Sensitive' Memos," *NYT*, 7/2/1974, 22

321 *"the most extreme"*: Krogh, *Integrity*, 2
"Someday when you": NT 920-3, 5/16/1973, 4:55 p.m.
"I think what we've": Waters, "The Agony"

322 *"My motive was"*: Timothy S. Robinson, "Admits Justice Obstruction in Ellsberg Trial," *WP*, 6/4/1974, A1
a different matter: During his confirmation hearings for Attorney General,

Kleindienst falsely testified that Nixon hadn't ordered him to drop an antitrust case against ITT Corporation.

doubt on the testimony: Adam Liptak, "New Look at an Old Memo Casts More Doubt on Rehnquist," *NYT,* 3/20/2012, A18

323 *"thin" and "illogical":* Rehnquist book outline, "Death in the Paw Paw Tunnel," Box 193, Rehnquist papers, HI, Stanford

324 *skip tracers:* Author interview with ACLU legal director Art Spitzer, 6/11/2015

"But in a very real": Dellums v. Powell case file, Box 1336, ACLU records, PU, Princeton

the largest judgment: The case was *Dellums v. Powell,* 566 F2d 167, decided August 4, 1977.

325 *Whitewater investigation:* In re Grand Jury Proceedings, U.S. District Court, D.C., 5/27/1998, 5 F.Supp.2d 21 (1998)

Mike Espy: In re Sealed Case, U.S. Court of Appeals, D.C., 8/29/1997, 121 F.3d 729 (1997)

energy policy: In re Cheney, U.S. Supreme Court, 6/24/2004, 03-475

326 *ordered the records destroyed:* The case was *Sullivan v. Murphy,* 478 F.2d 938 156 U.S. App.D.C. 28, decided April 16, 1973.

"overly cautious": Paul W. Valentine, "D.C. Paid $3 Million in 2 Years to Citizens in Lawsuits," *WP,* 9/21/1975, 25

"The White House": A Quaker Action Group v. Morton, 516 F.2d 717 (1975)

327 *"what was done in":* Washington Mobilization Committee v. Maurice J. Cullinane, Court of Appeals, D.C., 9/14/1977, 566 F.2d 107

"a singularly far-reaching": Ricardo J. Bascuas, "The Unconstitutionality of 'Hold Until Cleared': Reexamining Material Witness Detentions in the Wake of the September 11th Dragnet," *Vanderbilt Law Review* 677 (2005), 58. See also Michael Greenberger, "Indefinite Material Witness Protection Without Probable Cause," working paper, University of Maryland School of Law, January 2004

328 *"very often prevents":* Caulfield to Krogh, 3/11/1970, Box 6, EKP, NL

Nixon himself gave: NT 752-13, 7/25/72, 2:29 p.m.

329 *"This is the honest-to-God":* Neiburger interview

"people are here": "Capitol Bombing Affidavit Draft," Box 9, AGP, Michigan

330 *"Get the hell":* Gumbo interviews

Judy told listeners: "Tell Us All About Your Friends," Pacifica Radio Archives

Dohrn and Boudin: Collier and Horowitz, *Destructive Generation,* 105; Braudy, *Family Circle,* 240–45; Burrough, *Days of Rage,* 163–64

331 *"scouted the target":* Jacobs, *The Way the Wind Blew,* 129

"We may consider use": FBI airtel, Director to Albany, 12/22/71, Box 10, AGP, Michigan

"on several occasions": Manuscripts and Writings, Box 2, AGP, Michigan

"I was a shaper": Name and Correspondence Files, Box 6, AGP, Michigan

singling out Stew: Kathleen Rout, *Eldridge Cleaver* (Boston: Twayne, 1991), 148

332 *"were a wonderful":* Stew Albert, "Death of a Salesman," 9/1996, *Tikkun* 48

"The yippies and Weather": Bernardine Dohrn, "Eulogy for Stew Albert," *Monthly Review Online,* 6/6/2006

"Explain why the end": Manuscripts and Writings, Box 2, AGP, Michigan

333 *reveal the identities:* Froines interview

"When Mayday was over": Ibid.

334 *"cross the planet":* "Rennie Davis, Antiwar Activist, Now Focuses Life on Guru, 15," *NYT,* 5/6/1973, 57

"Now the facts": Michael Kirkhorn, "Radicals Plan New Maydays in Washington This Fall," *WP,* 6/28/1971, A2

"At some point": Dellinger, *Revolutionary Nonviolence,* acknowledgments

Dave was among: Paul L. Montgomery, "End of War Rally Brings Out 50,000," *NYT,* 5/12/1975, 11

335 *remains in touch:* O'Connor, Mallory, Butz interviews

336 *"I gave a little speech":* Babcock oral history, American Bar Association

"I do not believe": Diane Rogers, "Winning Ways," *Stanford Magazine,* 3/2003

338 *"I think it was contagious":* Cullinane interview

"It is difficult": Nixon, *RN,* 471

"a brotherhood of the misguided": Richard Nixon, *No More Vietnams* (New York: Arbor House, 1985), 19

"The most massive": Wood, *Unmarked Trail,* 113–15

339 *"repressive fascist":* Tim Weiner, *One Man Against the World* (New York: Holt, 2015), 261

"to move from the kid": Huston testimony, Senate Select Report on Watergate

340 *"I would tell him":* Krogh interview, 2/5/1997, Box 1, "Eye of the Storm" documentary film collection, Russell Library, University of Georgia

341 *58,276 Americans:* Michael E. Ruane, "Audit Finds Misspellings, Duplicates on Vietnam Wall," *WP,* 5/23/2019, B5

Selected Bibliography

Any study of the Vietnam antiwar movement has to begin with the encyclopedic and insightful work by Tom Wells, *The War Within: America's Battle over Vietnam* (Berkeley: University of California Press, 1994). I am indebted to the foundation and detail Wells provides about the underpinnings and events of spring 1971. Lucy Barber's excellent study, *Marching on Washington: The Forging of an American Political Tradition* (Berkeley: University of California, 2002), puts Mayday in broad historical and political perspective. Charles DeBenedetti, in *An American Ordeal: The Antiwar Movement of the Vietnam Era* (New York: Syracuse University Press, 1990), effectively traces the movement's ideological evolution, as does the rich collection of essays in *Give Peace a Chance: Exploring the Vietnam Antiwar Movement* (New York: Syracuse University Press, 1992), edited by Melvin Small and William Hoover. *Home to War: A History of the Vietnam Veterans' Movement* (New York: Crown, 2001), by Gerald Nicosia, is the most comprehensive study of the VVAW. Fred Halstead's engaging memoir *Out Now!: A Participant's Account of the Movement in the United States Against the Vietnam War* (New York: Mondad, 1978) is full of useful first-person stories. Among the analyses of the ideology and tactics involved in Mayday, and its broader implications for American dissent, L. A. Kauffman's *Direct Action: Protest and the Reinvention of American Radicalism* (Brooklyn, NY, and London: Verso, 2018) stands out.

Achenbach, Joel. 2005. *The Grand Idea: George Washington's Potomac and the Race to the West.* New York: Simon & Schuster Paperbacks.

Aguilar-San Juan, Karin and Frank Joyce, eds. 2015. *The People Make the Peace: Lessons from the Vietnam Antiwar Movement.* Charlottesville, VA: Just World Books.

Albert, Judith Clavir, and Stewart Edward Albert, eds. 1984. *The Sixties Papers: Documents of a Rebellious Decade.* New York: Praeger.

Albert, Stewart Edward. 2003. *Who the Hell Is Stew Albert?: A Memoir.* Los Angeles: Red Hen Press.

Ambrose, Stephen E. 1989. *Nixon, Vol. 2: The Triumph of a Politician, 1962–1972.* New York: Simon & Schuster.

Appy, Christian G. 2003. *Patriots: The Vietnam War Remembered from All Sides.* New York: Viking.

Ayers, Bill. 2009. *Fugitive Days: Memoirs of an Antiwar Activist.* Boston: Beacon Press.

Babcock, Barbara. 2016. *Fish Raincoats: A Woman Lawyer's Life.* Journeys and Memoirs. New Orleans, LA: Quid Pro, LLC.

Barber, Lucy. 2002. *Marching on Washington: The Forging of an American Political Tradition.* Berkeley: University of California Press.

Berg, Scott W. 2007. *Grand Avenues: The Story of the French Visionary Who Designed Washington, D.C.* New York: Pantheon Books.

Berger, Dan. 2005. *Outlaws of America: The Weather Underground and the Politics of Solidarity.* Chico, CA: AK Press.

Bingham, Clara. 2016. *Witness to the Revolution: Radicals, Resisters, Vets, Hippies, and the Year America Lost Its Mind and Found Its Soul.* New York: Random House.

Bowling, Kenneth R. 1988. *Creating the Federal City, 1774–1800: Potomac Fever.* Octagon Research Series. Washington, DC: American Institute of Architects.

Boyer, Gene T, and Jackie Boor. 2011. *Inside the President's Helicopter.* Brule, WI: Cable Pub.

Braudy, Susan. 2004. *Family Circle: The Boudins and the Aristocracy of the Left.* New York: Anchor Books.

Brinkley, Douglas. 2004. *Tour of Duty: John Kerry and the Vietnam War.* New York: William Morrow.

Brinkley, Douglas, and Luke Nichter, eds. 2014. *The Nixon Tapes: 1971–1972.* Boston: Houghton Mifflin Harcourt.

Bryan, John. 1998. *Whatever Happened to Timothy Leary?* San Francisco: Renaisence Press.

Buchanan, Patrick J. 2017. *Nixon's White House Wars: The Battles That Made and Broke a President and Divided America Forever.* New York: Crown Forum.

Burrough, Bryan. 2015. *Days of Rage: America's Radical Underground, the FBI, and the Forgotten Age of Revolutionary Violence.* New York: Penguin Press.

Collier, Peter, and David Horowitz. 2006. *Destructive Generation: Second Thoughts About the Sixties.* San Francisco: Encounter Books.

Collins, Judy. 2011. *Sweet Judy Blue Eyes: My Life in Music.* New York: Crown Archetype.

Crowley, Monica. 1998. *Nixon in Winter.* New York: Random House.

Dallek, Robert. 2007. *Kissinger and Nixon: Partners in Power.* New York: Harper.

Danielson, Leilah. 2014. *American Gandhi: A. J. Muste and the History of Radicalism in the Twentieth Century.* Philadelphia: University of Pennsylvania Press.

Davis, Rennie. 2017. *The New Humanity: A Movement to Change the World.* Las Vegas: BlissLife Press.

Dean, John W. 1976. *Blind Ambition: The White House Years.* New York: Simon and Schuster.

———. 2014. *The Nixon Defense: What He Knew and When He Knew It.* New York: Viking.

DeBenedetti, Charles. 1990. *An American Ordeal: The Antiwar Movement of the Vietnam Era.* Syracuse, NY: Syracuse University Press.

Dellinger, David T. 1993. *From Yale to Jail: The Life Story of a Moral Dissenter.* New York: Pantheon.

———. 1975. *More Power Than We Know: The People's Movement Toward Democracy.* Garden City, NY: Anchor Press/Doubleday.

———. 1971. *Revolutionary Nonviolence.* New York: Doubleday.

Deming, Barbara. 1974. *We Cannot Live Without Our Lives.* New York: Grossman Publishers.

Dickson, Paul, and Thomas B. Allen. 2004. *The Bonus Army: An American Epic.* New York: Walker & Co.

Dohrn, Bernardine, William Ayers, Jeff Jones, and Weather Underground Organization, eds. 2006. *Sing a Battle Song: The Revolutionary Poetry, Statements, and Communiqués of the Weather Underground, 1970–1974.* New York: Seven Stories Press.

Donner, Frank J. 1990. *Protectors of Privilege: Red Squads and Police Repression in Urban America.* Berkeley: University of California Press.

Eckstein, Arthur M. 2016. *Bad Moon Rising: How the Weather Underground Beat the FBI and Lost the Revolution.* New Haven, CT: Yale University Press.

Ehrlichman, John. 1982. *Witness to Power: The Nixon Years.* New York: Simon & Schuster.

Eisenhower, Julie Nixon. 1986. *Pat Nixon: The Untold Story.* New York: Simon & Schuster.

Ellsberg, Daniel. 2002. *Secrets: A Memoir of Vietnam and the Pentagon Papers.* New York: Viking.

Epstein, Edward Jay. 1990. *Agency of Fear: Opiates and Political Power in America,* rev. ed. London and New York: Verso.

Farber, David R. 1988. *Chicago '68.* Chicago: University of Chicago Press.

Farrell, John A. 2017. *Richard Nixon: The Life.* New York: Doubleday.

Fonda, Jane. 2005. *My Life So Far.* New York: Random House.

Garment, Leonard. 1997. *Crazy Rhythm: My Journey from Brooklyn, Jazz, and Wall Street to Nixon's White House, Watergate, and Beyond.* New York: Times Books.

Gentry, Curt. 2001. *J. Edgar Hoover: The Man and the Secrets.* New York: Norton.

Gilbert, Ben W. 1968. *Ten Blocks from the White House: An Anatomy of the Washington Riots of 1968.* London: Pall Mall Press.

Gilbert, David. 2012. *Love and Struggle: My Life in SDS, the Weather Underground, and Beyond.* Oakland, CA: PM Press.

Gilbert, Marc Jason, ed. 2002. *Why the North Won the Vietnam War.* New York: Palgrave.

Gitlin, Todd. 1987. *The Sixties: Years of Hope, Days of Rage.* Toronto and New York: Bantam Books.

———. 1980. *The Whole World Is Watching: Mass Media in the Making and Unmaking of the New Left.* Berkeley: University of California Press.

Gottlieb, Stephen E. 2000. *Morality Imposed: The Rehnquist Court and the State of Liberty in America.* New York: NYU Press.

Greenberg, Amy S. 2013. *A Wicked War: Polk, Clay, Lincoln, and the 1846 U.S. Invasion of Mexico.* New York: Vintage.

Greenfield, Robert. 2006. *Timothy Leary: A Biography.* Orlando: Harcourt.

Gregg, Richard. 1934. *The Power of Nonviolence.* Cambridge, UK: Cambridge University Press.

Haldeman, H. R. 1978. *The Ends of Power.* New York: Dell.

———. 1994. *The Haldeman Diaries: Inside the Nixon White House.* New York: G. P. Putnam's Sons.

Halstead, Fred. 1978. *Out Now!: A Participant's Account of the Movement in the United States Against the Vietnam War.* New York: Monad.

Harmon, Mark. 2011. *Found, Featured, Then Forgotten: U.S. Network TV News and the Vietnam Veterans Against the War.* Knoxville, TN: Newfound Press.

Hayden, Tom. 1988. *Reunion: A Memoir.* New York: Random House.

Herr, Michael. 1991. *Dispatches.* New York: Vintage Books.

Hines, Christian. 1866. *Early Recollections of Washington City.* Washington: Columbia Historical Society. Washington Junior League reprint, 1981.

Hoffman, Abbie. 2000. *The Autobiography of Abbie Hoffman.* New York: Four Walls Eight Windows.

Hunt, Andrew E. 2006. *David Dellinger: The Life and Times of a Nonviolent Revolutionary.* New York: NYU Press.

———. 2001. *The Turning: A History of Vietnam Veterans Against the War.* New York: NYU Press.

Isserman, Maurice, and Michael Kazin. 2015. *America Divided: The Civil War of the 1960s.* New York: Oxford University Press.

Jacobs, Ron. 1997. *The Way the Wind Blew: A History of the Weather Underground.* Brooklyn and London: Verso.

Kane, Rod. 1990. *Veteran's Day.* New York: Orion Books.

Kauffman, L. A. 2017. *Direct Action: Protest and the Reinvention of American Radicalism.* Brooklyn and London: Verso.

Kerry, John. 2018. *Every Day Is Extra.* New York: Simon & Schuster.

Kerry, John, and Vietnam Veterans Against the War. 1971. *The New Soldier*. New York: Macmillan.

Kissinger, Henry. 1979. *White House Years*. Boston: Little, Brown.

———. 2003. *Ending the Vietnam War: A History of America's Involvement In and Extrication From The Vietnam War*. New York: Simon & Schuster.

Kleindienst, Richard G. 1985. *Justice: The Memoirs of Attorney General Richard Kleindienst*. Ottawa, IL: Jameson Books.

Krassner, Paul, ed. 1999. *Paul Krassner's Impolite Interviews*. New York: Seven Stories Press.

Krogh, Egil, and Matthew Krogh. 2007. *Integrity: Good People, Bad Choices, and Life Lessons from the White House*. New York: PublicAffairs.

Kusch, Frank. 2008. *Battleground Chicago: The Police and the 1968 Democratic National Convention*. Chicago: University of Chicago Press.

Kutler, Stanley I., ed. 1998. *Abuse of Power: The New Nixon Tapes*. New York: Simon & Schuster.

Lukas, J. Anthony. 1971. *Don't Shoot — We Are Your Children!* New York: Random House.

———. 1976. *Nightmare: The Underside of the Nixon Years*. New York: Viking.

Lynd, Staughton, ed. 1966. *Nonviolence in America: A Documentary History*. Indianapolis, IN: Bobbs-Merrill.

Lyttle, Bradford. 2014. *Peace Activist: The Autobiography of Bradford Lyttle*. Indianapolis, IN: Dog Ear Publishing.

MacKenzie, Angus. 1999. *Secrets: The CIA's War at Home*. Berkeley: University of California Press.

Magruder, Jeb Stuart. 1974. *An American Life: One Man's Road to Watergate*. New York: Atheneum.

Mailer, Norman. 1994. *The Armies of the Night: History as a Novel, the Novel as History*. Reprint. New York: Plume.

Massing, Michael. 2000. *The Fix*. Berkeley: University of California Press.

Mollenhoff, Clark R. 1976. *Game Plan for Disaster: An Ombudsman's Report on the Nixon Years*. New York: Norton.

Moss, George. 2010. *Vietnam, an American Ordeal*. Upper Saddle River, NJ: Prentice Hall.

Nicosia, Gerald. 2001. *Home to War: A History of the Vietnam Veterans' Movement*. New York: Crown Publishers.

Nixon, Richard M. 1990. *RN: The Memoirs of Richard Nixon, with a New Introduction*. The Richard Nixon Library Edition. New York: Simon & Schuster.

Oudes, Bruce, ed. 1989. *From the President: Richard Nixon's Secret Files*. New York: Harper & Row.

Packer, George. 2019. *Our Man: Richard Holbrooke and the End of the American Century*. New York: Knopf.

Perlstein, Rick. 2008. *Nixonland: The Rise of a President and the Fracturing of America*. New York: Scribner.

Perry, Lewis. 2013. *Civil Disobedience: An American Tradition*. New Haven: Yale University Press.

Powers, Richard Gid. 1987. *Secrecy and Power: The Life of J. Edgar Hoover*. New York and London: Free Press; Collier Macmillan.

Prados, John. 2009. *Vietnam: The History of an Unwinnable War, 1945–1975*. Modern War Studies. Lawrence: University Press of Kansas.

Reeves, Richard. 2001. *President Nixon: Alone in the White House*. New York: Simon & Schuster.

Rosen, James. 2008. *The Strong Man: John Mitchell and the Secrets of Watergate*. New York: Doubleday.

Rosen, Ruth. 2006. *The World Split Open: How the Modern Women's Movement Changed America*. New York: Penguin Books.

Rosenfeld, Seth. 2012. *Subversives: The FBI's War on Student Radicals, and Reagan's Rise to Power*. New York: Farrar, Straus and Giroux.

Rout, Kathleen. 1991. *Eldridge Cleaver*. Boston: Twayne Publishers.

Rubin, Jerry. 1970. *Do It!: Scenarios of the Revolution*. New York: Simon & Schuster.

Schell, Jonathan. 1976. *The Time of Illusion*. New York: Vintage Books.

Small, Melvin. 2002. *Antiwarriors: The Vietnam War and the Battle for America's Hearts and Minds*. Lanham, MD: Rowman & Littlefield.

———. 1988. *Johnson, Nixon, and the Doves*. New Brunswick: Rutgers University Press.

Small, Melvin, and William Hoover, eds. 1992. *Give Peace a Chance: Exploring the Vietnam Antiwar Movement*. Syracuse, NY: Syracuse University Press. See especially Chapter 5: George W. Hopkins, "May Day 1971: Civil Disobedience and the Vietnam Antiwar Movement."

Snodgrass, Mary Ellen. 2009. *Civil Disobedience: An Encyclopedic History of Dissidence in the United States*. New York: Routledge.

Stacewicz, Richard, ed. 1997. *Winter Soldiers: An Oral History of the Vietnam Veterans Against the War*. New York: Twayne.

Thomas, Evan. 2015. *Being Nixon: A Man Divided*. New York: Random House.

Tracy, James. 1996. *Direct Action: Radical Pacifism From the Union Eight to the Chicago Seven*. Chicago: University of Chicago Press.

Ungar, Sanford J. 1976. *FBI*. Boston: Little, Brown.

Weiner, Tim. 2015. *One Man Against the World: The Tragedy of Richard Nixon*, 1st ed. New York: Henry Holt and Company.

Wells, Tom. 1994. *The War Within: America's Battle over Vietnam*. Berkeley: University of California Press.

———. 2001. *Wild Man: The Life and Times of Daniel Ellsberg*. London and New York: Palgrave MacMillan.

Wertheimer, Linda, and National Public Radio (U.S.), eds. 1995. *Listening to America: Twenty-Five Years in the Life of a Nation, as Heard on National Public Radio*. Boston: Houghton Mifflin.

White, Theodore H. 1975. *Breach of Faith: The Fall of Richard Nixon.* New York: Atheneum.

Wilson, Jerry V. 1975. *Police Report: A View of Law Enforcement.* Boston: Little, Brown.

Wood, Harlington. 2008. *An Unmarked Trail.* Petersburg, IL: H. Wood.

Young, Marilyn B. 1992. *The Vietnam Wars, 1945–1990.* New York: Harper Perennial.

Zaroulis, N. L. 1984. *Who Spoke Up?: American Protest Against the War in Vietnam, 1963–1975.* Garden City, NY: Doubleday.

Zimmerman, Bill. 2011. *Troublemaker: A Memoir from the Front Lines of the Sixties.* Garden City, NY: Doubleday.

Films

1971. Directed by Johanna Hamilton. New York: First Run Features, 2014.

Berkeley in the Sixties. Directed by Mark Kitchell. San Francisco: California Newsreel, 1990.

Fog of War: Eleven Lessons from the Life of Robert S. McNamara. Directed by Errol Morris. New York: Sony Pictures Classics, 2003.

FTA. Directed by Francine Parker. Los Angeles: American International Pictures, 1972

Going Upriver: The Long War of John Kerry. Directed by George Butler. Washington, DC: Thinkfilm, 2004.

Let a Thousand Parks Bloom. Directed by Leonard Lipton. Berkeley: Canyon Cinema, 1969.

Mayday 1971 Raw. Directed by Skip Blumberg. Washington, DC: Videofreex; Mayday Video, 2017.

Our Nixon. Directed by Penny Lane. Atlanta: CNN Films; Cinedigm, 2013.

The Weather Underground. Directed by Sam Green and Bill Siegel. Los Angeles: Docurama, 2002.

Underground. Directed by Emile de Antonio, Mary Lampson, and Haskell Wexler. Toronto: Sphinx Productions, 1976.

Reports and Journal Articles

Isbell, F. B., and American Civil Liberties Union of the National Capital Area. *May Day 1971: Order Without Law: An ACLU Study of the Largest Sweep Arrests in American History.* Washington, DC: American Civil Liberties Union of the National Capital Area, 1972.

Public Defender Service for the District of Columbia. *Legal Services During the 1971 Mayday Demonstrations.* Washington, DC: Public Defender Service, 1971.

Scheips, Paul. *The Role of Federal Military Forces in Domestic Disorders, 1945–1992.* Washington, DC: Center of Military History, U.S. Army, 2012.

Wald, Michael S. *Mayday Revisited, Parts I and II: A Study of the Legal System's Response to Mass Arrests.* Criminal Law Bulletin, 1974.

Index